Saving
Remnants

Saving Remnants

Feeling Jewish in America

Sara Bershtel and Allen Graubard

THE FREE PRESS
A Division of Macmillan, Inc.
NEW YORK

Maxwell Macmillan Canada
TORONTO

Maxwell Macmillan International
NEW YORK   OXFORD   SINGAPORE   SYDNEY

The Free Press
A Division of Macmillan, Inc.
866 Third Avenue, New York, N.Y. 10022

Maxwell Macmillan Canada, Inc.
1200 Eglinton Avenue East
Suite 200
Don Mills, Ontario M3C 3N1

Macmillan, Inc. is part of the Maxwell Communication Group of Companies.

Printed in the United States of America

printing number
1   2   3   4   5   6   7   8   9   10

Library of Congress Cataloging-in-Publication Data

Bershtel, Sara
    Saving remnants : feeling Jewish in America / Sara Bershtel and Allen Graubard.
        p.   cm.
    ISBN 0-02-903085-4
    1. Jews—United States—Cultural assimilation   2. Judaism—United States.   3. United States—Ethnic relations.   I. Graubard, Allen, 1938–   .   II. Title.
    E184.J5B496   1992
    305.892′4073—dc20   91-45468
                                                                      CIP

A version of Chapter 7, "The Jewish Radical," appeared as "The Mystique of the Progressive Jew" in *Working Papers,* vol. 10, no. 2, March–April 1983

To Ester and Menashe Bershtel
who never imagined such possibilities
and
To Moses Graubard
who takes them for granted

Contents

Acknowledgments

Books that endeavor to map social change are frequently collective enterprises. This one, more than most, depended on generous contributions of time and thought by many people. First, we wish to thank all those, named and unnamed, whom we interviewed, and all the others whose stories inform every page, notably Diane Balser, Jack Bershtel, Lynn Bershtel, Mordechai Bershtel, Sharon Bershtel, Jonathan Black, the late Paul Cowan, Rachel Cowan, Ellen David-Friedman, Stuart David-Friedman, Marion Faber, Thomas Farber, Gordon Fellman, David Gelber, Lynn Gottlieb, Melvin Gottlieb, David Gurin, Alan Jacobs, Blima Kagan, Vivian Kleiman, Katherine Lamb, Jeremy Larner, Kennie Lyman, Mark Mirsky, Thomas Nagel, Ann Popkin, Jan Rosenberg, Moishe Rosenfeld, Robert Scheer, Diane Schulder, the late Erica Sherover-Marcuse, Fred Siegel, Steven Siegel, Cheryl Stern, Joseph Stern, Sol Stern, Igor Webb, and Charlotte Weissberg.

Our profound gratitude as well to the following critics and scholars whose willingness to share their insights into Jewish life in America provided us with valuable background and helped us make sense of what we heard: Robert Alter, Steven M. Cohen,

Rabbi Ben-Zion Gold, Paula Hyman, Neal Kozodoy, Michael Lerner, Alan Mintz, Stephen Mitchell, Samuel Norich, David Stern, Judith Walzer, Michael Walzer, and Leon Wieseltier.

When we first began our research, in the summer of 1979, we did not foresee how long it would take to complete. That we persisted is in no small part due to Irving Howe, Christopher Jencks, and the late Paul Zweig, who first encouraged us to undertake this project; to John Simon and Robert Kuttner, editors of *Working Papers,* who published some of our earliest work; and to Barbara Anderman and, especially, Charlotte Sheedy, who were instrumental in turning our efforts into a book. A grant from the National Endowment for the Humanities allowed us to conduct interviews and do our research; of course, NEH support is not to be identified with endorsement of our conclusions.

We were particularly fortunate to have friends and colleagues whose rigorous criticism was always tempered by sympathetic support. A number of people read and commented on all or parts of various drafts of the book: for their many helpful suggestions we thank Eva Hoffman and Laura Slatkin, together with Edward Cohen, John McNees, Leslie Pockell, Don Pretari, Francine Prose, Sally Singer, Roslyn Schloss, André Schiffrin, and Daniel Zitin. Jonathan Cobb's careful reading was a model of generous criticism; his standards of clarity and coherence improved this book whenever we succeeded in meeting them. Amy Edith Johnson's advice and judgment were indispensable at every stage and every level; the value of her insights and formulations was matched only by the grace with which she offered them. Our greatest debt is to Tom Engelhardt, tireless editor and sensitive friend, who not only strengthened and shaped the manuscript—no small task—but whose questions and responses time and again inspired us to think further and more boldly.

Our sincere appreciation to Eliza Osborne, Gina Davis, and Emily Garlin for their assistance in preparing the book for publication.

At The Free Press, we thank Erwin Glikes, Edith Lewis, and above all, our editor Adam Bellow, whose care and intelligence carried this project through to completion.

Finally, to our families—Joanna, Claire, Andrea, and Stephanie Boudreaux; Moses Graubard; and Richard and Noah Ashur Brick—our deepest gratitude for countless acts of help, large and small, and for their patience and cheerful endurance.

Saving Remnants

And the remnant that is escaped of the House of Judah shall
again take root downwards, and bear fruit upwards: for out
of Jerusalem shall a remnant go out, and they that escape
out of Mount Zion: the zeal of the Lord of Hosts shall do
this.

—Isaiah, 37:31,32

Two American Jews, immigrants long ago and now
thoroughly assimilated, meet on the street in New York.
"So," says one, "what remains to you of being Jewish?"
"I still drink tea from a glass," replies the other. "What
about you?"
"I'm still afraid of dogs."

—Jewish joke

Introduction

The young musicians, a band called Ellis Island, played lively klezmer music as the guests wandered through the gardens of the rented estate (formerly the home of a California railroad baron). The music was a good indication that this wedding would be attentive to tradition. After all, klezmer melodies accompanied traditional Jewish weddings in the old country; and although this musical style had almost disappeared during the Americanization of the immigrant Jewish community, recent bursts of interest in ethnic heritage have spurred a surprising revival of klezmer music—and many other aspects of traditional Jewish culture as well.

The bride's white satin gown and the groom's elegant gray tuxedo, however, were universalist touches. Since the wedding marked a second marriage for both parties, the mood was a bit more easygoing than is usual at a formal wedding. The bride was present and available for greeting during the prenuptial milling around, while off to one side the rabbi was rehearsing the groom on the pronunciation of the unfamiliar Hebrew words he would have to recite during the ceremony.

In the course of the wedding itself, the rabbi explained each aspect of the ritual and the ceremonial objects used: the canopy, the rings, the glass that would be broken. He apologized to the bride's family, Eastern European refugees, but noted that courtesy to the groom's American clan, as well as to most of the guests, required careful explanation and translation.

1

The ceremony was lovely; everyone enjoyed. The groom's recitation was quite recognizable as Hebrew. During the party that followed the ceremony, both bride and groom were joyously hoisted up and carried around the room on chairs, another touch of shtetl tradition. There were some less traditional aspects of the ceremony as well: all gender inequalities were rigorously excised from the service, each partner made a special commitment to care for the other's child by a previous marriage, and, since one of the partners was not Jewish—the groom was the proud descendant of a southern Presbyterian family—the rabbi made a special point of referring to the populism and concern for social justice within that strand of Protestantism.

The various elements combined beautifully to lend the occasion the joyous solemnity and communal validation the bride and groom desired. No one assumed that the groom had gone through a conversion to conform to at least the letter of Jewish law. Nor was it assumed that a Jewish family had been created by the marriage, although the bride's background would certainly be an important part of the aura of the home—as would the groom's, for that matter. Their future offspring would be "half-Jewish," a vague but quite satisfactory state of identity shared by numerous children in the sophisticated urban milieu in which they would grow up.

What are we to make of this event? For some Jews, this wedding offers a contemporary version of an old and sad story, the forsaking of Jewish community. It is the intermarriage of a Jew with a "gentile," an act forbidden by Jewish law, and widely disapproved of even by Jews who are not religious but who feel a fundamental loyalty to the Jewish people and their history. In some cases of intermarriage, the non-Jewish partner converts formally, although conversion for the sake of satisfying requirements for a religious ceremony is almost never an expression of commitment to Judaism as a faith, and often no further involvement in Jewish religious activity follows the wedding. But in this instance, there was not even a pro forma conversion, and no articulated commitment, however ceremonial, to carrying on Jewish-community membership to the next generation.

In the past, it would have been unusual to have a Jewish ceremony at all in such a situation, since it is religiously forbidden to rabbis of every major denomination—Reform, Conservative, and, of course, Orthodox—to conduct a Jewish marriage ceremony except between Jews. But in recent decades, as the incidence of Jewish intermarriage began a rapid statistical climb, more and more rabbis became willing to violate the law out of desperation, so to speak, in the cause of Jewish "survival," justifying their actions by the hope that any gesture toward Jewish identification might be a sign of future involvement and should be encouraged.

Intermarriage figures for American Jews have increased more than fivefold over the past thirty years, the measure of a generation. Their rise is linked to salient decreases in Jewish-community life: synagogue attendance, Jewish education for children, organizational membership. All signify assimilation: the decline of Jewish awareness, knowledge, and allegiance, as Jews become "like everyone else." For those with a fundamental commitment to Jewish collective existence as a separate people, religion, and culture, the prospect of this scenario unfolding with ever-increasing rapidity evokes profound anxiety, expressed in ever more highly charged phrases like "internal erosion and corruption," "spiritual Jewish genocide," and the "end of American Jewish history."

Recently, however, a different, more optimistic view has gained currency. Although the statistical trends are obvious to all, some observers have pointed to changes in the "quality of Jewish life." In this view, even the California intermarriage has a bright side: the conscious desire to connect to a Jewish tradition seen as joyful and zesty, and the incorporation of rituals, customs, and music beyond what is required by the formal ceremony. The new interest in things Jewish is, according to this analysis, a sign of a growing concern for Jewish identity; indeed, it is part of what has been proclaimed as a diverse, widespread, and unpredicted Jewish revival.

Those who seek evidence of such a revival do not have far to look. There are the proselytizing Hasidim of the Chabad movement who invite passersby to pray in their Mitzvah Mobiles; the flourishing Orthodox congregations attended by young, prosperous, well-educated, and worldly people, many of whom have had no previous religious training; the groups of former New Leftists who gather for their own form of weekly Sabbath service combining ancient prayers and Hebrew songs with excerpts from socialist, humanist, and feminist writings. The growing attendance at High Holy Day services on college campuses, the enthusiastic memberships of gay congregations, the resurgence of interest in Yiddish language and culture, and the sustained concern with the Holocaust—all suggest that more and more Jewish-Americans are discovering, rediscovering, or intensifying some impulse to Jewish identity.

Such individual impulses hold out a larger promise. In his 1985 study of Jews in America, *A Certain People*, social critic Charles Silberman surveyed the Jewish scene and announced with exuberant confidence, "We are, in fact, in the early stages of a major revitalization of Jewish religious, intellectual, and cultural life—one that is likely to transform as well as strengthen American Judaism." He was hardly alone in his opinion that Jewish identity and community are generally strong and growing stronger, that apparent decline masks a promising transformation of Jewish life in America.

These two views—the pessimistic vision of the end of community and the optimistic anticipation of a new Golden Age—set the terms of Jewish debate on the nature of contemporary American Jewish life. If they seem like polar opposites, the only alternatives in a passionate argument about survival, they are actually points on a single continuum. For underlying both sides of the debate is the same limited and moralistic conception of community and commitment. Jewish self-identification and affiliation are taken to be the natural destiny of Jews: individuals moving away from the community are seen as "betraying" their heritage; returnees are "coming home."

This tension between communal decline and communal revival is the constant theme in Jewish self-description, the lens through which all evidence about Jewish life is viewed. History, including the history of the present moment, is frequently read as an adversarial encounter between the Jewish people and a succession of enemies who threaten their survival. In this dramatic discourse, the traditional self-image of the Jews as the "ever-dying people" faced with powerful forces continually threatening them calls up simultaneously their miraculous power to survive against all odds. In whatever difficulties the Jews find themselves, a "saving remnant," first evoked by the Prophet Isaiah, will always escape the threat and become the seed of Jewish continuity and renewal, happy confirmation of the mystical vitality of Jewish life.

Historically, most enemies in this tale were easily identified: the pharaohs, the Babylonians who destroyed the First Temple, the Romans who destroyed the Second Temple and expelled the Jews from their ancestral homeland into an exile that was to last two thousand years, the Catholic church and its Inquisition, and, of course, the Nazis. The Holocaust represents the most extreme expression of the traditional vulnerability of the Jewish people to the powerful forces of anti-Semitic hatred, the murderous antagonism of the outside world. Paradoxically, the survival fears fueling the current Jewish anxiety in America arise from quite a new source: the stunning acceptance of Jews in the larger society. Now, the threatening forces have become vaguer, harder to grasp, and more difficult to dislike, not pharaohs or Inquisitors, but values such as tolerance, respect for diversity, and cultural integration. Jews "cannot give up" in the "battle" against intermarriage, insists a New York Jewish-community leader, using characteristic adversarial imagery: "Throughout history, Jews have never given up the fight; if they had, there would be no Jews left today."

But the attempt to turn the American experience into the latest round in the old fight for survival against outside enemies has had the effect of obscuring the actual processes shaping culture and identity in American today. While this conventional way of thinking may have made a certain amount of sense earlier in the century, when Jews formed a more cohesive community beset by prejudice and discrimination, it no longer does. None of the givens of Jewish life in that past America still obtain: not a given community, not a given faith, not even a given enemy. The Jews are not *encountering* modern America; they *are* modern America, like other Americans whose origins are also rooted in immigrant cultures from around the world. Jews have traditionally seen themselves as special, a perception that has sometimes led Jewish observers to assert that Jews might remain more resistant to assimilative pressures than other groups. This view has proved to be an illusion. American Jews, highly skewed toward membership in the educated, urban, middle class, are, on the contrary, particularly well placed to experience just those aspects of modernity that characteristically draw people out of traditional communities: the primacy of choice, individual freedom, psychic and social mobility, separation of private and public worlds, multiple loyalties.

If we look at the wedding again, from this perspective, its apparently contradictory meanings can be explained. An instance neither of betrayal nor of reaffiliation, the wedding is not primarily a Jewish event: it is a modern—and above all, a modern American—event. Once we look beyond the traditional interpretations of decline or renewal, what is striking in this case is the freedom of choice and the spirit of incorporation and inclusiveness that govern every aspect of this occasion, from the selection of partners across religious and ethnic lines to the composition of the ceremony, which combines the old world and the new, the shtetl and Los Angeles. Whereas in times past, whether in 1840s Europe or 1940s America, such a mishmash would have been unthinkable, now it is possible to "have it all"; individuals can selectively choose privately satisfying components from which to fashion a public form. The ceremony is deliberately made up of traditional elements, bits and pieces of religion and culture, and it is the presence of these elements, given by the tradition, that provokes talk of revival. But, in truth, the actual elements matter less than the fact that they can be chosen without regard to religious law or cultural coherence, and combined into an individually constructed design. The experience, like the locale, is there for the occasion; it can be enjoyed for what it offers; it may signal a long-term allegiance, but it can also be left behind.

This wedding may seem idiosyncratic—too "California," too "New Age," the participants completely secular, without any ethnic attachment. But it has been our observation that the qualities at the heart of this event affect the lives of *all* American Jews—the unaffiliated, to be sure, but also the organized mainstream, the newly returned, and even the Orthodox. Moreover, they call into question the central terms that the Jewish community uses to interpret its condition: assimilation, anti-Semitism, Zionism, loyalty, faith.

Over the last ten years we have observed and participated in a variety of activities spanning the Jewish community. We have spent evenings in Hasidic homes in Brooklyn and observed Yiddish classes in Berkeley, visited Purim services in New York's gay temple and celebrated the Sabbath at campus Jewish centers in Boston and Los Angeles, attended a secular bar mitzvah in a Santa Barbara backyard and synagogue discussion groups in suburban New Jersey. We interviewed hundreds of people throughout the country: Orthodox Jews from Chicago, Zionist Jews from Peoria, Marxist Jews from Vermont, Reform Jews from Indianapolis, newly observant Jews from Atlanta, and unaffiliated Jews everywhere. Our focus was on adults who came of age in the postwar period of acceptance and integration and who consequently have defined their Jewish identity in the context of American social and cultural history rather than, for example, the immigrant experience. We asked them to explain however they could what being Jewish meant to them, what part it played in their lives and in their sense of themselves. Since our aim was to understand the interplay of modernity and tradition, we sought out and talked with those who were actively engaged intellectually and personally with just those issues.

We ourselves are members of the group from which the interviewees for this book are drawn. Both of us came from intensely Jewish homes, Orthodox in one case, secular, socialist, and Yiddishist in the other. One of us, the child of parents who had survived the Holocaust, arrived in this country at age ten; the other was an active Zionist youth leader, national president in the mid-1950s of the country's largest Zionist youth group. Both of us went on to college, graduate school, and professional and personal lives that had no explicit connection to Judaism, Jewish culture, or the Jewish community.

Although our particular origins may not be typical, the adult destinations we arrived at seemed quite ordinary for our generation. And so we were surprised, in the mid-1970s, to discover an increasing interest in Jewish identity. Both of us knew people who proclaimed themselves "revived," and others, more tentative, who expressed curiosity about Jewish ritual, a new awareness about anti-Semitism, and the like. Further, a strengthening seemed apparent across the whole spectrum of Jewish practice and identification. We remained puzzled at how to place this new intensity in what appeared to be a continuing climate of assimilation, and our attempt to uncover the connections between such apparently disparate phenomena as revival and assimilation became over time a broader inquiry into the Jewish condition in America.

In a field crowded with sociological summaries and philosophical abstraction, overly simple survey responses, and generalized historical overviews, we found that extended interviews in which individuals could articulate what being Jewish actually meant in their lives provided the nuance and complexity the subject demanded. These interviews were the pleasure that sustained us over years of work, our sources of reflection, and, most of all, the evidence that continually modified our interpretations. For the more we listened, the more the dichotomy of decline and renewal through which Jews have insisted on understanding their fate in America seemed to lead us only to dead ends, kept us from hearing what people were telling us. The interesting questions, we became convinced, were no longer the traditional queries of the Jewish community: the continual "How are we doing?" or, as in the title of one recent account, "Where are we?" What needed to be asked now was: What happens to traditional loyalties when givens become options? What force can—or should—such loyalties have in a culture that makes the quest for personal fulfillment a central value? If assimilation is a matter of choice, why should it be a subject of lament? What sense can the warning about becoming "like everyone else" retain in an integrated and constantly shifting cultural milieu in which "everyone else" is also subject to multiple possibilities of choice and identity?

In the face of these questions, images of the "ever-dying people" and the "saving remnant" offer the comfort of familiarity. But they cannot help us understand what is happening today or what will happen tomorrow to the Jews in America. The idea of a saving remnant that will preserve Judaism and the Jewish people against all odds is no longer enlightening. It is not that such a remnant does not exist. It is, rather, that we live in a society and during an age that creates remnants of all traditional cultures, groups, and beliefs. Jews, like other Americans, are free to stitch together these remnants into something that incorporates traces and patterns of the past, that suggests—for the time being—the seamless and organic tradition of generations. And they can do so over and over again. But these creations and re-creations, no matter how vivid and compelling, cannot escape the fragility that modernity imposes on any enterprise essentially dependent on individual choice and commitment.

The Unaffiliated

America is God's Crucible, the great Melting-Pot where all races of Europe are melting and reforming! Here you stand, good folk, think I, when I see them at Ellis Island, here you stand in your fifty blood hatreds and rivalries. But you won't be long like that, brothers, for these are the fires of God you've come to—these are the fires of God. A fig for your feuds and vendettas! Germans and Frenchmen, Irishmen and Englishmen, Jews and Russians—into the Crucible with you all! God is making the American!

—Israel Zangwill, *The Melting Pot* (1908)

The tale of the Jews in America is the epitome of the ethnic success story. The account of how millions of poor and persecuted Jews from the old country—where they had been pariahs and victims, hated and isolated—came to a land where they could be free and equal citizens, and of how they seized that opportunity and rose to an unparalleled level of achievement, has been told thousands of times. The celebration of Jewish progress in America has not, however, been unqualified. Jewish commentators, religious and secular, have expressed fears that successful integration into American life would mean the attrition of cohesiveness, the erosion of culture and religion, and, perhaps, ultimately, the effective disappearance of a sizable and thriving community. Through the years of rising prosperity and Americanization, those fears have come to seem increasingly well founded. However comfortable the American experience was for individual Jews, for the long-term prospects of Judaism—and for the future of the Jewish people—there were grounds for worry, even despair.

The latest estimates place the total number of American Jews somewhere between five and a half and six million. This figure represents a notable increase from the estimated two and a half million Jews who emigrated from Europe between 1880 and 1924, and makes the contemporary American Jewish population the largest group of Jews ever to live within a single political jurisdiction. Indeed, it is almost twice the number of Jews living in Israel. But approximately half of this group are not part of the American Jewish community. They are "unaffiliated": although they may be classified as Jewish, they are not members of the organized community. They do not practice Judaism as a religion, although they may occasionally attend a Passover Seder or light Hanukkah candles. They make no special effort to associate with other Jews, and they belong to no Jewish organization or group. Many would marry or have married non-Jews. They know very little about Jewish history or culture—although they may have been sent to Hebrew school or Sunday school during childhood—and they are not inclined to learn. They do not give their children a Jewish education. They do not contribute regularly to the local federation of Jewish charities, an act generally considered an important affirmation of symbolic as well as practical Jewish-community membership. They will not deny that they are Jewish, but this may be their only act of Jewish identification.

This massive disaffiliation is typically a third-generation phenomenon. From the time of the great immigration from Eastern Europe to the rising prosperity of the second-generation "gilded ghettos" in the 1940s and 1950s, Jews have Americanized with exceptional speed and success. But, like other immigrant groups, they did so as a community. Certainly, there were always individuals who left, but they were definitely the exception in an America intensely conscious of group identity, with widespread and powerful prejudices against ethnic and racial minorities. Even in the 1950s, ethnic separation was the normal condition.

But in the last three decades, disaffiliation has accelerated dramatically. Intermarriage, always the best indicator of integration into the wider society, marks this sharp increase. Significantly, the rate of intermarriage for American Jews remained quite low through the first and second generations, much lower than the expressed anxiety in the sermons, novels, dramas, and stories of the time indicated. *Abie's Irish Rose* was a rare bloom in the 1920s, when that play was a Broadway hit. Even into the 1960s, the intermarriage rate was still below 9 percent, hardly higher than for the first immigrant generation. But over the past thirty years that rate has soared to the 50-percent range nationally. Figures are even higher among highly educated professionals and in communities with small Jewish populations. (A recent local study done in the Denver area showed a startling finding for eighteen-to-twenty-nine-year-olds: of Jews who married, 72 percent had married non-Jews.) Obviously, the intermarriage phenomenon is not confined to Jews. It takes two to intermarry, so the willingness of Jews to marry outside the community is matched by a decline in exclusive feelings among non-Jews. (Roman Catholics too are intermarrying much more than they used to—mainly with Protestants, of course—at a rate estimated to approach one-third within the larger urban archdioceses.)

Today, the largest and fastest-growing group of American Jews are the unaffiliated. Although they may be described in sociological terms like synagogue membership, observance, and intermarriage rates, they are not at all a neutral category. Their existence in such large numbers represents both an achievement and a threat.

From one perspective the unaffiliated stand for the fulfillment of modern universalist ideals. The Enlightenment concepts of a secular national state, religious toleration, and universal citizenship offered emancipation to Jews—that is, they could, as individuals, finally become full members of the nation in which they had been living a separate community existence. Emancipation meant that Jews, in theory, could maintain their Jewish religious involvements, while becoming culturally and politically part of the national community —"Germans of the Mosaic persuasion," as the phrase went in the most important emancipated Jewish community. Even more radically, it meant—again in principle—that a Jew could go further and reject all involvement with Judaism. Any individual could simply give up Jewish identification and disappear as a Jew.

The United States was the great exemplar of this Enlightenment vision—a nation of immigrants whose culture would emerge from a mélange of peoples and whose principles of toleration were enshrined in its founding documents. Although there was always a disparity between the ideal and reality—the "melting-pot" ideology, for example, was used to justify forcing ethnic minorities to conform to the dominant "Anglo" image of the good American—the values of freedom, choice, and mobility remained vivid and powerful in American society, a challenge and inspiration for the millions of new Americans, Jews as well as others. As one

Jewish-American historian has recently concluded, "Only in twentieth-century America has emancipation been fully achieved."

According to modern democratic ideology, which values individual rights and social equality, the possibility of choice about community affiliation marked a great moral advance. But for those who also valued the continued existence of the Jewish people, with its own particularist religion, culture, and history, choice presented great peril. It was in this post-Enlightenment period that assimilation became the most contested issue within Jewish life and that the Jewish critique of assimilation was first formulated.

Jewish spokesmen warned of the danger. For example, Arthur Ruppin, a German-Jewish scholar who pioneered the sociological study of Judaism, ends his report *The Jews of Today* (1913), the earliest demographic survey of worldwide Jewry, with an unscientific cry of anguish: "The structure of Judaism, once so solid, is crumbling away before our very eyes. Conversion and intermarriage are thinning the ranks of Jews in every direction, and the loss is the heavier to bear, in that the great decrease in the Jewish birth-rate makes it more and more difficult to fill up the gaps in the natural way. . . . *We see in the assimilative movement the greatest danger that has assailed Judaism since the Dispersion.*" Even after the Holocaust and in the face of Israel's precarious situation, the late Rabbi Meir Kahane, repeating the claim that assimilation is the true modern danger to the survival of Judaism, gave pungent expression to the community's intense anxiety about assimilation, calling it the "subtly soft disease that is raging throughout the American and Western Jewish body and which threatens it with oblivion."

Besides its threat to the community, assimilation was also taken to have serious negative consequences for the individual. Whatever the liberal ideals of tolerance and acceptance seemed to promise, the social reality included widespread and powerful prejudices. In order to be accepted in an anti-Semitic world, a Jew would have to hide his Jewishness —through name change, avoidance of Jewish family and friends, and even conversion to Christianity—and would inevitably feel shame, disloyalty, loss of self-esteem, even pathological self-hatred. Moreover, the assimilating Jew, by severing his connection to his people and past, would trade a rich, authentic ethnic and religious life for alienated rootlessness. Only by seeing the error of his ways and returning to his people and faith could the prodigal hope to become whole again.

In schematic form, this is the standard critique of assimilation. While literal exemplars were rare even during the historical period that generated this critique, it continues to provide the terms by which the Jewish community judges its prodigals, and, often, the prodigals judge themselves. Powerful though this schematic analysis may be, it is—at least now—profoundly misleading. Among the millions of unaffiliated American Jews today, it is difficult to uncover anyone who resembles the classic stereotype—who actively repudiates even the classification "Jewish." Estimates place the number of "repudiators" at below 5 percent of the Jewish population, and even this proportion is declining.

This is not to say that there are no tensions or confusions for the unaffiliated in their chosen assimilated lives. Although individuals who fit the schematic picture are rare, what is easy to find among unaffiliated Jews today are many of the emotions connected with that traditional image, including a feeling of impoverishment, anxiety about betrayal of one's self and one's people, a sense of vulnerability. These feelings have been taken as signs that the unaffiliated are not totally "lost" to the appeals of Jewish commitment. But what significance do such feelings really have? How heavily do they weigh in the balance with all the other qualities that make up an American identity? Indeed, can the word "assimilated," with its historical, moral, and psychological connotations, still give an accurate sense of the lives and minds of the growing numbers of unaffiliated Jews in America today?

1

Assimilation, the American Way

Being unaffiliated certainly does not preclude strong and prideful assertions of Jewish identification by contemporary Americans. The expressions of such identification are as varied as the individuals themselves. Michael Stone,* a New York–based motion picture production manager in his early forties, is married and the father of a young son. Jewish concerns affect his political views, social relations, image of family, intimate commitments, even his sense of physical security. If not actually obsessed with Jewishness, he is emotionally involved with the issue to a striking degree.

"Fear and Pride"

The Six-Day War was a catalyst for what is now my paranoid and proud split feeling about Jewishness. The '67 War is the first Israeli war that I remember. I was aware that this time Israel could have gone out of existence. I had never been a Zionist. I'd never been actively interested in Israel. This changed after 1967. I didn't go around shaking my friends who were less concerned, who just didn't care. But I was profoundly affected by it. I read books on the founding of Israel, which means something since I'm not a great reader. I also read books on the Holocaust, and I sent

*Pseudonym.

17

money to Israel. I knew people who went down to the embassy
and went to Israel, and I was tempted.

I identified a lot with Israel at that particular time. And I am
very suspicious of that feeling. I see it almost exclusively in
psychoanalytic terms, as a neurotic reaction, paranoia mostly. This
was the biggest threat toward the most Jews anywhere in the
world, and, as I saw it, it happened largely *because* they were
Jewish. There were lots of other reasons for the war, I know, but to
me it was because they were Jewish. I felt threatened by the war.

It's true that the idea of threat, of vulnerability, was the major
content of being Jewish when I was growing up. I don't remember
specifically being sat down and told, "The Holocaust happened
and you're Jewish, so you'll always be threatened in some way."
But I grew up with a very strong sense of that. My grandmother
told me stories of being a child in Russia and seeing the cossacks
come through her town and literally cut off people's heads with
swords. She came to America after a pogrom in 1903, I think. And
she told me that story a thousand times. I felt the threat as a kid
even though I lived in Scarsdale. Once, at an ice-skating rink in
Rye, I got beat up, and the theme was that I was a "kike." I was
seven or eight. It was a little scary, but it wasn't really a big deal.

I have a rifle now—and people are appalled that anyone who is
intelligent and liberal would have a rifle—and I'm going to
Vermont next week essentially to master it and become very good
at using it, and I'm going to buy some pistols, and bury the pistols
and ammunition. I am comfortable enough with how weird that
seems, although I can imagine what my analyst would say. And I
would absolutely consciously use those guns to defend myself and
my family. I wouldn't hesitate to shoot people who were coming
after Jews, if that happened again. Which is, I think, a highly
neurotic fear, and yet I'm comfortable with it. It's not that likely.
It is even highly unlikely. But the fact that the possibility exists at
all means somebody—me—should do something about it.

The other half of feeling threatened as a Jew is feeling some
justifiable, rich pride in being Jewish. My parents always made it
clear that there was a disproportionate contribution in the sciences and arts and letters from Jews. I knew at a young age that
Einstein was Jewish. It was good to be Jewish, to belong to that
group, to be hardworking and productive.

I find myself very surprised now that I want to know right away,
Is this person Jewish? And I think, How fucked up. I'm like my

grandmother. She'd see somebody on TV: "Gabe Pressman, he's a Jew," she would call out. I like working with Jews. I do feel an instant connection to people who are Jewish. I think ultimately there is a bond among Jews.

For five years I lived with a non-Jewish woman. Her father, a German Jew, came from a family so well established and wealthy that the fact that they were Jewish hardly crossed their minds. He married a Lutheran German woman whose brother-in-law died in Hitler's army. She fled with him, and they escaped through France and came here and changed their name, and became Unitarians. The father, as a result of fleeing Hitler, completely turned his back on anything Jewish and did his best to be American, to be German, to be anything but Jewish.

When I fell in love with this woman, I would get very confused by the German thing. She wasn't just Christian, she was German. There was nothing Jewish about her whatsoever. I listened to more German during those five years—the German language is definitely creepy to me, and I hate listening to it. I am amazed at the intensity of my reaction; I can't stand listening to German. Anyway, the relationship came to a point where either we were going to get married or it would end. I knew it wasn't right. Part of it was that there was this fundamental lack of trust, this missing shared identity. It wasn't really a matter of attitude. She wasn't totally sympathetic to the plight of Israel, but more so than most of my radical friends, who *were* Jewish. And it wasn't a matter of observance. I certainly don't observe anything.

In fact, except for funerals, I haven't set foot in a temple for fifteen years. And before that there wasn't much either. I went to Hebrew school for three years to have a Reform bar mitzvah. I had no choice about that. But after that, there was a choice, and I stopped right away. I hated Hebrew school; it wasn't special, like sports or wrestling practice, and it wasn't fun, and my family in no way reinforced it as a value. My parents felt the obligation to send me, for the grandparents. Both my grandmothers kept kosher homes, the Sabbath, candles, everything. But we rarely went to their houses for holidays or anything like that. My mother rejected all observance. Both my parents understood Yiddish, yet neither ever spoke it to the other. My mother had a very strong Jewish identity, but no religious identity whatsoever. I know if I took a quiz I would probably get in the bottom tenth percentile of right answers about basic Jewish observance.

So what divided me from my girlfriend wasn't observance, certainly. Or even the absence of paranoia, though she certainly felt none of that. All of her lovers had been Jewish. That was no problem for her. She didn't believe any Christian things. Her whole shtick was the California feeling thing. Modern American. She was really assimilated. I can't be terribly articulate about what was missing between the two of us. I felt strongly that I was a Jew. She clearly wasn't. She resented tremendously my even raising these feelings. If we went to see a film about Jews—I remember we went to see *Night and Fog*, a great date—I could count on our getting into an argument, a displaced argument about how she was dressed or why I was late. I would be very affected by the movie; she would be very defensive and not so affected by the movie. Then, at one point, I asked her whether she would convert if we were going to get married. I actually asked her! I was surprised to hear the words come out of my mouth. Very surprised. What a provocative, almost hostile thing to say to her. And that really was the end of the relationship. Because she said, "Absolutely not!" And she was insulted that she wasn't good enough the way she was. The problem was basic. I was saying, I'm a Jew, it's important to me, and on some level, she could never share it. Though the "it," the shared "it," the content of the "it" that's so important— that's what I can't define. In a sense, even if she had said yes, it wouldn't have made her Jewish. It wouldn't have solved anything. Because, in fact, there wasn't anything she could convert to that was Jewish in my sense. She would have converted, we would have gotten married, and we would have been divorced in a year. It would have been an exercise in futility.

When I met Jeanie, my wife, I thought it was great that she came from a more Jewish home than I did. We had an Orthodox marriage ceremony. She said if we were going to get married, then it should be civil or Orthodox, either was fine with her, but there was nothing else, because if it's not Orthodox, then basically it's not Jewish. I was in the position of having to assemble ten men who knew their Jewish names, which was no small problem. And I had to memorize a passage in Hebrew, which was like classical Greek to me. It was very awkward. Still, I ended up feeling very good about the whole thing. I liked it because it was authentic and serious and real.

I wish we did more. I had thought that maybe we would run some modified Jewish home, which for me would be a heightening of observance. Well, Jeanie's not interested in that at all. She came out of a rigorous Jewish home, and it was a matter of either embracing it or rejecting it—and she rejected it. My own background was so much more watered down, there wasn't much to reject, so I'm sort of stuck in the middle. Jeanie refuses to romanticize Jews—Israelis, grandparents, Orthodox rabbis, any Jews. I automatically give extra points to people if they're Jewish; she takes points away. In fact, I'm lucky to be her husband. I feel I'd have a much less confused relationship to Judaism if I had been born into that world, if Orthodoxy had been closer and I had rejected it cleanly. I would have listened to all of the Yiddish; I would have been involved in the life, the culture; I would have been oppressed by the religion. I would have rejected all of it. Without the generation of my parents between me and that world, I'd have a much clearer idea of where I stand.

I am romantic about it, I'm sure. A high point of my life, and not just professionally, was our re-creation of the Lower East Side for a film I worked on. All the stills that you see about Jewish life on the Lower East Side, we made them move. This is what it must have been like when my grandparents went to community banquets at Beethoven Hall on Second Avenue. Of course, I wasn't able to read the street signs and the Yiddish lettering, but I knew they were authentic. And I loved it. I yearned for it. I had no trouble getting up at four in the morning to work on the set. Not that I would exchange my life now for that. I know the problems were overwhelming—it was dirty, it was crowded, it was poor, it was oppressive. But it was perfect for me: like stepping into a still photograph every morning, then going home every night.

I've heard of groups of people meeting to learn more about Judaism. I have friends who have been in groups like that. But I can't see myself there. I guess I don't want it enough. The truth is, I'd probably study Italian—we're planning to go to Italy—before I'd study Judaism. Partly, I suppose it's that I don't really have religious feelings. I don't believe in God, so that's a problem. It is the underlying problem. To learn the blessings and light the candles and all that if one doesn't believe in God seems just like putting on a costume, nothing more. The inner thing has to be belief. I know there are people who think rituals do some good, independent of any faith. I don't think so. I guess all this means I'm assimilated, but I don't really like to admit it.

So I'll probably end up wanting to push some lame thing on our children in terms of their Jewish education, something not far from what my parents did to me. I'll take the kids aside to talk. They'll grow up with a sense of Jewishness, a sense of some justifiable fear and pride. I'll tell them about anti-Semitism and the Holocaust and the vulnerability of the Jews. It is part of the survival indoctrination of children to know that they are particularly vulnerable because they are Jews. And Jeanie will cook Jewish food sometimes and tell stories about our grandparents. But, in truth, our children will have even fewer opportunities for observance than I did. My mother, after all, will be their grandmother. They will never ever hear her speak Yiddish. And maybe they'll totally reject my vision of pride and fear. I feel strongly that I am Jewish, and my kids will have a less strong feeling of that, and I think in the generation beyond there will be none. They'll say, "Yeah, my grandparents were Jewish." It will be a fact of birth, nothing more than that. I anticipate being sad about it.

And then again, maybe all that's lost are some feelings that are so tied up with my own personal psychology that they just may have nothing to do with the next generation. They might feel a lot less paranoid; that would be a gain. It is a burden for me. Having guns is not such a terrific thing.

Leslie Epstein offers a more cheerful version of Jewish identification. A well-known and respected novelist in his early fifties who teaches writing at Boston University, Epstein is married, with three children. After growing up in Hollywood (his father and uncle wrote the screenplays for *Casablanca, Arsenic and Old Lace, The Man Who Came to Dinner,* and other classic films), Epstein achieved literary fame with his novel *King of the Jews,* a modernist, black-humor tale about the bizarre leader of the Jewish Council in one of the ghettos set up by the Nazis. For Epstein, the thinking that went into the book was connected to his own reflections about being Jewish and what it meant to him.

"Mozart Was Jewish"

Being a Jew in Los Angeles was very different from being a Jew in New York. In L.A., the sun was shining and nothing had anything to do with Judaism. I was a Hollywood brat, and I grew up with Christmas trees. We did occasionally go to my grandparents' house for Seder. It was the typical scene with all the eight- and nine-year-old cousins running around, and people dipping their fingers in the wine and that was it. I also went to Sunday school for a while, but got thrown out. I can still sing a snatch of a song or two. But basically I preferred playing tennis. My parents didn't mind when I stopped going—they were happy not to have to drive me there. My parents had been given the typical strict upbringing, and they broke free and said, The hell with it, we're not putting our kids through that. They were the second generation. And I'm the typical third-generation Jew, groping his way back to what he never had—no roots, no knowledge, nothing to be proud of, nothing to offer up as my own. I was a Christmas-tree and Easter-egg boy who felt something was missing, and so I felt compelled to discover it. World War II broke out a year after I was born. The distance in time and space, in atmosphere and spirit, between the events in Europe and my life in America pushed me to write about the war, the Holocaust specifically. I was Jewish; I had to deal with it. I sprang toward this material at a very young age. Even as a fourteen-year-old, I was writing a story about Hitler. And the impulse that lay behind *King of the Jews* is that attempt to fill in the empty spaces of my knowledge and experience. Because I didn't know it directly in my life, I felt the need to counter it, to confront it.

The barriers raised against my Jewishness gave way very gradually. I used to spend a lot of time driving around on Hollywood Boulevard with friends. After a while, it wasn't O'Reilly and Hockenberry in the car with me; it was Fox and Rosenkrantz and Mosk. Once, at Yale, a bunch of us were sitting around a table and there was a guy there who tried to pretend he was black, he was so afraid of being Jewish. At some point, one guy said, "Well, there's no one at the table but us Jews," and this other guy turned deep red. He thought he'd been fooling people all this time. I can still remember that moment now, thirty years later. I kind of liked him saying that. I liked being included at that table.

The real change happened while I was at Oxford, of all places. It was in part the influence of other Americans there. So many were East Coast Jews. They were so secure about it. I wanted to be like them. But more, I think, it was simply that the time had come. I'm not a Jungian, but maybe there is a collective Jewish unconscious, some genetic program, that surfaced then. I knew this one guy who used to sit around the pub where we ate lunch, and one day he said only half-jokingly that if he ever had a sabbatical, he would devote it to proving that Mozart was Jewish. That stuck in my mind for eight years, and I eventually wrote a story about this little old man who had spent his whole life, from the time of his youth in Romania to his old age on New York's Lower East Side, proving just that. The evidence is impressive! I'm entirely in sympathy with the character.

When the dam broke, I became insufferable. I got this book with lists, like "Jews in music." It's pathetic. The big three: Mozart, Meyerbeer, and Mendelssohn. Jewish pitcher? Sandy Koufax. Sid Luckman? He was a Jew. I loved this poem about Hank Greenberg. He was playing for the Detroit Tigers, hitting fifty-seven, fifty-eight home runs, and Detroit was in the pennant race. Came the big day, Yom Kippur, and Greenberg refused to play, jeopardizing both the pennant and his chance for the home-run record. Edgar Guest, I think, wrote the poem, and the refrain is: "We shall miss him in the outfield/We shall miss him at the bat/But he's true to his religion/And we honor him for that."

Plus I went to Israel. In fact, on the boat there I met a German girl, and we were together for four years. She even came to America to live with me. She was going to Israel for all kinds of complicated reasons. Her father was a Communist and an anti-Nazi, but he was drafted. There were pictures of him in uniform. She would weep over that, she would weep over the Holocaust, and somehow that history brought us together. It was crucial to both of our identities. I don't think you can be Jewish and not feel that the center of things is the Holocaust. I think it will prove to be to Judaism just what the Exodus was. And I'm convinced that in another couple of thousand years it will be remembered in the same way. But as much as I admire the Jews for groping for a way of incorporating the Holocaust into Judaism, ultimately I feel the Holocaust belongs to the whole world. That if it makes any claims on us, it does so on all of us. The Jews are the paradigm of what could happen to everybody. And their experience exposes what everyone is capable of. I really dislike people saying things like "We should do more, go to temple more, because of the Holocaust." The Holocaust does make some claim on us, but it's not on the level of synagogue attendance.

In some crazy way, not formally, I've come to feel intensely Jewish.

My wife is Jewish, but that wasn't a factor in our marrying. I wouldn't have cared if I had married a Catholic. I don't know if she ever went to Sunday school. We never talk about it. We were married in city hall. I don't go to synagogue. I've been to a fair number of them, to give talks about my book, and I was dismayed by the rabbis. They were so mediocre. But beyond that, I'm just not drawn to religion. I was walking near the Boston Common a while ago, and this guy came right up to me and said, "You Jewish?" I drew the line; I'm not hiding anymore! So I said, "Yes." He tells me to take this lemon and hold this twig* and follow him into his mobile van. He says: "Say this after me. . . . You speak Hebrew? No? So say this after me. . . ." And I did it. I guess I was charmed. I think religious people are crazy, but charmingly crazy.

I've seen Orthodox children. Through the windows of the apartment we lived in on the Upper West Side, I'd see these poor pale kids pathetically trying to play handball and missing by about three feet, and they'd look up with their little pale faces. I was moved by them. That could have been me, I would think. I know everyone claims to be from a long list of rabbis in the old country; I do, too. I have this photo of the rabbis in my family, and I think, had the world gone differently, I would have been one of these kids with the *peyes* [earlocks] and the pale faces and unable to catch a ball. But I have to admit that I prefer Hank Greenberg. My wife feels this much more than I do—she feels "Yech," and I get angry at her for saying "Yech," but I also feel contempt for their awkwardness and paleness. They're very sad. They don't have a childhood. They're missing so much—a childhood, sports, America. I would have been very upset if my kids had chosen that. No, I suppose I am assimilated, rebelliously. For me, what it comes down to is some tribal thing. I feel comfortable around other Jews. It's for this tribal reason too that I suppose I would feel a twinge if my daughter married—as she probably will—a non-Jewish person. Judaism has been around for thousands of years. The thread has gone on for so long, has been woven into such a marvelous tapestry, been almost lost so often. What a shame for it to end.

Our children were raised a little more Jewish than I was. We always had a Christmas tree. Christmas is a fabulous thing for kids; I remember presents piled up under the tree. I'm not going to take

---

*The citron and palm branch used in the ritual celebration of Sukkot, the Feast of Tabernacles.

something so beautiful away from them. But we also started having a little Hanukkah celebration. I'd read from a book about the holiday to the children, and they'd listen patiently. We also had Thanksgiving. And we used to have Easter—though that was downplayed a bit. We had a chocolate-Easter-egg hunt, but the resurrection of Christ we stayed away from. Mainly, I tried to make a point of bringing up the fact that they're Jewish. We'd get out of the car and I'd say something like "All right, Jews, pile out." The kids had friends who were more actively Jewish, who went to Sunday school, but they always said it wasn't for them. They saw that these kids were miserable, forced to go by their families. I wasn't going to do that. But who knows what the fourth or fifth generation will be like? I believe in this strange historical-genetic process. Something will work out.

I think *King of the Jews* was a contribution to awareness and continuity. After I finished it, I thought I was done with being a professional Jew, a "Jewish" writer. The result was that my next book, *Pinto and Sons*, took eleven years, and began to take off only when I discovered that the main character was a Jew. In fact it began to write itself only when I let him tell it in his own voice—which turns out to be a lot like mine. And not just the voice, but the themes—mainly about the fate of Indians in California—are the same: destruction and betrayal. I'm a Diaspora Jew, and I'm interested in endings.

Author Paul Berman offers an exceptionally creative example of Jewish identification. In his early forties, he lives in New York and writes regularly on history, literature, and politics for the *Village Voice, Dissent, Tikkun,* and other journals. But for a time he was also a contemporary version of a figure straight out of the Lower East Side "world of our fathers" so central to Jewish-American nostalgia.

"A Yiddish Journalist"

Like a lot of kids who are intellectual, or maybe like all kids, I grew up feeling like an oddball. I was crazy for reading and ideas. I had political passions. Other kids were interested in these things, too, but maybe not so much as me. And I used to wonder what made me different. I went through all the answers—being a liberal, having parents who liked Franklin Roosevelt in the heart of Republican Westchester County. And at a certain point, it dawned on me that most of the other oddballs like me happened to be Jewish. Maybe I wasn't odd at all. Maybe I was just Jewish.

This occurred to me in my early twenties. Before, "Jewish" was never the primary way I identified myself in the world. My Jewish education was a mess. I went to Sunday school at the Reform temple, and I hated it. I found the whole thing nonsensical and repulsive. We read Bible stories in a dumb book, with horrible illustrations. We sang stupid songs and were taught the Hebrew alphabet. This went on for a few years. Then, when I was twelve, I found a book in a bookstore by Bertrand Russell, called *Why I Am Not a Christian*. It immediately struck me that his argument was applicable to Judaism, and I insisted on quitting. I refused to be bar mitzvahed. I declared myself an atheist and I said I wouldn't go along with a ceremony I didn't believe in. My parents didn't force me. Possibly my father was disappointed on religious grounds, but relieved on financial grounds. My mother was content to have me refuse on religious grounds, but, I think, she was sorry to miss the social occasion. There wasn't much feeling about it, really.

During high school and college I had mixed feelings about Jewish topics. I didn't necessarily adore the Jews in my little world. In the sixties, when I was not exactly a fountain of knowledge, the Jewish community seemed to me a reactionary place from which little was to be hoped. My idea of Jewish types was that they were small-minded and self-interested. But then, during the Six-Day War in '67, I took a certain pleasure in Israel. I went out to San Francisco, for the "Summer of Love," and I was probably the only hippie in existence who put up a poster of Moshe Dayan. My friends didn't notice it, except for one, who made me take it down.

My conscious recognition of myself as this Jewish type came from reading literature, which I began to do seriously in the early seventies. That was a Jewish event, maybe, to learn about your personality from books. I read all sorts of novels, and I saw myself in the old Jewish world of the Lower East Side of fifty years before, where a certain characteristic personality—at least in the novels —was someone whose life revolved around a passion for ideas: Marxist ideas, or literature, or religion, or whatever. I was living on St. Mark's Place and Avenue A and was fervent for libertarian socialism, and I went on sort of a Jewish kick. A lot of people were doing that in those days, and I wasn't as enthusiastic as some.

Even so, I started eating pastrami, knishes, bagels, blintzes. Jewish foods and Jewish shops, which before had only seemed mediocre to me, suddenly seemed meritorious. I saw excellences in your average Jewish delicatessen, where before I'd seen only heartburn. I began to hang out at restaurants like Ratner's, Second Avenue. I'd find myself at Ratner's at four in the morning discussing Stalin's foreign policy with the waiters, and whether Balzac was as great a writer as Tolstoy, and things like that. The soup was watery, but if I was down, it cheered me up.

Just about then, along came the editor of the *Freie Arbeiter Stimme,* the Free Voice of Labor, which was the oldest Yiddish paper in the world, part of what used to be an international network of Yiddish anarchist publications. He asked me to write. So I wrote something, and I gave him pieces I'd written for other journals, which he then translated and published. I was thrilled, really delighted. Because I was worried by my new interest in Judaism. Wasn't it just an affectation? Wasn't it fake? But *he* was certainly, indisputably Jewish, and *he* wanted *me,* fake that I was, for his paper. He was the first editor to be enthusiastic about me. So I wasn't a fake. I was for real. What could be more Jewish than a Yiddish journalist living on the Lower East Side? So what if he didn't know a word of Yiddish!

I've thought about learning Yiddish. It would have been nice to be able to read my own articles. But, in the end, the urge to learn was, for me, a sentimentality. Yiddish is dead now, and it was even deader then, because there weren't so many Soviet immigrants. The oldest Yiddish newspaper in the world folded. Of course, seeing any virtue in the food at Ratner's was also sentimental, an affectation. But it was within reasonable bounds. Learning Yiddish is more serious than eating blintzes. Finally I did take up a good old-fashioned New York language, but it was Spanish.

When I look back on the little fad for Jewish things that I went through, I'm happy about it, and happy that I didn't get more carried away. There's an ethnic overemphasis today, part of the cult of "difference," which got its start in the seventies, and mostly it depresses me. If someone comes along and pigeonholes some opinion of mine as merely Jewish, I get indignant. I don't want to go through life with a label on my forehead. If I were religious, I suppose I might understand issues of Jewishness and

Jewish identity in a more profound way. But I've never managed to make head or tail of Judaism. I appreciate a certain mysteriousness in Jewish history, and I used to wonder what relation might exist between the rabbinate of ages past and the Jewish intellectuals of today. But I don't understand these things, and I've let the questions go—for the time being.

What seems quite remarkable in these interviews is the degree to which these unaffiliated American Jews are concerned with questions about Jewishness, as well as the impressive variety of their modes of identification. Even in this small sample, almost every aspect of Jewish connection—except religious faith—is evoked: ethnic pride in being a member of this notable and distinctive historical people; nationalist concern for Israel and its security; nostalgic affection for the old immigrant Jewish culture and tribal insistence on special bonds with other Jews; a mystical belief in Jewish historical survival—albeit in modern terms of a collective Jewish unconscious or a genetic program; unabashed delight in Jewish heritage and accomplishments; intense aware-ness of the Holocaust and anti-Semitism; appreciation of Jewish rituals and holiday celebrations; even sentimental images of Jewish food. The hints of concealment, denial, avoidance, shame —so characteristic of the traditional image of assimilation—are clearly marginal. On the contrary, these individuals express little sympathy and occasional contempt for any signs of flight from Jewish identification. The German Jew who fled to the United States, changed his name, and converted to Unitarianism—simply to hide Jewish origins, it is presumed—evokes moral outrage. Even the interviewees' own parents do not escape some degree of censure for having let their heritage slide.

Still, intermingled with positive assertions and staunch identifi-cations, a different and more plaintive tone is audible: a longing for something more; a sense of loss, of having missed something important; perhaps even vague guilt connected with obligations to the survival of the Jewish people. The expressed longing is for a warm traditional home, for the depth that ceremony and ritual give to daily life, for the rootedness that knowledge of and participation in a rich and ancient heritage can bestow. The community that most easily engages these feelings is the crowded and lively Jewish world of the immigrant decades, imagined as a vivid, coherent society, vibrant with political and intellectual life—waiters who argue about Balzac and Tolstoy, cultural events at Beethoven Hall (attended by workers, writers, and capitalists, all mixed together), the sounds of Yiddish and its cultural "feel." None of these memories are part of this generation's Jewish experience, not even secondhand. The images come through books and films about a period of Jewish life now long gone.

In recent years, these expressions of yearning among the unaffiliated have been interpreted as symptoms of a larger and deeper discontent. In his moving memoir, *An Orphan in History*, Paul Cowan records a midlife journey that took him back to his Jewish origins. The search for his past led him to a growing involvement in Jewish religion, culture, and community and to a fervent commitment to encourage others to embark on this journey as well. For Cowan, and for the generation he hoped to speak for, the losses that assimilation imposed on American Jews were profound: spiritual life, historical continuity, sense of membership in a "people." He summed up the feeling that provided the poignant title for his story: "I know that, for my part, I am reacting to the rootlessness I felt as a child—to the fact that for all the Cowan family's warmth, for all its intellectual vigor, for all its loyalty toward each other, our pasts had been amputated. We were orphans in history." Cowan's account, with its wrenching, violent images of an "amputated" past and "orphans in history," dramatizes the author's understanding of the price of the lost connection to a living, creative, and spiritually sustaining Jewish tradition and community.

Another memoir, Anne Roiphe's *Generation Without Memory: A Jewish Journey in Christian America*, also records newly discovered feelings of loss and presents a historical and anthropological vision that both explains and deplores the assimilated state characteristic of large and growing numbers of Jews. Several years earlier Roiphe had achieved a measure of notoriety in Jewish circles because of her essay in the *New York Times* celebrating the joys of Christmas in her completely assimilated Jewish home. For her, as for Cowan, her former life—now seen as evidence of betrayal or, at best, self-deception—arouses remorse.

In her story of assimilation and its discontents, Roiphe deplores the skimpiness of her Jewish identity. Her account is suffused with feelings of loss and guilt. She conjures up a "parade of assimilation," generations of modern Jews in Europe and America shuffling along from authentic and rich ethnic and religious community to the homogenized, alienated, individualistic condition of secular life. Roiphe sees deep, even "biological," needs to belong to a tribe, to have rituals and ceremonies, to be rooted in an ongoing history. Her inquiry tries to illuminate certain questions that to her now appear central:

> If one leaves the tight world of one's ancestors, if one abandons the synagogue, the High Holy Days, the Sabbath Queen, the Torah, the Talmud, the Midrash, what replacements are made in the building of the soul? How are the crises of life marked: birth, marriage, death? How are festivals managed? Men and women need ways of living within ethical frameworks, ways of passing on to their children their morality and their lifestyles. What do we do—we who once thought only of abandoning the ways of our parents and parents' parents and gave no heed to the necessary replacements, substitutes, we would need to make— what do we in our empty apartments do to make furniture and fabric for ourselves?

Roiphe's metaphor-rich speculation on the spiritual price of assimilation presents a contemporary version of the litany repeated for more than a century by committed Jews attempting to counter the growing movement toward disaffiliation. Community is missing, a sense of deep connection to one's people, and this feels bad. Guilt and anguish are ascribed to a conviction that collectively "we" assimilated Jews gave up something wonderful; consequently, "we" are in a sense responsible for our own deprivation, for the lack of spirituality, for the alienated individualism that the unaffiliated accept as natural, even seem to choose.

The figure of a transgenerational superindividual conjured up by this "we" appears frequently in accounts of Jewish history. "The Jew," or more precisely, "The Modern Jew," gave up traditional faith in a rush to become like the others, to grab for the glittering prizes of acceptance and upward mobility. In so doing, he surrendered invaluable resources in exchange for deceptively attractive and seductive freedoms that brought little more than alienation.

Though rhetorically powerful, this presentation is satisfying neither as history nor as analysis. "Assimilated" is a term with at least two important senses. As an adjective, it describes a finished condition, a process completed. But "assimilated" can also be understood as the past participle of an active verb describing a process that its subjects consciously undertook. Many young American Jews are assimilated in the first sense. Very few of them, however, assimilated in the second, active sense; their parents and grandparents did it for them. The deliberate move to assimilate—variously painful, disturbing, exhilarating, and liberating—was the story of the immigrant generation and their children. For many members of the third and fourth generations—including Cowan, Roiphe, and our interviewees—being assimilated was their only reality. They were American from the start.

Conflating the two senses of "assimilated" slights the actual experience of the separate generations. For one thing, if the individuals who intentionally left the traditional community are allowed to speak, a different version is heard. Many parents and grandparents who forsook the traditional religious Jewish community did so not because they were blinded by the enticements of materialism or because they were ashamed of their origins but because they *wanted* to leave the "tight world of [their] ancestors." They did not believe in the fundamental tenets of Jewish faith and scripture, the ceremonies, the prayers or festivals, and they did not want to continue as part of a religious community they found oppressive, at odds with the liberal values that were transforming traditional and particularist communities everywhere. These young Jews did not simply jettison furniture and fabric, incapacitating themselves for the acts of birth, marriage, and death. Nor did they find themselves bereft of morality, or of a means to transmit that morality to their children. Often, for example, the children of religious Jews from traditional Eastern European communities embraced a universalist ethic of socialism, in its broad democratic and humanistic sense—precisely the morality central to the immigrant Lower East Side image that appeals so strongly today to many unaffiliated American Jews. To call their spiritual apartments "empty," to imagine that they had no "substitutes" for religious conceptions of morality, to conclude that these people were merely "abandoning" the ways of their parents, is a simplistic projection that ignores the actual content of the visions that they chose to follow.

The rhetorical construction is also false as a description of the evolution of the Jewish community. Typically, what happened to immigrant groups—Jews as well as others—is what sociologists call "acculturation": newcomers became Americanized, but they did so *within* their ethnic community of origin. Acculturation did not equal assimilation, if assimilation is taken to mean the dissolution of the community, the "melting" of individuals into the general population, where their ethnic identity effectively dissolves. According to Milton Gordon, the leading sociological analyst of assimilation, the "massive acculturation" of American Jews through the first half of the century was not accompanied by "structural integration," and the great majority of newcomers and their offspring held fast to a communal life shared with their fellow emigrants. Jews may have been exceptional in acculturating faster and more successfully than most other ethnic groups, but, like the others, they essentially stayed with their own.

Jewish families left their immigrant areas of "first settlement" by moving in the company of other Jews and establishing new Jewish neighborhoods—"gilded ghettos," in effect—that kept their fundamental ethnic character even as their members adopted American customs. The institutions in these second-generation communities were those of mainstream America: fraternal orders, mah-jongg groups for women, high school and college fraternities, basketball teams, Boy Scout and Girl Scout troops—with the difference that they were exclusively Jewish. Jewish kids played football, chewed gum, listened to *The Lone Ranger* on the radio, joined gangs, went to libraries and movies, became plumbers, lawyers, scientists, salesmen, secretaries, and teachers. But most Jewish boys had a bar mitzvah, most Jewish children learned some Hebrew or Yiddish, and went to Sunday school; few had close non-Jewish friends as they grew up. Intimate social relations with gentiles were exceptional. Many adults, now completely integrated into the non-Jewish world, remember that during their childhoods no non-Jewish adult ever entered their homes for a social occasion. It is this insular Americanized Jewish community that provides the characteristic ethnic setting for novels like Meyer Levin's *The Old Bunch*, Daniel Fuchs's Williamsburg trilogy, and Philip Roth's *Goodbye, Columbus* and *Portnoy's Complaint.*

There was certainly a diminishing of Jewish culture, learning, and intensity as Americanization proceeded. But the vision of the melting pot had not been fulfilled. Group acculturation did not mean the dissolution of Jewish community and identity. As the second generation was succeeded by the fully acculturated third,

however, significant shifts took place. As a development parallel to
the acculturation process within the community, the 1950s saw
the growth of a more radical kind of assimilation, one that went
beyond Americanization and took individuals out of the community in ever-larger numbers. Looking at this decade, Gordon noted
the emergence of an unaffiliated subsociety that he categorized as
"intellectuals and artists." These people gravitated to cosmopolitan centers. They chose friends and spouses without regard to
ethnicity or religion. Over the next decade, this category grew
rapidly, and by the early 1960s it had come to encompass far more
than an intellectual subculture. This was the period when the
postwar Jewish generation—at rates approaching 80 percent—
was entering colleges, an environment that characteristically
undermined particularist loyalties. For rapidly growing numbers,
with respect to choices of career, friends, lovers, spouse, politics,
and neighborhood, ethnicity was fading as a determining factor.

From a historical perspective, it becomes clear that the rhetorical presentation of assimilation misperceives not only the experience of the earlier generations of American Jews, but also that of
the contemporary generation. The Jews who left the acculturated
communities with their attenuated Jewish involvements were not
relinquishing anything very substantial. They hardly abandoned a
rich, powerful fellowship of faith. Again and again, our interviews
depict the actual encounter with the Jewish community in negative tones. Hebrew school was trivial or unpleasant; bar mitzvah
was dutiful, an occasion for presents; the cultural atmosphere was
materialistic and philistine. Most of this generation had only a
smattering of observance: occasional visits to the synagogue, a
Seder here and there. Since there was so little Jewish culture or
learning or religion to begin with, there was finally little to reject.

In contrast with earlier generations, the emotional content of
this disaffiliation story is rather bland. Not much happened, really.
The story of *The Jazz Singer*—who painfully breaks away from a
traditional religious and ethnic Jewish home, knowingly violates
the basic religious laws of the community, and causes great
anguish to his beloved parents—or the more recent literary
dramas of Orthodox rebels provided in Chaim Potok's novels are
not illuminating for this recent generation. Today's unaffiliated
Jews relinquished their ethnic attachments with relative ease.
Their story cannot readily be made into tragedy or melodrama,
though comedy remains possible.

Having been brought up thoroughly Americanized, the children and grandchildren of immigrants could hardly give up what they never had. Consequently, any feelings of guilt seem baseless. Moreover, their apparent yearning for Jewish connection seems equally ambiguous. The fact is that in their grown-up lives they do not look to Jewish affiliation to address the concerns with roots, alienation, and lack of community that they share with their non-Jewish counterparts. They are not unaware of the availability of a Jewish community, religion, and culture, or of the claims of some—like Roiphe and Cowan—that "returning" to their people and religion will answer those concerns. But statistics confirm the cumulative impression of our interviews, namely, that community involvement and religious Judaism have little appeal for the mass of the unaffiliated. Whatever meaning their regret has, it does not move them to join synagogues, keep Jewish homes, become members of Jewish organizations, or give their children Jewish educations.

Even specifically Jewish yearnings can highlight how stable unaffiliated identities are. For instance, when Michael Stone misses the traditional Orthodox home he never had, what he is disappointed at losing is the exhilarating experience of breaking away cleanly. Stone's Jewish actions—occasionally giving money to Israel, choosing a wedding ceremony that is not only Jewish but Orthodox—are discrete moments that add up to no pattern; he steps in and out of such moments easily. And that is the ideal relationship he desires to maintain to Jewishness, whether the lost Yiddish world of his immigrant grandparents or the Orthodox rituals of his wife's past—not a return but an occasional journey into a static reconstruction. As he says of the movie set on the Lower East Side, what he really likes is "stepping into a still photograph every morning, then going home every night." Nothing in his daily life will be determined by this intermittent if intense consciousness about Jewish identity.

Essentially, Jewish identifications are desirable only when they express the values that the unaffiliated hold anyway. So, for Paul Berman, his ideal Jewish community is one that embodies and reinforces his personal cultural and political values, not those of the Jewish home in which he grew up. The Jewish community he "joins" is the left-wing, secular, intellectual culture that flourished in the early decades of this century. As Berman well knows, this culture is now only a memory. The "Yiddish journalist living on the Lower East Side" is a phantom figure; neither the Lower East Side, nor the anarchist movement, nor Yiddish culture exist anymore. It is all a beautiful construction that can have no weight in the real world; learning Yiddish seems to him just sentimentality.

An unproblematic inclusiveness marks the relationship of the unaffiliated to both religion and cultural heritage. For Leslie Epstein, Christmas is one of the few "traditions" in his and his wife's families. To express his Jewish identification, he simply adds the reading of the Hanukkah story to the December revels of modern secularity. And since the reason for any celebration is its significance to the individual, no issues of coherence and contradiction are raised. Combining Christmas and Hanukkah is easy, unproblematic, simply part of American family life. Indeed, the Jewish acts mentioned in our interviews are typically gestures, episodes, enhancements—pinches of spice in the melting pot.

The characterization of unaffiliated Jews as a "generation without memory" is, then, revealingly inaccurate. No guilty or repressive amnesia characterizes the large and growing part of the Jewish generation that chooses not to participate in organized Jewish life, religious, cultural, or political. As we have seen, they remember all too clearly the minimal symbolic Judaism of their parental homes, the trivial education about Jewish history and culture offered them in their Sunday schools and bar mitzvah– preparation classes. They are more correctly seen as a generation without the experience of relatively coherent and unacculturated Jewish life; without knowledge of Jewish culture and history or the desire to acquire such knowledge; without religious commitment or the inclination to will themselves into gestures of faith. In fact, as with other Americans, their traditions, their memories, come from elsewhere: radio, TV, movies, pop music, sports, politics, public school and its message of mobility and meritocratic achievement in an open society.

Memory can be created; indeed, there is, if anything, too much "memory" in America, too much made-up, synthetic, mythologized memory. The search for roots is a national pastime, and not just for Jews. To "recover" Jewish memory, Jews can see documentaries about the Borscht Belt or Jewish anarchists; they can read accounts of the Lower East Side (as in Irving Howe's World of Our Fathers and E. L. Doctorow's Ragtime) and oral histories of immigrant Jews "out West," just as other American groups can, in *The Godfather, Roots, Bury My Heart at Wounded Knee,* and many other works, ranging from the popular and sensational to the learned and serious. But such efforts cannot create the experience of community that seems to be what they seek. And though people—Jewish or not—may yearn for roots as a balm for their discontents, such yearning itself is only one part of the person, and usually not the part that has real power. "Yes, I would like to be religious, but . . ." or "I wish I were part of a real Jewish community, but . . ." are the formulations that keep coming up. And what follow the "buts" are the beliefs, commitments, and attitudes that are central to the lives of these individuals: a secular, universalist perspective, tolerance in culture and politics, a defense of freedom of choice in life-style and identity. This modernist worldview is the birthright of the unaffiliated; they are not likely to want to give it up.

An observer looking for signs of return among unaffiliated Jews may see their nostalgia for Jewish roots and their creative gestures of Jewish identification as evidence of real potential for Jewish activity. But as we have seen, the interests and concerns voiced by the unaffiliated as they talk about being (or feeling) Jewish are seldom signs of a deep discontent with their current lives or identities; nor do they indicate a change of course of any Jewish significance. And when it comes to the fundamental questions of choosing a spouse or transmitting one's culture and community to offspring, Jewishness remains marginal, at best, for the unaffiliated. Under closer scrutiny, the yearning and the sense of loss dissolve into insubstantial musing, leading sometimes to a gesture of identification but seldom to genuine affiliation.

We should consider the possibility that these feelings are less the expression of a real desire for connection than a residual defensiveness stemming from the negative connotations carried by the traditional image of assimilation. Michael Stone expresses his discomfort with having the word applied to him but admits that the description is accurate. Leslie Epstein says that he is assimilated "rebelliously." To refuse the sociological label while admitting its accuracy must be seen at least in part as an avoidance of the taint of betrayal associated with the classic image.

Although unaffiliated Jews can give imaginative form to their individual gestures of identification and can offer complicated personal arguments to the effect that, appearances notwithstanding, they are not *really* assimilated, the solidity of their assimilated condition is brought out sharply by contrast with the account of someone who makes no gestures, refuses to see assimilation as requiring a complex defense or as a description needing rebuttal, and even expresses resentment toward the Jewish community's moralistic call for affiliation and participation in organized Jewish life.

Sam Silverman* was born and raised in Philadelphia in the early 1940s. He went to the University of Pennsylvania, and then served in the army. Stationed in Japan, he met and married a Japanese woman. He now lives in Philadelphia and works as a journalist. His understanding of his own Jewish experience leaves remarkably little room for sentiment and nostalgia.

"A Democrat and a Dodger Fan"

My idea, when I grew up, was that every Jew was a Democrat and a Dodger fan. That was being Jewish! It all went together. I remember one day in 1952, my mother wakes us up and says, "Eisenhower's president." Oh, my God! That's it! We're in big trouble, Mom! A *Republican* president! Oh, this could be the end of civilization as we know it. See, I thought Adlai Stevenson was Jewish. I mean, who knew?

Jewish is artifacts. Jewish is being a Dodger fan and being a Democrat and talking in a certain way and using certain kinds of words. My grandmother would listen by the radio, and she would hear a Jewish word. She would say, "Oh, did you hear that?" Eddie Cantor would come on and she would rave, "Oh, my God, it's wonderful." Why is it wonderful? Well, it means that other people are Jewish, too, and they're even on the radio. That's good, huh? That reinforces a sense of identity. You don't go to synagogue. Absolutely not. But there's no question that you're Jewish.

Every kid in school, he knows he's not Christian. All the kids are singing Christmas carols at Christmastime. But I know I never said "Christ" when it came up in a song. I'd never say "Christ is born"; I'd say "*Mmmm* is born." Also, I'd never go to school on Passover, or Rosh Hashanah and Yom Kippur. The last two were especially terrible because they were in September. You've just

*Pseudonym.

started school, and then you have to take a stupid day off. For what? Not to go to temple, or anything like that. We'd go to the zoo. Or shopping at Gimbel's department store. We absolutely never went to services—except when I was about to get bar mitzvahed; then we went briefly. You had to have a bar mitzvah; that's the other thing Jewish kids did. So I went through it. And I was so alienated from it. I couldn't figure out what any of it had to do with me. I liked the bourbon and the honey cake at the Kiddush, that was about it. *"Gut Shabbos, gut Shabbos,* eat, eat, eat." That was Jewish religion. And then sometimes right after, we would go downtown shopping at the Food Fair. They would have these little brown 'n' serve sausages, you know, a little sample. I'd just gone to services, now I was eating pork in the supermarket. Even to me, it seemed very, very strange.

Hebrew school, too, was strange. There was no time for me to learn anything for my bar mitzvah, except for a few blessings you say before and after reading the Torah. Though the rabbi did give me a little extra stuff. Like *tefillin*—which I looked up in the dictionary, and it said "phylacteries." So much for that. But whatever it meant, it was the weirdest thing in the world. The rabbi got this little thing out of a box and did it up and put it around me. You know the joke about how it looks like you're taking your own blood pressure? Clearly I could never learn how to do that myself. It's like learning how to change a tire; it's very hard. I never did it again, of course. Anyway, we had my bar mitzvah in the backyard, a whole big party, with pickles and watermelon, pastrami, cold cuts, and hot dogs. There was a certain vestigial religious element to all this, but it had nothing to do with God. Never anything to do with God. Religion was the community. Or the idea of being Jewish.

As kids in school, we never really talked about being Jewish. You knew you were, but it wasn't an important area of concern. I never particularly felt a bond with other kids just because they were Jewish. There are an awful lot of *shlubs* around who are Jewish, let's face it. I mean, *shlub* is a Jewish word, right? And there was never any real sense of anti-Semitism or apartness, except that people would say, "Oh, Jews are so smart," and stuff like that. There were some nasty kids who would say bad things to you, like "kike," occasionally. But only in the sense in which they would say, "Fuck you, asshole," if they wanted to push you out of the way when they were going down the hall. I mean, which do you prefer? There were certainly no attempts to make trouble for people because they were Jewish.

I think that at the time I was going to school there was still this tremendous wave of liberalism about Jews. There was war guilt. There was Israel. *Exodus* was coming out, and *The Source,* and all those things made people say, "Oh, gee, Jews are really special people." This is very dangerous. I'll never forget Bill Russell, on some TV show, saying how much he hated the idea that blacks had natural rhythm. He said, "If you once give blacks the concept of natural rhythm, then you can also say that they're kind of slow, or they could never make good quarterbacks because they don't have the intellect. So please don't tell me I'm terrific at this and I have a great singing voice." Very sharp guy. "Oh, Jews are so smart." And they're devious and clannish, and they're all rich. I remember reading the *American Mercury* in the library when I was in high school. Very anti-Semitic and racist. It was fascinating to me to see direct anti-Semitic utterances. Like, "It's no coincidence that the flag of the United Nations and the flag of Israel are the same color." Or stuff about the "Rothschild-Rockefeller conspiracy." Now, I knew this was crazy. First of all, I knew Rockefeller wasn't Jewish. And second, I knew I didn't have any money. Where was the conspiracy? I'm Jewish and they never tell me about it? I'd feel a lot better if I were in on it.

Look, I get sentimental about some Jewish things and Jewish songs and stuff like that. But I think it's as much being sentimental about childhood as about being Jewish. I was never more Jewish than when I was a kid growing up with my grandma. I grew up so closely with her that I even used to confuse Yiddish and English. I remember I once went to this kid's birthday party, I must have been five, six years old—and they're having birthday cake. I dropped my fork, and I said, "Can I have another *gappel?*" Everybody looked at me and said: "What's the hell's the matter with him? What's a *gappel?*" Or I would say "cloysepin" instead of "clothespin," things like that. She was really Jewish, my grandma. Not religious, but as Jewish as any grandmother could ever be. And I can still imagine her making onion *bulkes* [rolls] and stuffing a kishke. Always food, right? That's my childhood. That's what I look back on. It's not exactly Proust, but that's how I get sentimental. More delicious than a madeleine.

But when I actually think about Jewishness, I don't like it. I don't like nationalism. I don't like sectarianism. I think it's a tremendously divisive force. I've always felt this. I remember one day in school, when I was about eight years old, this kid comes up to me and says, "Al Jolson died." I had seen *The Jolson Story*, and I felt awfully sorry and sad too. And he says, "He was a good Jew." And I thought, How disgusting! I mean what a sectarian attitude—a "good Jew." He sang "Mammy" like nobody's business, but—a "good Jew"? What is it with this crap? I thought that even then. And I always remembered it, and it just made me sick. I thought it was just horrible. A "good Jew." It really makes me mad.

And so does all this stuff from the rabbis that "Jews are assimilating; you shouldn't marry non-Jews." Well, too bad. So make it so they won't. Don't make a law against it. It's like Prohibition. If their Judaism was strong enough, then they wouldn't marry outside Judaism. It's as simple as that. Moses did it, and his sister gave him a hard time—and she got leprosy. So you see. And all the complaints: "You should be more Jewish. It's a sin that people aren't more Jewish." Hey, what is this "more" Jewish? Come to think of it, I don't even like some of the Prophets, jumping up and down saying, "You guys really should go back to worshipping God." I mean, what's in it for us? Well, what's in it is this mystical covenant about being the chosen people. That's why you shouldn't marry goyim, that's why you should keep kosher. It's a horrible idea—I don't like it at all. I don't believe I'm a chosen person. And I'm Jewish. The point is, people keep what means something to them. I'm against suppression. If there were a situation like in Russia where people are not allowed to observe Passover, that's a very bad thing. However, if there's a big slackening off in the purchase of matzoh in the United States because people are just not eating it, well, that's the way it is. And *zol zein*, you know, let it be.

I like to say "*zol zein*," come to think of it. It makes me feel good. It's again like childhood, and I still enjoy doing a lot of things I liked doing as a child. But if I had a child and the kid never said "*zol zein*," but said "*shga ta genai*"—that's Japanese for "can't help it"—then that would be OK too. I felt very bad when the Dodgers went to Los Angeles—this is not a non sequitur. I feel about as bad about the decline of Judaism in the United States. And I feel really bad about the decline of the Democratic party. I feel a real yearning for the New Deal and Franklin Delano Roosevelt. The Dodgers are in L.A.; Judaism is falling apart. To me, these have similar significance. Now, some may say, "The decline of Judaism is much more important than the fact that the Dodgers moved to L.A." Not to me, not to me! And I think other people should reassess their values.

Of course, I feel a pang that I'm losing something. I'm losing a tradition. My parents don't speak Yiddish as well as their parents. I speak almost no Yiddish at all. I feel something is lost. But I don't feel guilt about that. I feel regret. I could learn Yiddish, but it's not the same thing, because to learn it means to make it artificial, something that's not part of you. The people who are taking Yiddish courses, they're going to pronounce Yiddish the way I would pronounce Japanese. It's like learning the blues from records. It's a kind of blues. And the people who do it really love it. But it's not the blues. The blues is the blues. You can't learn it from a record. It's too bad; it's lost. And I regret that loss. But if I step back, I think it's perfectly normal—because much is taken, much is given. You get something else.

People who become religious in their adulthood are almost inexplicable to me. I don't know why they need it. I'm not talking about people who believe in God. I'm talking about people who are looking for a sense of community. It's like a lot of people are attached to the folklore of the mailman going by the old Main Street: "Hi, Grandpa." "Hiya, Doc." *Our Town.* Thornton Wilder. But they should've read *Winesburg, Ohio.* Or Kafka. Because this is nothing new, the so-called alienation of society that we're suffering from, and the fragmentation of the individual, and the breakdown of the family. The farmers all moved to the city. Why is that? Because they didn't want to be on the farm anymore. They hated being on the goddamn farm. "Oh, the old family farm." Let it go. If there's no need for it, let it go. Sure, I love those old houses with the verandah, the swing on the back porch, grandpa, grandma, the picnic table out in front. "Won't you have some fried chicken?" Well, I never had it in my own life. Most people never had it. And you can't re-create it. People have to get a sense of community from themselves, or from their common interests. I would no more join a Jewish congregation to get it than I would join the Kiwanis Club.

Everything changes. Nothing stays the way it is. So? What's the big deal? Why is that a terrible thing? What's so terrible about that? If Jewishness disappeared completely off the face of the earth, what would be lost? Jewish folk songs? People who wanted to could still listen to them. Jewish literature? It would still be there for those interested in reading it. People would still keep talking about the Haggadah and Queen Esther. It's mythology, just like the Roman and Greek myths, and they're still part of our culture even though we don't believe in Apollo. The Jewish Law? Nobody would follow the Law? Nobody would be kosher? Oh, my God, where would we get a good pastrami sandwich? Well, that's how it is. What will happen is that Judaism will evolve itself out of recognition. Somebody from the generation before will say, "That's not Judaism." So it's something else. What would be lost is a certain feeling. Undoubtedly. But is that a bad thing? I assume something will replace it. I'm not a Dodger fan anymore. I feel that lack, I must admit. But I still like baseball.

Look, if the whooping crane ain't gonna make it, the whooping crane ain't gonna make it. No hatcheries are going to do it. That's what these rabbis are trying to do, make hatcheries for whooping cranes.

Silverman demonstrates a striking immunity to the tradition-hunger, the ritual-hunger, and the wholeness-hunger that can agitate even securely unaffiliated Jewish-Americans. He is even able to contemplate the disappearance of the Jewish people with equanimity. But in terms of actions, nothing different follows from Silverman's unsentimental attitude than from the more defensive and emotionally charged questionings or prideful assertions of the others. He does neither more, nor less, than they do. What distinguishes him from the others is the absence of particular feelings: the mixture of images and sentiments, nostalgia, yearning for a lost world and guilt for having lost it, and the tone of defensiveness. Once these feelings are cleared away, the reality of assimilation stands out sharply.

But not as it is ordinarily conceived. The episodic but intense involvement with Jewishness and Jewish identification found among the unaffiliated is at odds with the traditional paradigm of assimilation, which emphasizes the abandonment of identification and repression of Jewish connection. This gap between the traditional image and reality does not mean, however, that assimilation is not the proper designation for the unaffiliated—only that the traditional "either-or" construction does not capture the contemporary nature of either assimilation or identification today.

Currently, the millions of unaffiliated Jewish-Americans, along with other hyphenated Americans, find themselves in a historically unprecedented situation, where nostalgia for a lost world coexists easily with integration into the larger culture, and where feeling ethnic requires no communal affiliation.

Assimilation, conventionally defined as the total abandonment of ethnic expression and connection, has clearly not been the fate of Jewish-Americans, nor of many other Americans who can cite the source for the adjective before the hyphen in their ethnic classification. Yet those adjectives, the various ethnic pieces, do not typically add up to anything more than an enhancement of integrated American lives. What exists now is best described as a post-assimilation state in which the most powerful forces shaping consciousness and identity are no longer commitments to or rebellions against religious or ethnic groups, as in the old assimilation paradigm, but free choice, psychic as well as physical mobility, and individualism—which may even include some degree of ethnic and religious identification.

Although this description does not apply to all Americans by any means, the number living in this cultural state is growing rapidly. The character of this developing post-assimilation culture can be brought out vividly by considering the children of Sam Silverman. They will hear stories of past generations of Jews in America, of immigrants, ethnic food, and jokes. They will know their father is Jewish and have some sense of what that means, just as they will know that their mother is Japanese and hear stories of her origins. They will be true Americans, close to the melting-pot ideal, mixed in many ways, with "roots" in the ghettos of Eastern Europe, American urban life, traditional and modernized Japan.

Will it be analytically fruitful to use the old concept of "assimilation" to explain their situation or to predict their commitments and loyalties? Assimilated from what and to what? Although objectively describable as Jewish-Japanese (or vice versa) Americans, they will be natives of a culture not definable by traditional group membership categories. Their parents are still aware of the change of milieu and culture that separates their own childhood and youth from the world of their adult lives; for the children, that post-assimilation culture will be the given—the only one they know.

2

In Search of the Self-Hating Jew

It has been a constant theme in the debate about assimilation that disaffiliation from the Jewish community would cause psychic conflict. The risks are grave: not only the loss of community, but also the shame and self-betrayal that must follow the repudiation of one's people. "The Jews have wanted profoundly to be Americans, Englishmen, Germans, even Poles," wrote novelist Ludwig Lewisohn. "Can such things be done? Can they be done without inflicting an inner hurt, a wound to the moral fiber?"

In Europe, where assimilation commonly required hiding one's origins and often conversion to Christianity, the effects of flight from Jewish identity could and often did impose a painful psychological burden. There is evidence for this burden not only among Jews but also in the history of other stigmatized groups whose acceptance into the larger society was possible only at the cost of hiding, denying, or repressing their ethnic or racial origins.

For Jews, this plight acquired its name in Germany during the years preceding Hitler's rise to power. In 1930, the German-Jewish philosopher Theodor Lessing identified the syndrome in his widely noticed study *Der Jüdische Selbsthass* (Jewish Self-Hatred). Lessing presented case histories of "self-hating" German-Jewish intellectuals, including several, like Otto Weininger, who escaped the "curse" of Jewishness by committing suicide. The

45

voices of these pathetic figures rise to an ecstasy of self-loathing. One ends his confession this way:

> There exists today hardly a more tragic fate than that of those few who have truly fought themselves free from their Jewish ancestry and who now discover that people do not believe them, do not want to believe them. Where, where can we go? Behind us lie revulsion and disgust, in front of us yawns an abyss. . . . And I feel as if I had to carry on my shoulders the entire accumulated guilt of that cursed breed of men whose poisonous self-blood is becoming my virus. I feel as if I, I alone, had to do penance for every crime those people are committing against Germanness.

Although such extremes of feeling were hardly common, self-hatred in some degree was a palpable danger for all who felt ambivalent about their Jewish origin or experienced it as an unwanted burden. Could this situation be relevant to America, a country with a sharp separation of church and state, a melting-pot culture, and even an official commitment, first voiced publicly by none other than George Washington, to oppose the anti-Semitism so prevalent in the Old World?

Generations back, the answer was clearly yes. Here is how Ben Hecht, co-author of *The Front Page*, began his 1931 novel *A Jew in Love:*

> Jo Boshere (born Abe Nussbaum) was a man of thirty—a dark-skinned little Jew with a vulturous and moody face, a reedy body and a sense of posture.
>
> The Jews now and then hatch a face which for Jewishness surpasses the caricatures of the entire anti-Semitic press. These Jew faces in which race leers and burns like some biologic disease are rather shocking to a mongrelized world.
>
> People dislike being reminded of their origins. They shudder a bit mystically at the sight of anyone who looks too much like a fish, a lizard, a chimpanzee or a Jew. This is probably nonsense. The Jew face is an enemy totem, an ancient target for spittle and, like a thing long hated, a sort of magic propagandist of hate. Its persistence in the world is that of some repulsive and hostile fauna, half crippled, yet containing in its ineffaceable Yiddish outline the taunt and challenge of the unfinished victim. This, of

course, is true only of the worst looking Jew faces and the worst Jew haters.

Boshere was not quite so bad as this. The racial decadence which had popped so Hebraic a nosegay out of his mother's womb was of finer stuff than that glandular degeneration which produces the Jew with the sausage face; the bulbous, diabetic half-monsters who look as if they had been fished out of the water a month too late.

These bloaters are surely a vicious drag on the vanity of the race, and nobody winces at the sight of them so much as the Jew.

This is strong stuff, European in tone. Even in America, it seems, being Jewish was experienced as a burden, something to be regretted, escaped, hidden—often literally, by changing hair, nose, name, accent, cultural traits, and religious affiliation. Indeed, in 1946, when Sidney Hook was a philosophy professor at New York University, he reported to the Fortieth Annual Meeting of the American Jewish Committee on the results of an informal poll that he took every year in his philosophy classes at NYU. He said that when he asked his students whether they would have wanted to be born Jewish, *not one* of them had ever answered in the affirmative.

In the same period, Kurt Lewin, a German-Jewish psychologist who emigrated to the United States, published several essays on the psychology of self-hatred that are still read and quoted today by psychologically-minded writers on issues of Jewish identity. In "Self-Hatred Among Jews," Lewin theorized that in any underprivileged group there will be a number of persons ashamed of their group identity, since assimilation means internalizing the values of the majority, including the majority's negative images of one's own minority group. Jews of this sort will try to move as far as possible from things Jewish, a condition he called "negative chauvinism": "The more typically Jewish people are, or the more typically Jewish a cultural symbol or behavior pattern is, the more distasteful they will appear to this person. Being unable to cut himself loose from his Jewish connections and his Jewish past, the hatred turns upon himself." Lewin described Jews as marginal persons standing between groups, subject to an instability and uncertainty of identity capable of causing self-hate. This perspective was codified in a widely used social psychology textbook in which self-hatred is analyzed as the interaction of three factors:

those of high status define one's group as inferior, one experiences discrimination because of group membership, yet the attitudes of the majority prevent one from leaving the group.

"The conflict between assimilation and identification for Jews exacts a price in discontent, alienation, and various forms of self-hate," writes Judith Weinstein Klein, a psychotherapist in California who has developed a detailed theory and practice of "ethnotherapy" specifically for American Jews, whom she considers particularly afflicted by self-hatred. In this latest formulation of Lewin's perspective, Klein is extending the work of psychiatrist Price Cobbs, co-author of *Black Rage*, who developed therapy groups for blacks to repair their self-images of inferiority. Klein makes use of Lewin's notion that belonging to a stigmatized minority group leads members of the group to express hostility toward themselves or their group rather than toward the more powerful majority. Because they have been raised in an "assimilated cultural environment," she asserts, most American Jews experience self-hatred and negative chauvinism to some degree. For the blatant self-haters of earlier decades, such feelings were neither obscure nor unconscious. In the current situation, however, these traits usually manifest themselves, according to Klein, in ways that are masked to the individual's consciousness. Of course, viewed through such a psychosocial lens, any unaffiliated American Jew is potentially vulnerable to the accusation of self-hatred—and one's own testimony to the contrary can be taken as no more than proof of the point.

But, as Lewin noted, such self-hatred is not inevitable; and Klein agrees. Since the troubling element is, as Lewin put it, "uncertainty about the ground on which [one] stands and the group to which [one] belongs," psychic health for minority-group members requires "early, clear, and positive feeling of belonging to the group." Klein's ethnotherapy groups (like others around the country) are intended to accomplish this identification, which the second- or third-generation family typically failed to provide. In a lengthy account of her work that appeared in the *San Francisco Chronicle*, under the heading "Helping Jews to Like Themselves," Klein summarized her experience. "Over and over," she said, she found that "the Jews who were the least comfortable with their Jewishness tended to date non-Jews, have non-Jewish friends, avoid Jewish organizations and traditional holiday observances, and be displeased with what they felt were unattractive Jewish features, like dark curly hair or big noses." Klein noted that after undergoing ethnotherapy, a significant number of her clients were able to feel "more comfortable" with their Jewishness. The evidence of their progress was that they were dating Jews for the first time, joining Jewish organizations, or becoming active in political causes that involved specifically Jewish concerns. "Anytime that people move from a passive to an active stance," Klein concluded, "it breeds higher self-esteem. That's what the groups are all about."

Jeremy Block* was born in Baltimore in 1940, and moved to California when he was a boy. A veterinarian, he lives with his wife in San Francisco. He recalls having felt deeply ambivalent about being Jewish throughout his life.

"My Parents Are, But . . ."

There was a period when I would not have said I was Jewish, but by the time I was in my late twenties, if it came up, I just said "Yes," and didn't explain. I went from "No, I'm not" to "My parents are, but . . ." to just saying "Yes." Over time, I started to feel Jewish. I felt Jewish, but confused. Before I started in the ethnotherapy group, there was the feeling of not being comfortable about being Jewish, somehow not feeling right. I became aware of wanting more contact with things Jewish. I've always felt like an outsider.

My family was ethnic Jewish, agnostic. My grandmother used Yiddish words, I remember. My mother's family also used Yiddish expressions, told jokes. There were occasional Seders, but at other people's houses. I've always felt antireligious and antiritual, and I still do. After my mother and I finally settled in Hollywood, she got me to go to the Reform temple for a year to get confirmed. I was already fourteen and hadn't been bar mitzvahed.

My wife is an artist. I met her at UCLA twenty-three years ago—we're still married. She came from a farm in Iowa, Midwestern, very American. "You ain't got no ethnic," I tell her. She was transferring to Berkeley, so I got a job as a vet there, and we've lived in the Bay area ever since.

Sometime in the early 1980s, I heard about ethnotherapy and

*Pseudonym.

went to a lecture by Judith Klein, where she talked about her thesis work and showed a video about the groups she ran. She talked about Chicanos and Asians and how every ethnic group has similar problems about their ethnicity, not just Jews. I gave her my name, and months later I got a notice about a group being organized. I went to the first meeting where there were about ten or twelve people. I remember being amazed at how WASP-looking half of them were, with names to match, like "Ross." We talked about that.

At the first meeting, people would say why they were there. Mostly there was stuff about confusion, a sense of lacking and loss, with some saying they wanted to be more a part of a Jewish community. The leaders asked "What is a Jew?" and we went around and answered, and there was a whole list of things like "hard to get along with," "being good fathers," "being emotional," things like that. After going around, Judith pointed out that no one had said "a fighter." Then people talked about what being Jewish meant to them. It was validating to hear how other people were feeling confused. I remember, at an all-day session near the end of the group, Judy was looking at all the food. She said she remembered that when she had done some event with a gentile woman and she had been looking at all the food, the other woman said, "Don't worry, it will all get eaten." She then said, "That's the gentile way of looking at it; the Jewish way is to worry whether there will be enough."

In the day-long session, one of the exercises we did was to stand up in front of the group, say "I am a Jew," and then say whatever came to mind, and then repeat "I am a Jew," and whatever else, over and over. When I did it, to my utter shock, from God knows where, I ended up crouched behind a chair, with my hand making like a gun, saying, "I am a Jew, and if you try to hurt me because of that, I'll kill you." I listened to myself saying that, and I thought, This is really strange. Maybe it was part of my sense of being an outsider—which is partly Jeremy and partly being a Jew.

I remember that when the group was singing "Hava Nagila," I went into the kitchen, and the guy who was the group's co-leader came in and pulled me over to the group, which was all right. It was just that I don't like that kind of ritual, like I don't like sitting around the campfire singing campfire songs. I don't like ceremonies. I don't celebrate my birthday, or Christmas. I don't like religion, but I think I have less antipathy toward Judaism than other religions, because I understand more about the historical things now.

The summing up was about what you got out of the group and what you were going to do with what you got, about feeling better and more comfortable about being Jewish. I said I wasn't sure what to do or where to go, and I went over all the things I didn't want, like the rituals and the religion, and I even asked "Does anyone have any suggestions?" and one of the guys said, "You want a Jewish volleyball team."

A couple of years ago, I learned about something called the Society for Humanistic Judaism and I thought, This is for me, and I went to a lecture and to a couple of their events, like a picnic. But even this was still too much about religion and rituals. I think my desire for the Jewish thing is part of my desire for a group bigger than myself. I don't belong to any groups or movements.

What I came to after the group was that I was going to acknowledge more consciously that I was Jewish, with my Jewish and non-Jewish friends. Like I would use a Jewish word, or tell a Jewish joke and explain it to my non-Jewish staff, or say to a non-Jewish friend, "Pretty good for a gentile"—things like that. I did join the local Jewish community center, but I only went to a play there, and to a lecture, which was a report about politics in Central America. And I did become a member of an organization called American Veterinarians for Israel, which really exists, and I actually went to Israel a few years ago. My wife was in Italy and we arranged to meet in Israel. I expected a kind of Jewish gemütlichkeit, or Jewishkeit. I said I would let myself be open to the rush of Jewish experience. But I didn't feel that at all. I thought I was in a Levantine country, Middle Eastern, and the tension was palpable—I would never want to live there.

I talked the group up a lot, to all my Jewish friends, and they all said it sounded interesting, but none of them took me up on it. I think that it helped me feel more that there is something like a shared common experience of being Jewish, though I can't really explain what this is. But for an illustration, this insurance guy came to see me, and he was a Jew, and I knew he was a Jew, though he didn't say it and he didn't trade on that, and I thought, If I'm going to do business with an insurance agent who I don't know, I'll do it with him. Part of me said, I trust this guy, he wouldn't cheat me. Now intellectually, I knew this was silly. Still, if someone came to my door and said, "Help me, I'm Jewish, and I saw you had a Jewish name," I think I would help him. . . . Don't tell anyone I said this. The more a person is like me, the more I'm likely to help him.

———

When Jeremy Block was infected with what he has learned to call self-hatred, he had no involvement in the Jewish community; now that he has been cured, he still has no involvement—though he does occasionally tell Jewish jokes. Apparently, for him there is no serious tension between his previous life and a new Jewish identification.

And why should there be? The fact that an American Jew today has many non-Jewish friends, dates and marries a non-Jew, and is uninvolved and uninterested in Jewish community affairs should not be taken to imply a pathological condition for which the recommended therapy is becoming "more" Jewish. While self-hatred could plausibly explain certain behaviors of a self-hating individual ("tending to date non-Jews," "avoiding Jewish organizations and traditional holiday observances"), such behavior in a given individual does not—particularly in the present-day American context—provide a basis for ascribing self-hatred. Although a self-hating Jew would definitely display behavior of this sort, a contented and even proudly identified Jew can, as Block does, show the very same characteristics—not joining Jewish groups, marrying a gentile woman—but not for the same reasons, and not with the same meanings.

Ethnotherapy makes a strong claim: That a proud and open commitment to Jewish identification is the path to psychic health for unaffiliated American Jews. That Jews who are deeply engaged in Jewish culture and religion, who gain joyful and satisfying experiences from their Jewish identification, who are knowledgeable and well integrated in a Jewish community, will be much healthier psychologically than assimilated Jews, for whom Jewish identity is by definition problematic. As Irving Levine of the American Jewish Committee said while a guest with Judith Klein and two other ethnotherapists (of non-Jewish ethnicities) on the Phil Donahue show, "It isn't a question of chauvinism or whatever; it is a question of good mental health."

Levine, we suggest, was being somewhat disingenuous. It may not be "chauvinism" that is in question, but the worry of all Jewish organizations about the growing trend toward disaffiliation must be part of the reason for the American Jewish Committee's support for Klein's kind of therapy. Given the low levels of knowledge of and interest in Judaism as a religion or a cultural heritage among the unaffiliated, it is understandable that Jewish-community professionals should grasp at that most modernist of beliefs, the therapeutic ideal, to shore up Jewish commitment. In the therapeutic approach, psychic discomfort may be traced back to problems in self-image, which, whatever else goes into its construction, certainly includes one's ethnic, racial, religious, regional, and class backgrounds. Being Jewish could not fail to have some meaning for an American Jew. But to make ethnic assertion—the stronger, the better—a crucial sign of mental health is a highly ideological claim with little empirical or theoretical support.

The traditional self-hatred perspective simultaneously overrates the peril of being Jewish in contemporary America and underrates the scope of positive self-images available to Jews today. Even unaffiliated American Jews who know very little about Judaism, Jewish culture, or the Jewish community are aware of the favorable stereotypes about Jewish character—Jews are smart, sensual, responsible, clever, and so on—commonly found in the broader cultural milieu, which is to say, in the books, movies, and TV shows that are shared by all Americans. In ethnotherapy's own terms, such positive notions of Jewishness should provide psychic supports for personal self-esteem powerful enough to complicate the theoretical dynamics of classic Jewish self-hatred.

Janet Freed* is a magazine editor in her late twenties. Though apparently in need of some powerful ethnotherapy, she in fact offers a striking illustration of just how complicated those dynamics have now become.

"Half-Jewish"

In the last three weeks, I've all of a sudden become Jewish. I got an invitation to a lecture at the Anti-Defamation League. And for some reason I thought, I'm going to do this.

I grew up without much Jewish identity. My parents both came from Brooklyn, what they would refer to as a "Jewish ghetto." And they definitely wanted out of that. Wherever they lived—in

*Pseudonym.

Long Island, New Jersey, or Washington, D.C.—they purposely moved to non-Jewish neighborhoods. My father is a physicist who does work for the Defense Department, and my mother works for the Welfare Department. We kept up some Jewish connections. We would go to Seders at my grandparents and to cousins' bar mitzvahs. In our own house, we had a menorah for Hanukkah, and my mother sometimes lit candles on the holidays. For a while, we even observed Yom Kippur; we would fast and go to temple. That is, my mother would. My father wouldn't. He was an atheist, and he always told me the whole thing was bullshit. My brother wasn't bar mitzvahed. By that time we had stopped going to temple even once a year. The issue of bar mitzvah never came up. My father just got him a dog for his thirteenth birthday. My sister and I occasionally went to the youth group at the temple, even though we didn't belong. Why anyone wanted to bake cookies and sit around talking about what it means to be Jewish today! I thought it was really boring. I much preferred going to Bloomingdale's. And I did.

When I went to Harvard, I started going out with all sorts of men. I went through a whole preppy phase. I dated preppy men and had preppy girlfriends and wore turtlenecks and pastel colors and played field hockey. It was so different. Because even though I was raised in non-Jewish neighborhoods, I still had a very Jewish family. Especially my father—not in a religious sense, but heritage-wise and in speech patterns and attitudes. "Jews are the best and the smartest" or "Jews don't concern themselves with athletics." "There are two kinds of people," my father would say, "people of the body and people of the mind." Italians and other Christians are mostly people of the body; Jews—you guessed it—are people of the mind. Also, everyone in the family always expressed their emotions fully. We had screaming arguments— yelling and screaming all the time. I called my father names, which I never found in any non-Jewish household. We were always talking about problems and moaning and whining. That is Jewish to me: whining. And I whine to this day, and I hate it.

I think my parents subtly encouraged me to go out with non-Jews. My mother always had an eye out for this social thing. She wanted me to have the best, which to her meant being accepted in WASP society. And I was, sort of. For a long time, I was involved with a very WASPy guy from Connecticut. We'd go to his family's house for weekends, and there would be soccer, football, baseball . . . and drinking. The men all worked in investment banks, and the women all sat around talking about their gardens, or the "weather" side of the house. I was the first Jewish girl he had gone out with. He liked it. He used to call me his "little knish." I think he found me exotic and sensual.

Being with him was sort of a dream come true. When I was younger I used to have this fantasy that I was a Jewess in medieval England, just like Rebecca in *Ivanhoe*. And I would be captured by some Anglo-Saxon prince; but I would be so wonderful that, instead of being put to death, I would become part of the court. I would be the Jewess, his mistress, whom he couldn't marry because I was Jewish. It was exciting and dramatic. In this fantasy, there was also this Jewish man from the ghetto in London who tried to rescue me with his Jewish warriors. I was supposed to be engaged to him. He was sort of a tribesman, a young Charlton Heston. And I was fond of him . . . but I really adored this Anglo-Saxon prince.

I adored my boyfriend, and I wanted to be part of his world. I was impressed with the status and social standing of these people. They had made American society and were a real part of it: a kind of aristocracy. They were it. They had class. Jews could be just as rich, but they were vulgar. The WASPs had manners. They would never scream at someone over the dinner table. They wouldn't come to dinner in their underwear, which my father did now and then. They would always hear you out, and not say, "Oh, come off it, cut the crap, okay?" They'd say, "Oh, that's very interesting; maybe we could talk about that later on," or something like that. I admired that so much. I never actually denied that I was Jewish, though I was very aware of trying not to be. I wanted to be elegant and athletic and worldly, just like them. My sister had an even worse case of it than I did. She came back from college totally ashamed of my family: why were we never raised to be athletic, and why are you overweight, Dad, and why do you use that vulgar language and yell at the table? She convinced our father to send our brother to a very WASPy boarding school to get him away from his bad heritage.

But I didn't ever quite fit in. My boyfriend's father was very anti-Semitic. Not in a malicious way. More in the sense that Jews are different, they're from another planet. He is a physician, and sometimes he'll barter services if people can't afford to pay. He was treating the little girl of some Jewish people who owned a restaurant, and they were giving his family a free dinner, since they couldn't afford his fees. The dinner was lovely. The people gave us menus without prices, came over and chatted with us, and were charming and attentive. After we left, just outside, the father commented, "You know, those are the nicest people—for Jews." I just couldn't believe it. I stuck my friend with an elbow. His father didn't even know I was Jewish. I told him to mention it to his father, and nothing like that ever happened again. But in that crowd, anti-Semitic jokes were always coming up, or comments about how Jewish someone was. What they meant was that Jews were very smart, but wily. They believed what I suppose are all the old stereotypes, which hold true to a certain extent. A lot of them weren't aware that I was Jewish, or it never occurred to them that I would mind. And I wasn't sure what I felt; they did it in such a casual way that my objections felt wrong, overly defensive.

Ultimately, things didn't work out, because I was denying more than just a label. I was denying myself. I was the only one in the group who liked to read, and yet I never did. I really didn't care about tennis, but I was totally ashamed that I wasn't good at it. And I got very sick of the whole WASP thing. I found it repressive and sort of silly. I never really fit in with those women—I still don't know which is the "weather" side of the house, or why. And I don't care. You couldn't really get inside those people. And finally, I didn't want to be them—they were just too boring.

I love the image of the Jews as smart. And though the Jewish way of life has its great drawbacks—it tends to make you a bit spineless, passive, and cowardly—at least it doesn't make you repressed. It encourages you to express what you think and feel; and once you do, and someone else responds to you—well, that's communicating and thinking and ideas are born and things get made and civilization is advanced. Well, I don't care a whole lot about civilization being advanced, but I do care about communicating. That's important. So I wanted to get more involved in Jewish things to see if that was for me.

I enjoyed my evening at the Anti-Defamation League meeting. The people were young professionals, and I liked that. But, frankly, I kind of OD'd on the Jewishness. I got a little heavied out by the amount of Jewish people. I mean—everybody there was Jewish. And not just Jewish, but ethnically Jewish! And I just . . . oh, enough with the Jewish, already. I mean, it's just like when you're in a place where everybody is Puerto Rican, like 14th

Street. You know, no matter how you feel about individual Puerto Ricans, there are just too many Puerto Ricans there. And this was just too Jewish. Still, I did meet two guys there, and they each asked me out, and I'm going out with both of them.

On a date with one of them, we went to temple. I was curious about the Jewish heritage and culture, and I wanted to see what the religion was all about. I didn't go to try and believe in God—that's a personal thing, and it doesn't concern me. In fact, I was nervous about going because I don't like all that hysterical religious stuff. I think it's harmful to be too religious. It instills in you a belief in something that is not reality.

I mean, look at the Hasidim. I feel no relation to those people at all. They have so many bad qualities. They disregard what's going on in the world and live in this medieval society. They're pasty-faced. That's almost the worst thing. They're white as a sheet. They don't get any exercise, which is good for you. I don't want to be associated with them, and they just embarrass the hell out of me. The Hasidim give Jews a bad name—whereas Jews can be beautiful and clean, and they don't all screw through holes in a sheet. The Hasidim play into the sense that Jews are different, that no matter how assimilated they get, they can never really fit in; they will never be acceptable, or accepted. And I hate being associated with them.

But to my surprise, temple was wonderful. The religion really appealed to me, because it believes in God as an ideal to be lived in this life. It's very humanistic and commonsensical. It deals with the here and now, not with saving your soul. I'm not interested in saving my soul. I care about the here and now. It was a lovely ceremony, the welcoming of the Sabbath: "OK, the week is done, and now it's Friday night; let's be peaceful and sing these pretty tunes and think these nice thoughts." I loved reading the Reform prayer book. I felt a real sense of community with the people there, even though I didn't know any of them. It was a very attractive, upper-middle-class, New York Jewish group. I felt like I was part of it.

I wouldn't mind going again. I suppose I'm still sort of going through a Jewish phase; but I suspect I'll transcend it. I'm already getting a bit sick of it. I'm not a preppy WASP, obviously, but I have the feeling from the little evidence I have—the temple, the Anti-Defamation League—that I'm not the other thing, either. The truth is, I'm finding, I don't belong to either camp. I thought I would have more in common with someone who was Jewish—but frankly, I'm finding I have less. I'm most comfortable in the middle ground, which is probably why I enjoy half-Jewish people so much. I realize that most of my close girlfriends are half-Jewish. And the one guy I really liked recently was also half-Jewish. What I liked about him was that he was Jewish, but not too Jewish, by any means. He was warm and bright and intellectual and a wheeler-dealer, but also extremely polite. He didn't come on too strong, and he knew how to hobnob with everybody.

In some basic way, the truth about me is that I am half-Jewish. I want an amalgam. My parents always said, "Being Jewish is wonderful; you just have to get away from the bad parts." And I think you can. After all, there are people who are Jews who come from old families. There are old Jewish families who have class, and I like the idea of belonging to them. I like the idea of being engaged to "Skip Rothschild," say, and going to a classy temple, and hearing all the Jewish ladies saying, "Oh, that's Skip Rothschild's fiancée." That's my ideal.

There is no need to dig deep into Janet Freed's psyche to find the characteristic tones of self-hatred: they are impossible to miss in her self-presentation. They color her youthful fantasy of a romantic Anglo-Saxon prince and her adult aspirations to enter the WASP elite. Her self-image involves a perpetual struggle against a whole complex of negative traits that she associates with Jews: "all the old stereotypes," as she puts it, "which hold true to a certain extent." Jews are vulgar and excessively emotional, given to yelling and whining. They are awkward and unhealthy, spineless, cowardly, uncivilized. Religious Jews are the worst: "medieval," "pasty-faced," unhealthy, and a personal embarrassment. More than anything, Freed yearns to escape from her "bad heritage" of Jewish tribalism into the neutral social world of good manners and elegance that she associates with the refinement and wealth of the WASP aristocracy.

At first glance, Freed's story seems merely a contemporary reprise of *Remember Me to God*, Myron Kaufmann's popular novel of the mid-1950s that portrayed the anguished Richard Amsterdam, a middle-class Jewish Bostonian who yearns to be accepted into the world of gentile Harvard (the novel is set in the early 1940s). His obsession with marrying a Radcliffe girl, his goal of membership in an exclusive Harvard club, his attempt to slough off Jewish traits, and eventually his decision to convert to a respectable and genteel Protestant denomination—these classic elements of Jewish self-hatred are the substance of Kaufmann's novel.

But the classic description hardly fits Janet Freed. Not only does she not deny her Jewish origin: she insists upon it as a source of pride. Jews are smart, unrepressed, interesting, and serious. They care about the essential things, they read, they communicate their feelings. Jewish religion, in its Reform aspect, is rational, "humanistic," "commonsensical," concerned with the "here and now." Freed even attends a meeting of the Anti-Defamation League. (A self-hater at the ADL? America really is different.) Indeed, Freed does not ultimately *want* to get away from all association with Jewishness. Secrecy, name change, denial, and, finally, conversion are not the direction in which the force of her internalized self-hatred will push her. She wants to be what she feels she is: "half"-Jewish. She wants to have access to the sources of pride Jewishness offers, but also to participate totally in the non-Jewish world. She wants the "middle ground," as she calls it, a combination of the brains associated with Jews and the classiness not so traditional in their heritage. The truth is, Freed wants everything, and in a world where a "Skip Rothschild" can exist, she has a good chance of getting it.

The noteworthy thing about Janet Freed is not what is obvious and repellent—the disturbing reiteration of some of the classic self-hating symptoms—but rather that these symptoms coexist easily with a cheerful insistence on a positive Jewish identity. Sidney Hook's test would find no parallel today. The universal sense of stigma evoked by his casual classroom poll is no longer apparent among unaffiliated young American Jews. Though some might still say they wished they had not been born Jewish, more would probably assert that they felt good about being Jewish, or that it was not a matter of importance—certainly a new circumstance for Jews.

The historically new desire to be half-Jewish reflects this destigmatization of Jewish identity in American society. The figure of the half-Jew conjures up a kind of ethnic equilibrium, a harmonious state in which there need not be any impetus to greater identification, but where there is no hiding. As one Jewish father told us, describing the situation of his own biologically half-Jewish daughter: "Caitlin doesn't want to be *Jewish*, she wants to be what she is. She's perfectly satisfied being the child of an Irish-Catholic mother and a Jewish-Slovak father. She likes the fact that she is all these different things; she doesn't want to be one thing. Now and again she thinks, Wouldn't it be nice to be this one thing? but basically, no."

The ideal of the half-Jew, whether as a real or an imagined identity, offers a much truer picture of the realities of assimilation today than the reduction of all nuance to an inevitable conflict between assimilation and identification, as posited by Klein and other proponents of self-hatred theories. In an anti-Semitic climate, full acceptance into the majority culture required abjuring Jewish identification. When Landauer, the "German" friend in Christopher Isherwood's *The Berlin Stories,* finally comes out with the tormented confession that he is a Jew—having changed his name and tried to pass as a gentile in order to get ahead in Weimar Germany—he reveals the wrenching experience he has suffered in posing as a "real" German and that he must suffer again as he reassumes his Jewish identity. But Freed's decision to enter a "Jewish phase" makes no demands on her, psychic, social, or ritualistic. In the synagogue she attends, she hardly feels out of place or a member of a despised and underprivileged minority. The parts of Judaism she likes and wants to own—intelligence, expressiveness, humanism, sensitivity—are completely in line with what she believes in: they are the basic values of secular culture. Far from conflicting with her self-image as a cosmopolitan, middle-class, intelligent professional, this kind of selective identification may even enhance it. Freed's sense of belonging, acquired without much effort, serves quite effectively to bolster her self-esteem, which is so dominant an issue in considerations of self-hatred and identification.

The basic problem with the ideological constructions of assimilation that automatically assume conflict or pathology is that they fail to take into account historical change. The difference between Janet Freed and a Landauer, say, or a Richard Amsterdam—even between Freed and her own parents—is a matter not principally of different personalities or perspectives but of changes in social context, changes that render theories of assimilation based on notions of underprivileged minority status, stigmatized identity, and self-hatred outdated and misleading. These theories may have accurately reflected social conditions in an earlier period in America. Certainly they reflected reality in Europe, where they were originally formulated. But they simply do not apply to young unaffiliated Jews in the United States today who live in a situation where choice is not constrained, where being Jewish is not fraught with peril, and where neither flight nor commitment has serious life consequences.

Nor do these theories provide an enlightening description of the experience of young adults emerging from acculturated second- and third-generation Jewish homes and communities who did not change their names, get baptized, have nose jobs, or even merely hope that people would not notice that they were Jewish. In the contemporary context of free social acceptance, being unaffiliated with the Jewish community has not typically been a source of profound conflict, as the Klein/Lewin model insists, much less a necessary generator of self-hatred. The simple fact is that for a Jewish-American today, nonaffiliation is not a sign of a deep, often hidden pathological state—not even a mild one. "Identification" is not the opposite of "assimilation" in a post-assimilation society.

The therapeutic perspective that sees such a conflict as inherent in the Jewish condition, even in societies with a high degree of group integration, rejects this relatively cheerful reading. But it seems hard to deny that as the notion of stigma becomes less and less appropriate, so must the idea of a heavy psychic cost for uninvolvement in Jewish-community life lose its force—except as a contemporary version of the classic call to Jews to return to their heritage. One can issue this call in traditional rabbinic tones, in cultural terms, or in the modern jargon of mental health or "human potential." "Hatred" is a loaded word, especially when applied to the self. Given the contemporary anxiety about impaired self-esteem, it is understandable that some in the organized Jewish community would both seek to excite and hope to tap the powerful modern revulsion against the taint of self-hatred in order to stimulate Jewish assertion and return. But though lingering traces of stigma can still be found, these psychological hangovers from conditions that no longer obtain will prove far too ephemeral to inspire Jewish-community affiliation.

3

Anti-Semitism, the Ultimate Tie

Obviously, the malaise of Jewish self-hatred was essentially dependent on the enduring force of anti-Semitism, since the underprivileged Jewish minority's negative opinion about itself was generated by the low esteem the majority had for Jews, and the sense of marginality was provoked by the great difficulty of either cutting loose from the stigmatized minority or becoming part of the majority.

In the 1920s, 1930s, and 1940s, when anti-Semitism in the United States was at its most virulent, it was not hard to find evidence of self-hatred among American Jews. One did not need an ethnotherapist to ferret out instances of obvious psychic repression and what Kurt Lewin called "negative chauvinism" in autobiographies and novels of the time, such as the widely read accounts by Ben Hecht, Ludwig Lewisohn, Fannie Hurst, Waldo Frank, and other writers. But by the 1960s, when Philip Roth wrote of Alex Portnoy's compulsive quest for the blond *shiksa*, self-hatred was already more a comic hang-up than a pervasive psychological disorder of Jews newly integrated into American society.

What had changed was the level of anti-Semitism in the general culture, manifested by derogatory stereotypes, social and economic discrimination, insulting jokes and epithets, beatings, and once, in the deep South early in the century, a lynching. Starting in the 1870s, the growing number of American Jews, prospering and attracting notice, encountered a rising level of prejudice and exclusion in almost all areas of social life. Hotels in upstate New York announced: "No Jews or Dogs Admitted Here." College quota systems limited Jewish enrollment. An Ivy League ditty of the 1920s gives us the spirit of those days:

> Oh, Harvard's run by millionaires,
> And Yale is run by booze,
> Cornell is run by farmers' sons,
> Columbia's run by Jews.
>
> So give a cheer for Baxter Street,
> Another one for Pell,
> And when the little sheenies die,
> Their souls will go to hell.

Indeed, the pattern of discrimination in higher education became part of Jewish folklore: Princeton was said to have a very low quota, Harvard was better; medical schools were very hard on Jews—they had to score well above comparable non-Jews to get accepted; engineering schools tended to be anti-Semitic; the chemical industry was anti-Semitic; and so on. Similar strictures applied to neighborhoods and house buying. "Restrictive convenants"—housing contracts that prohibited the owner of a house from selling to Jews—became widespread as upwardly mobile Jews began to move out of their ethnic neighborhoods into gentile urban and suburban communities. (Even when restrictive covenants were not written into contracts, there often existed "gentlemen's agreements" not to sell to Jews.)

In the world of work, it was well known that banks and insurance companies hired few Jews. In the want ads of one New York newspaper, the phrase "Christians Only" began to appear at the turn of the century. In 1911, the frequency of this phrase was three per thousand ads. In 1921, it was forty per thousand; and by 1937, almost one hundred.

Jews were hardly alone as objects of discrimination during this period, nor did they suffer most from it. Prejudices of all sorts were thriving. This was the time of hysterical anxiety about

"100-percent Americanism," when xenophobia was respectable, supported by pseudolearned, pseudoscientific monographs by distinguished white Anglo-Saxon writers, for example Madison Grant's *The Passing of the Great Race* and Lothrop Stoddard's *The Revolt Against Civilization: The Menace of the Underman.* Jim Crow laws and lynchings became standard methods of social control in the South. This was also a time of violent labor struggles, and the fear of radicals attached itself to images of "foreign agitators" and foreign ideologies—bomb-throwing anarchists, for example. The Ku Klux Klan was reborn and grew rapidly into a national organization with millions of members. The Klan purveyed a sweeping form of prejudice, stigmatizing Catholics, blacks, "swarthy" Southern Europeans, and Jews. Anti-Jewish prejudice, however, had some special characteristics. Other European immigrant groups saw prejudicial feeling decline as they assimilated. But anti-Jewish attitudes actually increased as Jews successfully acculturated and sought greater acceptance by the wider society. One important factor behind this unusual trend is that Jews were perceived not only as inferior (the usual view of disliked minorities), but also as having secret power: they were widely believed to belong to a vast conspiracy that controlled international finance, caused wars, and precipitated economic depressions. During the 1920s Henry Ford spent millions of dollars publishing his anti-Semitic newspaper the *Dearborn Independent,* and distributed millions of copies of *The Protocols of the Learned Elders of Zion,* the notorious czarist-police forgery describing a Jewish plot to take over the world. The stereotype that Ford perpetuated, but hardly created, focused on the sinister aspects of Jewish power—unscrupulous skill in business, evil intelligence.

Under the impact of the Great Depression, social antagonisms intensified further. Agitators like Father Coughlin, a popular radio preacher of the 1930s, found that anti-Semitism was useful in gaining adherents for his anti–New Deal movement, mainly in the small towns and rural communities of old America. Blaming the "international Jew" for the Depression became a kind of folk wisdom. This period also witnessed the peak of job discrimination. It is a surprising fact that Catholic colleges, with 3 percent of their professors Jewish during the 1930s, had a higher proportion of Jewish faculty members than did non-Catholic colleges. This was the time when Jews changed their names and joined churches to get business opportunities, and when it was considered sensible for a Jewish girl to wear a crucifix if she were applying for a sales job in a New York department store.*

Despite the knowledge that Jews were the most prominent victims of Nazi violence, anti-Jewish feeling in America continued to climb steadily during the war years. It is a remarkable fact that in 1940, 63 percent of Americans agreed that Jews as a group had "objectionable traits"; in the years 1940–45, up to 48 percent said they would actively support or at least sympathize with an anti-Semitic campaign—whereas only 30 percent said they would oppose one; and as late as 1944, 24 percent in one poll said that Jews were "a menace to America." Even in 1950, after the high rates measured in the early and mid-1940s had declined, 57 percent still said they would *definitely not* marry a Jew, while an additional 16 percent said they would *rather not* marry a Jew. According to Charles Stember, who made an intensive study of a large number of polls about anti-Semitism in the early 1960s, anti-Semitism "massively declined" in the United States during the period 1945–62. To illustrate with only one comparison: in 1950, 10 percent of those interviewed said they would not like at all having Jewish neighbors, 20 percent said it would not matter too much, and 69 percent said it would not make a difference; the comparable figures for 1962 were 3, 8, and 95 percent.

The decline of anti-Semitism has continued since 1962, when Stember published his analyses. The most recent large-scale national survey of anti-Semitism, commissioned by the American Jewish Committee in 1981, reported a significant decline since 1964, when a comparable attitude-and-belief survey was conducted by a social-science research group at Berkeley. The 1981 study found that the number of Americans who hold negative images about Jews has fallen off sharply; indeed, positive images have become considerably more widespread than negative ones. The great majority of non-Jewish Americans now say that Jews are unusually hardworking, have a strong faith in God, are warm and friendly, and have contributed much to cultural life. (Of course,

---

*A Jewish joke from that period evokes the pathos and pain of such situations: An immigrant Jewish businessman with a heavy accent goes to court and petitions to have his name changed to O'Brien. A month later he reappears before the same judge with a request to have his name changed again, this time to Kelly. The judge, naturally surprised, asks why he wants his name changed a second time. "So," explains the Jew, "ven I say my name is 'Kelly,' end dey esk vat it vas changed from, I can say 'O'Brien.'"

positive images may reflect prejudice as surely as negative ones, but they do represent a countertrend to anti-Semitism.)

This change is generational. According to the American Jewish Committee report, young people are relatively free of prejudice (16 percent of eighteen-to-twenty-nine-year-olds, compared to 31 percent of those fifty-five and over). "It is the changing of generations, then, and not the changing of attitudes, which is primarily responsible for a decline in anti-Semitism." The recent publicity about racial incidents on campuses, even at traditionally liberal colleges like the Madison campus of the University of Wisconsin, might suggest a growth of racism and other prejudices among young people. At present the question is open, but it should be noted that the incidents are taking place in a social context that has changed greatly over the past decades. Minorities are much more present on campuses, itself a sign of declining prejudice in these institutions; the reactions from many other students and from the school administrations have been strong and unqualified in deploring even the "prank" racism of fraternity parties as well as the uglier incidents; and the strictures against the expression of racist and stereotyped attitudes have become much more exacting. As far as Jews are concerned, no serious signs indicate that the decline of anti-Jewish prejudice has been halted and that American Jews are finding new barriers to acceptance, on campuses or anywhere else in American society. The publicity about far-right neo-Nazi groups is naturally disturbing, but the existence of fringe organizations with hate philosophies has been a constant in American history; and as repulsively fascinating as such groups may be, the idea that they are somehow more revealing of the overall trends than the much more widespread signs of decreasing prejudice is unproven, to say the least.

Changing attitudes translate into social reality. Jews are far more accepted than ever before in the United States. It is impossible to find areas of systematic discrimination of the sort that all Jews encountered just a generation ago. There are now many Jews on college faculties, in formerly exclusive law firms, at the head of corporations like Du Pont, for example, once famous in Jewish circles for its anti-Semitism. Jewish movie stars no longer have to adopt names like Tony Curtis, Edward G. Robinson, John Garfield, Lauren Bacall, or Kirk Douglas. At Ivy League colleges, the old stories of strict quotas for Jewish applicants do not apply. (Asian-American students are complaining that they are the "Jews" of our time, kept out by quotas despite their qualifications.) Twenty-five to thirty percent of the students at Harvard College, for example, are Jewish, and the percentage is even higher at the prestigious graduate schools of law and medicine. The list of triumphs is long; Charles Silberman's *A Certain People* provides the most recent comprehensive scorecard of Jewish achievement and success in American life.

The generational changes in the degree of anti-Semitism cannot be overstressed. To take one more example: In 1947, the Oscar-winning motion picture *Gentleman's Agreement,* based on Laura Z. Hobson's best-selling novel, was considered a bold and serious work, a daring exposé of anti-Semitism. Through the eyes of a passionately democratic and egalitarian WASP journalist, played by Gregory Peck, we see how Jews suffer from ubiquitous prejudice. On assignment to do a series entitled "I Was Jewish for Eight Weeks," the journalist gets to feel what it is like being Jewish: constantly hearing slurs, kept out of fancy resorts, prohibited from buying property in towns like New Canaan, Connecticut. The effect of prejudice on individual Jews is poignantly portrayed by a secretary at his magazine, who has hidden her Jewish identity for years and has paid the price in fear, anxiety, and guilt.

But compare a more recent Oscar-winning film that also touches on anti-Semitism, Woody Allen's *Annie Hall* (1977), which was hardly considered bold or daring for dealing with taboo subjects. The Woody Allen character, Alvy Singer, is paranoid about anti-Semitism and hears it everywhere, even in an innocent invitation to share a meal: to his ears, "Did you eat?" becomes "Jew eat?" That his perceptions are distorted is a given; it's a source of humor. The conviction that every non-Jew is at least a little anti-Semitic would not, however, have appeared funny when expressed by a small Jewish man in 1937 or in 1947—not in Berlin, certainly; not even in New York.

Although the reality of anti-Semitism has changed, attitudes like Alvy Singer's are still widespread. For many unaffiliated Jews, this is the last and only source of continued connection to Jewish identity: the sense that anti-Semitism is ever present, forcing a fundamental identification. From this perspective, the statistical decline of anti-Semitism is not significant. Superficially, the facts of such decline are undeniable. But under the surface, things may be quite different. There is still the thread of anxiety, the fear that the depths are as dark as ever. In an informal survey of Jewish

students at New York's City College and at Yale in 1973, half said
that a Holocaust could happen here. More than two-thirds felt that
there was a great deal of anti-Jewish feeling in the country,
although a third of those who said so could not recall any personal
anti-Semitic experiences. The 1981 American Jewish Committee
survey that charted a significant decline in anti-Semitism also
found that Jews in general have an unrealistically pessimistic
assessment of non-Jewish sentiments, as measured by items like
acceptability of Jewish marriage partners to non-Jews, or acceptability of Jewish presidential candidates. (For example, when
non-Jews were asked about how much they would mind if their
party nominated a Jew for president, on a scale of "very much" to
"not at all," 9 percent answered "very much" and 59 percent "not
at all." When Jews were asked to judge how a majority of non-Jews
would feel about this question, only 7 percent predicted the actual
result, that a majority would mind "not at all," whereas 42
percent felt that a majority would mind "very much"—nearly five
times the actual percentage.)

Of course, surveys of this sort raise real problems of interpretation and credibility. Skeptics might argue that non-Jews are not
expressing their real feelings. But the assumption that non-Jews
are more anti-Semitic than they will admit—even to themselves,
some would insist—is as problematic as the assumption of sincere
survey answers. What is so striking in discussions of anti-Semitism
is how many people are willing to discount statistics and surveys,
preferring to trust their own intuitions, and how enormously these
intuitions vary, even for individuals whose own milieus and
personal histories seem quite similar. This extraordinary degree of
dissonance suggests how fraught with emotion the issue is.

Many young Jews today do not feel marginal at all. They are
generally quite at home in the universalist culture of modern
America. Nor do they express much nostalgia for ritual, tradition,
or tribal community. Since the Six-Day War, however, when the
perceived threat to Israel's existence awakened general fears of
Jewish vulnerability, a new concern has stirred some members of
this unapologetically unaffiliated group. The source is an increasingly strong sense of hatred by others—and a powerful defiance.
The forms may vary. Michael Stone's intense sense of personal
vulnerability, for example, generates the most extreme response:
buying a gun and preparing, even with the proper ironic disclaim-
ers, for a last-stand scene at an isolated house in Vermont when

"they" come for this particular Jewish family. Less outlandish (though equally significant) responses focus not on self-defense but on Jewish identification as a moral duty imposed by anti-Semites. As radical writer Stanley Aronowitz put it at the founding conference of the New Jewish Agenda (which brought several hundred liberal and left-wing Jewish activists together in Washington, D.C., in 1980): "Anti-Semitism is one of the repressed themes of this conference. It explains why many of us have come to a conference of Jews and considered becoming part of an American Jewish movement when before we wouldn't have."

There is no doubt that, for many Jews, the subjective consciousness of anti-Semitism has grown. One has only to note the proliferation since 1967 of films and books about the Holocaust. For some, it is precisely this sense of the menace of anti-Semitism that has raised their own Jewish awareness. Their responses may vary, but anti-Semitism has become the key to their sense of Jewishness, the only force that moves them to acknowledge or assert Jewish identity.

Ellen Willis is a writer for the *Village Voice*, well known for intelligent commentary on sixties culture and its aftermath: rock music, sexual liberation, radical politics, feminism. Over the past decade, Willis has increasingly addressed Jewish issues. One of her most famous articles, a long essay in *Rolling Stone*, described a visit to Israel, to the Jerusalem yeshiva that her brother had entered, and her feminist opposition to Orthodox Judaism. But Willis's fundamental emphasis is not on Jewish religion or culture; rather, it is the politics of anti-Semitism that concerns her.

Willis was born and raised in New York City, first in the Bronx and then, following the upward-mobility path common to New York Jews of that period, in a Queens suburb. As a child of the second generation, with Orthodox grandparents and comparatively nonobservant parents, she had some Hebrew schooling at the local Jewish community center and regularly took part in Passover celebrations. Here she describes the gradual clarification of her Jewish identity.

"We Are All Jews"

I started being aware of Jewish stuff primarily because of anti-Semitism on the Left. When I came back from working in a GI antiwar coffeehouse in Colorado, a friend from the feminist movement had become very involved in the Palestinian cause. I felt very tense about it, but I read what she gave me and I came to see that I really disagreed with the anti-Zionist position; and I also became aware of the double standard with respect to how Israel was criticized and the way that the PLO and the Arab countries were criticized. I remember too the tension I had with a close friend at the time who was passionately anti-Israel, and I felt that there was an anti-Semitic feeling behind it. He wasn't Jewish, and as far as he was concerned, it was just a political position. We were so tense about it that we couldn't discuss it directly. At one point he had a job driving buses of Hasidim from the city up to the resorts, and I remember him complaining and saying how he didn't like "them." And I felt there was anti-Semitism there. And he would say, "What do you mean? I like you, and you're Jewish"; and I would think, You're willing to tolerate me because I'm assimilated enough for you, but not Hasidic Jews. The point is, Hasidic Jews are totally alien to me: they're religious; they're very traditional when it comes to women. At the same time, we're all Jews. And if someone criticized them for what seemed to me anti-Semitic reasons—they look funny, et cetera—then I would identify with them. We are all Jews, all part of the same oppressed group.

Then in 1973, after the Arab-Israeli War, when anti-Israel sentiment became even more obvious, I wrote my first piece on anti-Semitism. It was a reply to an article about how you couldn't talk to Jews anymore because they were so defensive about the Middle East. An incredibly patronizing article, real liberal anti-Semitism, which I hadn't previously identified as such. Jews were so partisan about the Middle East that you couldn't talk to them, but the writer, of course—or rather Christians in general—was totally objective. Really outrageous. I got a lot of letters after that.

I became convinced that there was more and more anti-Semitism around, which is what always happens as economic and social crisis deepens. Almost all of a sudden, there was this great rise in anti-Semitism. A lot of it took the form of people being outspoken about stuff they had thought all along but felt guilty about saying. For example, you heard much more blatant comments about Jews having influence in the media. Now, with the breakup of the Soviet empire, we're seeing this enormous outpouring of right-wing nationalist anti-Semitism. It's as if Stalinism kept these feelings in suspended animation for all these years, and they haven't lost one jot of intensity. It's a classic situation: you have economies and societies in shambles, and frustration, anxiety, and rage focusing on the Jews—even where, as in Poland, there are hardly any Jews left.

It seems like such a negative thing to define Jewish identity in terms of anti-Semitism. But I've come to the conclusion that that's really a false issue, because the very identity of the Jews—who we are in history, what we represent—is totally bound up with anti-Semitism, with our status as feared, hated, and envied outsiders. Basically I think that anti-Semitism is an under-the-surface thing, and it is there all the time. On the one hand, I don't believe most of the people I know are active anti-Semites; on the other, I don't believe anybody growing up in this culture is totally immune to it. And I'm sure that a lot of people have bad feelings about Jews that they don't acknowledge—even to themselves.

I want my daughter to know that being Jewish is part of her identity, something she will have to confront, whether she likes it or not. Every Jew is a victim of anti-Semitism—a member of a pariah people. If I have any belief, it is that one should examine what one is. Anything else is impoverishing one's consciousness.

———

Eva Hoffman grew up in Poland, the child of Polish-Jewish survivors. Author of a highly praised memoir on changing cultures, *Lost in Translation,* she writes on a variety of subjects, from music and literature to politics and culture in contemporary Eastern Europe. Now living in New York City, Hoffman makes it very clear how a concern for anti-Semitism may exist apart from any other Jewish identification.

"A Fact of Birth"

My parents were the only survivors of their two large families. They hid during the war, first in a forest and then with a Ukrainian family. They came from religious homes, but they were both rebellious and considered themselves to be enlightened. We lived in Kraków until I was fourteen, when we came to Vancouver. I knew I wasn't Catholic, but I wasn't told I was Jewish until I was seven. My parents thought I shouldn't suffer from that consciousness. I remember my mother taking me out for a walk and breaking it to me, telling me that I shouldn't cross myself in front of churches.

About that time, we started going to synagogue once a year, on Yom Kippur. We would go to this down-and-out part of town, to this mysterious-looking building, a seventeenth-century synagogue, and the people were talking in Yiddish, in soft and usually very sad tones. It seemed very mysterious and terrifying. We spoke Polish at home, but my parents sometimes spoke Yiddish to each other. They didn't try to teach it to me. It was reserved for family secrets.

Being Jewish became an issue for my family because of anti-Semitism. My father was insulted on the street, and there were actually people who said that the only good thing Hitler did was what he did to the Jews. I remember being told: "Don't ever be ashamed. Don't let them get to you." I got this sense of honor about it—I was going to stand up for myself as a Jewish person. Because that's what I was. But I also remember my parents saying, "You are better than they are," and I recoiled from that. I think they were trying to protect me. They used to say that I should have only Jewish friends; that "they" cannot be trusted, "they" will betray you, "they" think this and that about you behind your back. I did not want to believe that; I didn't want to think of myself as a Jew first, a person second.

Today, I think of myself as completely secular. If fact, I am amazed at the persistence of religion. It is a historical fact that I find amazing. It's not that Judaism isn't deep enough; I feel the same about Christianity. I can see how all this was immense, and I can see that, as a thing to study, religion can be immense. But it just doesn't make sense to me.

Sometimes I feel not-American, but it is never an issue of feeling different because I'm a Jew. Any notion of community that I have is not connected with the Jewish idea. When I got married, I learned about suburban ethnic Jewishness from my husband's family. This kind of ethnicity struck me as superficial and easy, very facile, and I positively disliked it. I especially disliked the kind of claim to historical grandeur and historical tragedy, which seemed unearned and emotionally self-indulgent. There was an attempt to endow frozen kreplach and other Jewish food with some kind of significance, because significance was not coming from anything else.

So I don't feel any guilt or regret about my letting go of Jewishness or whatever it is that I feel. Just the other day, I had a rare Jewish-identified experience—at the Éclair Coffee House. There were these elderly people speaking Yiddish and they were gossiping. And I didn't like them. There was definitely something I recognized about them—the gestures and kvetching and so on, and I didn't like them in the way that you particularly don't like something that you recognize as yours. Look, I might have been one of the people in the shtetl who just *had* to leave. The Lower East Side doesn't appeal to me; between the *shvitz* and the racquet and whatever health club, I'll take the health club.

What I do feel a responsibility about is Israel; I feel it is crucial for Israel to survive. I hope I would do my part if there were a real danger and there were something I could do. And I also feel an obligation to fight against anti-Semitism, though I don't feel that anti-Semitism poses a deep threat here in America except for black anti-Semitism. I feel anger at Jews who say, "This does not exist" or "It has to be tolerated." I understand why it exists, but I think it is the duty of Jews to fight it. I remember leaflets that were given out during the teachers' strike in New York, and I felt angry at Jews who said, "This is a manifestation of black consciousness, and it has to be respected as such." I also feel anger at Jews who are more pro-Arab than pro-Israel.

I think, finally, my Jewishness is defined by anti-Semitism as much as by anything else. Anti-Semitism is odious and reprehensible, and you fight it by standing up for Jewishness. In a climate of total acceptance and no anti-Semitism, there is hardly any sense I would have of being Jewish. Apart from history and its possible impact on me, no. There is the concern for Israel, which is the same kind of loyalty, the sense that Jews should be protected from persecution. Otherwise, Jewishness is a fact of my birth, my history. It has no other charge, mission, claim, consequence, obligation, guilt, or responsibility.

Lois Brown* is a free-lance writer. She is in her mid-thirties and has lived in New York her entire life. She grew up in an affluent Jewish suburb on Long Island, the typical "gilded ghetto,"

---

*Pseudonym.

characterized by minimal symbolic Jewish religious education and observance, and intense ethnic identification. For years she avoided any contact with Jewishness. Now her sense of the depth of anti-Semitism inspires active Jewish assertion.

"The Lesson of Germany"

I remember as a girl I went to Hebrew school, and I liked it for a while. I had a kind of evangelical spell about the age of eleven, and after that I just said, "Yuck! Forget this!" My parents identified themselves as cultural, not religious, Jews, but the content of this, as far as I could see, was hating goyim. "Stay away from them, they're out to get you." Jew and non-Jew was *the* basic dichotomy in the world, not good and evil, moral and immoral, or beautiful and ugly.

The environment on Long Island was very Jewish. We were the dominant culture—a very, very strange way to grow up, given reality. It made me completely secure about being Jewish, which my parents were deeply insecure about. I never had that, so when I left the ghetto to go to college at Barnard, it never meant a damn to me. I still don't give a damn about whether somebody is Jewish. I don't think that way at all. I was always told not to marry someone who wasn't Jewish. And when I did actually get married—I was very young—I married someone who was Jewish. But since then, I've *never* been with another man who was Jewish. My mother is sort of amazed, and she doesn't quite accept the fact.

I think I wanted to be in the greater world, in the realm of ideas and historical reality. It didn't just have to do with Jewishness. It was sort of like reading Thomas Mann, or Conrad. There was this whole realm of moral values that had nothing to do with the way that I was. I wanted to be a person in that world, a world that is more than a ghetto composed only of Jews. I would never have denied being born a Jew, but whenever people would ask, "Are you Jewish?" I used to say, "No, I'm not Jewish, but my parents are, and I, you know . . ." I would bristle at that question, as I still do, because I think that it's very often a question that is asked for reasons that I don't want to cooperate with by answering. I think people want to limit and label and have an understanding of me in a shorthand that I don't like.

I remember the Six-Day War, but it didn't get to me emotionally. But something else did—really understanding what anti-Semitism was about. I think that the reason that this happened was that I began to study what had happened to Jews in the Second World War.

I've experienced bits and pieces of anti-Semitism in my life, and I'm extremely sensitive to it. In fact, now I might consider the question "Are you Jewish?" an anti-Semitic remark. Once I understood and truly believed that I was a target of anti-Semitism, no matter what I did, then I felt it would be wrong to ever repudiate being Jewish. It became a very important issue to me, a political issue, like feminism. It was gut-real, not just an analogy. I'm not *like* a black person. I *am* a Jew, targeted in some cultural political reality as contemptible, hateable, persecutable.

I don't think anti-Semitism is going to go away. I feel it, I see it, I taste it, I know what it's about. Fairly recently, I had this incident in East Hampton. I was sitting in my car by the bay. I had just come back from a run; and a kid and an older man were working on a house, raking leaves, talking. Actually, they were yelling to each other, and they didn't know anybody was around. And they were screaming about Jews, how they hated them and how they wanted to burn their houses down. I mean, it was just unbelievable. They went on and on about it. I didn't think there was any point in asserting myself, not because I was afraid—I don't really have that fear—but because there was really something very off about them. And mainly, I wanted to listen. I was so furious. It was like I could feel anger like a liquid in my blood. I wanted to feel that experience of my response to anti-Semitism. You don't often get that experience, because people are very careful. Most people know I'm Jewish, and they wouldn't say those things in front of me. I think that anti-Semitism, like racism, is as profound here as in the South, where one could hear things like that more easily. But usually it is much more subtle than the kinds of Nazi sentiments that I was hearing.

Here's what I think: While there is anti-Semitism, we should have Jews. I think that the most important thrust of anti-Semitism has been to get Jews to deny their Jewishness, and for there not to be any Jews. Having no Jews is the fulfillment of the most important program in anti-Semitic ideology. So there must be Jews, or anti-Semitism has succeeded.

For me the lesson of Germany and the German Jews is: always be ready to go. I have a diamond ring—the most portable way to carry out some wealth if you have to move fast. That's why I bought it. I'm serious. I have a holocaustic imagination, a wonderful capacity to imagine catastrophe—and I do. A lot. It is a component of my psychological makeup. It's like being hypochondriacal, with cosmic projection. It's cosmic hypochondria.

To be a Jew for me is to be conscious and aware, to be outspoken on anti-Semitism, to protest. Not to not identify is the most important thing.

Bruce Fried* is a short, well-dressed, voluble man in his early forties. An extraordinarily varied entrepreneur, Fried sees in the persistence of anti-Semitism a sign of the naiveté of social idealism.

"I've Never Felt American"

I've never felt American, even in Israel, where I was called an "Anglo-Saxon." I have no self-image of being American. I have an image of being Jewish. But my identification as a Jew is largely an abstraction. I have a smattering of Hebrew, I know a few words of Yiddish, but I'm not in a real Jewish community. If someone came to my door and asked for my help, made any claims on me because we were both Jewish, you know what I'd do? I'd call the police. I'm disdainful of middle-class Jews because they're conventional and vulgar. I find most Jewish women unendurable as romantic partners. The very qualities that make them likable as friends and colleagues make them impossible as spouses: assertiveness, aggressiveness, a mode of interaction that depends heavily on inducing guilt, manipulation, a belief in female equality accompanied by the conviction of male responsibility for the ills of life. As for faith, I have never had an iota of religious feeling in my life; it is as alien to me as being interested in baseball—I just can't conceive of it. Not only do I not believe in God; I can't imagine what could lead someone to the experience. I think the Hasidim are crazy. If my daughter married one, I'd go bananas, really. I think Hasidism is a sign of criminal insanity. My holding on to Jewishness as an identity is a visceral response; it's hard to shed. I want my son to be bar-mitzvahed, for example, but even as I say it,

*Pseudonym.

I recognize the irrationality of wanting something that is an empty form for me. I used to dream of having a Jewish men's club. What I was hankering for was the fraternity of the steambath, a place for candid discussion untrammeled by considerations of politeness, like in a Malamud novel. I wanted a community of Jewish businessmen with whom I could share and gloat and indulge my base instincts. And feel at home. See, I'm cynical about the possibilities of friendship in this world. You need some common background, and being Jewish is code for that. But it doesn't work ultimately. There is no *communitas* of any kind, anymore, anywhere. I know that.

My identification essentially comes down to ethnic chauvinism. I grew up in a home with no religious content. My parents are both second-generation, educated, American Jews. My father is a psychoanalyst, my mother a therapist and teacher. We had only the most cursory holiday observation. I was bar-mitzvahed, it's true. But that was the only purpose and the end of Hebrew school. My parents never professed any religious feeling. I suspect that they're atheists—if they ever bother to think about it. What they have is a zealous ethnic identity. They support Israel, give to Jewish charities. Most important, all their friends are Jewish. My father was in the Air Force and the Navy, and that was true even there. My parents' attitude is, You'll certainly get persecuted and you should know why. Which comes down to, Jews are the best, and other such thinly veiled expressions of superiority to the rest of the world: Jews are smarter, Jews are better family people, more concerned about their own children.

This sense of Jewish superiority was inculcated in me from infancy, practically. And indeed the level of educational and occupational achievement among Jews I know is astonishingly high. But it is irrational. It is untrue. At the same time, I can't deny that I believe it. I believe an untruth. That's what it comes down to. And I suspect I have communicated it to my children. I probably make many of the same remarks my parents did. I suspect I speak disdainfully about WASPs. I try to check it, just as I try to check my expressions of sexism, knowing full well that I am sexist. Because I think it is psychologically dysfunctional to teach this sense of identification to kids. But I also think it is an essential survival mechanism. I think they are out to get us all the time. By "they" I mean anyone who isn't of our kind—urban, intellectual, Jewish. It's hard for me to accept this we/they thing, when it comes right down to it. It's even possible that by "non-Jewish," by the non-Jewish "other," what I really mean is non-urban-intellectual. I have close non-Jewish friends. I have no non-urban-intellectual friends. And I basically think that all of these distinctions—ethnic, religious, racial—have contributed far more to the diversity of harm that human beings have done each other than to their enrichment. I wish there were some channel of expression that I did not think was wrong. I think all ethnic division is wrong. I think chauvinism is wrong. I think nationalism is wrong. I think religion is worse than wrong. It's morally wrong, philosophically wrong, intrinsically wrong. But it comes down to—like it or not—I am "Jewish," a label that has proven impossible to shed by choice.

I've had frequent anti-Semitic experiences. During antiwar marches in Chicago, where I was for college, the epithet thrown most frequently at both the black and white marchers was "kike." I saw the essential feelings of the American underclass in Chicago, and it is virulently anti-Semitic. Also, at Chicago, I studied with Hannah Arendt, and I became sensitized to the issue of anti-Semitism. I learned about the Holocaust—my parents had hardly ever mentioned it directly. I even thought of writing a book on it. The idea was: Is there a lesson to be learned? I keep having anti-Semitic encounters. In my printing business, I employ a photographer from the South who said to me, "I need a smart Jewish accountant." I regard this as an anti-Semitic remark, unconscious, if you will. And often, from the WASPy businessmen I deal with, I sense an element of disdain for voluble, aggressive, talkative Jews, like me. They make frequent anti-Semitic comments. Not the crudest kind, but rather remarks about excessive intelligence or nervousness or aggressiveness or the "Sammy Glick syndrome." Nobody ever talks about the "Lee Iacocca syndrome." I am seriously afraid of a recurrence of anti-Semitic persecution here in America. I think we are rapidly approaching cataclysm, general economic deterioration coupled with repression. Jews, like blacks and women, are high up on the list.

This anti-Semitism is a major contributing factor to my view that economic security is the only protection for me and my family. At least one could escape. I think it is too late for assimilation. The social fabric in every area has been so sundered that there is no protection to be gained from assimilation—just money. My father used to say "You should know what being Jewish is, because what if there is another Holocaust?" Well, in the end, simply knowing you are Jewish is not a survival mechanism. So what if you understand the reason for which you're being put to death? The moment you're dying, you don't care. For me the lesson of the Holocaust is: economic security protects. The *rich* German Jews got out. I want money, not "in" from the WASP businessmen I deal with. I have a classic Marxist analysis, only I've decided that instead of joining the proletariat, I'm going to join the capitalists. I used to be idealistic; I'm much more cynical now. I wish my energy and success could have been harnessed toward less selfish ends, like the general betterment of mankind. I wish I could be socially useful, but I don't think there is a way. The best one can hope for is to do well without doing harm. I'm somewhat defensive about my ambition and my economic drive—it *is* conforming to the Sammy Glick caricature—but basically I'll play it up. If they feel contempt for me, that's OK. They'll let down their guard, and I'll come out ahead.

The real Jewish survival trait is to do more than one thing at a time. The point is to cover yourself, just in case they come. I've made a lot of money in the last few years. I've been a teacher and an editor. I'm a licensed therapist. I'm an entrepreneur. I have my own print shop, and I'm a computer software designer. I'm in real estate. And on the side, I write books. And you know what? If you want drapes, I'll make you drapes.

What surfaces over and over again in these and similar speculations on Jewish vulnerability is the image of the Holocaust. It *could* happen here. A mental-health worker in a small town in California says that he is learning how to defend himself and his family. He does not, he assures us, want to sound like Meir Kahane and the Jewish Defense League, but "Never again." Lois Brown has her diamond; Bruce Fried, his money in preparation for flight; in the shadow of the Green Mountains, Michael Stone loads his rifle. They discount the statistics and surveys and insist instead on their own intuition of the ineradicability of anti-Semitism. Anti-Semitism, they are convinced, has not declined; only standards of politeness have changed. People now are unwilling to express the anti-Semitic beliefs they surely hold, because the Holocaust has made such sentiments inadmissible. To complicate matters, the potential content of anti-Semitism has been broadened to include opposition to Zionist doctrine, for example, or criticism of Israel. And its potential forms have changed as well: anti-Semitism has become more subtle and is now as much a matter of attitudes as of action, of unconscious values as of consciously held beliefs. Indeed, one hears that people may well be anti-Semitic—the way they can be self-hating—without even knowing it. The moral of the story is that complacency and confidence based on surveys, polls, and statistics are mistakes—potentially fatal mistakes. Alertness is called for: suitcases must be packed; passports must be valid. Vigilance is all.

In talk of impending anti-Semitic hostility, one cautionary tale is always invoked: the lesson of Germany. It is the last word, the final justification for anxiety in the face of the apparent decline of anti-Semitism in America. Briefly stated, the lesson goes like this: The German Jews thought (as we do today) that they were safe. They too believed they could assimilate. But look what happened. Don't make the mistake they made.

Of the six million Jews who perished in the Holocaust, only a small number were German Jews. The entire German-Jewish community numbered around 600,000 at its height, less than 1 percent of the German population. But the German Jews have achieved a symbolic importance far beyond their numbers. They stand as the paradigm of a Jewish community that aspired to integration and acceptance by the non-Jewish society. Their fate seems to offer a crucially charged message about the appropriate state of mind for a Jew in the modern world.

It is easy to see why the story of the German Jews hovers as a warning of particular relevance to the millions of well-integrated and apparently accepted and absorbed Jews of the United States. The German Jews, after all, stood for the ideals of emancipation in their purest form. The integration of Jews into German social and cultural life was genuine, remarkable, and matched historically only by recent developments on the American scene. The opportunities they enjoyed seemed to confirm most strikingly the validity of the Enlightenment vision that Jews could, individually and communally, become part of the non-Jewish world.

By the 1920s—after the Weimar constitution of 1919 made liberal toleration the official state doctrine—German Jewry was in a situation that can be made to look roughly similar to that of American Jewry today. The German Jews too had experienced four generations of life in a society where, however partial and insecure, integration and cultural assimilation had been an option, and, for many, a goal. The characteristics that we now see among American Jews were also often evident among German Jews in that brief period of Weimar liberalism preceding the Nazi ascendency. For a Jew to enter fully into German cultural life at that time, given the cultural and social isolation of Jewish communities in Central and Eastern Europe, meant immersion in the non-Jewish world. In politics, science, philosophy, the arts, all that we think of as modern culture was being created, and created outside of the traditional and inward-looking Jewish communities of Europe. Individual Jews did, in fact, enter this world, in quite disproportionate numbers, and often became successful contributors to the national secular culture. Many of these creative moderns of Jewish origin had little or nothing to do with Jewish life, and were indeed often antagonistic to all religion—recall the examples of Marx and Freud, those oft-named sources of pride and identification for contemporary Jews. Intermarriage, that crucial index of community acculturation and acceptance by the host society, was well past the 30-percent mark, only recently reached by American Jews. Jews were active in political groups across the spectrum, including Fascist parties. It is worth noting that there was a conservative Jewish organization that supported the Nazi "revolution" before Hitler came to power. These superpatriotic German Jews regretted only that "bad influences" had led Hitler to adopt a violent anti-Semitism, preventing them from following a movement that in every other respect expressed their own political and cultural ideals.

As in America today, the prevailing sentiment of German Jewry was not that of the Jews who changed their names, denied their origins, converted to Christianity, or in other ways expressed self-hatred. Nor was it that of the small number like Gershom Scholem, the great Jewish scholar, who left Germany in the 1920s to go to Palestine—Jews who commited themselves to Zionism and rejected the assimilated German-Jewish path. The popular novelist Jakob Wassermann conveyed the dominant feelings of German Jewry after four generations of emancipation in his widely read autobiography, published in 1921. There was no need to choose between being a German and being a Jew, he maintained; although anti-Semitism was ugly and troublesome, Germany was still a true home for the German Jews. Wrote Wassermann, "I am a German, and I am a Jew, one as intensely and as completely as the other, inextricably bound together."

The bonds between Germany and its Jewish community were soon shattered forever. Half of Germany's Jews fled Nazi persecution before the war; virtually all who remained were murdered. The destruction and dispersal have been taken as proof that emancipation was a disaster, that the promise of assimilation— equality and participation in the broader culture—was a sham. Even in periods of apparent social acceptance, anti-Semitism retains its potency. The German Jews, moreover, were not only victims of evil; they appear to have colluded in their fate by indulging in the illusion that, by becoming good Germans, they could win the acceptance of the non-Jewish world. Their fate, in this perspective, is thus especially poignant: these German Jews, who knew little about Judaism and had no active relation to the Jewish community, were persecuted and killed for something that meant nothing to them.

The contemporary applications of this interpretation are clear enough. The example of the German Jews proves that assimilation will never work. The Enlightenment ideals of citizenship and tolerance will eventually turn out to be a sham, at least as far as Jews are concerned. Anti-Semitism is ubiquitous and eternal, rooted deep in the gentile unconscious—a sleeping dragon that can easily be stirred to fury by, say, a doubling of crude oil prices. Meir Kahane expressed this reading of the historical path of modern Jewish assimilation with characteristic vigor:

> How we believed all the false prophets and how we drank eagerly from all the poisoned water. How we ran toward all the glittering frauds and away from the strong and eternal Jewish verities. How we believed in Reform and Assimilation and Enlightenment and Cultural Pluralism and Liberalism and Democracy and Socialism and Marxism and Participatory Democracy and Chairman Mao and Comrade Trotsky and Rationalism and the inherent decency of man. . . . All of it died in the flames of Auschwitz and the mockery of Stalinist trials and the madness of an irrational mob.

Here the lesson is broadened to a "German-Russian lesson," and the virulence of anti-Semitism in Nazi Germany and Stalinist

Russia is taken as simply the final expression of the basic truth that the quest for acceptance was doomed from the start. "They" will never let the Jews assimilate. Those who desire this impossible acceptance are pathetic, despicable, and living an existential lie for which they are sure to pay the price. Their potential fate seems, as a corollary, to offer an argument for Jewish identification. If the Nazis come again and Jews are again taken away to be killed, they should at least recognize the "Jewishness" others ascribe to them as an identity. Since one must be Jewish, better to do so with pride.

Given the polemical purpose to which the history of Germany's Jews is applied in this country, and the fears and anxieties it provokes, we ought to be as clear as possible about that history and what it may or may not mean. Certainly, the finality of the Nazi "final solution" to the "Jewish question" makes it difficult to avoid concluding that Auschwitz was the "destiny" of German Jewry—not simply the end of the German-Jewish community in historical fact but also its telos in terms of historical meaning: that the fate of the German Jews was the inevitable conclusion of the course of German-Jewish history.

Yet to make the Nazis serve as proof that Jewish assimilationists in particular were victims of a profound delusion would be a serious distortion. The truth about Nazi anti-Semitism was that everyone classified as Jewish suffered the same fate. The most Orthodox communities of Hungary and Galicia, those Hasidic Jews who had almost no intercourse with modernity and who maintained the faith with complete conviction, were destroyed along with those who thought of themselves as completely German and had given up any association with Judaism.

Nor does the fate of the German Jews yield any unambiguous conclusions about the "eternality" of anti-Semitism. For classical Zionists, of course, the implications are clear. Nazism confirmed Theodor Herzl's predictions that anti-Semitism would flourish, even in modern, liberal societies like Herzl's own Austria. A Jewish sovereign homeland was therefore necessary, for only in their own state could Jews live safely without depending on the uncertain tolerance of a gentile host society. It follows that prudent Jews should come to the Jewish state, the only place where they will not be subject to the anti-Semitic persecution that can break out in the most tolerant societies—such as the United States. Many American Jews have heard Israelis warn them that what happened to the German Jews "could happen here"—a supposedly definitive historical "truth" meant to promote Jewish national identification and its ultimate expression, emigration to Israel.

As common as this notion is, almost no one takes it seriously. For Jews who have stayed behind, so to speak, an acknowledgment of this historical truth seems primarily to involve guarding against complacency in societies where they seem to be so comfortable. From this perspective, the German Jews ought to have anticipated what happened; in theory at least, they should not have been taken by surprise. And Jews who decide not to go to Israel must—in America or Britain or France or wherever—take seriously the idea of anti-Semitism as perpetual and implacable. But what does this awareness amount to, beyond a commitment not to be surprised?

The question, finally, is whether this intensified Jewish consciousness based on a heightened sensitivity to anti-Semitism propels people toward "Jewish" activity. Thoughts about such a response to anti-Semitism are not new. In Germany, some Jewish leaders welcomed the mainly verbal anti-Semitism of the 1920s, before the Nazis gained real power. They seemed to think that anti-Semitism of this nonmurderous sort would slow down the headlong assimilation of German Jews and move them to join in maintaining a culturally vibrant Jewish community. As one leader of the Jewish community put it, "Anti-Semitism is the scourge that God has sent us in order to lead us together and weld us together." Jews should go back to their people, who in some mystical way will always be separate, a "people that shall dwell alone."

This image of ultimate Jewish isolation, however, is difficult for young, modern, unaffiliated Jews to integrate into their ordinary sense of the way things are, even when they are willing to speculate along those lines. Their dark view of the breadth and depth of anti-Semitic feeling may certainly lead to gestures of defiance and a commitment not to be fooled about the "enemy." It may even prompt a kind of political activity. But the vision they prefer is emphatically not that of an isolated Jewish community maintaining itself in a hostile world; rather, they believe that the integrationist and humanistic vision based on universalist values will actually prevail. Indeed, opposition to anti-Semitism—as to any form of persecution—is an indispensable part of that vision, more likely to support the universalist ethical impulse than to spark any specific commitment to or interest in Jewish culture, religion, or practice.

It is this view of anti-Semitism as symbolizing discrimination and prejudice in general, and of Jewish identification as a culturally specific way of reasserting universalist ethical commitments, that may account for the growth in Jewish consciousness among some leftists who had for years ignored their Jewish origins. Jewish identification as a moral imperative divorced from cultural and religious content received a surprising reaffirmation in a *Nation* article, "Am I a Jew? A Radical's Search for an Answer," by Peggy Dennis, veteran of more than a half century of full-time dedication to the Communist Party.

Dennis recalled her radical, Yiddish-speaking, immigrant family, whose commitment was to Communist revolution and the international working class. She considered it merely incidental that this political culture was expressed in Yiddish and took place in emigré communities where everyone happened to be Jewish. For many years she had no interest in any form of Jewishness. But a dawning awareness of anti-Semitism as a phenomenon not only of the capitalist countries, but even of Soviet Russia and the other Communist countries of Eastern Europe—where anti-Semitism had been officially abolished—moved her to affirm Jewish commitment: "I still have never been inside a synagogue. I still do not like matzos. I still have no ethnic affinity with Israel and am more critical than ever of the Israeli government, Jewish though it may be. I now know less Yiddish than I did as a child. I know no more of Yiddish literature, culture or history than I ever did. I am still not clear why I am, but I know I am a Jew. . . . While anti-Semitism and ethnic discrimination exist anywhere, I am a Jew." The idea of Jewish identification as an ethical imperative—valuable while there is anti-Semitism, but only that long—could not be stated more clearly.

As a force for Jewish identification, anti-Semitism is ambiguous. On the one hand, the objective fact of anti-Semitism gives it peculiar power. Anti-Semitism, however one analyzes its causes, is finally about what *others* do and think and say. It is their irrationality that creates the reality for Jews, and this cannot be escaped by the person who is, by sheer historical accident, born Jewish. As Sam Silverman says, "I'm a Jew only when Jews are attacked. Perforce, huh? If they put me in a camp, I'm a Jew. If they say I am, I am."

On the other hand, anti-Semitism does not make any "Jewish" demands on the individual. Having a valid passport or keeping a packed suitcase, investing in portable diamonds, learning to make drapes, or diversifying one's business are hardly acts that define Jewishness. Lois Brown may posit the survival of the Jews as a specific refutation of anti-Semitism, yet neither she nor any of the others quoted here speak of Jewish survival except in the most literal, physical, and individual terms, as "escape." They have no concern with religious or cultural continuity. In fact, identification based on defiance demands very little from the modern unaffiliated Jew in terms of knowledge, feeling, or experience. There is no question of learning to appreciate the Jewish heritage or coming to believe in or practice Jewish religion. The limitations of this kind of identification emerge poignantly when we consider that most Jewish activity: passing on the heritage. As Ellen Willis puts it: "I want my daughter to know that being Jewish is part of her identity, something she will have to confront, whether she likes it or not. Every Jew is a victim of anti-Semitism—a member of a pariah people." The "Jewish" message here is mainly negative.

But even these expressions of anxiety finally seem little more than ritualistic. Bruce Fried may claim that he has geared his whole life toward escaping from the inevitable debacle, yet one hardly has the sense that he is really poised for flight. Lois Brown may claim to live by the injunction "Always be ready to go," but one diamond ring is hardly a resettlement plan. The talismanic quality of their gestures and objects is quite revealing. In sum, they are responses to a fantasy. The fear of persecution or assault is to a large extent a hypothetical anxiety, a case of "cosmic hypochondria," or "holocaustic imagination," as Brown puts it; it is a metaphorical, psychological condition that has little to do with a sober assessment of the political realities of present-day America or the personal strategies that might be required were their horrifying vision to come true. For these American Jews, an insistence on the depth of anti-Semitism as the one ineluctable link to Jewish identity finally seems, in essence, a way of expressing proper respect for the seriousness of what Jews have suffered. Considering how recently the Holocaust occured, it is remarkable how little their intimations of anti-Semitism affect their daily lives—in choice of friends, work, mates—if not their dreams or conversations.

This is not to say that anti-Semitism cannot initiate an active involvement in Jewish communal existence. If an irrational, implacable anti-Semitism were indeed to arise in American society, many unaffiliated Jews might well react by affirming Jewish identification and by organizing to combat the antagonism and prejudice of non-Jewish Americans. The intensity of this reaction could motivate a serious commitment to the study of Jewish history, culture, languages, and religious tradition, as the returnees sought to give content to their newly asserted identity.

No one in the Jewish-community would admit to wishing for a revival of anti-Semitism. But the "I-told-you-so" satisfaction with which some people greet any anti-Semitic action, no matter how minor, suggests that for those who deeply believe in eternal anti-Semitism some overt signs would not be unwelcome. Such signs would expose the continuing illusion of Jewish safety and might stimulate the return of Jews to their own community. But in the absence of an obvious, undeniable rise in anti-Semitic sentiments and actions, anti-Semitism will not be a strong force for promoting Jewish-community affiliation, and evocations of eternal Jew-hatred will continue to lose even their residual rhetorical power. As the memory of the Holocaust and the German lesson lose their force—already the case for the next generation—then for the unaffiliated, even this tenuous basis for affirming a connection with the organized Jewish community will diminish to the vanishing point.

The negative vision of assimilation that the Jewish community has created over the past century associates guilt-ridden loss, pathological self-hatred, and a constantly threatening anti-Semitism. Though these ideas have some power, they have nevertheless been drained of substance and relevance. Their bearing on the Jewish situation is no longer what it used to be.

For one thing, social circumstances are far different from what they were when the debate about assimilation first took shape. The emotional residue of the complex experiences of Jews in Europe and America over the last few generations no longer has a substantial foundation in daily life. The guilt and regret expressed by unaffiliated Jews are vestigial remnants from another time and place. The nostalgia for a lost world is growing thinner, more sentimental, less vivid. Self-hatred has been domesticated, transformed from psychic distress into comic paranoia. The sense of stigma has diminished, and with it has gone the need to compensate with cultural self-assertion. None of these residual concerns—even when they are evoked by conversations or questions from interviewers, by films and books, by incidents in the news, by reports of happenings in Israel, and so on—suggests a basis for a meaningful Jewish revival among the unaffiliated. The awareness of anti-Semitism, potentially the most objective stimulus for renewed Jewish identification, is also the farthest removed from any specifically *Jewish* knowledge, faith, or commitment. Moreover, the belief in an eternal threat to the Jews is profoundly at odds with the universalist culture and personal experience of the many American Jews who honestly voice such anxiety about anti-Semitism. As such, it shows no clear potential for bringing them back now—and even less potential for the future. The anxiety about anti-Semitism that plagues even those who are securely integrated into American society is clearly not being transmitted to the new generation. To some this signals the erosion of the last strong source of Jewish feeling, and even the unaffiliated, aware of what being Jewish has meant in recent history, feel some sorrow at this prospect. But the thoughtful also recognize the irony of locating one's identity in such a gloomy outlook.

The discussion within the Jewish community about assimilation has been especially sustained and troubled, in comparison with other white ethnic groups. The special burdens of Jewish history fuel this preoccupation and account for its intensity. But although the rhetoric continues, there is no longer a real debate, and there has not been for some years. There is only one "side," the community's exhortation to active Jewish identification, affiliation, and involvement, accompanied by the litany of ills that Jews (and others) suffer when they assimilate.

No opposing assimilationist argument exists to answer this repetition of anti-assimilation rhetoric, as there was in Jewish communities in Europe during the last century. One might say that now people "vote with their feet," without bothering to argue, or even without noticing that they are supposed to be engaged in an argument. Moreover, this trend intensifies even as "roots" and "ethnicity" continue to be favored themes in the culture.

The negative vision that weaves regret and guilt over the world "we" have lost, eternal anti-Semitism, stigmatized identity, and accusations of self-hatred is unilluminating and historically outmoded; more to the point, it is unable to slow the trend to disaffiliation, despite the hope of the Jewish community that the moving testimonies of those who have "returned" may be only the expressive vanguard of a much larger and still invisible mass. What could slow the trend is a strong and vital Jewish community, whose culture, religion, and institutions would attract commitment and loyalty. A fair assessment of the community's prospects requires close examination of its current state and recent transformations.

The Community

The passage of the Jew into American life is a saga of the deepest human experience. It afforded dignity and safety and psychological space to a homeless, embattled people who had been strangers in many lands for much of their history. . . . The Jew spans the whole of American experience, sharing the marvelous incongruity of each citizen: his pride in his origins, his success as an American, and his simultaneous worship of Jehovah, Lincoln, and Babe Ruth.

—Stanley Feldstein, *The Land That I Show You: Three Centuries of Jewish Life in America* (1978)

The idea of a Jewish community distinct from the Jewish population as a whole is a modern phenomenon. At the turn of the century, on New York City's Lower East Side, for example, a simple estimate of the number of individual Jews would have been a good approximation of the size of the Jewish community. The essence of Jewishness was being part of that community. Although even at that time a small number of Jews dissociated themselves from the community and disappeared into the American scene, for most Jews "life was with people," so to speak. Indeed, membership in the community hardly felt voluntary—it was simply part of life. Most Jews lived in Jewish neighborhoods, belonged to Jewish organizations, worked for and with other Jews, spoke and understood Yiddish. These ordinary aspects of community bound Jews together, and transcended the most passionate conflicts. Atheist anarchists harangued religious Jews entering synagogues on Yom Kippur; Communists fought Socialists for control of Jewish unions; Zionists battled anti-Zionists— but these struggles all took place within the community.

Today, Jewish affiliation is the result of conscious choices and acts. In the old ethnic immigrant community, it took great effort to disaffiliate and break away; now a major effort is required to maintain affiliation. Many Jews no longer participate in organized Jewish communal life, and therefore even if it is appropriate to count them in a census of Jews, it would not be accurate to include them as part of the Jewish community. But using a very rough and generous minimum standard, we could define "community members" as those Jews who have some conscious commitment to the idea of the historical-ethnic community and who are willing to act in support of that commitment: by joining a synagogue, enrolling their children in Hebrew school, belonging to a Jewish organization, or regularly donating to Israel and to Jewish philanthropies. According to these minimal criteria, the American Jewish community comprises about half of the Jewish population.

Of course, affiliation takes many forms, and even within a community defined by such generously inclusive standards, intensity of involvement varies greatly. Certainly, there are American Jews who devote most of their waking hours to Jewish activities: religious Jews of all varieties; leaders and professionals who run the complex network of Jewish community organizations, charities, synagogues, religious schools, and publications; educators and rabbis; scholars and students of Judaica. For these active Jews, Jewish concerns and subjects are at the core of life itself. They live the year according to the rhythm of Jewish festivals and holidays; they are knowledgeable about Jewish culture and history; their deepest commitments are to the Jewish community, Israel, and the world Jewish people.

But for most of the roughly three million affiliated Jews in the United States, involvement is neither so active nor so intense. They often join synagogues for no other reason than to enroll their children in Hebrew school. The education offered by synagogue Hebrew schools, such as it is—and for the great majority, it is very little indeed—usually stops with bar/bat mitzvah or confirmation. Their religious observance generally consists of synagogue attendance on the High Holy Days, an occasional Sabbath or other holiday ceremony, a Passover Seder at home with family and friends, and Hanukkah candle lighting. But even at this level, the primary social identification is with the Jewish community. This act of identification and the variety of gestures and actions that express it—regular donations to the United Jewish Appeal, annual appearances at the synagogue for the Yom Kippur service—mark the boundary, however fuzzy, that separates the community from the unaffiliated.

The great majority of the Jewish community can be considered "mainstream." The mainstream vision of community is an inclusive one: being Jewish is something for which there are only minimal requirements. What is crucial for the mainstream is ethnic, cultural, and political identification with the community. Beyond this there are no standards of what it is to be a "good Jew," no judgments of quality or authenticity. That is to say, philanthropy is as Jewish as faith. Indeed, public support of Israel is incomparably more important for good standing in the mainstream community than any private matter of belief or practice, such as observing the Sabbath, keeping kosher, fasting on Yom Kippur, or studying Talmud or Torah. This principled inclusiveness differentiates the mainstream from the Orthodox, who represent a roughly estimated 8 percent of the Jewish population. Orthodox Jews do not accept this basically ethnic definition because it makes the religious core of Judaism a matter of choice, in no way essential to the concept of a "good Jew." To the Orthodox "community of faith," any secularized conceptions of Jewish identity and affiliation are totally inadequate, and although many Orthodox Jews do not deny the "Jewishness" of non-believing, nonpracticing Jews—religious law considers all born Jews as Jews, whatever they do, including converting to another religion—they do not agree with the mainstream, relativist sense that all ways of affirming Jewish commitment, identity, and community membership are equally worthy.

The relation of Orthodox Jews to the mainstream of the Jewish community is complex and ambivalent. Some refuse to participate in community affairs with non-Orthodox Jews; others participate grudgingly, with the underlying sense that the justification for such participation is the opportunity to win over others to the true path of Orthodox Judaism. And a small and embattled group are atypically "liberal" and do not insist on the superiority of their own way of being Jewish, adhering rather to the modernist spirit of individual choice that permeates the more secular mainstream.

Still, for all its internal rifts and tensions, the American Jewish community continues to display impressive vitality. This is especially remarkable in a third- and fourth-generation ethnic group that has been strikingly successful in its Americanization. Other groups do not have the equivalent of the 700-page American Jewish Year Book, which annually collects reams of information on the organizational life of the Jewish community. Religion, education, culture, community relations, overseas aid, social welfare, mutual benefit, Israel —these are just some of the subjects addressed by over 230 national organizations and their thousands of local affiliates. Of the Jewish mass organizations in America, Hadassah is the largest, with a membership of 375,000 women who support Israel while encouraging education for "intelligent and creative Jewish living in America," sponsoring Zionist youth movements and summer camps, and providing massive volunteer services for Jewish community activities all over the United States. At the other end of the scale are tiny and obscure sects of aging Jews who still uphold lost causes of the past, groups such as the Freiland League for Jewish Territorial Colonization, which until recently supported "colonization in some sparsely populated territory for those Jews who seek a home and cannot or will not go to Israel, and which promotes the development and use of the Yiddish language and culture." There are associations of strict fundamentalist Orthodox synagogues and Hebrew schools, and the explicitly atheistic Society for Humanistic Judaism. There is the anti-Zionist, anti-Israel American Council for Judaism, and there is also Herut-USA, Menachem Begin's militant wing of the Zionist movement, which claims Jewish sovereignty over all of the "promised land" of ancient Israel, including what is now the kingdom of Jordan.

Indeed, American Jewish activity spans the entire spectrum of political and cultural tendencies. There are hundreds of Jewish periodicals and journals, from scholarly quarterlies in Hebrew to local community newspapers full of gossip, pictures of wealthy charity givers, accounts of engagements, marriages, bar mitzvahs, and school graduations. Hundreds of millions of dollars for thousands of projects in the United States, in Israel, and elsewhere are collected annually and disbursed by a large and effective Jewish welfare bureaucracy.

The Jewish community, then, is certainly alive. But is it well? Sociologists correctly note that growing social acceptance has not led to the demise of the Jewish community, that the Jewish community "changed but did not dissolve during modernization." But the nature of the change still requires illumination—and here there are conflicting judgments.

In spite of the community's apparent vitality, its qualitative decline has been projected by many observers. "Everything has changed for the better in the last generation," wrote Conservative rabbi and community leader Arthur Hertzberg in the 1970s, "except one variable—there is less Jewish piety, less Jewish learning, and less commitment to the continuity of Judaism." And in 1989, summing up his major history of American Jews, Hertzberg judged that "after nearly four centuries, the momentum of Jewish experience in America is essentially spent." Statistics tend to support such a perspective. The most extensive community study (conducted by the Combined Jewish Philanthropies of Greater Boston) showed "sizable declines in almost all Jewish identification measures" between 1965 and 1975. According to the usual criteria—celebrating Passover, lighting Sabbath candles, keeping kosher, attending synagogue, joining Jewish organizations, giving to charities—the total of Jewish activities is going down. Moreover, the study found the decline most "precipitous" for young adults aged twenty-five to thirty-four. Though the data are not conclusive, in the decade and a half that has since passed no confident claim has been made that these trends are being reversed. Orthodox rabbi Stephen Riskin noted in 1984, for instance, that "82 percent of our children do not attend synagogue," that the intermarriage rate is "approaching 47 percent," and that there are "declining figures for congregational affiliation, Hebrew school enrollment, and membership in Jewish communal organizations."

Other observers reject this gloomy picture. They point to the impressive organizational diversity that remains, in spite of the past generation's rapid acculturation; they also point to an unexpected revival of interest, energy, and commitment throughout the community. If the indices of attrition have not changed, it is argued, then they are simply too grossly conceived to reflect the subtler shift that has taken place among the young-adult generation since the 1967 War, a shift demonstrated by a heightened interest in the Holocaust, newly flourishing synagogues in heartlands of unaffiliation like Berkeley, California, and Cambridge, Massachusetts, the proliferation of Jewish all-day schools, the influx of young people into leadership positions in organizations like the United Jewish Appeal, and the development of an elite of

American Jewish scholars. They point as well to the renewed energy apparent among the Orthodox, and some observers even claim an increase in their number. The *shtieblach*, the little Orthodox prayer houses, moribund for years, are once again busy; and more Orthodox youths are now studying in yeshivas than perhaps ever before in Jewish history. In New York City, for example, the number of yeshiva students doubled between 1965 and 1980. Orthodox communities are spreading; one can now find them in suburban areas like Teaneck, New Jersey, on Manhattan's trendy Upper West Side, and in pockets across the country.

More than the discussion of statistics and demography, the debate within the Jewish community turns on judgments about the "Jewish quality" of the culture, religion, and community that everyone admits has changed. But this moralizing approach once again obscures how the changes reflect cultural forces that are transforming *all* traditional groups and communities in the United States. What is the nature of community in an open, secular society, and what can membership and loyalty mean when identity is a matter of choice?

To address these questions, we first look at how participation in modern American culture has affected the mainstream Jewish community, particularly the traditional pillars of Jewish identity: Torah, Israel, and God, or—as they appear in mundane, mainstream form—ethnicity, Zionism, and synagogue. We will then consider the same developments within the Orthodox "community of faith."

4

Life in the Mainstream

"Jewish" as a sociological category is uniquely messy. Typically, ethnic and religious classifications are separate; one can be "Irish" as an ethnic-national identification, while being Catholic—most commonly—or Protestant or even Jewish, for that matter, as regards religious affiliation. But "Jewish" cannot be so neatly separated. Clearly, Judaism is a religion, and people identified as Jewish are popularly assumed to be adherents of this religion. But being Jewish is also an ethnic category. Jews are the only religious group that also is included in encyclopedias of ethnic peoples. This doubling of meaning permeates the character of the mainstream Jewish community.

Ethnicity

Although Judaism is a religion, most American Jews are not religious according to the tenets of Judaism in any of its forms. Less than one in ten follows the historic practice of Orthodoxy. The majority do not belong to a synagogue, and, of those who do, most do not attend regularly or observe Jewish Law. Although Americans are an exceptionally churchgoing people for an advanced industrial country, Jews fall considerably below the national rate of attendance. According to national surveys conducted in the early 1980s, 44 percent of all Americans claim weekly church attendance, while the reported rate for the subgroup of Jewish-Americans was only 24 percent. But detailed surveys in a

99

variety of Jewish communities during the same period found that even this figure was highly inflated, and in no community was "frequent attendance" (defined as at least once a month) anywhere near 24 percent. A detailed review of data by sociologist Jack Wertheimer in the 1989 edition of *The American Jewish Year Book* concluded that in most communities, between one-third and one-half of the Jewish population *never* attend religious services, or attend only on the High Holy Days. To give a specific example of this general trend, in Rochester, New York, with an old and established Jewish community, 14 percent claimed weekly synagogue attendance in 1961. By 1980, that number had declined to 2 percent. During the same period, the percentage of those who said they attended synagogue only on the High Holy Days jumped from 19 percent to 45 percent. Furthermore, the percentage of regular attendees would be considerably lower if the Orthodox were taken out of the calculations. Informed estimates put total synagogue membership—which is not the same thing as attendance—at below half of Jewish heads of households, far less than the figure for Christian Americans. (For comparison, Protestant and Catholic church membership is reported by national polls to be around 70 percent.)

The predominance of the ethnic dimension of being Jewish is a modern development, an obvious consequence of the declining force of religion. However, even in the traditional Jewish communities of Eastern Europe, where, according to idealized memory, premodern Jews lived lives of deep and untroubled religious faith, skepticism and unbelief were making powerful inroads during the nineteenth century. The essentially ethnic nature of the Jewish community in America has been evident from the early days of immigration. Nevertheless, Jews have subscribed to the typical American pattern of classification according to religion. *Protestant-Catholic-Jew*, as Will Herberg titled his popular sociological description of America in the 1950s—these categories allowed for distinctions while confirming a common American identity. To be sure, even then the religious classification was largely a cover for ethnic identity. But assertion of ethnic differences was more problematic, for Jews as well as for other groups. In a climate where acceptance by the majority culture was still hesitant and grudging, open ethnic assertion might lead other Americans to doubt the sincerity of one's commitment to becoming "100-percent American." As sociologist Charles Liebman points out, "One can hardly blame the Jew for taking the easiest way out of his dilemma—calling Judaism a religion for external and formal purposes and filling the form with ethnic or communal content."

In the last generation, however, Jewish public self-description has changed. In 1979, a survey of Los Angeles Jews noted that "Jews are defining themselves more in ethnic and cultural terms than as members of a religious denomination"; whereas a generation before most Jews would have defined "Jewish" primarily in religious terms, now less than one-fifth did. The essential ethnic character of Jewish identification is apparent even in the dominant patterns of religious observance. For most Jews, religious activity consists of synagogue attendance on High Holy Days and some observance of Passover and Hanukkah—but not the Sabbath. This pattern makes sense only when understood as an affirmation of Jewish identity rather than as a fulfillment of religious requirements. For example, the fact that Hanukkah, a minor religious holiday, has assumed such importance is due to its proximity to Christmas and reflects the ethnic-communal need to have something Jewish to offer children in the holiday season.

The shift in self-description parallels the growing respectability of ethnic assertion that began in the mid-sixties with the civil-rights movement and the rise of black consciousness. By the 1970s, the view of ethnicity as a social good was well established. As professor Stephan Thernstrom, editor of the massive *Harvard Encyclopedia of American Ethnic Groups,* pointed out at the time, "It is generally assumed that maintenance of ethnicity is desirable, that preservation of differences is healthy, and that loss of group identity is to be deplored." For the current generation of Jews, seeing blacks and other minorities asserting group pride certainly helped create a context for an open exploration and confident affirmation of Jewish identification without many of the anxieties of the previous generations. And the outbreak of the Six-Day War in 1967 added a powerful emotional stimulus to heightened Jewish consciousness.

The Jewish community today affirms its ethnicity in mixed tones of pride and anxiety: in its discussion of group political interests (chiefly related to support of Israel), its ongoing discourse about "who and what we are," and its preoccupation with issues of importance to group survival, such as intermarriage, birth rates, and Jewish education. Recently, there have been many signs of renewed ethnic vigor. One small but deeply symbolic part of this apparent quickening of Jewish activity has been a noticeable mini-revival of interest in Yiddish language and culture. Traditional Jewish religious life is not usually the favored focus for modernist nostalgia; secular, modern Jews, while sometimes intrigued by the ultra-Orthodox forms of Judaism, such as Hasidism, feel little sentimentality about that religious way of life, and less attraction to it. Nor is there any great regret for second-generation "Americanized" ethnicity. The world of Portnoy's mother, so to speak, the community of *Goodbye, Columbus* and Duddy Kravitz, is material for satire, even anger, but not for tender literary eulogies. For the representative modern, liberal, and integrated Jew of today, the "world we have lost" is the idealized *ethnic* community of the "world of our fathers," so lovingly memorialized in Irving Howe's social history. The signs of interest in that lost world are plentiful: there is the creation of klezmer bands with names like The Klezmorim, Ellis Island, and the *Nisht Geferlech* (Not-So-Awful) Klezmer Band; the establishment of a new Workmen's Circle I. L. Peretz Yiddish School, worthy of a long feature in the *New York Times;* the adulation of Isaac Bashevis Singer, the production of Yiddish plays, Yiddish film revivals, and the new popularity of Yiddish-language classes.

A Yiddish teacher in New York told us: "The people who are coming to the Yiddish classes I teach are mainly young adults. A very few come from Yiddish-speaking homes, or have married into Yiddish-speaking homes. Some are social workers who deal with immigrants or work in Jewish old people's homes. Then there's a whole bunch who just want to know some Yiddish, for emotional reasons. They believe they've missed out on something by not knowing it. I meet hundreds of people who tell me, 'My parents spoke it as a secret language so I wouldn't understand what they were saying.' And now, they want to be let in on the secret. Understanding jokes is another big reason. Someone from Ohio told me he wanted to understand Lenny Bruce. For a long time, American Jews felt embarrassed about Yiddish, or they thought it was some funny language their parents or grandparents talked, and they ended up knowing a few words like *schmuck* or *pupik*. After a thousand years of history, to end up with that! But over the past fifteen years, some of those people have begun discovering the incredible things that their grandparents, those cute little *bubbes* and *zeydes*, actually did."

There are, of course, the perenially popular entertainment hits like *Fiddler on the Roof,* various documentary films on old-country themes, and a stream of popular novels featuring the immigrant Lower East Side community: *Evergreen, Rivington Street, Union Square, Ragtime*—all of which testify to an intensive effort to recover and reanimate a sense of Jewish ethnic roots. Brandeis University now has a center for the preservation, restoration, and distribution of Yiddish films, and festivals devoted to these films have drawn serious attention and attendance in cities around the country. The organizers of various Jewish film festivals around the country have found that Yiddish films and films about Yiddish culture have especially wide appeal.

It is not surprising that ethnic yearning should attach itself to the immigrant Jewish world. This was, after all, the time when the American Jewish community was at its most culturally dense, rich, and complex. Immigrant Jews were a cohesive group, a people in an anthropological sense. The great majority shared a language, Yiddish, and a common religious tradition—even militant Jewish atheists had grown up learning Torah and Talmud. There was a rich popular culture and an active and respectable high culture; lively, well-attended Yiddish theaters produced not just Yiddish plays but also the classics of world literature—Shakespeare, Ibsen, Chekhov—in new Yiddish translations. Several Yiddish daily newspapers competed, reaching circulations in the tens and even hundreds of thousands, and each paper expressed a different ideological position ranging from Communist to Orthodox. There were Yiddish radio programs, and, in New York, a Yiddish radio station (WEVD). Jewish unions—like those of the clothing and fur workers—and local political machines had enough power in New York to elect a Yiddish-speaking Socialist congressman. There were Jewish sports leagues, Yiddish musical comedies, coteries of modernist Jewish intellectuals and writers engaged in passionate literary polemics in Yiddish journals and over the tables of Lower East Side cafés. When Sholom Aleichem died in New York in 1916, over 125,000 people lined the streets to pay their respects as his funeral cortège passed by.

It would be a distortion to idealize this immigrant community as uniformly idealistic, fervent, and intellectual. But it would also be a mistake to deny the powerful presence of a self-aware cultural transformation of Jewish life, begun in the cities, towns, and *shtetlach* of Eastern Europe and carried over to the new settlement in America. The idea of *Yiddishkeit* comprised a set of images that Jewish thinkers and writers articulated, images of a creative "national" culture that would translate the historical saga of the Jewish people, their religious traditions and texts, their sufferings and survival, into a modern form, absorbing universal concerns while affirming the worth of Jewish particularity. This vision was essentially socialist, humanist, and cultural, appreciative of the religious elements of historical Jewishness but deeply committed to a secular conception of Jewish life. (A small confirmation of this universalist spirit is the fact that the call letters WEVD commemorate Eugene Victor Debs, the beloved non-Jewish Socialist Party leader.)

The "father of Yiddish literature," the Polish-Jewish writer I. L. Peretz, was a key figure in the formulation of the ideals of *Yiddishkeit*. In his vision, Jewishness referred to the "Jewish way of looking at things," and this meant an inclusive humanist spirit of social justice and liberation clothed in Jewish forms and carried out in all phases of community life: home, school, theater, literature, politics. In its American milieu, the culture of *Yiddishkeit* flourished, imbued with what Irving Howe has characterized as "utopian expectation and secularized messianic fervor."

Sheva Zucker is one of the few within the current generation of young adults who experienced the culture of *Yiddishkeit* firsthand. A lecturer in Yiddish and Jewish literature at Duke University, she was an active member of an organization of Yiddish speakers called Yugntruf (Call to Youth), a group dedicated to preserving the remnants of Yiddish language and literature. Significantly, Zucker grew up in Canada, where immigrant assimilation lagged behind the American pace by half a generation or more.

"A Finer, Lovelier World"

Winnipeg is special, Yiddishly. There are fifteen thousand Jews in the city; there's still a Yiddish library and a Yiddish radio program. And that's nothing compared to what there used to be. Once there was a Yiddish daily newspaper; there were three

Yiddish all-day schools. One was from the Workmen's Circle, another was more Communist, and the third was the Sholom Aleichem school, more cultural, less political. On the other hand, you could count the number of people who were Sabbath observers on the fingers of one hand, and there is still only one kosher restaurant in the whole city. I remember my father used to say about potential husbands, "Better a goy than a rabbi."

My school was a secular Yiddish day school. Half the time was spent on Jewish history, Bible, and literature. I had a sense that what was going on in the Jewish part of the school day was very different from what was going on in the English part. I don't want to sound trite, but it was something about learning to be a mensch, a just and good human being. I still have this sense that certain kinds of ideas and ideals were filtered down to me in Yiddish. When I was younger, I even thought that if everyone spoke Yiddish, the world would be better. I guess I thought it meant that everyone would love each other, and do things like they do in Peretz stories. Like the rabbis who, instead of going to the synagogue, go chop firewood for little old ladies, to help them out.* People would be moral and good. They would help each other, and together we would all build, as Peretz calls it, *"a bessere, shenere velt"*—"a finer, lovelier world." What I learned is socialist, in a way. Yiddish became a kind of surrogate religion, a way of being Jewish that was modern and radical. Socialists would say that they are the best heirs to the prophetic tradition. One of my Yiddish teachers told me about one child who got Isaiah and Vladimir Medem, the great Socialist leader, mixed up because they both fought for social justice. It's true, of course, that once you get past the Peretz stories, there's a lot of literature that is cynical, exposing the class system in the shtetl, for example, which Peretz also does in some stories. But, as a child, I got the

---

*In the short story "If Not Still Higher," by I. L. Peretz, a Hasidic rebbe disappears on the holy days before Rosh Hashanah, and his disciples believe that he goes up to heaven to plead with God personally. A skeptic from Lithuania, the traditional home of Jewish skeptics, secretly follows the rebbe and discovers that in fact the rebbe disguises himself as a Ukrainian peasant and goes around the community doing simple good deeds, like bringing firewood to penniless widows. The end of the tale has the skeptic listening to the disciples regaling each other with stories of their great rebbe's ascent to heaven, to which he adds, under his breath, "if not still higher."

sweetness. And in my heart, I still believe in it, or I wouldn't be doing what I'm doing. I guess I still believe the world would be better if everyone spoke Yiddish.

To me, Yiddish says everything is not dollars and cents, everything doesn't have to be tied to practical values. Yiddish is beauty and warmth and compassion, and I believe my life was and is better because of it.

The Yiddish world that Sheva Zucker comes from has clearly vanished, at least in the United States, though the progressive values that were at its heart are still associated with being Jewish, and continue to animate the work of a number of activists in a variety of ethnic community institutions. Ursula Sherman is a founder of the Berkeley-Richmond Jewish Community Center, and her energetic activities as chairman of the board were instrumental in building this lively and popular institution.

"A More Communal Community"

When my daughter was in kindergarten, she thought she was the only Jewish child in the world. We had Seders at home, a Hanukkah menorah, but nothing public. So we joined the synagogue—we figured our daughter should know she wasn't in fact the only Jewish child in the world. But we didn't particularly like this shul—it was cold, it was dull, it wasn't community-involved. A group of us formed something called the Underground Prayer Committee, and we did our own services—this was in the sixties. We wanted to change the congregation—we got draft counseling, support for the grape boycott. Then in 1970 there was a group of "flower children," Jewish, and they wanted to have a Seder, and they finally had it in the basement of the Free Church because there was no room in the synagogues. There was just no space anywhere, no Jewish space to do community things. We needed to find a way to make the Jewish community more "communal." So first we started a service for street transients, the Hillel Street Work Project, so called because it was housed at Hillel. It eventually became Berkeley-Oakland Support Services, a major organization, with shelters and halfway houses, and it is now a two-million-a-year agency for the homeless. It was originally a Jewish project. Similar things were then run by churches, and we thought there just had to be a Jewish component to helping the needy people on the street.

The second thing we did was create a Jewish place, a community center, which was my particular baby. We tried to connect up with what was happening in the community. We developed a kosher nutrition project—not because we wanted to be kosher, but because it was the one way of getting elderly people to come. And it worked: people came from all over the place. And we did a nursery school which was also a big success. We started regular Sunday brunches and discussions. We did a series of dialogues with Jewish and Palestinian speakers. We did another series, with discussions and a concert, about Jews and blacks—good crowds, but very few blacks. We now run a Jewish music festival, with Sephardic as well as Eastern European music; we have workshops to learn about the music and the culture it came from, so it's more than just a music festival. We also have a film series. We had an extraordinary event with a young Belgian filmmaker who had made a film about the rescue of Belgian-Jewish children in the war. And there were four hundred people that Saturday night, and people stayed and talked till after eleven. That is what I like. I want to move the world toward being a better place, by doing things like that.

We've acquired a good reputation for our programs. They're controversial, they upset people. But the sad part is we're always broke, and we're always trying to get funding. The Federation of Jewish Charities people, the community leaders, don't come. I think for them Jewish culture is totally tied up with Israel. But you have to have a vibrant community, with a lively community life, otherwise you might as well pack it in. I have the feeling that the Federation doesn't understand this—that unless you nurture your own community, you'll never have anything. Somehow that message doesn't get across. Also, young people—it's hard to get them to come.

I'm old-fashioned. I want difference to be preserved and the Jewish component to be part of the difference. And that component has to do with helping and being involved in social issues. I think if you're going to be ethnic, you probably won't be establishment, you'll probably be on the Left. I believe in the message of the prophets, like in the saying "Justice, justice thou shalt pursue," and Hillel's old idea of "If I am only for myself, who am I?" and that you have to keep working at the task, even though you can't complete it. I couldn't tell you I believe in God, but I do believe in the perfectability of humans, and I think you can help that with this kind of communal renaissance.

Deborah Kaufman is in her mid-thirties, a lawyer, the mother of a four-year-old. She lives in the San Francisco Bay area, where she grew up. In the seventies she was active in radical politics. Today she works full-time as the director of the Jewish Film Festival, which she sees as a way of fostering a renaissance of Jewish culture in the Jewish community.

"My Favorite Jewish Holiday"

There is a way to be Jewish that isn't about religion, or Zionism, or federated Jewish community life, but about culture: art, music, film, whatever. Every year at the Jewish Film Festival, we ask people to fill out evaluations. Some people have written things like "The Jewish Film Festival is my favorite Jewish holiday" or "My pre–Rosh Hashanah is the Jewish Film Festival"—they relate to it in a ritualistic way, which is wonderful. Our audiences have increased enormously. We had 18,800 people at the showings in San Francisco and Berkeley last summer, people from everywhere: Toronto, Los Angeles, New York, and one person who regularly flies in from London. This is part of their calendar, the Jewish Film Festival.

The role of the festival is to act as a free-speech device inside the Jewish community—because the big fight we have with the Jewish establishment is that we are too politically "left-wing" for them. We invited Mubarek Awad, a Palestinian human-rights spokesperson,—and we're still suffering the consequences. The Jewish foundations cut back on our funding, saying that having a Palestinian speaker was a "slap in the face." We see the festival as a catalyst for debate about important issues in the Jewish community, an opportunity to hear sides not normally heard in that community, like the Palestinian side. The Jewish establishment is very provincial in understanding how most Jews feel about most contemporary Jewish issues, whether it is the Middle East or women and Judaism or homosexuality, or any of these issues. But we know that what our audience appreciates us for is opening up all the issues.

I work full-time in a Jewish organization, I belong to a synagogue, sort of, I go to Israel all the time, and I'm deeply involved
in Middle East peace work. Still, most of my best friends are not
Jewish and have no connection to anything Jewish. And in my
head, I still don't see myself really in the Jewish community. Our
views are too different. I'm outside the mainstream, by choice.

Though there still are activists like Ursula Sherman and Deborah Kaufman who insist on the connection between ethnic Jewishness and left-liberal values, they find themselves increasingly on
the margins, poorly funded, little encouraged by the larger
mainstream community. Yet undoubtedly there are people with
strong ethnic feelings in that larger community, even if they do not
share a left-liberal vision of ethnic culture. But what does Jewish
ethnicity in the mainstream look like today? What are the "Jewish
values" that it represents? What now distinguishes the "Jewish
way of looking at things"?

Apparently, not very much. Community acculturation over
the last two generations has steadily eroded the particular
Jewish content of ethnic life. The process of absorbing American mores and institutions—exemplified a generation ago by the
lavish temples of the "gilded ghettos," Jewish high-school fraternities, Jewish businessmen's associations, Yiddishized versions
of hit-parade tunes, like "K'nok Around the Clock" and "How
Much Is That Pickle in the Window?"—has moved with the
times, becoming more inclusive and, along with the community,
definitely more upscale. The political content of the original
ethnic vision has faded. Today, what is done under the label
"Jewish" is hardly distinguishable from what other middle-class
Americans do.

Except that what is done is done with other Jews, at Jewish
places, and under the sponsorship of Jewish organizations. A
community-newspaper account of a festival of "Jewish arts, crafts,
and recreation" in suburban Los Angeles quoted the chairman of
the event praising the gratifying turnout as "an exciting barometer
attesting to the vitality of Jewish life." The report continued,
"From the baseball clinic and autograph signings of Los Angeles
Dodger Joe Beckwith to the music of the Dave and Udi Guitar
Duo, it was a day of fun-filled family activity." In another story,
this one describing programs planned by the Los Angeles Jewish

Centers Association, we find that "the roster of activities runs the gamut from a babysitting clinic to karate." The purpose of this wide array of activities, the director noted, "is to get as many people as we can involved in a Jewish setting."

A vivid expression of what the texture of ethnic culture has become can be found in "Jewish-living" magazines like the slick 100-plus-page insert for the *Jewish Exponent*, the weekly newspaper of the Philadelphia Jewish community. Imitating the "good living" magazines that serve the sophisticated tastes of the urban middle and upper middle class, the insert is crammed with advertisements for cosmetics, jewelry, beauty salons, fur and leather boutiques, expensive condominiums, luxury car dealers, Oriental carpets, and other accoutrements of the contemporary good life. An editorial letter from the outgoing president of the *Jewish Exponent*—positioned between ads for women's evening wear and diamond necklaces—concludes with the assurance that, "like you, I shall remain a dedicated reader and participant in the adventure shared by all of us—the Jewish experience."

To be fair, the magazine is not all advertisements. The "Jewish experience" presumably is found in the articles and features, not the ads; and in these the word "Jewish" is applied liberally. There is the obligatory piece on physical fitness and exercise—not about the goyishe Canadian Air Force program, but about "The Israeli Army Fitness Strategy." A short story tells about someone growing up Jewish. One "think piece" is by a convert to Judaism (a common feature in Jewish publications), another compares the college experience in Israel with that in the United States, and a third offers a set of interviews with Holocaust survivors in Europe. The humor column is about Hanukkah; the contest column focuses on "Jewish Holidays and Festivals." The arts feature profiles a Jewish artist who uses Jewish themes. There is a gift-buying column that encourages "buying the best you can afford—for Hanukah"; commercial pride is rampant, and we are told that "the right Hanukah gift of quality is here. . . . Whatever you need, whatever your life-style, the one perfect purchase of quality exists here—somewhere."* The only items that do not use

---

*Throughout this book, in order to preserve the integrity of quoted material, the spelling of Yiddish and Hebrew words in quotations may differ from that in the text.

Jewish references, and so presumably are not part of the "Jewish experience," are the finance column on tax planning and the restaurant column on Italian cuisine.

Even the bizarre can be taken as proof of the enduring commitment of Jews to maintaining Jewish identification, however "American" they become. "It doesn't matter, I guess, where a bar mitzvah party is held as long as there is love and family and joy." So said Mr. Cohen after a sixty-four-member band, cheerleaders, and pompom girls from a local high school stormed onto the playing field blasting football marches and "Happy Birthday, Harvey." Mr. Cohen, Harvey's grandfather, made this observation in Miami's giant Orange Bowl, during a bar mitzvah party that was reported in the *New York Times:* "The grandfather watched family and friends lift Harvey to their shoulders as the band played a hora. He told guests that his own father had been held aloft in such a manner a long time ago in a Polish ghetto, as he himself had been embraced and serenaded that night in a crowded tenement flat near Avenue C, far from football fields and pompom girls."

For those who see ethnic health and cultural vigor bursting from the mainstream Jewish community, an incident like this signifies continuity and cultural strength rather than an embarrassing decay of tradition. The triumphant message is that no matter how successfully American they become, Jews will not lose their commitment to Jewish identity and community.

This buoyant sense of triumph is raised to visionary heights in accounts eagerly bought and read by the community they flatter. One of the most effusive of the celebrants is Max Dimont, a popular historian of Judaism, whose latest paean to American Jewish life proclaims, "American Judaism is destined to play the same role in the future of the Jews that rabbinic Judaism played in their past." Looking ahead, Dimont asks, "Are we perhaps already seeing the emergence of a new Judaism on American soil, just as some two and a half millennia ago a new Judaism began to emerge on Babylonian soil?" And he answers, "Everything points to such an outcome." After calling Jewish history "the greatest cultural and moral adventure in the history of man" and expressing an unrestrained pride in Jewish achievement—"Who else has dared to give the world God, Abraham, Moses, Isaiah, Job, Jesus, Spinoza, Marx, Freud, Einstein?"—Dimont assigns a world-transforming role to the American Jewish community: "It is our contention that American Judaism, as finally shaped by Jews, God, and American history, will be the Judaism which will affect the world."

This kind of cheerleading is good for comic relief, but little else. Dimont speaks of a "new Judaism" that will "affect the world," but what could it be? The special Jewish mission evoked in the vision of *Yiddishkeit*, for example, emphasized a set of values— brotherhood, toleration, social justice, transformation of economic and social institutions—and made demands on the individual and the community to build this *"bessere, shenere velt."* But the spirit of the community evoked and promoted in the magazines and popular histories has neither the old vision nor any distinctively new one to offer. As Jewish ethnic life, like ethnicity in general, has become increasingly drained of any particular meaning or perspective different from that of the dominant culture, its "special" trappings cannot help but become a form of "product differentiation"—the sort of style difference that people use to gain a sense of being unique without challenging the basic commonality. Ethnicity thereby becomes a symbolic assertion of difference without any serious content.

This inflation of group pride may seem innocuous, like rooting for the home team; and perhaps, like fan spirit, it serves a positive function in binding people together in the face of increasing social fragmentation. But it also has a dark side, not so easily laughed off. The positive cultural and religious achievements puffed up in accounts like Dimont's are only part of what makes for a strong sense of group identity. At least as powerful as the ethos of "us" is the continuing sense of the hatred and hostility of "them," the "others" among whom the American Jewish community dwells. In earlier decades, when anti-Semitism was widespread and strong, the derogatory sense of the "other" was widespread. For Jews, the gentile was a figure of contempt and derision. Of course, for those Jews who adopted universalist perspectives, especially the radicals, any assertion of ethnic superiority was ideologically condemned. But on a gut level, as a response to the hostility of the non-Jewish world, the reversal of stereotypes was easily understandable. Naturally, it was wise for a people without power to do this discreetly, either at home with other Jews, or else by using the disguise of humor.

In Yiddish-speaking homes in America, for example, children grew up hearing "Shikker Iz a Goy," an old Eastern European

Jewish folk song which tunefully asserts that the gentile is, in general, a drunkard. Many young adults can also remember their parents, or their grandparents, responding to victim lists in the newspapers with differential sorrow, depending on the presence of Jewish names. Daniel Fuchs, in his fictional trilogy of life in a Jewish section of Brooklyn during the early decades of the century, sketched a scene of the sort enacted in many Jewish homes. In *Homage to Blenholt,* a Jewish immigrant mother, Mrs. Balkan, overhears her American-born son talk about going to a funeral:

> "My God," she gasped with grief. "Who died?"
> "Don't worry for nothing," Max assured her. "It's nobody. They're burying a man called Blenholt today. He's not a Jew."
> "Still," she protested, relieved but broad-minded, "it's no picnic. Even a Christian is a person, too."

This kind of tribal sentiment has certainly diminished, but it is still a force, even among the younger generation. "Chosenness," a key concept in Jewish religious thought, has a mundane translation in the Jewish sense of inherent superiority to the host peoples. An especially bald assertion of Jewish superiority can be found in a book called *Why the Jews? The Reason for Anti-Semitism.* Written by two young "missionaries" dedicated to bringing indifferent Jews into full-time communal involvement, this book—ostensibly an analysis of anti-Semitism—dismisses without serious argument all attempts to explain it on the basis of psychological, economic, historical, social, cultural, or political factors as well as all discussions that treat anti-Semitism within the broader context of racism or other forms of group prejudice. No, anti-Semitism is unique, just as the Jews are unique, and the only valid account of anti-Semitism is what the authors call the "Jewish" explanation. Jews have always had a God, religion, set of values, culture, and way of life so superior to others that non-Jews, forced to face their inferiority, come to hate the Jews. With this forthright claim to Judaism's superiority over all other religions and value systems—the real point of this book—the authors hope to attract strayed Jews to active Jewish allegiance.

This subtext appears not only in documents like this one, but in a quieter, less examined way in the thinking of some members of the mainstream community. Even for those not learned in the actual content of Jewish texts and doctrine, the feeling of a basic superiority to an ineradicably anti-Semitic "other" can be powerfully active in binding individuals to the community.

Arlene Segal* is a good example of almost undiluted Jewish ethnicity of this sort. A nurse, with a husband and teenage daughter, she is in her mid-forties and has lived in New York all her life.

"Jewish Culture Is Unique"

Last year, my daughter, Ann, went out with a boy who was a Syrian Jew who had moved to the United States and had gone to a yeshiva. They went to a ball game, and at the game they got into a conversation, and he said he didn't think he would feel funny about marrying out of the Jewish religion. And that made Ann make up her mind never to see him again. I was glad she did this because it says to me that Ann likes who she is, and is proud of who she is. I like the fact that she is comfortable with her Jewishness, that she asserts it and doesn't hide it. She said that she didn't respect him. She just didn't know how anybody who knows what it is to be Jewish could consider doing that. Because then you assimilate, the Jews dilute, die out. And that's bad.

I was born after the war, but I always identified with the Jews in the concentration camps. What I identified with particularly was their resilience and their . . . survivability, if there's such a word, their transcendence, their staying power. And that's been a sustaining theme in my own life in small ways, and in large ways. What's strong about me, what's secure about me, has roots in my Jewishness.

I like who I am. I feel comfortable in my own skin, and I like that I'm assertive and have confidence in myself. In a society which doesn't particularly like Jews, either you can get very defensive and shrink because you don't want to make waves, or you can be the opposite. And I've become the opposite. I have contempt for apologetic, defensive Jews, for those who consider it a great accomplishment to have gentile friends, to feel that they "belong." I feel self-conscious saying this, but I really think that Jews are superior. That has certainly been my experience—in the people I've met, and also in the disproportionate contributions

*Pseudonym.

Jews have made to civilization. Names like Jesus, Marx, Freud, Einstein, Brandeis, Salk, Levi-Strauss—the whole ethic of Judaism is to contribute. I think it's a function of their Jewishness that these people have made these contributions, because that's the way Jews are raised—to value the intellect, to value contribution.

I do think it's hard to be Jewish. I have the deepest feeling that people don't like Jews. It's not just paranoia. At the hospital I worked at, I was constantly confronted with what I knew to be sometimes subtle, sometimes not-so-subtle, forms of anti-Semitism. For instance, if a woman was in labor and she was complaining, she was referred to as "Oh, you know that type from the Island," which was code for "Jewish." And when the holiday season came around, and every single crack in the wall was filled with a Christmas bell, or a Christmas tree, or a Christmas something, I wanted to put up some of the symbols of Hanukkah. Well, those were relegated to a small corner. I mean if you're just the slightest bit sensitive, you'll notice anti-Semitism—like in a comment about your name, or a so-called friendly comment about how smart Jews are. And you meet with people and they're telling ethnic jokes and you know the minute you leave the house they're going to tell their Jewish jokes. . . . Of course, I have to admit that I tell ethnic jokes too.

I feel strongly that I'm Jewish. I vote totally according to Jewish issues, and what's best for Israel. I give money to Israel, and for years I've made phone calls for the Federation and UJA to solicit funds for Israel. I admire all the people active in these organizations because they are part of a network that ensures the continuation of the Jewish people. I feel an instant bond with people who are Jewish. If someone came to my door, and said, "Look, I'm Jewish, I need help, take me in"—I would. And if I ever needed help, like in a foreign country, I'd immediately go to a Jew.

But I don't feel the need or the desire to participate in a lot of the rituals of Judaism. I just don't see how they would give me any kind of peace or inner strength. I've gone to synagogue, and I've tried, I've really tried. But I don't get it. We joined the synagogue so Ann could go to Hebrew school. But we don't do much else. Being Jewish in our house is not a very arduous, unpleasant experience. It's more a kind of feeling, a positive identity kind of thing. We have a Passover Seder, but it doesn't have much to do with God or religion. The point is that Jews all over the world are sitting down on this night, as they've done throughout history, to remind themselves of the meaning of Passover—what happened then and what still happens: anti-Semitism, and the desire of the larger society, the world, to deprive the Jews of their rightful freedom.

For me being Jewish is not observance, it's not God, and it's not synagogue; it's being a part of a particular history, a people, a culture. Living a Jewish life might be defined as living by the letter of the Law, like going to synagogue and saying certain prayers and having a kosher home and all those ritualistic things. But I feel living a Jewish life is living by the precepts and values and morals that the Jewish religion propounds: being honest, working hard, contributing. These to me are Jewish things. If I read a newspaper and see that some guy got indicted, I'm always glad if that person's not Jewish, and always pained if he is.

I think the Jewish culture is unique. There would be a terrible void in the universe if the Jews died out. And a large part of this uniqueness is the quality of survival. I guess really its uniqueness is survival. Look at all the other cultures that have died out. The fact that the Jews haven't been destroyed is very important to me, and to my sense of pride. I'm proud that I belong to this group of people who have survived in spite of oppression, persecution, and terrible threat.

Arlene Segal insists that her sense of herself as Jewish is confident and unproblematic. Her Jewish identity is exclusively ethnic; she is not concerned with God or synagogue or observance. Her link is with the people. She feels an instant bond with other Jews and has a Seder to affirm her connection to Jews all over the world and throughout history; she is hypervigilant about signs of anti-Semitism. Above all, she is proud of her group and committed to its survival. But this sense of group, however intensely felt, is not the equivalent of a distinctive ethnic culture. What is usually thought of as the content of a culture—history, language, art, ritual, tradition, philosophical assumptions—these do not draw her attention and commitment. The list of achievers she cites to prove the unique superiority of the Jewish essence is exclusively made up of people who were only marginally Jewish and whose contributions were to world, not Jewish, culture. (To be fair, the list offered by Dimont—who is thought to know a great deal about Jewish culture—is no different. Of the Jewish heroes he nominates for glory, from Abraham to Einstein, the most recent participant in Jewish community life is Jesus.) Indeed, on closer examination, it turns out that the uniqueness of the Jewish culture, whose disappearance, Arlene Segal says, would cause "a void in the universe," basically consists in its survival.

Arlene Segal's combination of intense loyalty and sparse knowledge captures the general state of popular ethnic feeling among Jews today. The group undeniably exists, but its cultural meaning has been reduced to hardly more than pride in survival and achievement (usually achievement that has little to do with being Jewish), and a conviction, spoken or not, about the superiority of "us" to "them."

Of course, such tribal sentiments are not officially emphasized. In polite and guarded Jewish public discourse, the powerful sense of "us" and "them" is expressed more obliquely in a constant litany of Jewish accomplishment. It is just this self-congratulatory glorification of the group that can disturb thoughtful individuals actively engaged in Jewish life.

Leon Wieseltier, a Jewish scholar and respected literary critic and political writer, strongly supports Jewish group consciousness, and even a politics of Jewish interest. But he finds the *alrightnik* smugness of mainstream Jewish group pride deplorable and ignorant. It is not the thinning out of the culture that draws his criticism—historical forces are not apt subjects for blame—but the refusal of the community to acknowledge the crisis, its preference for inflated pride and defensive boasting over serious engagement: "The most important question to many American Jews is whose is it, ours or theirs? Jewish or non-Jewish? American Jews are very proud that Maimonides was a 'Jewish thinker,' but they don't have a clue about what he thought. Maimonides himself was not proud that he was a 'Jewish thinker,' because he was too much a thinker and too much a Jew to bother with that kind of idiotic pride. American Jews think life can be satisfied by just being Jewish, whatever that means. They admire everything Jewish. Nothing Jewish is foreign to them. Of course, if they knew anything about the Jewish tradition, many things would have to be foreign to them. If *Kabbalah*, and *halachah*, and philosophy, and Spinoza, and Sabbatai Zvi are not foreign to you, then the only thing you see in all of them is that they are Jewish. The traditional Jews who take these things seriously and see that they have some content are the first to admit that a lot that is Jewish is foreign to them. What I'm saying is more than that there is no interest in self-criticism within the Jewish community; there certainly isn't. It is that this is the death of the mind in some way."

Wieseltier sees the hollowness of this kind of community "pride." He says: "Gladness at being Jewish is not exactly an idea. It's an attitude at best. It's also an attitude almost completely devoid of content, except self-congratulation, and it becomes a substitute for real thought. Dwelling on the sheer fact of being Jewish offers people something they desperately need—a sense of importance. The Holocaust does that especially. And since the '67 War and the explosion of interest in the Holocaust, tendencies have emerged in American Jewish life that are not at all admirable —cheerleading, flag-waving, 'Jewishness without difficulty.' Jewishness has never been so undifficult as in this country. I'm not saying we need a little anti-Semitism to quicken the culture. It is historically false to say that it ever was anti-Semitism that quickened the culture. What's lacking in American life is not an enemy. It's that there used to be an interlocutor within, a goad, genuine internal difficulties and intellectual challenges. There used to be really serious and bitter battles of ideas that went on within Jewish culture, not just between Jewish and non-Jewish culture. But not now. Now American Jewish culture basically comes down to 'anything produced by a Jew is Jewish.' This is an insult to the intelligence. It is also not far from the Nazi idea. There was an obnoxious book published a while back, *The Ordeal of Civility: Freud, Marx, Lévi-Strauss, and the Jewish Struggle with Modernity*, by a sociologist named Cuddihy. He is one of those philo-Semites who you know will turn around someday and hate us. That book makes the argument that the thinking of Jewish intellectuals is Jewish, no matter what. But Lévi-Strauss doesn't have a Jewish bone in his body. He just comes from the Jews. There is no difference between that idea and the Nazi idea of psychoanalysis as a 'Jewish science.' 'Jewish psychoanalysis' is like 'Jewish geometry'—it's meaningless. Survivalism is a fine goal for Jewish politics. As a goal for Jewish life, though, it's a paltry thing compared to what was."

Ironically, for many Jews, what remains most vivid and "ethnically" alive is the Holocaust. The Holocaust destroyed the European Jewish community, and with it the reservoir from which American *Yiddishkeit* drew its élan and inspiration. Not that acculturation and the deepening integration of American Jews into American life would have been prevented by a continuing infusion of cultural energy from Jewish communities in Europe. But the process would have taken longer, and might have been more complex and surprising. The Holocaust destroyed most speakers of Yiddish, its writers and poets, actors and musicians, philosophers and critics. It destroyed any future. But remembrance of the tragedy cannot serve as a stand-in for a live ethnic culture.

Jewish-community leaders and activists use the Holocaust to bind Jews emotionally to the Jewish community, and to inspire identification and commitment to Jewish survival. In the theological writings of Emil Fackenheim, a prominent mainstream rabbi and philosopher, the duty to commit oneself to Jewish survival derives directly from the Holocaust. His argument—and others like it—is emotionally anchored in guilt, although this may not be its conscious intent. The claim is made that, since Hitler wanted to destroy the Jewish people, Jews have the moral duty of denying Hitler a posthumous victory. In other words, it is incumbent upon Jews to survive as Jews and continue Jewish peoplehood and culture, lest they become unwitting accomplices of Hitler.

Fackenheim's argument, presented as a serious philosophical and theological inquiry, is not widely known. But there are more popular forms of survivalist exhortation that echo his concerns in invoking the Holocaust. When discussing survival issues— assimilation, Jewish birth rates, intermarriage, and the like— Jewish-community professionals are not shy about exploiting the tragic power of the Holocaust. The use of a phrase like "self-inflicted mode of genocide" in an article on the low fertility of middle-class Jewish couples, or a reference, in a discussion of residential mobility, to formerly Jewish neighborhoods as *judenrein,* the official Nazi term for areas from which all Jews were forcibly removed, is deeply disturbing. "Endogenous Jewish Genocide" is the title of a paper delivered at a conference on Jewish population that discussed the impact of the Zero-Population-Growth movement on Jews. Although anti–Vietnam War student demonstrators were chastised for daring to invoke the Holocaust when they shouted accusations against the American government's military policies in Indochina, some Jewish-community spokespersons seem to feel that calling on the Holocaust is quite appropriate to make their survivalist points about the right number of children for Jewish families or the correct position on ethnic identification.

It is understandable that the Holocaust lends itself to survivalist aims. Like anti-Semitism, which has become the most potent or even the only Jewish connection for some American Jews, the Holocaust exerts a strong emotional force for Jewish identification. What is so poignant for those who actually knew and loved the culture that was destroyed is that there is so little positive interest in and knowledge of what the *Yiddishkeit* of that world meant. As Arnold Eisen, a professor of religion at Stanford University, ruefully comments, "I am afraid that we're educating a generation of students whose only knowledge of Jews is how they died."

What cultural meaning can the Holocaust have? Jewish classes on the Holocaust get a more active response from students than traditional classes on the Bible or Jewish history. But what is learned is not anything about Jewishness. What is transmitted is a message of victimhood and an idea of the Jews as the most special victims ever—a warning that once again comes down to the message of "us" and "them."

In this context, efforts to recover the images and texture of the old ethnic world—in music, film, and literature—are laudable attempts to recall a time when the Jewish community seemed vibrant with idealism and did not have to call on images of victimhood and massacre to ensure a sense of peoplehood and common culture. Yet the appealing remnants of the past only reinforce the realization that in the current mainstream Jewish community, Jewish labels have steadily replaced Jewish content. In a post-assimilation culture, ethnic memories are often vague, sweetly sentimental, and typically rather lightweight and malleable. Thus, idealists can call on a variety of images of the past to try to move the community to support political visions reminiscent of the *"bessere, shenere velt."* The more hard-nosed can evoke ethnic sentiments to support a politics of Jewish self-interest, emphasizing the importance of the Jewish bond (looking out for one's own) in a world where the "others" are hostile and not to be trusted. Such mainly symbolic ethnicity is characteristic not just of Jews, of course; political candidates of all origins now regularly make ethnic appeals, even as these differences become increasingly less substantive. Sociologists estimate that a majority of Americans are now "nonethnic." Polls show that most Americans do not claim to be more comfortable with people of their own ethnic classification and most are wary of emphasizing deep differences among ethnic groups because of concern for the social unity considered a good for American society.

For Jews, as for other groups, that rather unsavory part of ethnic consciousness—defensive, pumped up (often for dubious reasons), and chauvinistic—comes to the fore as the particular cultural content that infused ethnic communities fades under the force of continuing absorption into the common cultural mix. But even in its more positive form, symbolic ethnicity cannot hold the community together in an America where ethnic differences continue to decline in content, salience, and appeal.

Zionism

If the sentimental appeal to a romanticized (but not remembered) past cannot provide a living ethnic content for the contemporary Jewish community, what can? The mainstream answer is obvious: Israel. As a leading Israeli intellectual, Shlomo Avineri, writes in his history of Zionist ideology: "Today there does not exist one idea or one institution around which all Jewish people can or do unite—with the exception of Israel. . . . Israel is thus the new public dimension of Jewish existence. . . . As such it replaces the old religious-communal bonds that circumscribed Jewish existence in the past."

Zionism—popularly understood as the fervent support of Jews for Israel as the Jewish state—now appears at the top of the list of what being Jewish in America is all about. Charles Liebman has emphasized the fact that, of the limited amount of time an average "committed" American Jew gives to Jewish activity, "an increasing portion of that fraction of Jewish time-space, perhaps even most of it, is devoted to activity and thought surrounding Israel. This includes time spent in attendance at meetings and rallies, conversation about Israel, reading or hearing news about Israel, and, most significantly in the last decade or so, trips to Israel." Most Jewish organizations put a large part of their efforts into Israel-related programs: selling Israel Bonds, or supporting "adopted" Israeli institutions like the Weizmann Institute of

Science, assorted hospitals, and schools. Synagogue schools and Jewish all-day schools also give a large part of their educational time to Israel. Hard work within organizations is often rewarded with trips to Israel. Rabbinical students now spend at least a year in Israel as part of their training.

Support for Israel is the fundamental criterion of membership in the American Jewish community. Of course, it is possible to be Jewish without being committed to Israel or even to be actively opposed to the concept of a Jewish state as well as to its policies, a position that still has ideological and institutional form in the small but long-lived American Council for Judaism. But it is not possible to be accepted in the mainstream organized Jewish community if such views are publicly expressed. And it would not be possible to be a leader of any mainstream organization without a fervent public commitment to Israel, its basic political position, broadly conceived, and its present and future well-being.

This was not always the case.

Before the Holocaust, Zionism was a highly contested doctrine. The goal of establishing a Jewish state in Palestine was opposed by most groups within the American Jewish community: by secular, socialist, Yiddishist groups who believed in cultural pluralism in a friendly Diaspora polity like the United States; by the affluent, assimilated, German-Jewish elite who feared that the nationalistic principles of Zionism would adversely affect the acceptance of Jews into gentile America by raising ancient doubts about the sincerity of Jewish commitment to the host nation; by Jewish Communists and anarchists who saw Zionism as national chauvinism; by Orthodox Jewish groups who understood Zionism as a godless, secular movement.

But the Holocaust undercut all objections to the Zionist project of a Jewish state in Palestine. The reluctance of sympathetic countries like the United States and Great Britain to accept substantial numbers of Jewish survivors further strengthened the case for a sovereign Jewish homeland. Even articulate opponents of Zionist ideology were moved by the trauma of the Holocaust and the situation of Jewish survivors in the displaced-persons camps of postwar Europe. There was an almost universal wave of Jewish support for the new state in 1948. Most American Jews became outspoken backers of Israel, and Israel quickly became the center of American Jewish activity—the functional equivalent of the rapidly waning, mainly secular, ethnic culture of the earlier period of American Jewish life. It was as if, by a single cunning (and friendly) stroke of history, just as the rich and complex culture of Jewish immigrant life was being eroded by Americanization, and immediately after the destruction of the European roots of even the dwindling Jewish culture of American Jews, a new and powerful source of Jewish cultural vigor and ethnic continuity had miraculously emerged.

The role of Israel in the apparent rejuvenation of American Jewish life was gratefully acknowledged. In 1957, the respected American-Jewish historian Howard Sachar offered this appreciation of Israel's meaning for the continuity and flourishing of the American Jewish community:

> The doughty and courageous little state was more than a source of pride to American Jews, more even than a source of status and self-respect. It was also an inspiration for uninhibited Jewish identification, for increased interest in Jewish history and folklore, for creativity in Jewish literature, music, and art. For the first time in many years, children were learning Hebrew as a living language rather than as a burdensome inheritance from antiquity. College youth in increasing numbers were visiting Israel, attending its university, working on its farms. There was little likelihood that many of them would remain; but there was a great likelihood that many of them would bring the Israeli spirit back with them. It was a spirit of complete, unselfconscious, thoroughly affirmative Jewishness. Without this spirit, Jewish life in America with all its wealth, security, community democracy, and pragmatic realism, would hardly signify more than the dissipation of an unprecedented opportunity for corporate self-expression. With this spirit, the American-Jewish community bade fair to create a civilization of such enduring vitality as to preempt from medieval Spain the title of "Golden Age."

Motivating such exaggerated prose was the accurate perception of how necessary Israel was for giving content to American Jewish life. Nothing internal to the life and culture of the community compared with the intensity of Israel. This perception of Israel's central role has remained unchanged; indeed, in the post-1967 period, the sense of the dependence of Jewish community life on

Israel has only sharpened. As the prominent Jewish-American political scientist Daniel Elazar put it in 1976:

> Israel, both as a state and as the only Jewish country in the world, has become the touchstone of Jewish self-esteem and the measure of Jewish achievement for the world at large. As a result it has acquired an authoritative role in Jewish life that, for the moment at least, is unchallenged. Moreover, as the only place in the world where an authentic Jewish culture can flourish (at least potentially), it exercises an unequalled attraction upon American Jews searching for a meaning in their Jewishness. Even the more peripheral of American Jews are touched by the Jewish authenticity of Israel, while the more committed find the power of Israel in this respect almost irresistible.

The expectation that Israel could stimulate identification, pride, and participation has certainly been borne out. "If a single factor in the self-respect American Jewry does possess can be isolated, it is its pride in the State of Israel and its achievements," writes Rabbi Jacob Neusner. "Zionism lies at the foundation of American Jewry's capacity to affirm its Jewishness." The rebirth of the Hebrew language naturally had a great effect on Jewish cultural life and on Jewish education. Hebrew songs and dances were a rich source of energy and spirit for Jewish youth organizations, not just those that were officially Zionist. High-quality Hebrew teachers' colleges and Hebrew-speaking camps created a network of lively institutions that nourished the current generational elite of American Jewish scholars who now staff the numerous Jewish studies programs in American universities.

But even more than the maintenance of cultural commitment and engagement, the image of a "Golden Age" held out the hope of a Jewish culture and community appealing enough to bring back the Jewish youth who were increasingly drifting away into the larger integrated society.

Beth Greenbaum* is an exemplary model of how Israel has worked its power for the mainstream Jewish community. For them, she is an ideal, a paradigm of what should happen to young Jews in an American Jewish world invigorated and sustained by its

*Pseudonym.

ties to Israel. In her life she expresses just that reversal of the assimilation process for which Jewish-community activists hope and pray. She is an attorney, working as counsel for a major Jewish institution. She grew up in Council Bluffs, Iowa, where the Jewish community numbered only in the hundreds. Although her parents had a fairly strong Jewish consciousness and were involved in community activities, Greenbaum herself did not attend Hebrew school and recalls that she preferred to be with her non-Jewish friends.

"Zionist, Israel-Oriented, Like Me"

When I was a young person back in Council Bluffs, I didn't want to be Jewish. I didn't want to be set apart, to be different. I wanted to go to church and sing in the choir and be like my Christian friends. The Jewish things that we did have at home were not presented in a living way. We always had a Passover Seder, and I hated it. We rushed through it as quickly as possible to get to the meal. And the worst was when we went to my uncle, a rabbi with a small Conservative congregation in a town in Illinois. The Rosh Hashanah service was long, three and a half hours, all in Hebrew, and I didn't understand a word, and there was no children's service, where it was explained.

When I was sixteen, I really wanted to get away from home, and the Reform synagogue's youth organization had this program in countries abroad, so I signed up. The England part was filled, and all that was open was Israel, and first I thought, Ugh, all those Jews. But I had a friend who said I really should go, so I took a chance. And I fell in love with the country. It's hard for me to articulate what happened, but I think I began to feel myself part of a five-thousand-year history, and a part of the Jewish people. I think there are chords within each of us that may remain unresponsive all our lives unless triggered by the right stimulus. I believe that my core was Jewish and that I had been absorbing Jewish feelings all my life through my parents, relatives, whatever, that I had suppressed them, and that being in Israel was just the right stimulus. Maybe it was being in a place where Jews were people like everyone else. I didn't have to hide my Judaism. I didn't have to be embarrassed about being a Jew. Not only were the people around me not embarrassed about it, they were proud of it. After I returned, I felt a difference in my being Jewish. I talked about Israel all the time. I did not have that sense of being apart anymore. Since then I've been back to Israel seven times, including right after the Six-Day War and the Yom Kippur War.

Now all of my friends are Jewish, mainly from my work with the United Jewish Appeal. All of them are also very Zionist, Israel-oriented, like me. Look around my home. Over there are four books on Jerusalem, a book, *The Israel I Love*, another book, *Israel: The Reality*. A Turkish coffeepot bought in Jerusalem. A vase made of hand-painted Israeli glassware. Next to it is something I got as a gift, a piece of gray slate, with an olive tree with the Hebrew word *Shalom* engraved on it as the branches. Over there are four pictures, prints of tapestries by an Israeli artist, taken from biblical themes. Behind that is the *Encyclopedia Judaica* and a platter from the Old City of Jerusalem. And the *Second Jewish Catalog*, books on Jewish Law, Jewish literature, and numerous books on the Holocaust.

I've gotten to know more about the religious tradition, which I appreciate, like the atmosphere of Shabbat. But I'm really not at all religious in the believing-in-God sense, though I think it is important to belong to a synagogue, and I do. When I go to services and pray, I pray because I'm in touch with the tradition. The prayers mean something to me on that basis: that I am saying the same words that Jews have said for thousands of years. That link with my heritage is very important to me.

I started keeping a kosher home when I moved into my present apartment. I had taken a course called "Basic Judaism," which teaches you all the different things: Shabbat, Passover, keeping kosher. The rabbi who taught the course talked about keeping kosher in ways I'd never thought of, as a sanctification. And so I began to see keeping kosher as a link to thousands of years of Jewish history. Written Jewish history goes back three thousand years, and those people kept kosher. The whole concept is that every time you pick up a dish, every time you eat food, you have to think about who you are, that you are a Jew, that you're setting yourself apart from the rest of the world, that you are sanctifying your belief and your faith by keeping your home kosher. And I wanted a home where every Jew could eat; I didn't want someone to feel uncomfortable thinking there was a possibility of *treyf*, food that wasn't kosher.

But I don't feel I have to move to Israel. I believe that when the state of Israel was created in 1948, the Jews of the world—the Diaspora—and the Jews of Israel entered into a partnership, and that partnership guarantees that the Jews of the Diaspora will provide the financial support necessary to maintain Israel. But not necessarily to live there. I meet Israelis who say that a Jew who doesn't go to live in Israel is not a good Jew. I have no patience with that idea. It's like saying that you can be a good Jew only if you pray three times a day. At one time in my life, I did feel defensive about not going to live in Israel, but not anymore. No Jew should ever be forced to live anywhere. We were forced to live in ghettos for thousands of years.

Beth Greenbaum may be younger than most leaders of national Jewish organizations, she may be part of the new generation, but she is carrying on the traditions that have characterized American Zionism from the time of Louis D. Brandeis's leadership in the 1920s onward: philanthropy, political support, visits, artifacts, admiration, and praise—"partnership" combined with a firm denial of Zionism's fundamental demand for *aliyah* (settlement in Israel).

This "Zionistic" perspective differs profoundly from the central doctrines of classical Zionism. No one in the mainstream community disagrees about the importance of "the land of Israel" in Jewish doctrine and history. After all, traditional Jewish religion is clearly the religion of a particular people, a people "chosen" by God. To this people God gave not only his revelation, the Torah, but also a particular piece of land. Almost all of the holy writings and a good deal of religious ceremony—the Temple service, the sacrifices, the holiday festivals, the harvest festivals—are bound up with the idea of the Jewish people living and worshipping in this land. There is perhaps no single line of Jewish ritual that is recited more universally by Jews, even by those who are almost entirely nonobservant, than the ending of the Passover Seder, which is the most widely observed of all Jewish customs: "This year we celebrate here, but next year in Jerusalem."

The aspiration to return to the land is echoed in Israel's founding document, the Proclamation of Independence: "Exiled from the land of Israel, the Jewish people remained faithful to it in all the countries of their dispersion, never ceasing to pray and hope for their return and the restoration of their national freedom." But contrary to this sweeping claim, many of the "Jewish people" had long ceased to "pray and hope" for any such goal.

The most powerful strand in modern Jewish history had been the struggle to find acceptance in civil society, while retaining some form of Jewish identification. Since the French Revolution, when Jews were first emancipated—offered citizenship—the "Jewish question," which asked whether the Jews could truly be integrated into the larger nation, had been the central issue in European Jewish life.

Zionism was one answer to this question. It appeared as a political movement in the second half of the nineteenth century, when modern nationalism was achieving a broad ideological ascendency in Europe. The Zionist answer to the Jewish question was that, whatever individual Jews might prefer, the circumstances of modern history would compel the reaffirmation of Jewish nationality due to the inevitable failure of Jewish emancipation and assimilation. The negative vision underlying Zionist ideology was that the Jews would never really be accepted; that, on the contrary, anti-Semitism would survive, grow, and sooner or later flare up to murderous dimensions—not only in the relatively benighted Eastern European regions where pogroms were a perpetual danger, but also in the enlightened and liberal cultures of Western and Central Europe, where legal emancipation for Jews had been achieved.

But there was much more to the Zionist answer than just physical security through political sovereignty. There was the matter of the Jewish soul, which Zionists believed to be more insidiously threatened than Jewish bodies. The psychocultural dimension of Zionist doctrine emphasized the distortions of the Jewish character caused by oppression. Ironically, the concept of the warped Jewish personality mirrored much of the anti-Jewish expression of the period. Zionist doctrine and anti-Semitic polemic met in their acceptance of the idea that Jews as a people had developed undesirable traits due to their "unnatural" condition of weakness and dependence; that Jews predominated in unsavory economic practices like money-lending and financial speculation; and that Jews did not follow productive and culturally sound pursuits like agriculture and manual labor. Further, according to the Zionist perspective, the attempt to escape their condition through assimilation guaranteed an unhappy spiritual fate for those Jews who embarked on that journey. Not only would failure be the final result; the attempt itself would extract a high price in the form of self-hatred. "Cultural Zionism" emphasized that the land and political sovereignty were only means, not ends in themselves; the real end was the salvation of the Jewish spirit threatened by the poisons of attempted assimilation in an anti-Semitic world.

The founder of cultural Zionism, Ahad Ha'am (a Hebrew pseudonym meaning "One of the People," the pen name of Asher Ginzburg), characterized emancipation and assimilation into European culture as "slavery in freedom." He wrote: "Do I envy these fellow-Jews of mine their emancipation?—I answer, in all truth and sincerity: No! The privileges are not worth the price: I may not be emancipated; but at least I have not sold my soul for emancipation."

For Zionists, just as for anti-Semites, Jews were essentially a foreign people, one who could never be absorbed by the nations they dwelled among. The Jewish question, in both its psychological and its political aspects, could be resolved only when Jews normalized their historical situation, bringing their long exile to an end, reconstituting a sovereign community in their ancient homeland, renewing their culture in their own language. Despite their ideological differences over the form this community might take, all Zionists agreed that only a Jewish national home, with the Jewish people ingathered from their exile, could repair the powerlessness, psychological ills, and cultural decay of modern Jewry.

The twentieth century gave horrible confirmation to Zionist predictions. The Nazi slaughter of European Jewry, from the completely assimilated to the most pious, exceeded by far even the gloomiest of Zionist warnings. But this confirmation has not been taken as validating the basic principles of Zionism. Ironically, most American Jews do not accept the Zionist vision even when they are "Zionists." They do not think of themselves as living in "exile," always strangers, rejected by the non-Jewish majority, ultimately under the threat of extinction; nor do they accept the problem of the "Jewish soul" that gave form to the Zionist ideal of the redemption of the Jewish people. They feel neither psychologically unhealthy nor culturally warped. Despite their official Zionism, the truth is that they have never seriously supported the idea that Jews are at grave risk in the United States or that they are obligated by any imperative to settle in Israel.

Perhaps the best way to apprehend the gap between classical Zionism and its American version is to listen to someone who believed the vision and tried to live out its demands. Earl Brownstein* came of age in the intensely emotional period of Israel's founding. An American boy, growing up in Brooklyn, he joined one of a number of Zionist youth movements, and entered a lively, contentious world in which competing groups were divided by the specifics of their ideologies, and yet united by their fervent commitment to build the Jewish state. For him, Zionism offered a powerful and plausible reading of Jewish history that made tough demands on anyone for whom Jewish identity and involvement were major concerns. At present he lives in California, where he is a Jewish-community professional, the director of the local branch of an important national Jewish organization.

"My Heroes Were the Irgun"

When I was ten years old, I was on an outing at Coney Island. There were some abandoned buildings, part of the boardwalk, and in one of the buildings there was an exhibition of photographs of the concentration camps. A big sign said, "No children allowed," so naturally I crawled under the sign. I'll never forget the impact of seeing what the Nazis had done to people who I later learned were Jews. This was probably the most formative experience I had. I remember swearing that if people were doing this to Jews, I would find out why, and if there was anything I could do in my life to make sure it didn't happen again, I would do it. I couldn't believe that the photographs were real—the bodies all piled up. It is still very vivid. I asked my parents what it was all about, and they were very evasive. So I went to the library to read about it. I had trouble understanding a lot of the words. I remember then seeing people around Bensonhurst wearing uniforms with Jewish insignias. At first I thought they were some kind of Boy Scouts, but they turned out to be the youth movement of the Revisionist Zionists, Betar. They were in a campaign to collect weapons from the Jewish veterans of World War II. They had gotten lists from sympathetic chaplains. I started going door-to-door with them. We even stored weapons in my basement. It was a very exciting and dramatic involvement.

*Pseudonym.

My own background was fairly conventional. My father took the family to synagogue to observe the High Holy Days. He was a mild Zionist—collecting money for the Mogen David Adom, the Jewish "Red Cross"—the "send-an-ambulance-to-Israel" kind of Zionism. Though I joined Betar, I could have been recruited by any Zionist youth group. I made no ideological distinctions. A year or two later, we started getting into physical confrontations with young people from other movements, mainly the really far-left Hashomer Hatzair; and then we started hearing stories that in Palestine, people from the Left had been turning over our Irgun people to the British. In public school, as kids were getting involved in the different movements, they would sit in their own groups, they wouldn't talk to each other, there were fistfights and bloody noses. On one occasion, the windows of our meeting hall were broken by the other side.

During those years in Betar, from age ten and a half to nineteen, I lived for the movement. It changed my life in every way. Most of the leadership of Betar was drawn from people with an Orthodox education. I decided then that if I was going to be Jewish and Zionist, I should find out what the religious part was all about, and I adopted, without much understanding, most of the trappings of Orthodoxy. This was hard on my parents. I remember one incident, when I was a little over thirteen. I came home and decided to break all the dishes in the house, because they weren't kosher. We lived in a fourth-floor walkup, and I started to throw all the dishes out of the window into the backyard. This brought the neighbors up to see what was going on. My parents weren't home, and the people asked whether I'd flipped out. I said, "No, no, it's all right. I'm just religious."

In the summer, I went to a Betar camp in Liberty, New York. We learned jujitsu, how to cut through barbed wire, how to use rifles. While our contemporaries knew all the latest hit songs and movie actors, we were singing songs of the early pioneers in Israel. I developed an interest in soccer, the national game of the Jews in Palestine. My heroes were the Irgun people sent to recruit arms and money. There were some ideological discussions, but mainly there was the idea of love and appreciation for the Jewish people, and the concept Menachem Begin talks about, learned from his master, Jabotinsky—*hadar*, which means dignity. We learned about bringing dignity and honor to the Jewish people. Our expectation was that, although we had been born in the U.S.

through historical accident, we would be spending the rest of our lives in our true homeland, Israel.

My group went in 1956, right before the outbreak of the Sinai War. We were going to be the saviors of Israel. We were sent to a Betar settlement first. None of us had training in agriculture. It was very tough—mainly rocks grew there. Reality was tough too, and our group broke up and we went our separate ways. I joined the Israeli army—Nahal, the "Fighting Pioneer Youth" division —and served in a kibbutz near the border. By 1959, I knew I was coming back to the United States. Everyone has different reasons for staying or coming back. I never developed roots. I had no family there as others did. I started feeling pangs of loneliness. Even though I felt Israel was my country, I wasn't comfortable there. I began to feel there was more to being a Jew than the nationalistic aspect.

I felt like a failure when I came back. My magnificent dream was just a dream. The truth was, the day-to-day difficulties of life had overwhelmed the ideology. But even now, I still feel guilty about living here. In the back of my mind, I feel I'm not complete unless I live in Israel.

Brownstein recalls a time when Zionism was still a living doctrine, and the sharply conflicting visions of what Israel should be, what values and ideologies would shape its politics and culture, were part of an active intellectual ferment—a genuine community ferment—at the heart of American Jewish life. Such debate is not ongoing in the mainstream American Jewish community today. Fragmentary youth movements still maintain the true Zionist faith, insisting on the repressed content of Zionism as a doctrine that should threaten the bland allegiance that American Jews call "Zionism." These groups repeat the core Zionist analysis that insists that the duty of each Jew who wishes to live an authentic Jewish life must be to move to Israel (or feel guilty about not doing so). Although they are officially honored and praised by American Jewish-community activists, and especially by Israeli political groups that continue to pay lip service to Zionist doctrines embodied in the founding ideology of Israel, they are essentially disregarded. Not surprisingly, their pronouncements take on a tone of angry complaint, moralistically scolding the official Jewish community that honors—and ignores—them.

In the past, political differences among the youth groups were intense, matching the profound conflicts among the adult movements here and in Palestine. But as the youth groups declined in their ability to draw new recruits, the differences between them became less important than the threat to their survival, and the groups moved to unite in order to display a greater presence to the mainstream Jewish community. More than a decade ago, in 1979, representatives of all of the various tiny Zionist youth groups, from left-wing socialist movements dedicated to the ideal of kibbutz life to supporters of right-wing ultra-nationalist expansionist factions, gathered to create a united Zionist youth front. (To get a sense of proportion, it should be noted that the total membership of all the Zionist youth groups put together is below one-tenth of 1 percent of the American Jewish population.) Calling themselves "Telem," an acronym formed from the Hebrew words for "Movement of Zionist Fulfillment," the representatives issued yet another demand to American Jews to rededicate themselves to Zionism's historic and as yet unfulfilled goals. Once again chastizing the adult Zionist organizations for being deaf to true Zionist demands, the founders of Telem delivered a defiant manifesto, reaffirming the classical Zionist ideals. The preamble of the manifesto expressed the essential claim: "The return to Zion has always been the dream of the Jewish people. Zionism, the national liberation movement of the Jewish people, envisions the continued building of the state of Israel based on ideals and ethics rooted in the Jewish tradition. The Zionist dream was not completed with the establishment of the state. Zionism sees the return of the Jewish people to the state of Israel as an essential component in the continued building of the Jewish liberation struggle." In 1988, the *Telem Update* reiterated the need for "increased free-choice aliyah," and "challenged" American Jews with the slogan "Is Aliyah Only for Oppressed Jewry?"

Now, quite obviously, the return to Zion is not the repressed dream—let alone the waking desire—of the vast majority of American Jews. The basic Zionist premises—that Jewish identity is fundamentally national, that this national people should live in its own land and create its own culture in its own language, and that assimilation is deplorable as well as harmful to the individual and to the Jewish people—are not even seriously contemplated by more than a small number of ideologically engaged Jews who continue to argue about such issues. Even the new leadership elite of the Jewish community, people such as Beth Greenbaum, can be uncomprehending of the theoretical force of Zionist claims. Her contention that, since Jews were forced to live in ghettos, no one should ever tell any Jew where he or she should live, misses the point of the Zionist ideal of an end to exile.

But it is perfectly consistent with the "Israelism" that has become the dominant center of American Jewish life. Charles Liebman captures the essence of this distinction: "Support for Israel becomes not merely support for a state thousands of miles away or for its inhabitants; rather, support for Israel is the symbol of one's Jewish identity, like staying home from work on Yom Kippur. It has nothing to do with Zionism, with a national Jewish self-definition, or even with knowing very much about Israel itself or modern Jewish-Israeli culture."

One rabbi of a flourishing New York congregation offered his sardonic version of Israelism in action. "Israel is very important to the people in my congregation," he says, "but I don't know what more beyond that. They make trips—our synagogue alone sponsors trips for three thousand people a year. Israel means identity: People have an emotional experience when they go to the Wailing Wall. It means status. If they go on a UJA mission, it means even more status. You know up front that you are going to get a pitch for funds. What is the selling point? On Monday you'll have breakfast with Abba Eban, and on Tuesday you'll be in the Knesset to talk to Shimon Peres. It's bullshit. You'll have breakfast with Abba Eban, only it's him and five hundred other people. But at home, telling your next-door neighbor in Scarsdale, you're not talking about the five hundred people, you're saying 'Abba Eban.' Israel has become the prestige ladder inside the Jewish community. You get invited to a luncheon with Foreign Minister Arens. It's a fundraiser for Israel, costs you a $1000 pledge, and the UJA guy is there, and he'll take a picture of you and Arens and that picture will be in the Jewish-community paper that week. This is un-Jewish, as far as I'm concerned. It's a putdown of the person who can't afford to make the $1000 pledge. And it really gets me; the one thing these people will not do is publicly criticize Israel—but that's it. They may not come to shul on Yom Kippur or do anything else. The only 'law' they always observe is: Never criticize Israel."

The point here is not to accuse the "phony" American Zionists of having betrayed the real Zionist ideals—such consistency would be a dubious virtue when based on premises as out-of-sync with today's reality as those of classical Zionism. The point is rather to suggest that the rise of Israelism signals a further decline in the cultural vitality of the mainstream Jewish community. Zionism's deep and radical questions about the conditions needed for a creative Jewish culture and community have now been silenced—and replaced by a single minimalist demand: support and be proud of Israel.

The great irony of the current situation is that the actual achievements of the Zionist movement are what undermined its core analysis. Rather than the existence of a Jewish state providing the ideal conditions for the voluntary ending of the exile, Israel has provided the inspiration and content for a Jewish life in the Diaspora that can seem healthy, safe, and happy to Israel-inspired Jews. Not only does Israel give the community a focus for Jewish activity that requires little in the way of Jewish culture, knowledge, religion, or group life, it also creates, or did until recently, the psychological conditions of Jewish pride and uninhibited Jewish identification, the very situation that Zionists considered impossible to achieve for Jews living in the Diaspora.

The fragility of this arrangement is illustrated by the response to the Six-Day War, certainly the most powerful and mobilizing Jewish experience in recent times. Particularly for the generation that came of age after the founding of Israel, the June 1967 war between Israel and her Arab neighbors was the most intense time of Jewish consciousness in recent decades. What seemed especially noteworthy about the response to this event was that it was shared by considerable numbers of Jews who had previously been rather uninvolved in any Jewish activities. The war is even credited with having moved indifferent, unaffiliated Jews to active concern with the Jewish community. Some observers saw in the intense emotional tone of those weeks an almost miraculous interruption or even reversal of the accelerating pace of disaffiliation among the younger generation. Like the establishment of Israel twenty years earlier, the Six-Day War was presented as a dramatic turning point, an event whose positive impact on Jewish-community life would be felt for many years.

Nathan Glazer, in an epilogue to the revised 1972 edition of his excellent study, *American Judaism*, summed up this perception: "Interest in Jewish religion and in Jewish issues among young Jews seemed to have reached a nadir in the early 1960s. But in the latter part of the decade, one overwhelming event, the Israeli war of 1967 and its consequences, transformed the scene, leading Jews to a new intensity of self-consciousness and a new level of concern for Jewish issues." Especially remarkable was the response of politically engaged young Jews. As Glazer noted, "American Jews, among them even the Jewishly indifferent youth whose energies had for so long been engaged by the cause of the Negroes or the poor or the Vietnamese, suddenly discovered that the fate of Israel, of Jews of different language, culture, and state, meant more to them than these other causes."

A judgment like this now seems exaggerated. After all, the really intense time of the antiwar movement and the struggle for civil rights came *after* the Six-Day War, and even young American Jews who had become anxiously concerned with Israel's fate when that fate seemed threatened (and this included a large number of student radicals who had no active connection to the Jewish community), reverted to their normal pattern of commitments and concerns once it was obvious that Israel was in no imminent danger of annihilation.

There is, however, enough anecdotal evidence from young Jews about their intense experiences to explain how a judgment like Glazer's could have seemed plausible at the time. There were dramatic "conversions," returns to a sense of primary identification with a Jewish-community, accounts that were understandably highlighted by the media. In our interviews, we frequently heard about the catalytic effect of those June days on Jewish identification. But statistics indicate that the outpouring of intense support for Israel came mainly from American Jews who were already involved in Jewish-community life. (This situation was even more sharply pronounced during the 1973 Yom Kippur War between Israel and Egypt and Syria.) Unaffiliated and well-integrated American Jews, including the radical Jewish student youth to whom Glazer referred, usually felt sympathetic to Israel when Israel seemed especially threatened, and most of this group were relieved and even proud after the Israeli victory in 1967. But there is no convincing evidence of a major shift to involvement in Jewish-community activities for this group, or of a massive emotional return of unaffiliated youth to the Jewish community.

Within the community, the outpouring of support was very

impressive. In monetary terms, the 1966 level of donations to Israel—$64 million—quadrupled in 1967 to $242 million, while sales of Israel Bonds went from $76 million to $190 million, a 250-percent increase. For several years after the 1967 emergency, contributions stayed at a much higher plateau than their pre-1967 level, before declining to a normal rate. Even more striking than the rise in donations was the sharp increase in American Jewish emigration to Israel. In 1967, 1,700 Americans settled in Israel. The trend accelerated remarkably, as the number climbed to 4,300 in 1968, 6,700 in 1969, and 9,200 in 1970. But after 1970, the rate leveled off and then declined. Of those who made up this mini-swell of aliyah, at least 50 percent have returned to the United States, and the migration problem that now attracts the most attention is the increasing number of Israelis leaving Israel for the United States and Canada, a number considerably greater than the diminishing trickle of American Jews going to Israel. Fewer than two thousand American Jews now emigrate to Israel yearly. In a macabre footnote to this trend, the *New York Times* noted a number of years ago that "far more New York Jews were brought to Israel for burial in 1985 than came for purposes of immigration."

The waning of involvement in recent years is apparent as well in the fate of organizations devoted to Israel's welfare. Leaving aside the tiny youth groups, who, as we have noted, have less and less influence on the community, the large adult groups like the Zionist Organization of America, the Farband–Labor Zionist organization, or even the giantess of Jewish organizations, Hadassah, the women's Zionist organization, all continue to decline in membership and élan, and there is no serious claim from inside the community that these groups are having great success in attracting the new generation of adults. The same steady decline can be observed in the other Israelist organizations that have been so prominent in American Jewish life, such as B'nai B'rith, the American Jewish Congress, and the Women's American Organization for Rehabilitation Through Training. The flourishing of a new young leadership core, exemplified by Beth Greenbaum, should be recognized, but in an appropriately illuminating way. A leading sociologist of Jewish-community life, Steven M. Cohen of Queens College in New York, characterized this elite group as a "packet of energy in a decaying system." Another important scholar of American Jewish culture, Alan Mintz, of the University of Maryland, noted a "quickening of activity at the top of the pyramid structure of Jewish life," but also pointed out that "the great bulk are being washed into the sands or are maintaining a very low level of identification."

Still, for the foreseeable future, Israel will continue to be the most powerful focus for community-wide cultural and ethnic activity, especially as the related strands of community activity, like the cause of Soviet Jewry, lose their hold on emotional Jewish commitment. And that is the problem. What is starkly clear is the vicarious quality of Israelism as the main content of Jewish ethnic activity, the dependence of American Jewish life on what other Jews do: what they sing, who they fight, what their political needs are, what they claim "Jewish" could or should mean. This dependence for energy and interest on concerns that are external to the actual daily life of the American Jewish community becomes much more risky for the future of that community as Israel's situation changes rapidly and drastically. In the past, the perceived precariousness of Israel's situation was the greatest spur to activity and commitment; the more turmoil and trouble, the deeper and more widespread the involvement of American Jews in Jewish activities. But this is no longer so.

Beginning with the 1982 invasion of Lebanon, continuing with the rise of the Right and the increasing power of ultra-fundamentalism in Israeli politics and culture, and intensifying with the struggles of the *intifada*—Israel has become an increasingly problematic object for the sentimental identification that has served the mainstream community for over four decades. The ultra-Orthodox who help shape state policy can no longer be considered merely picturesque, their customs presenting quaint scenes for the cameras of Reform Jewish tourists. The image of the heroic, democratic underdog around which Jewish pride has crystallized has sustained serious shock from such revelations as Israel's military and commercial links with South Africa, the Iran-Contra scandal, the Sabra and Shatila massacres during the Israeli army's occupation of Beirut several years ago, and current documented violations of human rights in the occupied West Bank and Gaza. The possibility that the Israeli government might modify the Law of Return and limit the definition of "who is a Jew" to exclude those converted by Reform and Conservative rabbis, and so directly negate those denominations' claim to

Jewish legitimacy, cannot help but complicate the long-standing and unquestioned allegiance of the mainstream.

In an article, significantly entitled "Marriage," novelist Anne Roiphe movingly articulates the fear, confusion, and distress of American Jews faced with the new reality of Israel. "What of the occupation, the settlers, the claim to Judaea and Samaria?" she asks:

> Are we really so proud of the expansionists and the religious nationalists and the rubber bullets that don't seem to be made of rubber at all? . . . What if Israel becomes a state that is nondemocratic, non-Western, not like us at all? Will it still be our Israel, our place of last refuge, the center of a spiritual dream that we own, have always owned, and can only abandon by abandoning ourselves? . . . Where is the point where divorce is contemplated? How much violence to their inner selves will American Jews tolerate in order to hold on to their dream of an Israel that redeems, that promises the future?

Such fears and outrage about Israel are certainly a new and important development for the self-image of American Jews.

In the days when the vision of Israel could attract unalloyed ethnic pride and enthusiasm—the new state in 1948, the Six-Day War in 1967—the underlying problem of dependence could be evaded. Acculturated ethnic communities need outside infusions to provide energy and content, and the Israel of those heroic years served this function well. But the Israel of today is much less useful for this purpose. Sentimental identification can be easily shaken, and contemporary developments in Israel have disturbed, embarrassed, even alienated American supporters, rather than provided the source of the "complete, unselfconscious, thoroughly affirmative Jewishness" that, in Howard Sachar's phrase, was to enable the American Jewish community to create a new "Golden Age." An event like the Gulf War, with its threat to Israel, can momentarily revivify the old sentiments of unqualified support, but as the aftermath of the war has shown—the continued move to the right, the insistence on establishing more settlements, the weakening of the Israeli peace movement—the long-term problems for the connections between Israel and American Jews remain the same.

American Jewish-community activists are appropriately frightened at the prospects of losing Israelism as a content-provider. "Without Israel," writes Anne Roiphe, "the American Jewish community would spin its wheels and like the Edsel be taken off the line. Without this profound connection to Israel, American Jews would be impoverished, diminished—spiritually and psychologically—and vulnerable to a major identity crisis." As Israel is less and less able to serve as a fount for American Jewish energy, it is less and less capable of providing the content for a Jewish community whose substance continues to dissipate.

Synagogue

Of course, there is always religion. And Jewish mainstream community life has an obvious religious dimension: synagogue membership and attendance, religious education for the children, observance of holidays and festivals, practice and ritual. The usual classification of Jewish denominations is Orthodox, Conservative, and Reform. For the mainstream community, Reform and Conservative are dominant. These are the primary forms of Judaism that arose in response to the Enlightenment, the scientific revolution, liberalism, democratic ideas, and other major developments of modernity.

Reform Judaism was created in Germany by German Jews who wished to participate in the secular culture of modern Europe. Eager to abandon the "tribal" features of Jewish existence in return for access to "enlightened" European culture, these modernizing Jews needed a way of being Jewish *and* modern. They fashioned a form of Judaism compatible with the values of the bourgeois cultural milieu into which they sought entry. This required dropping the entire structure of traditional practice and the creation of a modern service, modeled on the decorous worship of middle-class Protestantism, with a choir, responsive readings, a sermon in the vernacular, and, in some congregations, Sunday services. Reform also eliminated the powerful particularism of traditional Judaic religious notions. By selective choice of texts and new interpretations, reformers "discovered" that the essence of Jewish tradition was precisely in those universal ethical truths that had become the widely accepted coin of modern liberal thought. For example, the Messiah was no longer envisioned as a God-sent figure who would restore the Jews to their rightful place of sovereignty in their own land, but as the symbolic expression of a general moral and ethical spirit that would enlighten all peoples. Mention of "chosenness" was eliminated from the ritual, and the concept was reinterpreted to avoid any sense of superiority or God-given privilege; instead it meant that the Jews were to be an ethical light unto the nations.

Reform Judaism grew in the United States along with the rising German-Jewish population during the second half of the nineteenth century. But within the Reform camp, there was a more traditional-minded, historical perspective that, while it would not accept Orthodoxy's rigorous position on ritual and doctrine, still valued much of the traditional practice of Judaism. In the United States, these adherents of the middle ground evolved Conservative Judaism at the beginning of the twentieth century. Much traditional ritual—Sabbath observance, *kashrut* (dietary laws), the wearing of skullcaps and prayer shawls in synagogue—was retained. But a good deal was either dropped or observed with less rigor. Conservative Judaism gained force because of its appeal to the new masses of Eastern European immigrants, for whom Reform was too radical a departure: it did not reflect their Jewish experience, or their class, or the cultural conditions in the urban ghettos of the United States. For the rising numbers of Jews who had no desire to continue traditional Orthodoxy, but who still felt ethnically and religiously Jewish, Conservative Judaism was a satisfactory solution. In the decades after the Second World War, when the prospering Jewish community moved up into the middle class and out to the suburbs, and when the synagogue became a "community-center" institution that could provide a focus for Jewish identification, the children of the Eastern European immigrants responded favorably to Conservatism's combination of traditional rituals and reform spirit. As a result, Conservatism emerged as the most popular of the Jewish denominations.

In recent decades, the differences between Conservative and Reform Judaism, though still articulated by rabbis and scholars associated with each denomination, are hardly significant to the great majority of those belonging to Reform and Conservative congregations. No honest observer suggests that more than a few synagogue members practice the ritual requirements still considered valid by the ideology of Conservatism. Meanwhile the modernist appreciation for traditional symbols has softened the classical Reform opposition to the ritual use of skullcaps and prayer shawls, so that one can now observe many students at their graduation from Reform rabbinical school adopting these very symbols of what the movement had rejected in its early years. In addition, the anti-Zionism that was so powerful a strand in classical Reform's opposition to national particularism has been superseded by the enthusiastic acceptance of Israelism. So there is hardly any serious difference now between Reform and Conservative realities. Although the Conservative movement remains the most popular denomination, Reform has been growing substantially while Conservative membership has been slipping. That is because Reform remains the more adaptive to modern conditions. Indeed, it is the part of the mainstream religious world that first ordained women rabbis, first welcomed gay congregations into its synagogue association, and most actively participates in movements of social reform. But though Reform has been gaining within the community, it is subject, along with Conservatism, to the broad forces discouraging affiliation.

Synagogue membership has dropped below half of the number of Jewish households, and, even for the diminishing number of members, synagogue attendance continues to decline. The proportion of Jewish children enrolled in Hebrew schools has been continually falling from its high point in the 1950s, and the proportion of Jewish youth receiving Jewish education is currently at an all-time low. Further, it is widely admitted that the quality of this education—aside from the growing day-school movement— is poor. If not for the large numbers of Israeli immigrants needing jobs, the pool of Hebrew-school teachers would be almost dry. The strikingly diminished attendance at synagogue services and the undistinguished quality of Jewish education are matched by declining revenues and a long-term decrease in applications to rabbinical schools.

Statistically, synagogue membership is closely tied to Hebrew school, bar and bat mitzvah, and, for Reform congregations, confirmation. Families of school-age children show much higher membership levels than families without children or families whose children have passed the relevant ages. (One 1950s study of a typical Jewish suburban community found that only 19 percent of families with children below school age belonged to synagogues. Affiliation went up to 56 percent during the early school years and peaked at 87 percent for the bar/bat mitzvah years. After that, the rate sharply declined.)

Aside from its religious and instructional role, the synagogue also functions as a community center. Synagogues provide facilities for a wide range of recreational and educational events. They offer lectures, classes of all sorts, from macrame and yoga to current events, and encounter groups. Local chapters of Jewish organizations like B'nai B'rith, the American Jewish Congress, and Hadassah hold their meetings in the building. There are synagogue youth groups, Boy Scout and Girl Scout chapters, dances, fairs, craft shows, concerts—and, of course, the Hebrew school.

That there has been a steady decline in synagogue membership, religious participation of synagogue members, and Jewish education for the young is not a matter of dispute. But in spite of the persistence of this trend, some observers have found grounds for a new optimism about mainstream Jewish religion in America. During the past decade, a revival of synagogue life has been noted in the Jewish community. In 1980, *Present Tense*, a journal published by the American Jewish Committee, announced "The Reawakening of Jewish Religious Life in America" in a series of articles on the state of the synagogue. According to the editor of the series, American Jewish religious life had indeed become bland and empty. But "the new militancy of the Reform movement and the spread of *havurot* [fellowship groups] into even the most conventional synagogue settings" testify to a religious resurgence. The writer agrees that it is "ironic that this renewed sense of optimism and activity parallels double-digit intermarriage, an all-time drop in synagogue attendance, and fears of drastically declining revenues for communal and religious institutions." Yet, despite these problems, he expresses confidence in the "health, soundness and certainly the endurance of Jewish religious life in America." Moreover, he foresees a transformation in religious life that is "truly staggering"—a prediction apparently confirmed by a 1991 *New York Times* front-page story on the rabbinate as a "bright new career choice." "More and more young Jews are picking careers as rabbis," proclaims the article, which describes an "explosion of interest in rabbinical training" as Reform and Conservative seminaries accept their largest classes in a decade; the article goes on to suggest that the trend "may signify a movement away from the materialism of the 1980s toward more spiritual concerns."

Such developments in the synagogue and the rabbinate place the Jews within the religious revival noted in Christian America during recent years, which some sociologists view as an expression of spreading dissatisfaction with modern secular culture. For example, in a 1984 essay in the *New York Times Magazine,* several intellectuals offered reasons for their own "Return to Religion." Daniel Bell, a distinguished Harvard social theorist, argued that the secular alternatives to religious faith, like politics or art, have lost their ability to move people, and that faith in science and belief in human progress have similarly been undermined by the horrors of twentieth-century history. Bell speaks eloquently about the coming "resacralization" of modern culture. According to Robert Bellah, a University of California sociologist, the senior author of a widely discussed study of American character, *Habits of the Heart* (1985), and himself an active Episcopalian: "There is a reaction against extreme individualism and self, a preoccupation with and a search for roots with a capital R, which takes people back to religion. Tradition is on the agenda with a positive force." The reasons cited for the renewal of Jewish religiosity evoke the same desire for tradition, roots, community, in addition to certain specific catalytic events. The Six-Day War, the movement in support of Soviet Jewry, the rise in ethnic consciousness—these new developments have reversed the secularizing trend, we hear, and have generated a new and exuberant rise in Jewish energy.

But if one looks closely at the array of causes called on to explain the perceived ferment in Jewish religious life, it is hard to miss the fact that none of them are actually religious. While they may plausibly account for the observed heightening of ethnic consciousness—and there is evidence of such a development—it is not obvious why they should stimulate *religious* consciousness.

Rabbi Eric Kessler's* little temple is doing well. Housed in a modest structure in a newly gentrified big-city enclave, the temple draws impressive numbers of regular attendees—mainly young, single, professional, and culturally sophisticated. According to Rabbi Kessler, since 1978, when he came to the synagogue, the Reform congregation has grown considerably, and the median age

*Pseudonym.

has dropped about twenty years. He estimates that about 10 percent of the congregation are "Jews by choice," people who have converted, mainly because of marrying a Jewish partner.

"People Want Community"

I'm not sure why the number of people coming to services and joining the temple has been increasing. Maybe there is a sense that society is so big, so impersonal; people want community. Most of my congregants are not coming primarily because of theological belief in God. I encourage them to lead a vibrant Jewish life, to make Judaism a guiding force in terms of their moral choices. And I explain about the spirit of Torah, which is there to elevate life, to make it more humane. I think the Torah has to be rewritten every day by every person.

We're very much involved with social action and the community. We think of ourselves as a social-activist congregation. I'm very involved in the abortion-rights movement, for example. I'm the vice-president of a senior citizens' coalition in the neighborhood that serves hot meals to disadvantaged old people, Jewish and non-Jewish. And I'm the vice-president of the nursing home.

I think that I see my own relationship to God in the framework of striving to be a better person, to make the world better. In a more theological sense, I don't think I have ever experienced God. It takes a long time to open yourself up enough to permit God to enter. I hope for it. I've even thought about putting on *tefillin*, with the hope that over time, doing the rituals, the prayers, something would happen, I would be touched. But I can't get myself to enter that discipline.

There is an argument we used to carry on in rabbinical school, and it still goes on, over the rabbi's role, and the whole notion of universalism versus particularism. Should a rabbi be in a prophetic role, looking out for all people, or should we just be looking out for the Jewish people, be involved exclusively in issues of the Jewish poor and Soviet Jewry and things like that? Personally, I don't think they are mutually exclusive. I think Judaism calls for balance in all dimensions of life. I think Judaism represents a value system that is at odds with the idea of good as what is good for *me*, get all the gusto, all that Madison Avenue hedonism. Because Judaism says we as a people have a messianic role. We in the Reform movement have a wonderful idea about the Messiah. We do not believe in a personal Messiah. We believe that the Messiah depends upon you and me. When all humanity learns how to get it together and really live on the premise that we're all created equal, that we're all sisters and brothers, that will be the Messiah.

Alienation, isolation, impersonality, the desire for community: these might plausibly help support a local efflorescence of synagogue attendance in an urban neighborhood favored by a young, single, sophisticated population. But such a situation is hardly characteristic of mainstream Jewish-community life. Are comparable unpredicted flourishings observable in a typical, stable, family-oriented setting, like an upper-middle-class Jewish suburb?

Barry Friedman's suburban, nonaffiliated, "traditional progressive" synagogue in Livingston, New Jersey, is a very successful institution. Membership is high; the building is large, architecturally impressive, set on extensive, lovely, and well-kept grounds. Attendance is up, and young, affluent, and well-educated Jews are joining and participating in gratifying numbers. The Hebrew school is large and lively. Rabbi Friedman has an explanation for his success.

"Judaism Does Not Stagnate"

You have to give people a reason to come to the synagogue and declare their Jewish identification. When I first started here in 1968, Rosh Hashanah and Yom Kippur services began at nine, with a small group racing really fast through the Hebrew liturgy. The majority of the congregation came at eleven, when the rabbis and cantors took the Torah out of the Ark and there was some English and chanting. When we moved out of Newark into the suburbs, we attracted younger, more educated, more Americanized people. I had to really think about whether our service was meaningful to *this* congregation. Nothing was translated, and so it couldn't make sense to them. Maybe it satisfied the old-timers, but the congregation wasn't made up of those people anymore. The people here now, if you ask them if they believe in God, would say yes, because that's the American way. But God doesn't play a role in their lives. "Yes, I believe." But if you probe, you learn, no, it isn't really an issue for them.

So I rewrote the High Holy Day morning services. I kept traditional liturgical elements chanted by the cantor, which had nostalgic value. But I added other things, some poems, a piece by Einstein that was very religious in spirit, a few of my own writings. And we started the service at ten in the morning. The room was completely full. Why? There was English, it was meaningful, it was aesthetic. People wanted to be in the synagogue and we had been keeping them away. And what do you do to fill the entire Yom Kippur day? There isn't enough in the prayer book to carry you through to sunset. So I put together a collection of meditations and readings—Hasidic stories, Rabindranath Tagore, Stephen Vincent Bénet, and Martin Buber—very beautiful things. We hired a string quartet to play relaxing classical and liturgical music and put benches outside in the gardens, so if you want to go out, go out. You want to talk, there is a place to go and talk. The congregation loved it and it fits with Yom Kippur. It makes you feel a nostalgia for times past, for people past, you feel a sense of community and yourself as part of the community. You can be with people, or be alone, think about your *bubbe* and *zeyde*, whatever.

I began experimenting with services right after I came. I got a first-rate composer as music director, and we began to compose services in an American mode, whether it was rock or jazz, whatever. Our guiding principle was the biblical verse "Sing unto the Eternal a *new* song." Any idiom in good taste was fine with us. Hardly anyone had been coming to synagogue on the morning after the Passover Seder; the traditional service didn't mean much to them. So we took that service, with its powerful theme of freedom, brought in the American Revolution and the idea of the heroic with the Warsaw Ghetto Uprising, and wrote a service around these themes. We took music—from Beethoven to Yiddish melodies—and brought in part of the brass section of the New York Philharmonic. That year, more than two thousand people attended our Passover morning service! The point is, if you give people something meaningful, done on a level that doesn't embarrass them, they'll come and eventually they'll care and understand what the service is all about. But it has to be a class act, or it's embarrassing, and they won't come again. It can't be a bar mitzvah band playing Beethoven. This is the suburbs; people can go to

New York, hear first-rate performances. The people here are much better educated than the earlier generation, they're very sophisticated.

I say that a synagogue should be all things to all people. For years, our congregation has sponsored a community forum on contemporary issues. We live in a community and we feel we have to contribute to the community. At the beginning, I needed someone who could give the series real visibility. The organizers had tried Jane Fonda several times. She refused. Jane is an old friend from the peace movement, so I called her. She was coming to New York, so she said, "Fine, no problem." We gave the honorarium not to her but to the Campaign for Economic Democracy. She sold the entire series, 2,500 tickets. She spoke on the changing politics in America—a good subject for a synagogue.

One Friday night a month we have a sermon lesson. There is a theme for the year. This year's theme is "problems in the community"—the aged, the young, the sick. We look at what Judaism has to say about these issues. So one Friday we might talk about the implications of welfare cutbacks in the light of Jewish values. Another Friday night we might have a creative service: we've had a "shtetl service" and one modeled on the classical German synagogue. We did one service with the synagogue music of the Renaissance composer Salomone Rossi. We got a prayer book from Italy of that period, duplicated it for each member, and that Friday-evening service was the Renaissance of Salomone Rossi. We've even invited the community in for an ecumenical Thanksgiving service, presented as a Broadway review. More than two thousand people attended that one.

We changed other things too, not just services. Take the religious school. At home, our children, unlike in my generation, have their own rooms, with TVs, stereos, VCRs, and air conditioning. Why would they want to come to the synagogue to go into a hot cellar, with old, boring teachers who rarely touch on anything relevant to their lives? So when we built the new school, we put in a room with air hockey and Ping-Pong and candy machines, so that when the young people come out of public school, before they start religious-school classes, they can relax in *their* synagogue, in *their* own room.

Attendance has gone way up. When we left the city, we had 350 families. Within three years of opening our suburban temple, with the new program and Hebrew-school approach, we went up to

950 families, and the age level of the congregation went from about sixty-three to thirty-six. What did it? I would like to think it's that we had the courage to make a statement—that Judaism does not stagnate, that it can incorporate anything of value. We built a program that could appeal to people on their American cultural level.

We brought the sons of the Rosenbergs to the synagogue. I thought they had something to say about politics and McCarthyism, the cold war, their own experiences growing up with that history. It was great. We brought Roy Cohn and *Screw* magazine publisher Al Goldstein to talk about their First Amendment court cases. We brought Rita Hauser to talk about the controversial meeting with the PLO that Hauser and other American Jewish leaders went to. We brought Prime Minister Shamir and people from the Peace Now movement. We've scheduled Mrs. Anwar Sadat as a speaker. We've discussed abortion, civil rights, antiwar resistance, the right to die, and the way our society treats the old, the sick, the disabled. We do this because it should be done, and if we didn't do it, who would?—and that is religious. If you want to be in the tradition of Isaiah, you've got to go out on a limb. The Jewish tradition says, go out on a limb, baby, and you pay the price; but "justice, justice shall you pursue."

The growth and vigor exemplified by such thriving congregations seem to offer evidence of new religious energy. Young, modern, and sophisticated congregants, including significant numbers who had previously and quite self-consciously avoided involvement in organized Jewish activity, are coming to the synagogue, and in surprisingly large numbers. However, such occasional successes do not really indicate a religious revival—a new and surprising quest for "resacralization"—but, ironically, a more successful secularization of Judaism. There is nothing in such worship services that challenges any secular perspective. Religion in the sense of ethical values, "going out on a limb," or the Messiah as universal brotherhood—these humanistic equivalents of religious concepts are perfectly in line with the spirit the new congregants bring with them from their local mall, neighborhood, or workplace, from their familiar daily life-styles in prosperous America.

As surveys keep showing, a large majority of American Jews who affirm their religion as Jewish believe that Judaism fundamentally means being a good person and being ethical; the more sophisticated sometimes vaguely cite a passage from the Talmud, where God says something like, "Better that you follow my laws and not believe in me than the opposite." This is the essence of the Judaism to which they adhere. And "following my laws" is generally understood to mean not the explicit Jewish ritual laws or even the moral requirements that could be derived from the Torah and Talmud, but the overarching injunction to be a good person. (The individual will judge for himself what constitutes being ethical, and for the great majority of American Jews, "ethical" generally connotes modern liberal values.) There is nothing in the service to offend one's modern and naturalistic beliefs, nothing like what Christians have to affirm if they accept dogmas like Original Sin, the Immaculate Conception, the Virgin Birth, the Resurrection, and other challenging theological doctrines. There is no serious attempt to apply religious concepts and laws so as to decide on the right position, the appropriate path, for a religious Jew. The message conveyed by most mainstream worship services is that Judaism in its modern garb conforms to what is already considered good and right on modern rationalistic, ethical, and epistemological grounds. The idea is that people can find their secular values underlined and given "spiritual" confirmation from within the Jewish tradition.

Our use of the notion of secularization for what is ostensibly religious activity, and is considered to be such by those involved, requires some attention to this much-contested concept. The term "secularization" refers to the modern trend by which increasingly larger areas of social and individual life are rationalized, and religious concepts are restricted to ever-smaller areas of consciousness and social life. Economics, politics, nature, the interpretation of psychological and moral phenomena—in all these areas, naturalistic concepts have come to dominate. Even in the realm of ethics, so central to religious thought, it has become an important principle of "secular humanism" that what is moral is to be ascertained by reason, and only when traditional religious notions echo what reason affirms can religious support for ethical truths be invoked.

In other words, secular people—and this includes many who consider themselves "somewhat" religious—do not use God as an explanation of what happens in the world, nor do they justify their moral judgments by citation of religious doctrine. When they get sick, they do not see the illness as God's retribution for some transgression; they do not consider earthquakes and hurricanes to be signs of God's displeasure; and they expect the weather report to be based on meteorology, not divination. When they argue for the morality of a course of action, they do not say, "This is what God has decreed."

This secularized public world is shared by all sorts of people, from avowed atheists to the religiously indifferent to the devout who attend church daily. And what makes this possible is that religion has become—in principle—an individual matter. A December 1989 special state election in San Diego illustrated the depth of this new understanding of religion. In a heavily Republican district, the Democratic candidate—a Catholic woman who supported a pro-choice position on abortion—was denied communion by her bishop on the grounds that her position was deeply offensive to Catholic doctrine on this very serious matter. The wave of support for the underdog Democratic candidate, including support from many Catholics, carried her to a narrow victory that she would have never otherwise achieved. In secular society, toleration of differing religious creeds makes the public claim to exclusive truth improper; those who maintain religious affiliation and participate in religious ritual will not, it is assumed, cite the dogmas of their own particular religious affiliation as the source of authoritative knowledge in any of the public spheres. Secularization means that religion loses the monopoly it once held, when religious authorities could impose at least public profession of belief and orthodox practice on everyone within their jurisdiction. Without this monopoly, religions become subject to a most modern pressure, the dynamics of "consumer preference," as sociologist of religion Peter Berger puts it. Religion now has to compete with everything else for our private time and interest. And the competition is conducted in the secular forms of the market, where other vendors also hawk their goods.

The obvious market for mainstream Judaism is solidly middle-class, educated, sophisticated, and largely secular. To compete successfully, the suppliers of the goods or services—in this case, the religious professionals—must take into account the tastes of the consumers. Consequently, mainstream Jewish religion has drastically reduced its supernatural element, traditionally considered the essence of religious belief. One does not ask congregants about belief in God. As Rabbi Friedman says, "It isn't really an issue for them." In any case, it is not the sort of thing a Reform or Conservative rabbi attempts to inspire in his or her "flock." The result is that, even in the synagogue, religion—in the sense of faith, belief, acceptance of doctrine, and ritual practice— becomes a private matter. Congregants are not to be questioned or judged on this score, by the rabbi or anyone else.

The ceremonial aspects of religion—the services, ceremonies, traditions, holidays, the rabbis and cantors, the rites of passage— these are available for each person to use for whatever reason, religious or not. Weddings, bar and bat mitzvahs, and funerals take up a large share of a rabbi's time, and it is not even necessary to belong to a synagogue to receive such services from the rabbi. The offer of a Jewish connection is an open one, although, of course, the religious professionals do hope that even very occasional participants in Jewish ritual will be drawn into the congregation.

The goal of the religious professional, then, must be to get people into the synagogue, without worrying about the traditional religious ideas of faith, saving souls, bringing congregants to repentance, perfecting their religious practice, and so forth. Those Jews who choose to come—a diminishing minority, as recent studies have confirmed—will come as typically modern and secular Americans. The synagogues that flourish are the ones (like Rabbi Friedman's) that know how to appeal most effectively to the current social and cultural tastes of their clientele, which is to say, the tastes of middle-class American consumers. Success in these terms comes from shaping and bending Jewish forms and labels to take in more and more of the contemporary and popular aspects of the broader American culture. As Rabbi Friedman says: "I'm trying to get them into the building. So if I give you Edwin Newman and Jane Fonda and Itzhak Perlman playing Bach in a synagogue and what have you, all these things are Jewish. Judaism is not limited to this place or to the observance of a ritual. Judaism is the way you live your life from the time you get up in the morning to the time you go to sleep. We have a creed of the congregation which says that we will take everything from our tradition which is meaningful, and change that which needs to be changed. We are not embarrassed that we find meaning in things ancient, and we're not so insecure that we're afraid to innovate."

One recent synagogue innovation that deserves a special mention is the *havurah*. Inspired by the small, anti-establishment, religious fellowships that were created in the late 1960s by young Jewish intellectuals in the large university communities in Boston, New York, Washington, Los Angeles, and Chicago, a few innovative rabbis encouraged the development of havurot within their own congregations. These groups attempt to incorporate some insights of the counterculture—Jewish version—in order to make the synagogue more attractive to young Jews who may be alienated by the anonymity and impersonality of the large suburban congregations. By 1981 havurot existed in at least one-quarter of the synagogues in the United States, and one writer could speak of the "havurization" of the American synagogue. Academics have already produced studies and dissertations on the subject. A leading sociological commentator on the movement, Professor Bernard Reisman of Brandeis University, offered a visionary conception of the meaning of the havurah: "As the members involve themselves in Jewish programs and activities, they are transformed from a friendship unit seeking personal gratification to a fellowship pursuing purposes which move beyond individual and material needs. . . . In their programs of Jewish study and celebration, the havurah members . . . achieve a sense of overriding purpose which moves beyond the ephemeral and mundane and gives meaning and direction to their lives. In short, they experience a sense of transcendence."

The Silver family* lives in the San Fernando Valley, Los Angeles. Dan Silver is a businessman. Eileen Silver is a skilled potter. Their two boys are fourteen and twelve. The family is active in a large Reform congregation, a synagogue with a membership of approximately nine hundred families. Eileen Silver is the president of the havurah council at the synagogue.

"The Synagogue as Havurah"

Eileen The havurah movement has been very big at temple. It is an auxiliary of the temple as much as the sisterhood and brotherhood. Those are fund-raising organizations. The havurah isn't.

*Pseudonym.

Dan The basic thing is to make a little clique within a big structure. My feeling is that if you're a new family in this big congregation, you feel left out. But if you belong to a havurah, you become friendly with this small group and it gives you an identity with the congregation. Plus you meet people through your havurah because people there know other people. And then there are havurah activities where you meet people from other groups. In our temple, the havurah was started by a woman who had talked to Rabbi Schulweis or some of the leaders of the havurah over at Valley Beth Shalom synagogue. We now have about twenty groups. When someone is interested in joining a havurah group, they fill out a form, and then Eileen, as president of the council, tries to place them where they would fit in most comfortably.

The way we got involved was, some friends said, "We're having a havurah meeting, come." We didn't know what it was. I turned up my nose, but we went. The first meeting was led by the cantor, and he tried to do some things to open us up about our backgrounds. He asked about our parents and about whether we did any Jewish things when we were growing up. There were eight or nine couples, most were strangers. Our group has been together now for almost a decade. There are ten families. We've taken in some new ones and some have dropped out. There is a nucleus of four families who have been together for the whole time.

Eileen Each family is given one month to plan the activity for that month's meeting. We had August, and we planned the havurah garage sale. Everybody brought stuff, and we made money for our little treasury. We had a Hanukkah party, and a Purim party, and a theater party for the adults only. We also have a family havurah Shabbat. The Hanukkah thing was great. You never saw the sanctuary so full for Friday night. Every seat was full, and each havurah was responsible for bringing three dozen jelly doughnuts, because jelly doughnuts are the traditional food that is served on Hanukkah in Israel. The reason is that the doughnuts are cooked in oil, and the rabbi made sure we knew why we were serving the jelly doughnuts. We have some adult-education activities, but I haven't taken any of them. We have gone to some of the cantor's things, like family counseling and communications skills. These also bring in people.

Dan We're sports-oriented in our havurah. One month we went to a Dodgers game together. And one month there was a beach party with lots of games. And once there was a swim party. There is a volleyball tournament for all the groups. Our group has won that tournament three years out of four. And there is a games night, which we've won twice. It's getting to be a joke among the havurah groups about how competitive we are, but it's a fun competition. About half our group plays in these. Once we had a bike rally, with clues and searches.

Different havurot have different purposes. There is one group that plays bridge. And "Big Wheel" likes to go bike riding. Some do religious things and read books, but not that many. I play raquetball with someone from Rabbi Schulweis's congregation, from the original havurah group, and he says they're very social also.

We're really an activity havurah.

Jeremy (fourteen years old) There is the high-school havurah. It's called PJY—that stands for "Proud Jewish Youth." We just went to Disneyland last Saturday. And there is a junior-high havurah, and the Hillelites, the younger kids. When you get to PJY, you're almost managing yourselves. You elect a president and a treasurer. And you sponsor things for the temple. Like we raise money for the temple with a "bagel brunch." People sign up and we deliver the stuff.

Most of the kids I know in public school didn't keep on in their Hebrew schools after bar mitzvah, but most of the kids from my class at temple are staying on. They are going on for confirmation. There is a special group for those who are staying on, called Havurat Noar, that's more religious-oriented. The first topic was about Jewish identity: what is a Jew? We talked about different definitions, like you know, Ben Gurion—that anyone who says he's a Jew is a Jew, and if you're religiously a Jew, and all that stuff. And we voted, but I forget what won. If other people classify you as Jewish, then you're Jewish. Or if you are Catholic and say you're Jewish, but you're not. Or you have to have a Jewish mother. Stuff like that. I forget what it came out to be.

Anyway, we do lots of other things, too. We celebrate holidays. And there are family services once a month, more child-oriented. The rabbi plays the guitar and sings songs. But we go through the Torah and stuff like that. I just signed up to lead the Torah. The service is short, and the birthday kids go up on the stage and get blessed.

Eileen I think the younger Jewish population is becoming more aware of their Jewish heritage today. More than I was. I don't remember anything about the Holocaust when I was growing up. My parents didn't talk about it. I never saw movies or read books about it. But these days, children are required to learn. And the result, I think, is that they are growing up much more aware of their Jewish identity than I was. There was nothing like what Jeremy has at Havurat Noar offered to us, nothing to entice us into going further with our studies.

Jeremy We discussed the Holocaust one day. I remember one of the girls started to cry. Our leader read us about this kid, and we discussed how this kid felt, and how Jews fought back, and the Jewish army in the Warsaw Ghetto. One day, as we came into class, the teacher tied a red or yellow string around each student's arm. And then he said, "Work! Reds can do what they want, but yellows keep working." And then he turned around and yelled, "What are you doing? OK, yellows can get a drink," and stuff like that. And later we talked about what it was like being shut up in the ghetto and not being able to do what you wanted.

Undoubtedly there are synagogue havurot that are deeply engaged in religious and cultural study and celebration. But not all that many. The havurot are another effort on the part of Jewish professionals to appeal to essentially secular American Jews. The perception that more intimate groups within anonymous large organizations help develop commitment to the organization is a sound one, as shown by the success of "quality-of-work-life" circles in innovative corporations. The spirit of encounter groups, so widespread in our culture, may also be enlisted to attract the therapeutically minded to the synagogue. But neither of these motivations expresses a religious perspective. Despite the official enthusiasm, and the occasional lively temple, the claim of a "staggering transformation" of religious life seems like whistling in the dark. The evidence of flourishing synagogues means simply that some synagogues—by means of innovations like havurot and

Itzhak Perlman playing Bach—have been relatively successful in re-creating themselves in the image of their new middle-class members. The very recent rise of the rabbinate as a "bright new career choice" is obviously the result more of a combination of economic and secular causes—newly high status and salary, and the appeal of a "helping profession"—than of spiritual concerns. Rather than a resurgence of religious life, these trends signify only the continuing secularization of Judaism.

Another sign, if an ironic one, of the triumph of secular consciousness in mainstream Jewish life is the almost total disappearance of organizations and doctrines that once battled militantly against religion. It is difficult to imagine now the fervor of the secularist assaults on the religious "superstitions" of other Jews—such as the Jewish-anarchist balls on Yom Kippur night or the Bund's Yom Kippur picnic and outing up the Hudson to Bear Mountain. Why bother?

Sheva Zucker, raised in the milieu of antireligious *Yiddishkeit,* now attends services. She explains: "I don't have the feeling that I am betraying something by stepping into a synagogue, which people like my father thought. They were very Jewish, and could even read Torah, which they had learned as kids. They were so familiar with the religion, they could hate it and leave it. I think it would have been fun to go to a Yom Kippur ball back then, when there was a real fight and you, *dafka,* had to go and do *something* on Yom Kippur. But now I think it would be obnoxious. I wouldn't go to work on Yom Kippur. I fast. I am looking, as a secular person, for a meaning in all the Jewish holidays. I think fasting is a powerful experience—it puts you in a different frame, very passive and reflective, and it is good to do that once a year. So why not do it on Yom Kippur, along with other Jews? I used to have trouble with all the praying and God. But now I think it is nice to be with those people, and some of the prayers, especially on the High Holidays, are very beautiful. There is a meaning that Rosh Hashanah and Yom Kippur can have for everybody."

But Zucker's "return" is clearly not religious. The only reason she can feel comfortable participating in religion is that her secular attitudes are no longer at odds with the religious spirit of mainstream Judaism. Contrary to Bell, Bellah, and other prophets of resacralization, the continuing existence—even "flourishing"—of religion does not refute the idea of secularization as the dominant process in our culture. And in comparison with mainstream Protestantism or Catholicism, Judaism has come especially far. Many Jews—from articulate atheists to those for whom God "isn't really an issue"—can now attend religious ceremonies tailored to appeal to their secularized tastes and values.

The intriguing question is why the flourishing is not more general, why, despite the enthusiasm and creativity, the trend toward nonaffiliation keeps growing. One answer is that the competition is too strong. Why go to synagogue to see last year's Woody Allen movie if the new one is playing around the corner? Why go to synagogue to hear Itzhak Perlman play? And what if he is not coming to *your* synagogue? What if tonight your synagogue is offering the cantor's wife singing selections from *Fiddler on the Roof*? In short, why take the trouble to go to synagogue for the very activities that a host of organizations and businesses and entertainment venues are specially skilled in providing?

Religious conservatives argue that it is precisely this attempt to compete with commercial institutions by imitating their secular attitudes and values that has caused and will continue to cause the decline of religious Judaism and increasing disaffiliation from the synagogue. The effort to appeal to a secular audience on its own terms, as they see it, has led to disaster: on the one hand, liberalized religion cannot beat the competition; on the other, it cannot attract people truly moved by religious impulses. They point out that the successful religious movements of recent years, represented by evangelicals like Jerry Falwell, the Ayatollah Khomeini, and other fundamentalists, take an outspoken anti-secular stand.

Within Christianity, neoconservatism is thriving religiously as well as politically. In a study called *Why Conservative Churches Are Growing*, a prominent Protestant theologian notes that religious vigor today is lodged in fundamentalist churches or in the more traditional, conservative wings of the mainstream churches. The Pentecostal and the Charismatic movements—both of them antimodern and antirationalist—are the fastest-growing parts of Protestant Christianity, and have become significant even within Catholicism. After a steady decline in the number of applicants to seminaries and religious orders, there has been a reversal—but only for the stricter orders. And there are other phenomena that have both troubled and encouraged religious observers, such as the appeal of various cults to thousands of young and educated Americans—Jews, Christians, and the "unchurched." The desire for an all-encompassing spirituality, the quest for God, the willingness to accept religious authority and to dedicate one's life to a religious community—these yearnings, which the cults address in ways that are deplored by mainstream religious professionals, are taken as evidence of a widespread religious hunger among modern secularized Americans. According to traditionalists, the liberals have actually driven such seekers away.

Within Judaism, the equivalent of neoconservatism is Orthodoxy. If you are Jewish and want the "old-time religion," it is always there. But the mainstream American Jewish community is not susceptible to the appeal of Orthodoxy. The liberal synagogue cannot count on religious fervor to give intensity and depth to Jewish involvement, and so its success will depend on winning the affiliation of Jews who define their identity essentially in ethnic and cultural terms.

Winning that affiliation is an increasingly formidable task. The difficulty is easy to explain. Since synagogue membership for the mainstream Jewish community has increasingly become a function of ethnic involvement, as the ethnic impulse diminishes, so does the urge to join a synagogue. In a post-assimilation environment, where ethnicities take on the symbolic status described earlier, and where mobility and individual choice are paramount values, the difficulty of attracting and keeping members will naturally increase. In spite of the talk of religious revival, market conditions are not favorable for the long-term prosperity of the synagogue.

Given the erosion of both the ethnic and religious foundations of active Jewish-community affiliation and commitment, one can easily understand the doomsday predictions, evoked most catastrophically in a much-discussed article on Jewish demography by the Harvard-based Israeli sociologist Elihu Bergman. By pessimistically extrapolating current trends, he projected a Jewish community in the year 2076 of ten thousand, and by making somewhat more optimistic assumptions, a maximum community of slightly less than a million. The implications of even the optimistic prediction for the support of presently existing Jewish institutions and organizations are obviously disastrous from the point of view of Jewish-community survivalists.

But apocalyptic dirges are somewhat premature. In fact, American Jewry is not about to disappear as an organized and self-aware community. Whatever one's judgment of the quality of Jewishness remaining in the ethnic culture, Israelism, and the synagogue, the mainstream Jewish community serves important social and private functions for considerable numbers of American Jews. The network of philanthropic organizations still provides a supportive community, important in an individualistic and mobile society that steadily weakens communal ties. Israel still serves as a vivid source of content and a symbol of ethnic identity, however troubled and disheartening its current situation may appear. And the synagogue continues to fulfill communitarian, ritual, and religious needs for those who want this institutional expression of Jewish identity.

For the long term, the key factor is the critical dependence of the American Jewish community on the power of outside forces, rather than on the strength and fecundity of internal cultural resources, ethnic and religious. This dependence can be vividly revealed by a simple "thought experiment." Imagine three conceivable (though admittedly unlikely) developments: the growth of a social-democratic welfare state in the United States; the peaceful settlement of the Middle East situation; and the effective disappearance of anti-Semitism in the United States, Europe, the Soviet Union, and the Middle East. If there were a real welfare state on the Swedish model, for example, that gave decent care to the needy, the sick, and the elderly, eliminated poverty, provided a national health service, and so on, there would be no need for the philanthropic network that provides activities for many members of the organized Jewish community. If Israel were in no political or military danger, and did not need American Jewish financial contributions, the greatest source of Jewish community activity and concern would disappear. And if there were not enough anti-Semitism to talk about, even that gloomy incentive for Jewish assertion, awareness, and community action would be gone. The weakness of the internal sources of Jewish identification and community cohesion would then stand out far more sharply.

For devout Orthodox Jews, however, none of these developments would be threatening. On the contrary, they could pray that "it should only come to pass in our day." And an Israeli Jew might echo such sentiments in modern secular Hebrew. But for a Jewish-community survivalist of the mainstream, such joy would be tempered by the realization of a bleak future for organized Jewish life in America.

5

The Resilience of Orthodoxy

The Orthodox do not fit neatly into the prevailing picture of the Jewish community. They do not represent just another variety of ritual practice in the tolerant milieu of mainstream Judaism, where it is a sacrilege to claim that one way of being Jewish is superior to other ways. In its own eyes, Orthodoxy is real Judaism, the only true Judaism—unreformed, unadapted, uncompromised —the faith and practice of the Torah and the Talmud that Jews have carried on for thousands of years, often at the price of torture and death. At the unshaken center of the Orthodox faith stands the covenant between God and his chosen people, Israel, the giving and accepting of the Torah. The central belief of traditional Judaism is that God communicated his commandments to the people of Israel at an actual time and place. The promulgation of the Ten Commandments at Mount Sinai, seven weeks following the Exodus from Egypt, and the recording of the "written Torah" by Moses during the subsequent forty-year period in the desert are the basis for the entire structure of religious law that tradition-al Judaism applies to all areas of life. In addition to the written Five Books of Moses, the Pentateuch, Judaism also bases its belief on the oral tradition that God communicated directly to Moses, who in turn taught it to the religious leaders of Israel. This "oral Torah" was finally codified and written down in the second century A.D., forming the basis of the Talmud.

The Talmud works out the application of God's word through a complex process of commentary, and much of Jewish religious thought is concerned with arguments over the interpretation of cryptic and ambiguous biblical pronouncements so as to put these "laws" in operation. For example, the biblical commandment against boiling a kid in its mother's milk is the basis for the separation of milk and meat; this injunction has been expanded into a complex set of dietary laws that Orthodox Jews must scrupulously observe.

The detailed exfoliation of interpretation takes in the whole range of human behavior. The overall term for the body of Jewish law is *halachah;* the word may also refer to the final, authoritative decision on any question. *Halachic* law governs not only the complex ritual requirements of religious practice—when and how to pray, what blessings to make over myriad daily activities—but all social existence as well: diet, sexuality, business ethics, social life, entertainment, artistic expression, clothing, personal appearance, and so on. The ultimate goal of this demanding way of life is the creation of a sanctified Israel, a holy people. The fulfillment of all 613 basic "commandments," or *mitzvot,* is the concrete expression of this sanctification.

Although the religion contains statements of ethical standards that are taken to apply to all people, the full weight of the Law applies only to Jews. In fact, many of the requirements—like dietary laws—act to separate Jews from other people. In much of Jewish history, and for a large number of Orthodox Jews today, physical as well as cultural separation from non-Jews is central to the faith and practice of Judaism.

Orthodox Judaism, with its commitment to carrying out the Law in all its detail, its concern for strict ritual practice, and its intense concentration on the holy writings and commentaries, displays an impressive continuity of doctrine and practice that cannot be claimed by the reformed modes of Judaism. After all, the idea behind "reform" was that serious changes in doctrine and practice were needed to make Judaism appropriate for new conditions. Still, Orthodoxy has certainly changed over the centuries; it is not nearly so monolithic as its adherents sometimes claim.

The last two hundred years have seen an intense dialectic of accommodation and isolation within Orthodoxy, between the "modern Orthodox"—eager to participate in contemporary culture, ordinary in dress and way of life while adhering to Jewish law—and the "ultra-Orthodox"—violently opposed to any accommodation with modernity, including modern political Zionism.

Within the American Jewish community, Orthodoxy in all its forms was and still is characteristic of the first generation. Reform Judaism, the creation of middle-class, intellectual, modernizing German Jews, barely touched the Jewish masses of Eastern Europe who made up the bulk of the immigration. Those who attended synagogues after they came to America at first went to Orthodox congregations, often made up of immigrants from the same town in the old country.

Many immigrants abandoned Orthodoxy as they Americanized, and their children continued this trend. The National Jewish Population Study of 1970 found that 26 percent of first-generation Jews called themselves Orthodox. For second-generation Jews, the figure fell to 9 percent; and only 3 percent of the third or later generations classified themselves as Orthodox. A 1975 survey in metropolitan Boston found that, of second-generation Jews with Orthodox parents, only 6 percent called themselves Orthodox; there were almost no second-generation Jews without Orthodox parents who themselves were Orthodox.

In recent years, however, Orthodoxy has demonstrated a remarkable resurgence. Whereas a generation back it was reasonable to expect Orthodoxy to effectively disappear, now its "share" among American Jewish denominations is holding steady. Orthodox Judaism appears tough and lively, able not only to keep its own often numerous progeny, but even to attract previously unreligious Jews.

This kind of story makes good copy. For more than a decade now, tales of resurgent Orthodoxy have generated interest in national and local media, beyond the strictly Jewish publications. In 1984, the *New York Times Magazine* announced this startling revival and described it in glowing terms. Under the title "American Jews Discover Orthodoxy," the article featured a mix of long-term and newly Orthodox Jews who combined traditional religious commitment with impressive success in the secular world—people like Zalman Chaim Bernstein, chairman of a multi-billion-dollar investment firm; Allan Leicht, TV writer and producer of the show *Kate and Allie;* and Nobel-laureate physicist Arno Penzias.

Ultra-Orthodox groups also earned respectful descriptions,

most notably in a 1985 three-part *New Yorker* profile of the Lubavitcher Hasidic community. These and other stories emphasized the depth of community strength and commitment as well as the remarkable ability of such fundamentalist sects to attract new members from every part of the secular world. *Pittsburgh* magazine, for example, featured a couple who had given up a million-dollar granola business to enter a two-and-a-half-year program in a Hasidic seminary, and who currently work full-time for the group. Leaders of the Pittsburgh Orthodox community explained this decision in what are now familiar terms. "What is happening," said Rabbi Eliyahu Safran of Congregation Poale Zedeck, "is that the Jew is becoming what he always was. This is the return to what we've always been." Such returns may involve truly radical transformations. In his Harvard class's *Fifteenth-Anniversary Report*, amid the stories of professions and families, honors and public office, one alumnus told about his surprising decision. After recounting his successful career as a physical chemist and Ivy League professor, author of several books and recipient of major scientific awards, he described his current situation: "I am now a full-time student of Talmud at Yeshiva _____ in Brooklyn. . . . I am also the unpaid and under-utilized Secretary-Treasurer of my wife's store, 'New York's Top Designers in Women's Fashions at Brooklyn's Bottom Prices.' The store and my Yeshiva are less than a mile from our home. We walk back and forth together and often share lunch. We have now managed to arrange the integrated whole life which we value."

There seemed to be no limit to Orthodoxy's possibilities. Both the *New York Times* and *New York* magazine featured stories about a rather unorthodox Orthodox synagogue on the Upper West Side of New York, the Lincoln Square Synagogue, notable for its surprisingly liberal tone and its policy of welcoming new members who want to try out Orthodox Judaism. That hundreds of chic, professional, well-educated young Jews were suddenly coming to an Orthodox synagogue, sitting in separate—but equal—sections for men and women, learning how to follow Orthodox Jewish laws that few of the attendees had ever known in their own Jewish homes, was indeed remarkable, and signaled a "new Orthodoxy."

These personal odysseys and flourishing congregations are spread across the whole spectrum of Orthodoxy. However, despite the publicized accounts of Orthodoxy's newfound appeal, there appears to have been no significant increase in the number of Orthodox Jews in the United States. In the last fifteen years or so, the period of visible resurgence, they have remained at a level that even by the most generous of estimates falls below 10 percent of the Jewish population.* But even maintaining its small proportion of the Jewish population is of great importance for a community that had steadily been losing numbers for decades. For all the sensational stories of intellectuals, professionals, and hippies finding their way "back" to Orthodoxy, the Orthodox resurgence is a matter not primarily of gaining new adherents, but of holding its own, of internal creativity, institutional strength, and a growing confidence in its ability to pass on the true faith to the next generation.

This is a new story for Orthodox Judaism in the modern world, especially in the liberal, integrationist cultures of advanced industrial societies, and it suggests tradition's victorious resistance to the forces of subversion. But the story is more complex. The struggle with modernity, a struggle that Orthodoxy had been steadily losing since the Enlightenment, has hardly been settled. Across the spectrum—from the antimodern "ultra-Orthodox" through the mainstream "modern Orthodox" to the liberal "new Orthodox"—the tensions between accommodation and isolation continue to pose profound challenges, creating conditions of risk and fragility even as the community celebrates its unexpected flourishing.

The Modern Orthodox

The vivid popular image of Orthodox Judaism is skewed toward the picturesque: rabbis with black robes and flowing beards; boys with long, curly earlocks; groups of yeshiva scholars, immersed in the detailed arguments of the Talmud, cosmically unconcerned

---

*As demographers point out, the concentration of the Orthodox in New York gives the movement an exaggerated visibility that overstates its actual share of the national Jewish population. In Boston, for example, between 1965 and 1985, the proportion of Jews who identified themselves as Orthodox fell from 14 to 4 percent. And except for the New York area, between two and three times as many Orthodox Jews are over sixty-five as are between eighteen and forty-five years old.

with the mundane doings of the rest of the world. New Yorkers in that city's diamond district daily see hundreds of such Hasidim from Brooklyn and upstate New York, resembling their ancestors in Eastern Europe two centuries ago in dress, gesture, language, and isolation from any significant contact with contemporary culture.

But the picturesque image is a distortion. Most Jews who came to this country during the great period of immigration were associated with some form of modern Orthodoxy: they were not Hasidim. Today, the modern Orthodox are, so to speak, the mainstream—and the majority—of the Orthodox world. Committed to "a synthesis of Torah Judaism and secular learning," as Rabbi Shlomo Riskin has phrased it, or to "Torah and Science," as in the motto of Yeshiva University, modern Orthodoxy developed during the nineteenth century in response to the stunning impact on Jewish life of emancipation and the possibility of participating fully in the non-Jewish secular world. In the United States, such participation was an essential principle of the dominant liberal ideology, and Jews enthusiastically took up this opportunity from the earliest days of the American republic. The ultra-Orthodox of European Jewry, fervently opposed even to attempting the delicate and risky process of modernization and synthesis, had fought against modern Orthodoxy in Europe, and viewed the democratic spirit of America as a temptation that pious Jews should avoid. During the first wave of mass immigration, for example, the Rabbi of Slutsk, addressing a meeting of Orthodox congregations in New York, chastised his listeners for having emigrated to this "*treyfa* land."

As the American Jewish community grew and acculturated, the steep decline of ritual practice and even nominal Orthodox affiliation seemed to bear out the gloomy predictions of the antimodern separatists. But in the past generation modern Orthodoxy has enjoyed a growth of vitality and strength, of breadth and depth of organization. The numbers have not changed, as we have seen. But numbers aside, the increased solidity of the modern Orthodox community can be discerned in the impressive growth of institutions. For example, there were thirty Orthodox day schools in the United States and Canada at the end of World War II; four decades later, there were 522, with an enrollment of 95,000—between 1973 and 1982 the number increased by

20,000. The new availability of kosher food may be taken as an index of how an apparently decaying modern Orthodoxy has regenerated. In his overview of the state of Orthodoxy, Rabbi Reuven P. Bulka, a prominent spokesman for the observant community, rhapsodized:

> The once-treyfa land, the same place which some famed Jewish religious leaders advised against living in as it would endanger Jewish commitment, now boasts of an institutionalized kashruth which is mind-boggling when viewed in the historical context. Chinese, French, and Italian kosher cuisine is available in many major centers, kosher pizza is a staple in most vibrant communities, and many major national and local producers pay for the privilege of having their products endorsed as kosher. . . . Exotic holidays and cruises are today available with kashruth guaranteed. Hotels serving glatt-kosher meals followed by Broadway-type entertainment combine the best of spiritual and human flesh. . . . The once-treyfa America is now ubiquitously kosher.

This sense of triumph can also be seen in the spiritual and intellectual realm; the Orthodox can point proudly to the vitality and prestige of Yeshiva University and other respected institutions of Orthodox higher learning, the outpouring of scholarship in books and journals, the growth of membership in the Association of Orthodox Jewish Scientists, the visibility of Orthodox scientists and mathematicians at major universities, the presence of distinguished scholars in the secular humanities, like Heidegger scholar and City University of New York philosopher Michael Wyschograd, who is also an Orthodox theologian.

An upbeat tone is also evident in the most mundane, everyday aspects of community life. If we look at an issue of *Young Israel Viewpoint*, the newspaper published by the modern Orthodox Young Israel movement, we see the conscious adoption of contemporary ways of daily life. A matchmaker ad in the "Personals" column has a familiar form with an unusual content: "For Orthodox or Chasidic men, 26–40, from relig. fam. or returnees, who seek attractive, committed, healthy girls. College grads preferred. Write with references." One page contains ads designed to attract new residents to an Orthodox community in New Jersey:

LIVE IN BEAUTIFUL CHERRY HILL

Many Young Orthodox Families in a Vibrant Synagogue
15 Minutes from Philadelphia
Reasonably Priced Homes & Apartments
Nursery and Newly-Completed Mikvah on Premises
Direct Bus Transportation to Nearby Day Schools
Kosher Butchers, Bakeries

To spend a Shabbos with Us or for Information
Call Cong. Sons of Israel

And there are similar announcements from employment agencies, with names such as "Tradition Personnel": "WE HAVE MANY SHOMER SHABBOS JOBS AVAILABLE! Controllers, Accountants, Bookkeepers, etc." An issue of *Jewish Action,* a magazine for Orthodox Jews, displays an ad for "Temple Tracker," billed as "the definitive name in synagogue administration software." Sample features: Membership data management, accounts receivable, and *"Yahrzeit* Control." As spokeswoman Ellen Franklin explains, " '*Yahrzeit* control' means that the computer sends you a friendly reminder." (*Yahrzeit* is the Yiddish word for the anniversary of a close relative's death.)

"We've gone into areas that more traditional yeshivas have never before entered. We've set up a computer laboratory. We've offered courses in automotive mechanics," says Rabbi Dinovitz of Santa Clara's Kerem Hebrew Institute. "It's our belief that a good Jew, one who will have an impact on the world at large, must be well-rounded."

Joseph Steinberg* is a lawyer, working as an executive at Citicorp. Thirty-five years old, married for eight years, he is the father of a four-year-old daughter and a two-year-old son. He grew up in Queens, went to religious schools until college, then attended Columbia University. He spent two years at Oxford, and then went through Harvard Law School. Steinberg highlights the joys and satisfactions of the Orthodox life and the relative ease of integrating Orthodoxy and modernity.

*Pseudonym.

"Frum *from Birth*"

I'm "F.F.B." It stands for *"frum* [observant] from birth." It's a term I'd never heard until I read it in that *New York* magazine piece on the "new Orthodox" on the Upper West Side. But I think it's a good term because it points to something interesting. My sense is that people who became Orthodox after not being so tend to be much more serious about things. They don't have a kind of sense of perspective that people who have always been Orthodox tend to have. Because you know no one can keep all of the commandments of the Torah; you know you do the best you can. But it is easy to spot someone who wasn't Orthodox from birth; for example, they'll say much more often, *"im yirtzeh Hashem,"* that's like, "I'll see you tomorrow, *if God is willing."* Fine, OK, that's always implicit in anything anybody does, but these newly Orthodox tend to say it noticeably more—things like that.

I grew up in a dense Orthodox community, in Queens. My parents were modern Orthodox; my father is a history professor and my mother works as a consultant on early-childhood education at an Orthodox day school. I went to the same shul the whole time, from when I was born until I got married; and even for the first seven years of the marriage. Now that we've moved to Forest Hills, we are part of an Orthodox community, and we go to the shul there.

Pretty much everyone I grew up with was Orthodox. I had very little contact with the rest of the city, the non-Jewish part, until I went to college. That was really the first time I got to know people who weren't Orthodox, or who weren't even Jewish. College can be a difficult time. You come across many different influences, you learn about all the great Western thinkers, and if you're from my kind of background, you have a sense of your insularity. It's natural to question. I saw many of my Orthodox friends from Flatbush Yeshiva become less Orthodox. You are exposed to biblical criticism, and you think, maybe everything in the Torah isn't 100-percent true, or you wonder whether God really cares if I turn on a light on Shabbos, or whether the Torah was really written by God, or by people. You can make a good argument that it was written by people. Or evolution—I think there are ways that Orthodox Jewish scholars have attempted to rationalize, to say that the Torah is right *and* that science is right. Like "years" means thousands or millions of years—things like that. I'm a little skeptical of all that. I just don't know. I've had problems on an intellectual level. In a way, I'm close to an agnostic. I don't *know* if God exists—there are good arguments for it and against it. But I've lived my life on the basis that he does exist, and I guess we'll find out at the end. Who knows? Take AIDS—you know some people say it is a punishment from God. I say, maybe it is and maybe it isn't. Some people get annoyed at that—how can you *possibly* say, even suggest, that AIDS could be a punishment from God? But I just don't know. I'm not God. I think there are things in the world that may point to the existence of God—the creation of the state of Israel, the Six-Day War, other things.

But I view the intellectual side of religion and the practicing emotional part as two completely different things. None of the intellectual questions would make me give up this life. I think the strength of modern Orthodoxy for those who stay Orthodox is that it is like their skin—they don't think about it much, it is just daily life. You don't hear much discussion about the metaquestions, the deeper questions. About practice and law, people do talk and argue. And doing is more important than pure belief—that idea is in the Talmud.

I think questions are there for me and for a lot of people. But it hasn't affected my practice, in part because I'm not sure and there is a good chance that God does exist, but mainly because I derive tremendous emotional satisfaction and comfort from doing these things I've always done. I value very highly having order in my life, and doing everything the way I've always done it gives me a tremendous sense of order. Take Shabbos: I'll come home Friday afternoon, I'll take the kids to shul; most of our friends from the neighborhood are there with their kids; it's a special time for all of us. We'll come home, I'll make Kiddush, my wife will light the candles, we'll sing songs. We won't answer the phone or watch TV or use the car. It's a time when the family is together, doing things together. Like the holidays, which are very satisfying, the repeating of the cycles of the Jewish year. You look forward to each, and the year goes by that way. It is very different from the secular world and its calendar. Here there are real events, the cycle of Jewish time.

Davening [praying] every day also gives me a sense of order. I daven three times a day. And I make it a practice every day to learn one passage from the Talmud, one Mishnah, before I go to work. From my perspective, there is a core to being Orthodox—

keeping Shabbos, the laws of *kashrut, mikvah** for a woman—the fundamental laws. There are always questions about practice, for instance in the area of sex, about whether single people who go out are allowed to touch or kiss or hug. Certainly intercourse is forbidden. Some of the girls I went out with wouldn't even touch hands. Others did, and I was always unsure whether I was violating Jewish law. But I never asked a rabbi. I was embarrassed; it isn't the kind of question one asked. I just did it. It is a tough area. My guess is that more Orthodox people depart from the Law there than in any other area. Like you aren't supposed to practice birth control, but obviously many modern Orthodox do. It isn't talked about much. A person does the best they can. But none of these questions mean I have to stop being Orthodox. I have the deep satisfaction of the sense of community, the strong sense of family values. It is hard to imagine staying Orthodox outside the community, with its reinforcement and shared satisfactions. Probably the need to belong attracts a lot of the people who are coming to Orthodoxy. This is a very anomic world.

If my own children left Orthodoxy, I'd be shocked. I would be shattered, heartbroken. The disappointment would be beyond belief—I mean just leaving Orthodoxy, not leaving Judaism or marrying out. I would barely have contact with them; it would be the worst thing. Like if I ever found out that my son or daughter had stopped keeping Shabbos, I would be devastated. I would be devastated if my daughter stopped going to the *mikvah*. I would be quite happy if they became more Orthodox than I am. But not if they became Hasidim—I do think there is a lot of good in modern culture. My wife agrees with me on all this. She has a brother who married out, to a Chinese woman who didn't convert. They live in California; we have never met her. She wouldn't be welcome in our home. It would be a bad example for my children, for one thing. The values of Orthodoxy are at war with secular humanism, absolutely. With my wife's brother, it is a heartbreaking thing; they have a child, and she has cerebral palsy. And we won't have any contact with her, we don't send her gifts—because she's not a Jewish child. My deep sense is that being Jewish is important, and

Mikvah refers to the body of water in which Orthodox women immerse themselves for ritual purification to mark the end of *niddah* ("separation"), the prescribed period during and just following menstruation when sex is forbidden. Immersion in a *mikvah* is also required of Orthodox converts, male and female.

remaining Jewish is important, and for someone who is born Jewish and marries out of the faith and has children who are not Jewish—that is not something I can support. I can override compassion when it is a question of keeping the Jewish people alive.

I don't feel anything could pull me away from Orthodoxy. I think this is true for my wife also. I don't view Orthodoxy as being only as strong as its weakest link, its most difficult parts—the whole system is what is satisfying.

For all the apparent confidence of Steinberg's presentation, he is aware of troubling tensions and ambiguities: between Torah and Science, faith and skepticism, the laws of purity and sex, commitment to Orthodox Jewish survival and compassion. The complex balance that Steinberg presents remains difficult to achieve, as becomes clear in the more typical story of someone for whom the modern Orthodox synthesis proved difficult and conflicted. Norm Grossman's* wavering path vividly captures the tensions of combining modernity and Orthodoxy, the difficulties that cheerful accounts of a happy coexistence too easily gloss over. Born on the Lower East Side in 1947, Norm Grossman grew up in the dense Orthodox milieu of New York City, always the center of American Orthodox life. He attended Orthodox educational institutions up to graduate school, and belongs to an Orthodox synagogue. Short, peppy, and fast-talking, Grossman is a practitioner of that most modernist of professions, psychotherapy, and he lives on the Upper West Side of Manhattan.

"Your Dishes Will Go to Heaven"

My father came from Poland, with an Orthodox background. My mother's family was from White Russia. She didn't know anything about religion until she met my father. From the outside, our family always looked very religious. My mother learned how to do everything from my father. And yet, my father had his own way of being Orthodox. He would put on *tefillin* and a *tallis* to daven three times a day, and he would go to shul. But at the same time, he was a gambler. And in order to gamble on Shabbos, he was willing to break the Law—he would drive to the track, or use the

*Pseudonym.

phone to call his bookies. My mother would also break Shabbos, sneak into the bathroom to smoke a cigarette. But they were very involved with Jewish things. The whole family was. I had an uncle who was very high up in the National Council of Young Israel. He helped start kosher kitchens on campuses. My grandfather managed a kosher restaurant for twenty-three years. Our business was kosher restaurants and a kosher bakery. Naturally, we had rabbinical connections.

Where I grew up, rabbis didn't have beards and didn't speak Yiddish. I lived in a modern Orthodox environment. I thought Hasidim were strange. My teachers were Misnagdim, the rationalist rabbis who had always opposed Hasidim. I always felt like I was an American. I was very proud that my parents had grown up in America. I liked it very much that my mother wore makeup. Some of my friends had parents who had accents and spoke Yiddish. And they were embarrassed about it. Women in my family wore stockings without seams. In Hasidic communities, they have to have seams to show they are wearing stockings, or you might think that they're not. We were Young Israel–style modern Orthodox. The Young Israel philosophy is "synthesize": synthesize science and religion. We were Americanized; we would eat out—in kosher restaurants, of course. There were more religious, modern Orthodox types, like the Agudath Israel crowd. They were the black-hat crew, more refugee, more European. Most of them spoke Yiddish.

In our style, you dated. You didn't have an arranged marriage. You made out in movies. My first date was a rabbi's daughter. She was a hot number. Yeshiva University High School, where I went, was all guys. So you went home after basketball games. At Flatbush Yeshiva or Ramaz, they had dances afterward because they were coed. Our rabbis would give us tests on Sundays, or after New Year's Eve, to keep us out of it. Still, I'd go to their dances sometimes, to meet girls. Those schools were more liberal than ours; they had more Hebrew culture, more Zionism. At our school, we had daily *tzitzis** check. The first half of the day was Jewish studies; the second half was English. All day we washed hands, said blessings for this and that, said the blessings after the meal, went to afternoon prayers. Sometimes we'd go out to porno movies. I took off my yarmulka when I went in.

*A fringed "undershirt" garment required for males.

Sometimes you'd see a Hasid there; you'd say, "Oooh, oooh." Of course all of us masturbated. There is a law against masturbation. I rationalized: "That's the law. I'm just breaking it, I'm just weak, I'm just a sinner." There was this rabbi who had what we called a "masturbation inquiry commission." We used to joke about him saying, "I have the evidence right here in my hands."

But actually, I didn't feel I was missing much. The things you see in advertising, those were not for Orthodox Jews. I didn't mind. I didn't want to have cheeseburgers and milkshakes or to meet non-Jewish girls. Even when I became nonobservant, I wouldn't eat shellfish or pork. About lobster, I couldn't care less. My brother felt more conflict. After two years of yeshiva, he said that he couldn't take that crap anymore, he wanted to go to public high school. On Shabbos, he would go up on the roof with a pencil to write out practice Regents exams. I was a good boy; he was bad generally. They beat the crap out of him. I said, "Oh, no, I'm not going through that."

My brother was engaged to an Italian girl, then to a Reform Jew. The family really got on top of him, to make him break these off. Eventually he married a distant relative of ours, with a religious background. His kids go to a yeshiva, but he isn't religious. The kids know. When they lived in New York, they went to shul on Shabbos; but they always knew which way to walk home so they could go to the pizza place and not be seen.

My brother's story was pretty common. A lot of kids would become nonreligious around high school. I started being a little freer then too. I wouldn't be fully observant on the Sabbath. I did laundry, turned on the TV instead of waiting for the timer. I would write, or travel. Once I went to Nathan's Delicatessen with my brother. He said, "Eat it, it's not pork." Some people were more freethinking, intellectual. They had serious questions about God, religion. Not me, I didn't question. I was more dependent. I remember once I went to a basketball game at the Garden, when Yeshiva was playing, and there was a guy sitting away from everybody else, with a leather jacket, a DA haircut, eating a hot dog, with his arm around a girl. Someone said, "That guy used to go to Yeshiva," like he was a bad kid now. I didn't want that kind of disapproval.

I always wore a yarmulka. We would have nice ones, knitted, different colors to match your suit. It was part of our fashion. When the buckles in the back came in, we had yarmulkas with little Ivy League buckles. You would get your name crocheted on a yarmulka. I wore my yarmulka all through college, and even when I went to Europe for a month. I was very proud of it.

I met my wife during my first year of college. We went together all four years of college, and I started becoming more religious again. She came from an Orthodox family, but from a more intellectual background. She questioned more. I wasn't involved in politics in college. No antiwar stuff; I didn't want to join the Peace Corps. But she got involved. In her family they fought about politics at the table. My family fought about money. We got married after college, and I began to work for a master's degree in psychology at Brooklyn College. In the morning, I went to learn Talmud for a couple of hours. This was "draft-dodging yeshiva." If you were a divinity student, you didn't get drafted. That's why I went.

Our religious practices began to change at home. So many things were happening. My wife was affected by women's liberation. She was working as a teacher to support me in school. After I got my degree, she went back for a master's and then a Ph.D. Her master's thesis was on the women workers in the Yorkshire coal industry during the early years of the Industrial Revolution, a real esoteric subject. She was getting more involved in the secular world. She didn't want to identify with my achievements. She wanted her own achievements. We got less religious, looked for more fun things. She stopped going to the *mikvah*. She started having affairs. We even got involved for a very brief time in "swinging." She couldn't compartmentalize like I could: she thought that if she wasn't being religious, she shouldn't be burdened by all those rules and observances. In terms of my own personality structure, I could compartmentalize; I could say, OK, put that in that part of your mind, and that there. As a therapist, I did it all the time. Jewish law is against making out, against masturbation. As a therapist, I'd say to these kids, "Go do it, enjoy it." But you can't change the Law. It isn't man-made.

We were caught up in the zeitgeist. Our observance dropped off. We moved out of the heartland of Orthodoxy in Brooklyn, to only a few blocks away, but to where we could be anonymous. It was like there was no one checking. My wife was in a consciousness-raising group, and she joined NOW. We started smoking marijuana. When we first got married, we were going to have five kids. Then she didn't want to have kids yet; she wanted a career. All this time, our house was still kosher and the outside world thought of us as Orthodox.

After we split up, I didn't go to services much except for the holidays, and I didn't observe the Sabbath. I had already gotten more into being sensual, toward the end of the marriage, smoking grass and all that. Once, at Christmastime, I went with my non-Jewish girlfriend to her house, and they gave me chicken. I looked at it—I ate. It wasn't all right, but I did it. Then I started to eat more things that weren't kosher—McDonald's, or Colonel Sanders chicken. But my home was still kosher; I always maintained my two sets of dishes. When I brought Colonel Sanders home, I'd eat it on paper plates. "Yes," some rabbis would say, "your dishes will surely go to Heaven."

I knew I wasn't practicing what I should be, what was right. I would say to my Orthodox friends how beautiful Torah Judaism was. They would say, "Norm, you're so good at bringing people to Torah Judaism, and here you're not practicing yourself." But I couldn't anymore. I wanted to experience everything, to taste different kinds of life, not just foods. My father's side of the family never knew. My mother didn't care. She would tell me: "Your father, this Orthodox guy, screwed around. He wore *tefillin*, but he screwed around. That's Orthodoxy, that's Young Israel, that's Yeshiva . . . that's bullshit." She said: "My parents are more religious because they don't cheat in business, they love each other, they respect other people. This is more religious than going to shul or eating kosher food."

Even now I believe Torah Judaism is what Judaism is supposed to be, that all modifications are halfway compromises. I still belong to an Orthodox synagogue, but I don't always go. Though it makes no sense, I have to say I'm a nonpracticing Orthodox Jew.

———

Norm Grossman followed a well-trodden path of "falling away" from Orthodoxy. But he is not out to free himself from the religious constraints of his youth; he is not intellectually or morally opposed to Orthodoxy—as were the many thousands of young people who during the modern era left Orthodoxy because they simply did not believe its doctrines or value its way of life. On the contrary, Torah Judaism remains for him an ideal way of life. "I knew the right thing to do was to be Orthodox," he says. "To be Orthodox was good, everything else was not good." But the constraints of conscience, family, and community prove too weak when, as Grossman puts it, the zeitgeist seeps into his life. His ability to "compartmentalize" breaks down.

"Compartmentalization" is the sociological term for the separation of modes of thought and belief in order to avoid any awareness of cognitive dissonance or conflicts between attitudes and principles used in one sphere of life with those in another. For example, as an Orthodox Jew, Grossman believes the Law is given by God; as a therapist, he ignores it in the service of what he considers his professional responsibility. This ability to compartmentalize, which kept him within Orthodoxy for so long, far from being a particular aberration of his, has often been recognized as the key to modern Orthodox survival. Charles Liebman points out that compartmentalization, though theologically indefensible, is indeed necessary. He argues that "most Orthodox Jews have retained their ritual tradition and belief system virtually intact and at the same time have acculturated in language, dress, and education to American styles because they have been able to separate these two aspects of life so that they impinge on each other as little as possible." In another formulation, sociologist Samuel Heilman emphasizes that "the Orthodox Jew has learned how to 'inattend,' to dim his attention, and finally to 'disattend,' that is, to 'actively withdraw his attention and awareness from that which is dissonant.'"

Compartmentalization can seem successful and rather easily managed, as in the case of Joseph Steinberg, "*frum* from birth" and never really tempted to be anything else. The deep commitment to a way of life, in turn, helps keep the cognitive compartments secure. Steinberg neatly exemplifies the sociologists' image of how modern Orthodoxy protects itself from the intellectual threats of modernity. But the threats are not just intellectual. When the Orthodox way of life loses its unquestioned appeal, when the image of a "liberated" life seeps through the separations, the effects can be as subversive as the classic undermining of belief. Norm Grossman, unlike his wife, will still maintain that Orthodoxy is sacrosanct, the only true Judaism. But he is strongly drawn to experiences and a life-style that are incompatible with Orthodox principles and practices. In his current state, practice depends on mood. Grossman might or might not turn on the TV on the Sabbath; he might or might not keep kosher. He ascribes his wavering practice and his weakness in the face of temptation to a failing in himself, his psychological inability to live up to his stated Orthodox principles. For Grossman there is no equivalent of the joyful and supportive Orthodox community that enfolds Joseph Steinberg and his family. And where Steinberg is determined to transmit Orthodoxy to his children and would be devastated if they deviated from it, Grossman only says that he would give his children an Orthodox education "because even if they don't keep it up, they should know what Torah Judaism is." For the present, Grossman remains committed to the idea of Orthodoxy; but the compartments are crumbling, and the prospects for passing on the commitment are dim.

As these two stories show, modern Orthodoxy, for all the celebration of its successful accommodation to modernity, remains vulnerable to subversion by freedom of choice, the excitement of experimentation, sensuality, the quest for social justice, tolerance. These aspects of the modern spirit must be kept at a proper distance even as the Orthodox use the technology produced by that spirit. Orthodox students may use computers to study Talmud; they may attend the best secular universities, participate in all the professions, and dress in the latest fashion. But these visible signs of modernization should not be taken as evidence that the Orthodox project of selective modernization has been accomplished. The underlying tensions remain, and those who cannot manage their compartments neatly and who therefore drop out of Orthodox life will remain as expressive of the Orthodox encounter with modernity as the Wall Street bond salesmen who meet for midday prayers in their well-appointed offices and leave early on Friday to prepare for the Sabbath. The goal of modern Orthodoxy, to avoid isolation but prevent integration from undermining the faith, remains as formidable as ever.

Underneath all the newfound confidence, an awareness of the strain is evident. Although popular accounts of the Orthodox revival may celebrate the scientists, financiers, and professors who arc able to maintain a successful and even enthusiastic balance, this is not the dominant tone within the community itself. The mainstream Orthodox are well aware of the need for constant vigilance against the dangerous attractions of modernist ideas. "Judaism, as I understand it," comments Charles Liebman, who is himself an Orthodox Jew, "is threatened by contemporary currents in American life. Fewer and fewer areas today are even neutral to Jewish values. Literature, theater, art, scholarship, politics—all seem to undermine what I consider to be the essentials of Judaism. More than ever before, the values of integration and survival are mutually contradictory."

Orthodox publications express a constant fear of attrition and apostasy, coupled with exhortations to appreciate the threat. One such article, in *Jewish Life,* the journal of the Orthodox synagogue association, tells the story of "Jonathan Chaim Segal." This is the title of a fable about a small flock of seagulls, the Segals, who have forgotten that they were "chosen" thousands of years ago to bring the true message of life to the gulls of the world. A mysterious gull appears one day to teach the narrator of the tale about the ancient mission: " 'Jonathan,' he said softly, 'the tragedy of our people today is that they are looking everywhere in the Seagull world for meaning except within their own Segal heritage, where it really exists for them. . . . Within every Segal's heart lies the meaning and purpose of life,' he explained. 'He need not look elsewhere for it. He has only to take the Sacred Scrolls off the shelves and he will learn to fly again.' " This proselytizing exhortation is directed not to the mass of American Jews, but solely to Orthodoxy's own adherents, especially the young. The point is to encourage them to resist temptation, to hold on to belief in the superiority of Judaism and its ultimate truth. Within Orthodoxy today, this "looking everywhere" is under fierce attack.

The Orthodox community has lately experienced a strong move to the right. There is a feeling that the modernizing trends within Orthodoxy need to be stopped and reversed, indeed, that Jewish survival depends on a tough attitude: no more concessions to modernity, no more apologetic attempts to compromise. And this new attitude, far from confirming a successful synthesis, expresses a continuing tension and increased anxiety about the risks of accommodation to secular culture.

The option of "withdrawal," says Rabbi Irving Greenberg, "is the fastest-growing, strongest tendency in Orthodoxy today." Such withdrawal is apparent in every area of Orthodox life. "Mixed dancing," reports one observer, "once practiced even among Agudath Israel youth, is a thing of the past in most committed Orthodox groups. The formalistic requirements of 'feminine modesty,' such as covering the hair, are stressed far more than ever before. Observance of the laws of 'family purity' and *mikvah,* which once seemed to be on the verge of total desuetude, are rising." A young teacher actively engaged in the

Orthodox world of New York notes important changes in his community: "Day schools which had coed classes ten years ago are separated, even down to the first grade. There is a whole push away from college education, a definite feeling that secular education is at best a necessary evil. I've seen articles with titles like 'The Case Against College'—remember, college is seen as the number-one cause of assimilation and intermarriage. A lot of Orthodox kids, if they go to college at all, are encouraged to study computers or engineering and to avoid liberal arts. The idea is to stay apart, to tune out the worst features of the secular world, whatever leads to assimilation." In the mid-eighties, Yeshiva University held a symposium entitled "Why Do Yeshiva Men Attend College?"—a question that would not have arisen at the institution dedicated to "Torah and Science" in earlier decades of its existence. Expressing the new mood of anxiety, one participant commented, "Secular pursuits for their own sake are dangerous on many grounds, particularly because they may not aid in developing one's self Jewishly."

The new intransigence can be seen in the refusal of many Orthodox rabbis to be "ecumenical" toward their non-Orthodox colleagues and the increasingly shrill demand of the Orthodox rabbinate in Israel to refuse recognition to Reform and Conservative conversions. A tone of embattled exhortation marks Orthodox publications. The assault is far-reaching. Central aspects of modern culture—triumphs of the human spirit from the liberal humanist perspective—are seen as Jewish disasters by the tough-minded modern Orthodox. For example, the editor of *Jewish Life* exhorts Orthodox readers to keep up intellectual vigilance: "We must deal with the liberation of European Jewry; with the Enlightenment, which brought a cover of darkness to traditional Jewish life; with the struggle against Reform, against modernism, against assimilation, and against the false messianism of a return to Zion bereft of the Torah."

Not surprisingly, the situation is increasingly uncomfortable for members of the liberal wing within Orthodoxy. One prominent rabbi expressed a growing sense of isolation. "The enlightened Orthodox Jew," writes Marc Angel, "finds it difficult to be at peace. He generally does not live in a community which helps him shut off external influences. He does not have a large reservoir of friends who share the depth of his religious commitment while at the same time sharing his openness to literature, philosophy, or science. . . . Really, he is alone."

Still, even a liberal religious thinker, Jewish or Christian, would have to admit that in the religious "marketplace," a more rigorous Orthodoxy, determined to oppose powerful modern trends, will offer something other faiths cannot—if only to that part of the consumer population which is open to an antimodern attitude. As the rightward-leaning Orthodox see it, liberalizing religion will not help it compete with the broader secular culture, and it will have lost the oppositional appeal of the fundamentalist faiths. The appeal must lie in Orthodoxy's difference.

But while this move to the right may well be necessary for the group, the demand for strict adherence to doctrine and ritual practice, and for increasing intolerance toward other ways of being Jewish, precludes any serious possibility of reaching out to the larger Jewish population. The survival of a small, increasingly separate religious community is almost certain, a growth in numbers and breadth of appeal highly unlikely.

The Ultra-Orthodox

Perhaps the most discussed religious phenomenon of recent years is the startling rise of fundamentalism in the United States. This term has been used to describe a variety of movements: Eastern cults—Hare Krishna, Divine Light Mission, Soka Gakkai; the "Moonies"; Jews for Jesus; Pentecostalism and Charismatic Christianity. Despite their many differences, all these movements share the general desire for a religious creed and worldview that is totally integrated and opposed to the modern rationalistic and secular perspective expressed in the Enlightenment and embodied in the scientific revolution. More precisely, "fundamentalist" refers to the idea that the ultimate truth is known and contained in traditional, authoritative texts.

All Orthodox Judaism is essentially fundamentalist. Since the Torah is God's word, given only to the Jews, doctrine and ritual based on the Torah are sufficient and unchangeable. While modern Orthodoxy took on the task of turning fundamentalist Judaism outward, not all Orthodox Jews supported this project. The ultra-Orthodox continued to reject the modern synthesis and to insist on a sharp separation from the surrounding world.

Even within Judaism, the ultra-Orthodox have always sought

isolation. Hasidic rebbes originally discouraged Jews from migrating to America, the "*treyfa* land." They recognized that the modernity and mobility of an open society would draw people away from both piety and practice. Better to endure the oppression and anti-Semitism of czarist Russia or the Austro-Hungarian empire, where Jews, however poor and physically threatened, could at least live a complete Jewish life. Some ultra-Orthodox groups did come to this country during the great period of late-nineteenth-century immigration, but most came either right before World War II, in flight from the Nazis, or just after, as survivors of the Holocaust. Currently, the ultra-Orthodox number about 100,000, with their main communities located in Brooklyn, and smaller groups in northern New Jersey, upstate New York, Boston, Chicago, and Los Angeles.

For the rest of the Jewish community, the ultra-Orthodox were more or less exotic remnants. Their way of life was picturesque, but hardly an attractive option for young Jews growing up free and modern. But as the appeal of fundamentalist religion seemed to grow for numbers of young moderns in the larger culture, so did the Jewish version. It was noticed that a disproportionately large number of Jewish "searchers" were coming in from the secular cold to join the various Eastern cults. Why not go to Judaism for that kind of commitment? Some have, and this process has caught the attention of the media. The broad popular interest was significantly directed not at those who were born within and never left the community, whether in Belz or Brooklyn, but at those who had seemed firmly entrenched in secular modernity and then chose to turn away from the life they had known.

In the general media, as well as within the Jewish community, the Lubavitcher movement, *Chabad* (also known as Lubavitch), has been most successful in attracting attention and converts. Chabad is the largest and most effective, dynamic, and visible of the Hasidic groups. Its own literature takes pains to point out its crucial difference from other Hasidic groups: "While other groups concentrate on strengthening their community and preserving the Hasidic way of life, Chabad feels that it is necessary to bring the teachings of Judaism to all Jews and Jewish communities, wherever they may be." To carry out this mission, the movement sends out its Mitzvah Mobiles, gaudily decorated RV's that can be seen in metropolitan areas with large Jewish populations and near university campuses like Berkeley and UCLA. Chabad Houses have opened in several college communities; millions of leaflets have been distributed on streets, at colleges, and to non-Orthodox institutions and Hebrew schools. The growing energy of the movement is well captured in a 1982 profile of Rabbi Shlomo Cunin, the West Coast director of Chabad-Lubavitch. In sixteen years, we learn, Rabbi Cunin built Chabad in Los Angeles from a one-man office in a garage to a complex institution with a staff of fifty-six rabbis, twenty-two shuls, Talmud Torahs (religious schools for children), yeshivas, and a drug-rehabilitation center. Indeed, according to Rabbi Cunin, "Chabad is the second-largest Jewish organization in Los Angeles, following only the Jewish Federation Council."

The resurgence and revival among the ultra-Orthodox is found primarily in the Lubavitcher movement, and is undoubtedly linked to their creative proselytizing. The mission of the group is to bring *all* Jews back to true Torah Judaism and so hasten the coming of the Messiah. Thus, they welcome all Jews to their workshops, celebrations, and services without making any demands about commitment and practice. In every Jew, they claim, no matter how assimilated, a spark of the holy can be found, and it is the mission of Lubavitch to find that spark and fan it; from the performance of even a minor ritual, the rote repetition of a blessing in a Mitzvah Mobile, for example, greater observance may follow.

In preaching to the assimilated, Lubavitch represents something new within ultra-Orthodoxy. Proselytizing is traditionally a central task for fundamentalist creeds and cults, certainly within Christianity—think of tent meetings and TV ministries. But ultra-Orthodox Judaism has characteristically been separatist and inward-looking, even in relation to the rest of the Jewish community. Chabad's tolerant ambiance certainly sets it apart from the other, more isolationist groups.*

---

*Chabad has not escaped criticism from other Hasidic groups who find these forays into the modern world, even for good fundamentalist purposes, a threat to purity. Some years ago, the New York papers featured stories on what must have been one of the most bizarre community melées in the history of that city. The Lubavitcher community is centered in the Crown Heights part of Brooklyn, while the other of the two largest Hasidic groups, the Satmar, are

But from the perspective of the modern Jews they wish to reach, Lubavitcher Hasidism would seem extreme enough. The cultural distance from the intellectual world of modernity is enormous, however short the subway ride from Times Square in Manhattan to the Lubavitcher headquarters in Crown Heights. How a modern person can make that journey—and why—continues to fascinate and mystify the secular mind.

Fred Pinsky,* or Chaim, as he is now called, made the journey, and he is ecstatic when he talks about it. Pinsky, a smiling, chubby, and energetic man in his late thirties, sports a full, untrimmed beard in the manner of Hasidic Jews. He wears ordinary clothes, no tie, and *tzitzis* and a yarmulka. He lives with his wife, Rivke, in an apartment in Crown Heights, a block away from the Lubavitcher headquarters and main synagogue on Eastern Parkway. Pictures of the current rebbe and the *Alte Rebbe*— the founder—adorn the walls along with other religious pictures. One can see Jewish ritual objects throughout the apartment. The only books in the house are religious ones—the Torah, the Talmud, the Tanya (the founding document of Chabad theology), and other volumes, mainly in Hebrew. There is a Steinway grand piano. Rivke Pinsky* is an accomplished musician, a graduate of New York's High School of Music and Art. But now she plays only Hasidic melodies. They look forward with great eagerness to having children.

Chaim bubbles over with enthusiasm for his faith. A sense of the miraculous permeates his descriptions of Hasidism and his certain conviction of its truth, a truth that he wants other Jews to realize. As is part of the Hasidic tradition, tales of wonder constantly pop up in his descriptions and evocations.

---

concentrated in the nearby Williamsburg section. During the traditional Purim march of Lubavitcher men from Crown Heights to Williamsburg, the marchers were set upon by Satmar Hasidim, resulting in a brawl that required police action. According to the outraged Chabad spokesman, Rabbi Krinsky, the Satmar are the aggressors; they attack Lubavitcher synagogues, deface the Mitzvah Mobiles, and harass Lubavitcher proselytizers. "It's a one-way battle. We hold no animosity. But they wait for us, with garbage pails and sticks, slashing the tires of our Mitzvah Mobiles. It's their sin."
*Pseudonym.

"I Found Truth!"

Here is a Baal Shem Tov story about a grain of wheat. The Besht*
was riding in a cart, and his driver was about to take a drink from a
bottle of whiskey, and the Besht said: "Please stop! Wait! Let me
tell you. Once, there was a grain of wheat, and it prayed that it
would actually be planted, and then that it actually would sprout.
It prayed, 'Oh, let me sprout!' And it sprouted, and then it prayed
that it would actually get harvested and refined. And then it
prayed that it would be made into something holy, that could
return to God. And its prayer was granted. It was made into kosher
whiskey, to be purchased by a Jew, not into just any whiskey that
might be used for something sacrilegious. And *you* bought this
bottle, and the grain of wheat was so happy. And let me tell you
something else—the soul of your own great-grandfather was
there, his remains were in that plot of ground where the grain
grew, and he is in the grain, he came back as this grain"—Jews
believe in reincarnation, which I didn't know before—"so, when
you make a blessing over the whiskey, his soul will have peace
because you will help the grain return to the highest place in
heaven, and then the soul of your grandfather will have peace. So,
please make that blessing before you drink."

After that story, I'm sure the guy made the blessing. I'm like
that grain. I never knew that as a Jew I had a purpose. When I
started reading Torah, I said "Wow! It's like, messianism." The
world isn't finished. The idea of the Jew is to bring this world to its
completion. If the others would leave us in peace, if they had left
the Jewish people in peace, we would create a world where there
won't be wars, there won't be famine, there won't be the inhuman-
ity of man toward man. We can bring *Moshiach*, the Messiah. The
Jews have their special mission. The Torah was offered to every
people, but the others didn't want it.

Before I came to Lubavitch, I used to be a fairly typical secular,
urban Jew. I went to NYU, demonstrated against the war, smoked
pot, listened to rock and roll, read authors like Fitzgerald,
Hemingway, Camus, and Sartre, and really wanted to be a writer. I
hung out in Europe and actually tried living a writer's life. But one
day when I was traveling through Spain, I was robbed and

---

*The acronym for the Baal Shem Tov (Master of the Good Name), as Rabbi Israel
ben Eliezer, the founder of Hasidism, was called.

stranded. And I made a vow. I promised God that if I got to America safe and sound, I would go to synagogue on the first Saturday after I got back. And then the miracle happened.

I walked into this old shul in Brooklyn, with nine old men there. They needed me for a tenth, for the prayer group, the minyan. I was helping them keep this, God forbid, dying minyan, in Brooklyn, alive! They were singing the old songs I remembered from synagogue as a kid. I thought—trips to Paris, to Greece, to Spain. Demonstrations and movements and Third World politics. And these people are still singing the songs and praying for the redemption. And suddenly I saw this chain, this unbroken chain, and I realized it was my chain and I wanted to be part of it. I wanted to be part of it because I *was* part of it. I just wanted to be myself.

I've been in Lubavitch for five years now, and I don't miss anything from the old life. At the beginning, some things were hard, like keeping kosher. At first, I said, "Give up Chinese food? Never!" I'd go to a Chinese restaurant and just order chicken or fried rice, and if I found some little red pieces of things that weren't so kosher, I'd push them aside and eat the rice and vegetables. Keeping my head covered at all times was hard. I started out wearing a beret; I didn't want to look distinctively Jewish. And observing Shabbos, that was hard. The idea that for twenty-four hours I wasn't going to pick up a telephone or turn on the television! But now, it feels so good. Once you keep Shabbos a few times, you always want to keep it. Shabbos is one-sixtieth of the world to come. In the world to come, you bask in the rays of spirit and pure essence and ultimate light, and you're closest to the Creator of the universe. So having one-sixtieth of that peace is a very, very beautiful experience. You want everyone to have it. When I first became Orthodox, I was really into making everyone Orthodox. Like when someone wasn't looking, I'd knock a mezuzah into their doorpost, and things like that. To tell you the truth, I don't miss my old life at all. I wish I didn't have to go into Manhattan to work in the computer store; I would sit in yeshiva learning from morning to night.

Studying Torah is the greatest! You know, when kids grow up outside Lubavitch, you want them to learn about Paris, about classical music, about all kinds of issues, you want them to broaden their minds. That's a very modern idea. Let them know about the wealth of knowledge. But when a Jew starts learning Torah, he sees that every branch of knowledge is contained within the Torah—there's philosophy, psychology, sociology, science, medicine, all the different branches of human knowledge. Worldly knowledge is actually inferior. The scientist says *this,* and the Torah says *that.* And in ten years, we'll see that science is wrong and the Torah is always right.

The only thing that is necessary to find out about the outside world is how to make a living in a way that leaves as much time as possible for studying Torah. Among us here there is no status success trip. What's really worthwhile is within the reach of each human being—how kind you can be, how good. There is no comparison of worldly things to Torah. Why go to a museum? All you see are naked women and crucifixes. That's not good. Music? Beethoven? Mozart? They don't turn me on the way Jewish melodies do. When I studied literature, it took me an entire novel to find one spark of one idea that I could catch onto to move myself toward. When I read Torah, I read one sentence, and I get more than I got out of an entire course of novels. Tolstoy, Dostoyevsky, Shakespeare, all of them. All of life's lessons are contained within the Torah.

Let me tell you something. The first letter of the Hebrew alphabet is *aleph.* The middle letter is *mem,* and the last letter is *tof.* When you put them together—the beginning, the middle, and the end—that spells *emes.* And that means "truth." It's been a long, hard journey. But I can sincerely say, in all humility, that, *baruch Hashem,* thank God, I found *emes.*

Rivke (Rachel) Pinsky grew up in a modern Orthodox family, though she had become nonobservant in her adult life before coming to Lubavitch. She went to graduate school, and she still has a copy of her master's thesis on D. H. Lawrence, the only secular volume remaining in the house. Rivke favorably compares the integrated religiosity of Lubavitch with the compartmentalized modern Orthodoxy she knew as a young person.

"The Torah Is a Beautiful Thing"

There was a lot of secularism in the modern Orthodox world I grew up in. My parents wanted me to be observant, but they also wanted me to have a well-rounded education: music, literature, science. I went out on dates, but not exclusively with Orthodox boys. My mother didn't feel that being Orthodox was so important, so long as they were Jewish. At the synagogue there was a suburban atmosphere, with a lot of value put on clothes and hairdos and makeup.

The spirituality was so diluted in that world. Sometimes it was so invisible, you could miss it altogether. I was always intrigued by the Hasidim. When I was a child, I would go with my mother to the Lower East Side to buy a mezuzah or a religious book, and I would see them. They had intensity, and I was awed. A child is very sensitive to the spiritual atmosphere of a person, and I was awed by those people. There was something great about them. They weren't out to impress anybody; they didn't have the latest styles.

I was in New York, working on my thesis. One of my sisters was in the psychology program at NYU. She brought home a brochure from Lubavitch describing Sukkot: its meaning, how to celebrate it and why. And there was a brochure about lighting Shabbos candles, and she had been given a free Shabbos candle. Some Lubavitcher women had approached her in the street as she was coming out of school, and asked, "Are you Jewish?" She was very offended. She was with friends, some were Jewish and some weren't, and she thought it was real chutzpah to ask her publicly if she was Jewish. But really, the only reason they ask is because they want you to do a mitzvah and to share with you. In the brochures there was an invitation to a four-day weekend for college students.

It sounded fascinating to me, as a purely cultural experience, to observe these people. My parents thought it was a nice thing to do; my mother's grandfather had grown up in the home of a famous Hasidic rebbe in Europe. The Friday night dinner and ceremony were similar to what I had experienced at home, except that they all seemed to be more into what they were doing. There was no political talk at the table, no sports talk, just Shabbos talk. A Hasidic story, maybe about an old Jew or a poor Jew, or just a Jew; or an explanation of part of the Torah. And on Shabbos morning, we went to the main shul on Eastern Parkway, where the Lubavitcher men daven. It wasn't formal, like a suburban synagogue, with nice carpets. This was very plain, unpretentious, bare wooden benches, bare wooden floors. I liked the plainness there—a person goes to shul to pray. You don't need a carpet to pray to God. You just need an atmosphere where you can be sincere. The cantor in the Young Israel synagogue, where I grew up, had this beautiful big strong operatic voice, and sometimes you wondered, Does he know why he's up there praying? It was too beautiful, too consciously musical. But at 770 Eastern Parkway, it wasn't like that. It was pure davening. You knew that the person leading the davening was standing before God and asking God certain things for himself and for the Jewish people.

What really impressed me was that after lunch they had a *farbrengen,* which is when everyone gathers to hear the rebbe speak. He was sitting at a long table, covered with a beautiful pure-white tablecloth. And around him, closest to him, were very old men; and then there were thousands of young and middle-aged men, craning their heads, straining to hear every single word. The rebbe was speaking in Yiddish, so I didn't understand, but I could tell he was giving a talk on Torah. I remember thinking, That something like this, something so heavenly, can actually exist in this world! When you have a *farbrengen* several times a month—who needs anything else?

I was very impressed by the women I met during this weekend. I had thought the women would be very drab. And I was amazed that the women were very intellectual, very bright, very pretty, well dressed, and just fascinating, dynamic women, more than any other group of women I had ever met. They had traveled all over the world, had looked into all possible life-styles. For the most part, they were women from secular Jewish homes, some from Conservative or traditional homes, but none from Orthodox. And then one woman mentioned to me that there were classes during the week that I could attend without any kind of obligation. I thought it would be interesting to go and learn more about Hasidism. So I went to my first class, and I was amazed at how personal the subject matter was. We studied a section of Torah that I had been taught as a child, but now it was taught with the Lubavitcher rebbe's interpretation, and it went into my personal life. It showed how Torah is not just an intellectual subject, which is how it was taught to me as a child, but that it is very real and affects me and other Jews directly. Chabad showed that everything in the Torah relates to our personal lives. Also, that there is a correlation between the part of the Torah that is read in any given week and what we're going through personally in that week. But this is very different from a horoscope. There is no magical quality to it; this comes from God. God gave the Torah to the Jewish people and we are meant to learn from it.

Over the next three years, after I finished my master's degree and I was teaching in a girls' yeshiva, I found myself going more frequently to classes and to Shabbos at Lubavitch. It's close, warm, friendly here, like a little village in a huge, anonymous city. I met people from the community, many of whom were *ba'alei teshuvah* [returnees]. During that three-year period, I got more into Lubavitcher ways. I began to dress differently—no pants, always a skirt or a dress, with the hem below the knees, and sleeves below the elbow. After I was married, I covered my hair—this isn't my real hair. And I began to study Tanya, a major interpretation of Torah written by the first Lubavitcher rebbe.

I think Judaism is a treasure, a heritage, that belongs to all Jews. The Torah is a beautiful thing. The Baal Shem Tov wrote that if a person loses something, you have to return it to them. And if a person loses their whole heritage, and they're not aware that they've lost it? It's my responsibility to try to return it to them. And even if they don't want it, you have to run after them and tell them, "But it's yours!"

Converts like Rivke and Chaim Pinsky have no difficulties with the denial of worth to the aspects of modernity they valued in their former lives. Art, literature, music, science—these all pale in comparison to Hasidic Judaism's encompassing truth. The miraculous is constantly hovering over their lives, mediated by the more-than-human figure of the rebbe, who has authority over the most personal aspects of the devotee's life: where to live, where to work, whom to marry.

For the more inward-looking Hasidic sects that seek only to stay as far from the modern world as possible while living physically within a city like New York, there is little need to address the modern spirit. But Lubavitch, as we have said, is a proselytizing group, imbued with a cosmic mission: to bring all Jews back to true Judaism and thereby prepare the way for the Messiah and the redemption of the world. This means engaging the modern world, responding to challenges to religious fundamentalism. These responses sometimes take a form that both amuses and irritates the skeptical observer, just as they would have affected the Rivkes and Chaims before they joined Lubavitch. In *The Purifying Waters*, a pamphlet extolling the virtues of *mikvah*, Chabad attempts to coopt the feminist opposition to ritual purity laws, "Is it true only oppressed Jewish women use the *mikvah*?" Chabad answers, "Surprisingly, the feminist stereotype just won't wash." Rather than defending *mikvah* solely as a command of God, the pamphlet tells us that this practice achieves that most modern of feminist demands: good sex. We hear that *mikvah* "undoubtedly" leads to "happier, healthier, more exciting sex lives" and "re-creates the feeling of a bridal situation. . . . like a honeymoon every month." Two thousand years before Masters and Johnson, Judaism understood the importance of periodic abstinence to promote sexual fulfillment.

Feminists are not the only target of Lubavitcher efforts. Showing an admirable command of current vocabulary, Chabad reaches out to disaffected youth. "Get re-jewvenated!" urges an ad in a student newspaper. "Get *chai*!" The talks offered include "Jewish Mysticism and Life Styles" and "Jogging Through Genesis." In another flyer we read: "The Jew is a seeker. He has tried every possible mind-blowing and mind-slowing technique that has been offered to him. Now it is growing dark, and he needs to return to his inner source of light."

Chabad also has something to say to intellectuals. In their very professionally produced newspaper, distributed free in Jewish communities around the world, the Lubavitcher editor explains the fallacy of modern biology and its supposed undermining of the biblical account of creation. Deploring the role of the scientific revolution in breaking the steady transmission of true Judaism, the editor explains that only the indoctrination of a conceptually mistaken worldview creates the impression that modern thought disproves traditional Judaic doctrine. He states: "This is a matter of absolute import for the Jew. He must realize that he lives in an alien civilization where the basic assumptions of its philosophical foundation deny the spiritual truths of Judaism. The reason why the conceptual model of the Ruling Rationality denies the existence of the spiritual dimensions of Judaism is not because of the fallibility of Torah, but because Torah lies beyond its scope of understanding."

The rebbe expands this perspective in a letter on evolution in the same issue. In line with the paper's proselytizing intentions, the editors highlight the fact that the rebbe has excellent scientific credentials, including an engineering degree from the Sorbonne. Combining religious authority with his knowledge of secular science, the rebbe presents the Lubavitcher answer to the theory of evolution, modern geology and astronomy, and related disciplines. The unquestionable assumption is that the Torah is absolute truth, from the mouth of God; and Torah declares that the world is a little less than six thousand years old. All doctrines to the contrary are mere speculation. Not only is there not a shred of evidence for theories of evolution, but even if it could be shown that species do evolve now, that would not contradict the truth that the world was created exactly as the Torah states. Nothing prevents God from having created a universe 5749 years ago, with all of the processes that we can now observe, with fossils exactly as we find them, with evidence of civilizations having existed earlier than the creation date, with oil and coal and other substances that would take millions of years to form by the processes we presently see in nature. As to why the biblical account is not accepted by scientists, the rebbe explains that it is a natural human ambition to be inventive and original. So the scientist avoids accepting the biblical account by classifying it as "mythology," since he cannot attack it on any valid rational ground.

It is obvious that such arguments cannot finally attract moderns to Lubavitch. *After* conversion, the truths of the Torah as interpreted by the rebbe can be unquestioned; but the move to this position could hardly be made by rational argument. The attraction is the way of life: the warm, friendly, intregrated life full of meaning, removed from the contradictions and pains of modernity. Because it wants to attract people, the Chabad movement is operationally liberal. It can tolerate all sorts of ritual deviations in those who approach gingerly or as observers hoping to explore some vague appeal of Jewishness at a Chabad House Sabbath celebration or other Jewish festival. As Chaim Pinsky told us: "Judaism is sweet. It doesn't make immediate demands. Do what you can, but come to us now, be with us. The rest will follow."

Of course, the rest does not always follow. Listening to the converted, one hears about the joys of that absorbing way of life and how the miraculous ways of God are constantly manifested in the world. Personal life becomes part of something much grander, more cosmic; all of the old quests for meaning are over. For the converted, the mission now is to bring this truth to other Jews and to accomplish the most important spiritual task: as Chaim Pinsky explains, if Lubavitch succeeds in its work, the Messiah will arrive in this generation. "The rebbe has been stressing ten major campaigns called 'mitzvah campaigns.' He has picked out some of the most important commandments, and he has said, if Jews will do these, *Moshiach* will come."*

How difficult it is to make the conversion, even when there are profound attractions—personal, spiritual, and communal—can be seen in the story of Susan Levy, a person who could not quite overcome the pull of modernity. Her attraction to Chabad on the one hand, and her profound resistance on the other, show the limits of the Hasidic way of life as the cure for stressful compartmentalization, while illuminating the broader appeal of the spiritual to questing young Jews.

A woman in her mid-forties, Susan Levy† is a student and teacher of linguistics. She is deeply concerned with the issues of Jewish identity. She has a doctorate in philosophy from Yale and other advanced degrees from Columbia University and the Sorbonne.

"I Felt This Yearning"

I grew up in Brooklyn, with my grandparents, who were from Poland. My grandfather considered himself a Socialist and read the *Jewish Daily Forward*. He made fun of my grandmother for keeping kosher. But he loved it. I went to a fancy Reform temple, to the Sunday school, and on to confirmation, but I didn't learn much. I finished college when I was nineteen, and started teaching in a junior high. With the money I earned, I took off for France, supposedly to study the influence of the symbolist poets on T. S. Eliot. I was half-assedly working toward a Ph.D. in comparative literature at Columbia. After I came back in 1965, I worked for a couple of years in a poverty program in Harlem, teaching literacy.

Then the Six-Day War broke out, and Israel was in the spotlight. I wanted to go, though I had never belonged to any Jewish organization, and I went that summer. I think a lot of latent and dormant feelings about my Jewishness were aroused. I fell in love with Israel, which was a big surprise. I had had the opportunity to

*In April 1991 newspapers carried a story about how the miracle of Israel's salvation during the Gulf War had led Chabad to publicly predict the coming of the Messiah by September 1991.
†Pseudonym.

go there many times before. But it wasn't sexy; it was all those Jews, and that didn't seem interesting . . . a country that was all Jews. But I just loved it. From the instant I set foot in Jerusalem, I felt elevated—walking on the stones in Jerusalem, you know, the usual things people talk about. I stayed for two years. For one, I was in an absorption center for new immigrants: Czechs, Romanians, South Africans, Americans. I quickly got caught up in the passion of that mission. It became important for me to teach. One group that I taught were Sephardic soldiers. This was their reward for being heroes in the war. They were being prepared to go to the university. I was swept up by the romance of my heroes, what they were striving for, what the country wanted for them. It was very exciting. I intended to stay in Israel. The idea of being wanted and needed—it was just a whole different experience of what my work might mean.

But I didn't stay. I came back. Why? I think I felt that finally, it was very provincial, that America was the place to become the Renaissance person I wanted to be. I taught for a while and then went back to graduate school, to Yale, to study philosophy. While I was living in New Haven, the Yom Kippur War broke out, in 1973. Again, I got on a plane and went to Israel. My passport wasn't valid; I didn't care. I was thrown off the plane in London. I had to go to the embassy to have the passport renewed. I remember screaming at the ambassador that he had to do it immediately, there was a war on. I went to my cousin's kibbutz, and picked oranges and taught English. After a few weeks, when it was clear that things were all right, I came back.

I've lived in Berkeley for fifteen years now. For the first few years, I was doing my thesis and teaching English as a second language. I wasn't doing anything Jewish. My grandmother would come to visit. I would send her to things while I was working. I used to send her to the big Berkeley temple, Beth El, and once they had a guest speaker, the director of Chabad House. He told the story of his life, how he had grown up in a very non-Jewish environment, had been a hustler, a Jew for Jesus, had run a head shop in San Jose—all before he found Lubavitch. My grandmother went up to tell him how much she had been moved, so he invited her to Chabad House. To please her, I took her there. It had never occurred to me to go. I thought that the Hasidim in Brooklyn were weird, strange, very other. The rabbi at Chabad had a wonderful voice, and though it seemed very strange to me, I got to love the services. I started going by myself to Friday-night services. But even when I was going regularly, I didn't think it was part of a process, that I would do anything else.

Then something happened. During High Holy Day services, I met this guy there. I thought he was really cute, a Hasid, with a long beard. He was an administrator at Chabad House. Even though I was a single woman, I hadn't looked at these men as men. Then this one guy . . . He was so articulate, and we had this kind of flirtation on. He would walk me home on Friday night, or on Shabbat during the day. I was waiting for him to call me up, and he didn't. Then another man called me and said that Avram wanted to go out with me, and I said, "Why are *you* calling me?" and he explained that this wasn't just going out; that they didn't do that; that it was a *shidduch.* I went over and this guy and his wife sat me down and explained that this wasn't to be a "relationship"—this was a *shidduch,* which is the exploration of the possibility of marriage, and that at any point if either person doesn't feel that it will result in a marriage, the whole thing is ended. And they said that they were our *shadchans,* which means that it was their purpose to protect me, and this was to be a safe process, not like the outside world, where people were so insensitive. The religious Jewish rule is that single people never touch. The way they explained it is, not only is it against the Law, but there are also emotional and psychological reasons: it is much harder to separate from someone you know with your body. So we were to see each other as people, and not be swept away by sexuality. Not touching was a "fence" to prevent intercourse, which is the thing that is really forbidden. The idea is that the more holy you can make things, the better, and the more fences, the better. That meant that we were not to be alone indoors. We would come to their house and have our dates in their living room, with them close by. We could be out in public together, but not in his apartment or mine. I thought it was crazy, but I went along with it.

While I was still involved with him, I went to the Lubavitcher women's yeshiva in Minnesota. There were these wayward girls, and prostitutes with hearts of gold, and women from Israel and South Africa. Everyone had a story—sex, drugs, whatever. After the first twenty-four hours, although I was still having conflicts about being there, I suddenly saw the light—Jews were supposed to live this way. This is what God had told the Jews to do, and it didn't matter what time and place you happened to be in; this was the mission of the Jews. It suddenly made sense to me. In the next twenty-four hours, I started yearning to do *nagelwasser*—this is the Hasidic custom of dipping your nails in water when you wake up. It is because of the impurities of sleep, which is likened to a deathlike state that you erase with prayer and with a pail of water that you leave next to your bed. We were living dormitory-style. Everyone had them by their beds, and I thought it was a weird thing to do. Someone had told me that it was really because you might have touched your sexual parts during the night, and that was the impurity you were going to take off. That association disgusted me. But anyway, I felt this yearning, like a mystical experience. I don't have anything to compare with it. It felt like my soul was starving and needed nourishment, and that it had a way to get nourished.

Actually, I never did *nagelwasser.* I fought it; and I left the yeshiva after a week. But it didn't really matter. They had gotten me. When I got home, I would stay up all night listening to the tapes of the rabbi whose lectures I had missed, lectures on the Tanya, and on *halachah.* I was addicted. When I came back from Minnesota, people told me that I was glowing. Something had really happened.

When I came back, I started separating from my old friends and connecting with the people in the Chabad community. There was like a Gestalt role-play of what it would be to be a Lubavitcher wife. The women of Chabad, with their *sheitls* [wigs] on their heads, would sit around talking about their own *shidduchs*, waxing nostalgic about the life-style. I had to be tutored all the time. I would call Avram "sweetie" or something; I didn't know that you couldn't do that, that even married couples don't, that intimacy is not to be displayed. I saw him almost every day, and during that time I moved away from my philosophy and linguistics friends. And the ones I would talk to would make it difficult. Most would say that he must have sexual problems; that no normal person would act like that. "How can you marry someone you haven't slept with? Are you going to wear a wig? Oh, Susan, come off it!" I couldn't integrate my life. My ambivalence broke up the relationship. But it was the most wonderful thing that had ever happened to me; I was very much in love. The relationship with Avram became the most profound and intimate one I'd had. I attribute this to the *shidduch*—there was automatic commitment, no game-playing. He was my boyfriend, from the beginning, which removed a lot of barriers. I became aware of how callous I had become in the New York system of dating that I was used to, what is considered courtship in this age. There was also the idea of the sacred, that it was not just his needs and my needs that existed. There were whole other levels involved. This was powerful. It opened me up in a way I hadn't been before. I felt safe.

It was mostly this experience that made me feel that they had a secret, that this was a better way to live, that the complexity of the other world was a very cruel complexity, having nothing to do with human souls and needs. I took the whole thing quite seriously. And at the same time, I kept saying that the whole thing was crazy. I thought, Are you kidding? I'm not going to put on a *sheitl.* But for a while, it got me. I became a member of that community. People there still think I am. They'll say to me, "Isn't it sad? The community is so small; we're dwindling." As if I'm part of those who are still in it.

I still love the ideas, the doctrines. As I see it, the particular Lubavitcher way of looking at things is to make Hasidism into a kind of alternative vocabulary for psychology. Everything is understood in terms of personal development, psychological processes. So the story of the Exodus from Egypt is the story of everyone's liberation from their own mechanisms that inhibit them from becoming what they can be. This captured me as a vocabulary, a framework for understanding the world, and I'm still drawn toward it. I've always had a spiritual leaning. One time I was into Saint Theresa; at another point, I was reading Saint John of the Cross. I had never read Torah before. Recently I went to Crown Heights, and I loved the scene—when the rebbe comes out, and the Hasidim are all standing around, and they part like the Red Sea, like a chorus line, to let the rebbe pass. When my grandmother was sick, I wrote to the rebbe. Yes, when things are tough, I turn to that. You might even say that I believe that he is responsible for the fact that she got out of the hospital when they said that she had almost no chance, and that she lived for almost two years after that. I'm not sure that the rebbe didn't have something to do with that.

But actually, I'm an atheist underneath. Belief in God comes with great difficulty to me. I can't quite get it. I remember, after being at Chabad House for a year, I confessed to the rabbi that I didn't believe in God, and he said, smiling at me, "Don't worry, you will." But I didn't. I do agree with them—practice is important. They're right, Judaism is not just a matter of belief. Practice is a necessary element in the system. And I've experienced it that way. The Shabboses that I have are an utter joy for me, beyond any of my anticipations. On Friday night, when I light the candles and put the timer on my electricity and walk to shul—I love it. But that doesn't seem to be enough motivation. I still can't accept it as the reasonable thing to do.

I think I had been in conflict about my Judaism. The Chabad thing made me accept it entirely and relish it. I got off on all indexes of Jewishness, no matter what. But the truth is that the Lubavitcher life-style is really very restrictive for me, and I don't want that.

What undermines the psychic energy needed for the leap out of modernity is the definitively modern quality of self-awareness. Susan Levy is always aware of the ambiguities of meaning and motivation; she is self-analytic, like any good modern, and she speaks the modern language of psychology—not instrumentally, the way Lubavitch does in its proselytizing efforts, but essentially. And once "faith" rests on modernist psychological justification, it becomes easier to leave it—one is not abandoning God, only revising the understanding of one's psychological needs.

Most deeply, Susan Levy is aware of how much depends on choice, her own choice. The sense of the miraculous cannot finally bring her over, even when she can acknowledge its appeal. Her skeptical, inquiring mind will not stop wondering. Levy has no problem going to Chabad House, and even appreciating the evocations of mystical spirituality. Yet it is difficult to imagine that she, or others like her, will make the leap to absolute faith, believe, for example, that the Messiah will arrive to end history if only all Jews perform certain ritual activities.

It is just this burning faith of the reborn in the simplifying and integrating doctrine of fundamentalist religion, a faith quite conscious of its negation of the most basic truths of modernity, that fascinates modern observers. Within the exceptionally secularized ambiance of modern Judaism, such developments are especially startling. But the problems of someone like Susan Levy suggest the limitations of this exit from compartmentalization. And, in fact, the number of young people moving toward fundamentalist sects like Chabad is small. Moreover, Lubavitch will find it difficult to retain all its converts over the long run. For most of them, self-consciousness is inescapable; *choice* is necessary to achieve and maintain an identity that is presented by the converted as an inherent, miraculous destiny. The tradition of Orthodoxy, especially the intensely antimodern Hasidic version, cannot regain the "taken-for-granted" character it had in different historical and cultural circumstances. The Lubavitcher proselytizers may insist that this is "what a Jew really is"; but all modern experience undercuts any such insistence.

For generations, in isolated communities in hostile societies, the destined, "given" quality of Orthodoxy was sustained by the social and cultural conditions of Jewish life. The community was the world; leaving was unthinkable, and often, in practice, impossible. The new Jewish converts in their Brooklyn yeshiva may adopt the dress, the beards, the ritual practice, the rhythm of daily life, and even the accents and verbal intonations of *shtetl* Jews. They may be immersed in the study of Torah and Talmud, spiritually isolated from the influences of the outside world. But the outside world remains right there. The subway that brought the secular wanderer to his Jewish destination—even miraculously, as the convert comes to believe—is still running a few blocks away. All the life choices that were available before entering the closed and integrated world of Hasidic Judaism are still there. A shave, a change of clothes, and a subway token are all it takes to re-enter that other world. The consciousness of this conditionality may be repressed, but it cannot be eliminated, and the power of a traditional community to sustain its returnees is constantly subverted by this fact of modern life. Enthusiasm is real and commitment sincere. But as the evidence of growing disaffiliation from all of the various born-again cults demonstrates, a commitment based on such subjective enthusiasm is profoundly fragile.

The New Orthodox

Ultra-Orthodoxy deals with the threatening tensions caused by modernity by building thicker walls around the Torah, keeping the ideas and life-styles of the surrounding culture far away. But why not move in the other direction, trying to absorb the freedoms of modernity while being genuinely Orthodox, all in a joyful harmony, without the vigilant defensiveness of the "old" modern Orthodoxy?

Recent developments suggest that this approach has real appeal. People are coming to Orthodoxy who do not deplore the emancipation of the Jews, the Enlightenment, the scientific revolution, or other forces that have undermined the solidity of the Orthodox faith. These modern returnees do not feel any tension between, say, the spirit of modern art and literature and that of Orthodox Judaism. They are not tempted to form socially isolated, inward-looking enclaves like the Lubavitcher community in Crown Heights or the Young Israel settlement in Cherry Hill. They are active participants in *all* phases of contemporary life, and they expect to continue this participation, even as they become Orthodox.

The "flagship" synagogues of this new style of Orthodoxy are found in the heart of high-priced, culturally sophisticated communities: the Bay Cities Synagogue, in Venice, California; the Beth Israel Synagogue, in Berkeley; and the most publicized, the Lincoln Square Synagogue, on Manhattan's West Side. Each of these synagogues had been in decline, reflecting the trend of Orthodoxy in general, and each has been transformed over the past decade by an influx of highly educated, prosperous, professional young people, mainly from non-Orthodox backgrounds and often with meager Jewish educations. The upsurge at the Lincoln Square Synagogue was first noted by the *New York Times* in 1981. The article emphasized that many of the new congregants were becoming "seriously interested in their Jewish identity for the first time in their lives." Profiled as a representative returnee was the well-known avant-garde composer Steve Reich. Raised in a Reform home, Reich "dropped out of Jewishness" after his bar mitzvah. "At age 39 he met Rabbi Buchwald [of the Lincoln Square Synagogue] and said he wanted to know more about 'what it means to be Jewish.' He now attends regularly."

The spirit of the Lincoln Square Synagogue is considerably more liberal than even the most moderate strands of mainstream modern Orthodoxy, and is many cultures removed from the Hasidic spirit. Historically, to participate so completely in modernity—in body and spirit—usually required a deliberate break with Orthodox Judaism. But in this new Orthodoxy, it seems possible to have everything: modernity and tradition too.

Benjamin and Naomi Stein* are active members of Lincoln Square Synagogue; Benjamin is a lay officer of the congregation and helps administer the institution. The Steins have been married for twelve years and have two daughters. Benjamin is an M.B.A., working as an executive in his family's business. Naomi is a social worker. Their Upper West Side apartment is elegant, tastefully decorated, displaying a serious and informed involvement with contemporary art.

"Judaism Isn't Guilt-Tripping"

Naomi My home on Long Island wasn't that Jewish. My parents sent me to a secular, cultural, Yiddish Sunday school. They didn't belong to any synagogue, but on Yom Kippur they went to a Conservative shul. I hated the Sunday school, but I probably got something out of it, a historical feeling maybe. In high school, I got involved with some kids who were in the youth group at an Orthodox synagogue, and somehow I ended up going to their summer seminar, where I met Ben. I was still in high school and he was in college. They gave an emotional push for Orthodoxy at the seminar. I liked the life-style, the structure it gives your life, the involvement in the group, knowing what is expected of you. It made sense to me. When I came back home, I became part of a group in the community which got together to observe the Sabbath. My parents thought I was going through a phase. My father had grown up in an Orthodox home and had rejected it. When he met Ben's father for the first time, he said, "Where did we go wrong?" Later, after my parents saw all these other kids on all these trips—ashrams, drugs, whatever—they saw that they were pretty lucky. Our life-style is not that different from their own. They can understand what we're doing with our lives, as long as they don't think about the ritual stuff. And there are the shared things, like baseball and ballet.

Benjamin Both of my parents grew up modern Orthodox. They are American-born and college-educated. My parents kept a kosher home in Long Beach and encouraged observance, partly to keep their own parents happy. I was sent to public school, but my three sisters and brother went to a yeshiva in Long Beach. I decided to go to Yeshiva University for college, maybe because I felt I had missed out, I hadn't given Jewish education a fair shake.

*Pseudonyms.

I felt that I wanted to get more exposure to textual Judaism. I think that if I had gone to Columbia, I would have been different. I think I could have become much more secular. Three out of five siblings haven't continued the observances we had at home.

After I graduated, I taught English—this was my major—at Yeshiva University High School for a year. Then I went to business school. Now I work in a family business, which gives me a lot of flexibility in doing Jewish organizational work. I work with six different Jewish organizations and schools.

Our religious perspective is Orthodox, or traditional. We are very involved with Lincoln Square Synagogue. We moved to the West Side because of the rabbi, Shlomo Riskin. I've known him for over twenty-five years. He was a teacher of mine and a very big influence on my life. Once I went on a study trip to Europe and Israel that he led. I had never seen anyone young who was an Orthodox rabbi. He took us on a walk to the British Museum, and we came to something he identified as the Rosetta Stone, and he proceeded to translate the Greek for us. And then, in Paris, he gave us a twenty-minute lecture on the look on Mona Lisa's face. When we went into a church in Rome a priest came running over to tell us to remove our yarmulkas, that it is a sign of discourtesy to have your head covered in a church. And Riskin said, "Do it." He thought it was proper. I was floored that a rabbi could negotiate the modern world so adeptly and still communicate his enthusiasm for Judaism and deal with it on an intellectual level.

I don't know if the perspective at Lincoln Square should be called "liberalism," but it is less rigid. People are accepting of the idea that you can be involved legitimately in Orthodox Judaism without living the old type of Orthodox life. One of the main arguments traditional Orthodox have against our synagogue is that it is tolerant of women's participation. Feminists would laugh at the idea that what we do represents anything like equality for women, but to some Orthodox it is scandalous. Increasingly, the perception among the Orthodox is that they must be apart, they must tune out the secular world in order to pass on their tradition. They want to stay away from all the parts of the secular world that lead to assimilation and intermarriage, like coeducation, dating, and especially college, which they see as the main culprit.

But the attitude at Lincoln Square is exactly the opposite. Lincoln Square Synagogue has 1,300 member units—700 families and 600 singles. There's a lecture series on Wednesday nights that usually draws about four hundred people. A few years ago the series was on sex—there were four or five hundred more than usual. We had to pipe it into extra rooms on closed-circuit TV. The synagogue earned an extra $18,000. Rabbi Riskin discussed premarital sex, homosexuality, marriage relations. People wanted to see how far he would go. He didn't go as far as most would have liked. He stressed the need for sanctity in relations. This is an area where the secular style has certainly buffeted Orthodoxy. The next year his talks were on aliyah—the responsibility of a Jew to go live in Israel—and attendance plummeted.

Naomi I'm actually quite troubled about the situation of the big singles population at Lincoln Square. There is a Jewish injunction against premarital sex, but there is apparently little difference between the secular and the Orthodox world in this regard. If I put myself in the position of a single woman, wanting to be part of our community and to uphold the values, I doubt I would be able to go out with most of the men in our community, from what I've heard about them. You might go to bed one date later than in the secular world. That's what it comes down to.

Benjamin For me, what is much more troubling is something like the Bergman affair. Rabbis are supposed to be an example. And here was this Orthodox rabbi who owned nursing homes, stealing money from old people and negating every precept that he is supposed to represent as a rabbi or an Orthodox Jew. He was convicted, but some parts of the community rallied around him, just because he was Orthodox; they said others did it too, why pick him out? And then there was the scandal about a computer-leasing company. One of the two guys was someone I had worked with. There was a bankruptcy and the suspicion that he had defrauded the company of $100 million. And the article in the *Wall Street Journal* said that these guys had led a fight in their Orthodox synagogue to have the *mechitzah* [the divider between the men and the women] raised, that it wasn't Orthodox enough. And to me, that is as bad as homosexuality, or anything else the Torah says you should be stoned for.

The thing that attracts me about Orthodox Judaism, not that I come near to having the ideal, is that there is a circumscribed set of behaviors that covers your whole existence. I think Judaism has survived precisely because of the commitment to Orthodox practice. Sure, I'll give lip service to the idea of the Torah as divine revelation. I think it is necessary as a premise to maintain the seriousness of our way of life. I'm willing to say that the people back then were hearing something. The issue doesn't trouble me. But the life-style makes sense in so many ways that I don't worry about theological problems.

Naomi We're not into a guilt trip. I don't think of Judaism as guilt-tripping. You could always put an element of guilt into it. For example, there is a clear Jewish viewpoint on homosexuality, yet there are homosexual members at Lincoln Square. There is an open attitude, there is counseling by the rabbi. I'm sure when he counsels them he shows a lot of understanding and deals with their situation respectfully. For my part, a person is a person; I don't care what he does in his private life. Sometimes it occurs to us that somebody is gay, but it doesn't matter. Who cares? Look, we also have members who are quite involved in the shul, who consider themselves Orthodox, but live in New Jersey and drive over on Shabbat. They've done it for years, and they aren't ostracized either. This is an accepting place. We don't ask questions about anybody's private life or their reasons for coming. Certainly there are things we can't do, like taking trips that wouldn't let us get to a shul on Shabbat to hear the Torah being read. We are required by Jewish law to hear it every Shabbat. I'm a social worker so I am aware of the conflicts around the ideas of therapy and psychoanalysis. Judaism is not really oriented toward the maximizing of someone's personal needs over community needs. For example, say you were counseling a young person from an observant Orthodox home who feels the need to explore, say, by doing things that would violate the Sabbath. Do you tell him the Jewish point of view only, as the right one? I would be inclined to present the ramifications of both sides. Or, take child placement, where the question is placing a kid from a kosher home in a residential center. They have kosher TV dinners available, but no kid would want them, it would make them outcasts in the group. What should one do?

But on the whole, for me too, this life-style makes a lot of sense on an emotional and intellectual level. I think people are being attracted now because they are looking for something to give meaning to life. People who have started coming to the synagogue tell us over and over—it sounds corny—that there was something missing from their lives, a sense of tradition, a sense of where they come from. There are some who make real sacrifices, like an actor we know—he was playing on Broadway. He started to come to the beginners' minyan, and he started studying. And then a few months ago he quit his show and went to Israel to study in a yeshiva, giving up his career. We've never had to make such sacrifices. And I worry about people who do. I worry about whether, in their emotional involvement, they are making the right choice for their lives. Maybe this is where I come into conflict with Judaism. I *should* think, They are adopting the Jewish life-style and they should be willing to give up everything to do it. But I wonder whether someday they may regret it.

Benjamin It's true, we haven't had to make any great sacrifices. I have a subscription to the New York City Ballet. And I love art. I work near 57th Street, and I have the opportunity to go to galleries a lot. I consider myself an amateur student of twentieth-century and contemporary art. I think ballet is a celebration of human potential. It is beautiful, and there is something almost religious about beautiful ballet and great art. What would I do if my daughters, who are taking ballet lessons, were really good and became ballerinas, and gave up Orthodox observance? Well, I wouldn't do anything. Whatever I could do, I'm doing now, and if it doesn't work, I'll accept it.

What is so striking about the "born-again" *ba'alei teshuvah* in an ultra-Orthodox yeshiva, even more than their obvious rejection of the physical trappings of modernity (in dress or life-style), is their withdrawal from the forms of modern consciousness: the arts and sciences, political and social activism, materialism, individualism, aesthetic appreciation, the quest for sensual and intellectual experience. The convert to fundamentalism rejects modern values as false, empty, and distracting. Shakespeare and Mozart shrink to nothing compared with a line of the God-given Torah. Modern Orthodoxy's task was to moderate this absolute stance in order to maintain the commitment of Jews who would not remain Orthodox in the ultrafundamentalist mode. Selective and guarded accommodations to modernity were sanctioned; permission was given to partake moderately, but along with it came a powerful compartmentalization of the spirit. It is understandable, as we have noted, that the tone of modern Orthodoxy toward secular ideas mixes negation, warning, and apologetics. Modern justifications for traditional religious claims need to be constantly updated and revised. The inevitable contradictions of religious doctrine with aspects of modern thought must be either explained away or compartmentalized so that the clash is muted or absorbed. Accommodation must always be vigilant so that the sharp distinction between Orthodoxy and those illegitimate modernizations— Conservative and Reform—is preserved.

But the new Orthodox joining the beginners' minyan at Lincoln Square do not seem to be touched by such concerns. In true post-assimilation fashion, they feel no guilt or ambivalence about partaking of modern secular culture à la carte. It is only the "unhappy" elements of that culture that are to be avoided: alienation, lack of community, loss of meaning and order, loss of roots.

Moreover, taking on the yoke of ritual does not prove all that disruptive to their lives. Since the startling transformation of Lincoln Square in the early 1980s, a large network of institutions devoted to supporting the Orthodox "good life" has sprung up in the neighborhood. Not only are there old-time kosher restaurants like Moshe Peking and La Differance, there are new upscale dining spots like La Kasbah and Benjamin of Tudela, as well as quality cheese stores and butchers, all making it possible for the new Orthodox to enter the religious life without leaving the old life—its tastes, habits, and material wealth—behind. As one of the new Orthodox put it, "The West Side is just right for us. It allows us to be uncompromising in our religious life without seriously compromising our secular life."

Although newcomers assert that "becoming an observant Jew invariably involves making sacrifices," these sacrifices do not add up to a very long list. There is the sort of inconvenience that Naomi Stein mentions, caused by the myriad ritual requirements of Orthodoxy. Some planning is always necessary: where to take a vacation, which restaurant to eat at, how to arrange work schedules so the Sabbath can be observed. But none of the essentials of the good life are sacrificed. Where Orthodox law would seriously affect the actions of individuals, as in the proscription of premarital sex, there is good reason to believe, as Naomi Stein ruefully admits, that this particular injunction can be finessed without threatening one's membership in the community. As for the individuals themselves, it is obvious that such picking and choosing, so characteristic of the liberalizing of Judaism in modern times, does not contradict their commitment to the new Orthodoxy.

This historically unique ease of combining Orthodoxy and modernity into a new Orthodox way of life or "life-style," as the Steins put it, is strikingly apparent in the unconflicted enthusiasm for central modern values like personal freedom, individualism, moral independence, and artistic creation. "Most new Orthodox parents," *New York* magazine tells us, "seem not in the least interested in circumscribing their children's intellectual development." Consider too, that for this state of mind, the exposure of human bodies in ballet and other arts—just the sort of thing that a strict modern Orthodox Jew, not to mention Chaim Pinsky, would find deeply troublesome—becomes unproblematic, an aesthetic experience that is "almost religious," as Ben Stein puts it. Such essential aspects of secular modernity are not seen as challenges to the ethos of traditional Judaism.

The generous spirit of tolerance can comfortably include people who do not offer even a compartmentalized lip service to the fundamental doctrines of Orthodoxy. Barbara and Walter Oppenheim* live in the beautiful Berkeley hills. Walter is a cardiologist and Barbara is an attorney. They have a four-year-old son. Theirs is a highly educated, professional, and sophisticated community. They belong to a newly flourishing Orthodox congregation where they feel quite welcome and at home even though they are not—and have no intention of becoming—Orthodox in belief or practice.

"An Orthodox Atmosphere"

Walter Both of my parents are from Orthodox backgrounds in Germany. They left Germany in 1935 and eventually got to the U.S. in 1941. They became what I like to term "superficial Orthodox." My father went to Orthodox synagogues, where all his cronies went. He participated in everything, but then, after the Sabbath services, he would go home and turn on the baseball game. My father took pains to hide that he wasn't observing from

*Pseudonyms.

his stricter friends. The reason he gave was that he didn't want to embarrass anyone else. I would argue with my father a lot. At one point, he called me anti-Semitic. He didn't want me to go out to the movies on Friday night, but it was all right to watch TV at home. I had an Orthodox bar mitzvah, and learned how to put on *tefillin,* but I never did it after that. And I wasn't really expected to. My father wanted me to be like he was, knowledgeable, able to perform. I'm still anxious about the exact phrase for greeting people on Rosh Hashanah and Yom Kippur. There was so much emphasis on the correct way that I am still afraid of rituals. I cower in the back during services, afraid that I'll be called up and not know the right way to do it. For me, there was never much joy in the rituals, in the synagogue or at home. The emphasis was always on doing it right.

I was raised to disdain Reform. I still don't like organs in Jewish services. And I've never liked English translations of Hebrew prayers. Not that I understand Hebrew. I can pick out some words, and understand sort of what the prayers say. But I don't like the use of the English language. It makes the prayers sound coarse, without beauty. Musically, I get a sense of the beauty in Hebrew. I myself don't actually pray, but I don't like the sharp curtailment of the service's length, for convenience, that they have in Reform. Conservative I think of as being in the middle, half in Hebrew, half in English. This is better, but still not what I think is really a Jewish experience, which is prayers in Hebrew and the Orthodox order of the service. I've never learned more. When I lived in New York, I often thought about taking courses at the Jewish Theological Seminary, but I always found other things that were more important. I had to take medical-school prerequisites, and then there were courses in music, history, language, general liberal arts. I still buy books on Jewish subjects and look at them now and then.

When we were going to have a child, we wanted to find a place where we could raise our child in a Jewish environment which was also an intellectual environment. We settled on Beth Israel in Berkeley. I like the fact that I can come and go as I wish. If you come late, no one bats an eye. If I have a *tallis* or not, no one cares. It is a cosmopolitan, intellectual community. The rabbi wants to elevate people to his standard but not browbeat them. There is a very low *mechitzah* between the men and the women. Barbara and I try to sit almost together, right on opposite sides, when we can. We like being together there.

I don't go to shul regularly. Often I'll arrange it so I'll arrive late. We've done some Shabbat at home, but not recently. Shabbat provides time for the family to be together, to pay attention to each other without distractions. I like the benefits, but I'm distractable. And there are still all the resentments from my childhood.

If I had a problem about ethical questions, say medical ethics, I wouldn't go to the rabbi to learn what Jewish law says, except out of curiosity. I think Judaism is part of my ethics. I'm always interested in the Jewish point of view. If it doesn't match my own view, I'm willing to think about it. But I don't think Jewish law is God-given. It was written by bright people, but some of it is based on superstition. I believe in God, not in a manipulating God, who directs lives and has a personality, but a superior, ordered, incomprehensible force—and I stop thinking beyond that. In fact, I'm really ignorant about Jewish things. I was asked the other day about the Jewish view of what happens when you die, and I really don't know.

Barbara My family was Reform, mainly because the Union Temple was down the block. When I came home from Reform Sunday school and said I'd learned about lighting candles, my parents decided to start doing it. Passover was always a lot of fun, though we never did the second part of the Seder, after the meal. I didn't want to continue my Jewish education after confirmation. I never found Reform satisfying—but I liked ritual.

In college I took a survey course on Jewish literature. I saved all the books and read them years later. The highlight for me was the prayer book edited by Rabbi Hertz. I learned about the medieval order of the Orthodox service. I liked it; it made sense. I'm sorry it was changed. The prayers are so appealing—though it's too bad you have to do them several times a day and repeat things. I like to do things once. I'd like to try a *mikvah*, or go spend a weekend with a Hasidic family. But I wouldn't want to get committed to something I'd have to do all the time.

For me, Orthodoxy has to do with an atmosphere in shul that allows me to pray. To be Orthodox is to feel that Judaism is a religion and not just a social event. I'd always had a very childlike conception of God as a personal intervener. Sometimes I wonder if my view of God doesn't come from the Irish maids we had in my childhood, who used to take me to mass. But for me, what's important is a certain kind of spiritual intention, not the details. I wouldn't want to keep kosher. I could give up the meat, but not Brie and Camembert. As far as I'm concerned, the solution to enjoying shul on Saturday morning is to go for a long run before, even if it means coming late. You come out feeling good, and the day isn't gone.

Even if the Oppenheims are not the norm for their congregation, their sense of feeling comfortable in the congregation flows from the new Orthodox spirit, from the fact that those most modern of liberal notions—tolerance, the worth of individual choice, the individual autonomy of moral decision—have seeped into such congregations: not into their officially stated tenets, of course, but into the attitudes of their members. The Oppenheims feel comfortable with open nonobservance. Similarly, at Lincoln Square, privacy is respected, and as the Steins point out, people come for their own reasons, even if they are not exactly Orthodox ones: to find a community that can ease the pain of alienation and isolation; to affirm a sense of history, tradition, and roots in a mobile, rootless culture; to create a realm of ritual for observing rites of passage in a society that is relentlessly secular and trivializing. And there is another modern value that attracts people like the Oppenheims to an Orthodox congregation: "authenticity." These congregants want their prayers in Hebrew; they prefer the medieval Orthodox order of the service. Orthodox Judaism is the real thing, the most Jewish thing. And it is valued as such. Innovation, in other words, is jarring aesthetically, not theologically.

But can even this ambiance of tolerance and authenticity attract substantial numbers to Orthodoxy, and hold them over the long haul? Do well-publicized, flourishing synagogues like Lincoln Square herald a widespread return to traditional Judaism—a return combining enthusiastic participation in all aspects of modern life with a new "style" of Orthodoxy capable of avoiding the difficult compartmentalization of traditional modern Orthodoxy?

It seems unlikely, for several reasons.

First, as in the mainstream synagogue, here too the resurgence depends on an increasing secularization of spirit. As one young Orthodox scholar puts it: "You can do anything nowadays wearing a yarmulka! It's easy to be Orthodox. These people wouldn't have considered trying to be Orthodox when there was a real conflict between being Orthodox and being American. What we're seeing now is not a revitalization, not renewed interest in real Orthodoxy, but a sign of how insubstantial it's all become." With most of the Orthodox world moving to the right, creating stricter and more powerful barriers, the new Orthodox will only become more isolated from the traditional spirit of Orthodoxy.

Second, the very ease of accommodation that makes this new Orthodoxy appealing to people who would not otherwise be tempted by traditional religious life brings with it a new fragility. The quality of commitment is shot through with the subversive ethos of individual choice. In this new, tolerant milieu, giving up Orthodox involvement or adopting a lenient practice are far easier than in traditional Orthodox communities. Community sanctions have weakened to the point where they hardly exist. Meanwhile, the force of internal sanctions—the feelings of guilt and betrayal expressed by traditional "leavers"—has drastically diminished, as it should in a post-assimilation culture that makes individual choice and authenticity the core of moral psychology. The incentive to join has now become largely a matter of one's own quest for meaning; should that quest lead away from the newly adopted Orthodoxy, then dropping it would also be the authentic (and easy) thing to do. The search for wholeness, meaning, roots, community, tradition; the appeal of spirituality; the power of charismatic leaders who can address this highly cultured constituency—all these factors can and do fuel flashes of revival like those of the Lincoln Square or Bay Cities congregations. But once again, the difficulty of passing on this "faith" shows why any expectations for a significant revival of Orthodoxy based on this accommodating style are likely to be disappointed.

Suppose the child of a liberal and tolerant new Orthodox couple absorbs her parents' love of ballet, takes lessons, shows real talent, and finds herself torn between a career as a ballerina and a life committed to the fulfillment of Orthodox law. Just how torn would she be and how likely to choose the path of Orthodox observance? The sanctions the parents can honestly exert are so much less even than Tevye's in *Fiddler on the Roof*, and we saw how his daughters chose. Not only would the parents not sit *shivah*, treating the child as "dead" for her dereliction, not only would the parents not cut off relations with the child, but such parents would go to see the child dance—though not on Friday night, of course.

For many, the commitment to new Orthodoxy is a self-conscious choice. And since the freedom to choose a life-style is a value for the parents, a value supported by the whole force of contemporary post-assimilation culture,—how can parents deny the same freedom to their children? If the children choose differently, where will the parents find the moral conviction for attacking such different—but no less authentic—choices?

Tamara Lemaross* teaches literature and Jewish studies at a large university in the Northeast. Married, with three adolescent children, and a member of an Orthodox congregation, she articulates with great clarity the difficulties and dilemmas of "choosing" Orthodoxy, of being an antimodern modernist.

"A Civilizing Discipline"

I have thought for many years that the Jewish agenda derives from the Enlightenment and the Emancipation. At that point, a very serious challenge was laid down to traditional Judaism. The great majority of young, intellectual Jews, thinking Jews, left Orthodox Judaism, broke with the Law and its manner of life, broke with their families, in many cases. Somehow it seemed to me that one has to go back there and ask the philosophical questions they were asking. After the Emancipation, the notion of "I am a Jew," the internal notion of who I am as a Jew, collapsed, and all that was left was "How does the world see me? Do I measure up? Am I morally upright enough?" This was the response to anti-Semitism, and it is so pernicious. It befouls the Jewish spirit. It corrupts the Jewish soul. I'd say that there has been an inverse ratio since the Enlightenment between the pressure of anti-Semitism and the health of the Jewish spirit. I find that the Jew grows sick in response to anti-Semitism. And I hate that illness. And I hate all the forms it takes.

I think that it's a very serious business, trying to define what we can still salvage from Judaism—especially without the presence of God. I have never in my life felt the presence of God. It's a very foreign idea to me, even though I love prayer. I love prayer, but I'm embarrassed by it. The only way in which I can relate to prayer is to think when I pray, These are the words that generations of Jews have spoken before me. I can be fascinated by the prayers, but I can't conceive of God, of a personal God, of a God acting in

*Pseudonym.

history. Still, I love the power of the idea, and I feel that it is necessary as a civilizing discipline.

What I find so admirable in Judaism is precisely the degree to which it begins with the notion of people at their worst, a rabble that has to be disciplined—and that is what the Law is for. It refines them through the generations, refines the notion of all the evils that man is susceptible to and how he can be disciplined. How does one make him a social animal? How does one make him a thinking person, sensitive to other people's needs? And the Law keeps building upon itself until you have a very highly disciplined people. The other pole of this process is the messianic notion that this is not enough, that one needs the dream of perfectibility. But what I think has happened is that things have gone completely to this other pole. Particularly, it seems to me that Jewish socialism and Jewish universalism and the Bund, and all those theories of perfectibility that were so powerfully attractive to Jews at the beginning of this century and that remain so powerfully attractive, are from that messianic pole. And I find that they're a very dangerous element in Judaism.

I think that Judaism is an alternative civilization, a very attractive alternative civilization, with content. The Jew who is raised with disciplining notions of Judaism has an advantage. The Jewish law that is taught to him from the cradle says: "It's not always what you want, what you feel like. This is the time; this is *not* the time. This is the place; this is *not* the place." I think that today people grow up without a notion of choice. They do not understand that there are choices to be made, and they do not understand that choices are tragic by their very nature, that they do impose certain restrictions on human beings. Jews ultimately respected the discipline because they were the people of God and this was God's Law.

The discipline of the Law still has force for those Jews who live within it. I would say of myself that I am a person who chooses to live within it. I make that choice consciously, voluntarily. For me, what is difficult about it is that I make that choice not before God but before my notion of the Jews. To me, the choice means practice. There is no abstract Jew. I know that people say, "I'm a Jew," and that's it. But it leads to nothing, and it's not Judaism. To be a Jew means that there are things incumbent on you to do and not to do. It imposes a set of imperatives. Certainly, these have changed over the centuries. The Law is malleable, retranslatable, for each age, for each stage. One does not talk about animal sacrifices nowadays. My friend and I study Torah every Saturday morning, and we're up to the laws pertaining to lepers. But with all of the arguing and commentary pertaining to the laws of lepers, people don't examine spots anymore. I suffer from eczema, so I see white spots breaking out. But I don't go to my rabbi and ask him if I should live outside the camp for ten weeks. Even the most Orthodox people who are so true to the body of law don't pay attention to every detail. Judaism is adaptable.

My father was a nonbeliever, though he went to synagogue regularly on holidays. He sent us to the Folkshule, a Labor-Zionist Yiddish school. My husband is also a graduate of this school. But when we had to send our children to school, we made a decision that I think was the most conscious choice of our lives as Jews. We decided not to send them to the Folkshule, and instead, to send them to a religious school, where the children are taught prayer and observance. So my children grew up knowing prayers, which I never grew up knowing. I learned them later on my own. The children will go through the religious school to the end of high school. Holidays are sacred to them. Friday night is sacred to them. Nobody is excused from being there for the lighting of candles, Kiddush, the meal. My husband wants us to keep the Sabbath in the sense of not engaging in any commerce. I'm sure that within the next little while, he and I will decide to do that. But this has been difficult because we both work and Saturday is the one day when the two of us don't. We can do errands. And so we haven't imposed that observance. But he is so reluctant to do these things that I've become reluctant too. If I do go to the store, I feel badly about it, as if I'm letting the side down.

We keep a kosher home now, but we've never kept kosher outside of the home. I was worried that the children would see this as hypocrisy. When they became older, I once raised the question. My children's response was "No, we are just so grateful that you decided not to do it outside home." They said, "You've given us the best of both worlds. We have a kosher home, so anybody can come to eat." We belong to an Orthodox synagogue, and we go there on holidays. My husband sometimes goes on Shabbos. I never considered any other kind of synagogue— basically for aesthetic reasons. Also, I'm a sexist. I love the play between the sexes, and I think this play is based on essential differences between men and women. One of the things I love about an Orthodox shul is that it is one of the few places where this distinction between men and women is visual, palpable, demonstrable.

I think the idea that in Judaism women are not equal is profoundly hostile. The notion that I belong to a sex considered inferior is an awful notion, in addition to being totally untrue. It's demeaning and degrading and ridiculous. I think role distinctions are healthy, especially in our culture, where no one ever says to you, "You cannot do something else." And I believe in the primacy of certain roles. The woman has to consider her primary function to be a wife and mother. Now she may choose, as an individual, not to be a wife and mother. But to say that just because I don't want to be a wife and mother, it is wrong to say that Women— capital W—shouldn't be wives and mothers, that men can be, this is wrong. In the long run, it leads to frustration and resentment. I see the culture moving in a certain direction, and I think it is very important to make the opposite case. It is the difference between tolerance and advocacy. To advocate the cause of homosexuality as a legitimate way of life is very different from being tolerant of homosexuality as social deviance. Judaism certainly should not lose its sense of this kind of distinction. My own views match those of the Torah, but I would not call upon the Torah about homosexuality, or about women either.

It would be very difficult for my children to give up being Jewish. The way we live it is so wonderful that they would be giving up an enormous amount. I know the pain that would be involved for them to give it up, and I have deliberately made that alternative difficult for them. I would be totally opposed to a mixed marriage unless the other person converted to Orthodox Judaism. But for all that, my children may still intermarry. They know that I'm not going to sit *shivah* for them and give them up forever.

The voluntary aspect is both a strength and a weakness. It's a weakness because there is not enough of a claim—can it remain attractive enough? But it's a strength *because* it has to compete: a free choice is a strong choice. I've never had any doubt that Judaism can hold its own. Sure it's difficult, but I'm not sure people don't like something that is difficult. To me, it is innately attractive, and I know that I can make it attractive to people with whom I speak.

Judaism as a way of life has real rewards, and I've given up intellectual questioning in that area. If I spent my life worrying about the primary principle, the philosophical grounds, as I was wont to do when I was younger, I couldn't do it. So at some point I stopped worrying. Maybe that is what Jewish identity is. In other areas, I am very critical; I try to rethink things. But Orthodox Judaism is not the place where one does that. I don't ask myself when I light the candles, as I did some years ago, Why am I doing this? What is the meaning of this? I don't anymore.

Tamara Lemaross finds in Orthodox Judaism a deeply conservative view of human nature, conservative in the sense of classical political theory. She energetically puts forward views about feminism, homosexuality, and other "liberation" issues that are opposed to the liberal and radical positions on culture and politics especially widespread among modern Jewish intellectuals. And since she holds the same values she sees in Orthodox Judaism, she can support those values. But she did not learn these views from Orthodox Judaism nor would she look to religious doctrines for foundations for such views. She honestly admits that she does not believe in God, so her beliefs cannot be founded on "this is what God commanded us." She appreciates the way Orthodox ritual and religious practice mesh with her views on human nature and moral good to form an alternative, antimodern, and conservative worldview. Her children have been brought up in this particular Orthodox style, where gratitude for not having to keep kosher outside the home is part of the pleasure of being Orthodox. Obviously Lemaross is deeply committed to Jewishness, and the binding power of Orthodoxy is important to her. But as her children are sure to see, many Jews have such a commitment without needing Orthodoxy to support it. They might very well find themselves with the same aesthetic sensibility as their mother, and so will find an Orthodox congregation pleasing. But whether or not they end up sharing her aesthetic and political views, they will certainly have absorbed the central modernity of their mother's idea: the importance of choosing for oneself. That their mother applies her critical, independent, secular mind to all areas of thought and culture except Orthodoxy is understandable, but it is a difficult prohibition to pass along.

Taking her own lack of religious commitment in stride, Tamara Lemaross expresses no problems, anxieties, or conflicts in her allegiance to Orthodoxy. But for those whose views do not mesh so closely with Orthodoxy's "alternative civilization," whose opinions on women's liberation, sexual preference, individual conscience, and social justice are in the liberal camp, life is much more problematic. Their options are those we have seen: either a tension-filled compartmentalization always threatening to collapse, or a fragile accommodation that pays lip service to Orthodox law while defending private freedom of choice.

For Jews who want to combine a commitment to Jewish identity and community with modern liberal values, the simpler way is just to reinterpret Judaism. This is the spirit that animates the "Jewish revival," a phrase used by the participants themselves. For the revivalists, only a different sort of creative absorption of the modern than had previously been found either in the mainstream Reform and Conservative communities or anywhere in the new Orthodox fringe can stem the historical decline of religious and ethnic Jewish culture and community.

The Revival

All right, Judaism can't be all things to all people, but I insist that every Jew has the right to construct his own ark, set sail, trim his vessel as he sees the mountain rising in the distance.

—Mark Jay Mirsky, *My Search for the Messiah: Studies and Wanderings in Israel and America* (1977)

How about a liberated frum *ballerina/writer/auto mechanic into Dylan, Shabbos, yoga, camping, Baal Shem Tov, polarity massage, existentialism, Degas and Torah.*

—"Personals" ad, *Sh'ma: A Journal of Jewish Responsibility* (1982)

Living Tree Kabbalah seminar. We do soul work with Jewish meditation and bioenergetics, toward becoming richer, more loving human beings.

—"Ongoing Groups" ad, *East Bay Express* (1991)

Within the broader heightening of interest in Jewish identity there has been observed during the past two decades a more precise and self-conscious movement of revival—a "movement of Jewish renewal," in the words of Arthur Waskow, a prolific publicist for this movement. For the activists of this revival, the goal is, in Waskow's words, "the renewing and remaking of Jewish thought and practice."

The key theme of this renewing and remaking has been creative incorporation. During the sixties, young Jews, to a noticeably greater extent than their non-Jewish peers, participated in the social and cultural movements that shook American life. Some of these young people were rather unusual for their generation in that they were very well educated in Jewish culture and religion and active in Jewish youth activities. They comprised the future elite of the American Jewish community. However, appropriate to the spirit of the 1960s, they found themselves in sharp opposition to the Jewish establishment, which they perceived as bland and out of date. They saw themselves as rare exceptions to growing trends of disaffiliation and assimilation, and for these trends they blamed the unappealing nature of conventional Judaism and the institutions and tone of the mainstream Jewish community.

For these young intellectuals, Judaism and Jewish identity were central values; but so were the new cultural, political, and social movements of the counterculture and the New Left. They not only wanted to maintain this range of commitments, they intended to integrate them. To accomplish this goal, they sought to institutionalize the sixties spirit, so to speak, to infuse Jewish life with a sense of participation, innovation, and hospitality to all of the most progressive movements of American life. By being creative, they felt that they would be true both to themselves and to the essential spirit of Judaism.

Waskow's chronicle of Jewish revival, *These Holy Sparks,* describes the movement's generative function. And, indeed, the effects of the revival's early "sparks" have been felt far beyond the small fellowship groups, the havurot, that were the revival's first organized expression. From the sixties onward, there has emerged a Jewish student movement, a Jewish counterculture, Jewish feminism, Jewish radical groups, groups of gay Jews, new forms of Jewish mysticism and spirituality. Many members of the early havurot have become rabbis, scholars, university professors of Jewish studies, teachers, organizers, and writers.

The movement is small, admittedly, but as sociologist Steven M. Cohen, an enthusiastic participant in the revival, asserts: "For the continuity of the Jewish people, it isn't a question of numbers, but of cultural and communal creativity. During the 'golden age' in Spain, the total Jewish population was 55,000."

All the intertwined aspects of revival—innovative spirituality, reaffirmation of radical Jewish political commitment, incorporation of the demands of women and gays for recognition and respect within Judaism—are characterized by the hope of stimulating and invigorating the existing Jewish community. The revivalists affirm the possibility of having it all—tradition and innovation, history and modernity, a sense of community and individualism—and of having it enthusiastically, without defensiveness or compartmentalization.

The revival has certainly shown continuing energy and verve. What is in question is how widespread and powerful this revival is, what supports it, what restrains and limits its force and appeal, and how likely it is to profoundly affect the quality of Jewish-community life and culture in America.

6

The New Spirituality

It is not surprising, of course, that the experimental spirituality that marked the sixties counterculture should have had an impact on Judaism. The young Jewish intellectuals who formed the future elite of the Jewish community—the children of rabbis and scholars, the leaders of Jewish youth organizations, the students at Jewish schools such as Boston Hebrew Teachers' College, Gratz College in Philadelphia, or the Jewish Theological Seminary in New York, the campers and counselors of the Ramah camps of the Conservative synagogue movement—were truly American as well as deeply Jewish. They, like their less-involved peers, were drawn to the spirit of the sixties, in politics, culture, and religion. The sixties movements were characteristically antiestablishment, whatever the establishment. The activist youth of this period who had grown up with religion, or who felt strong tugs toward religion, nevertheless shared a general critique of established religious forms as routinized, impersonal, prosaic, and dry. They sought a new spirituality, something creative, spontaneous, at times mystical, based on a personal and direct relation to God. The Jewish form of this quest was first articulated in Boston during the mid-1960s, when the original Havurah was formed. In this intimate fellowship of shared countercultural values, young, deeply committed Jews, often anticipating lives as rabbis, scholars, and activists, laid out the paths of a new Jewish spirituality. It was their example that inspired the widespread, though less adventurous, synagogue havurot.

Michael Strassfeld, co-author of *The Jewish Catalogs*, the popular how-to books of practical Judaism, was a member of the first Havurah, and he has remained a Jewish-revival activist. He is currently the executive director of Ansche Chesed, a synagogue on the Upper West Side of Manhattan, described in *Seven Days* magazine as "one of the hippest synagogues around." The article notes that the synagogue's "current incarnation came out of a young, Jewish revival movement, and is known for its participatory self-driven spirit. At 10:00 A.M. each Saturday morning the four-ring synagogue . . . simultaneously offers a service for every sensibility—intellectual, spiritual, formal, informal." Strassfeld remembers the central concern of the early revivalists with the creation of an intimate and supportive community, an alternative to the established institutional forms.

"The Boston Havurah"

The *Catalog* to a certain extent came out of the Boston Havurah, the Havurat Shalom, which began in 1968 in Cambridge and then moved to Somerville. It was started to be two things: first, a small religious fellowship, where people could be Jewish together, celebrate holidays, and study texts, as well as being a fellowship in the interpersonal area; and second, it was supposed to be an alternative rabbinical seminary. Its full name was "Havurat Shalom Community Seminary." That part of it never really took off. Some of the core founding members were graduates of the Jewish Theological Seminary. They were dissatisfied with the education at the seminary, which they found very academic, cold and dry. One of our members said that when he was there, he never heard anyone talk about God. The important figure for these people when they were at the seminary was Abraham Joshua Heschel. He was a theologian and a philosopher interested in mysticism, as well as a political activist, involved in civil rights and anti–Vietnam War activities.

The Havurah was a strange mix—the social action of Reform Judaism, the critical scholarship of Conservative Judaism, and some of the fervor and style of Hasidism. At first it was just men who were admitted, and their wives came along. By the third year there was more consciousness; my wife and I had to be admitted individually, and single women were joining. It was during the third year that a woman led the service for the first time. There wasn't even a discussion about it. After a while, it became un-remarkable. We were egalitarian. As someone said at a conference, this was a place where the men held the babies and the women held the Torahs. Usually we had about twenty or thirty members. And there was a real ideal of community, of being friendly with everyone. We had potluck dinners every Friday night. For about six months we did co-counseling. There were also agenda-less meetings for people to express their feelings. We had several encounter groups to discuss personal relations.

Politically we were all part of left-wing culture. One "refugee" from a very conservative yeshiva in New York came, and it was culture shock for him in lots of ways. He liked Nixon because everyone at his yeshiva liked Nixon. For us he was very strange. Partly the Havurah was a Jewish version of sixties left-wing culture, but it was also an attempt to be more authentically Jewish. We were against conventional forms, and against professionalism, but not against traditional Judaism. What we were doing was just as authentic as Orthodoxy.

The center of the week for the Havurah was Shabbat. The morning service began at 10:30. The prayer room had no furniture, just cushions. People would sit silently; there was a no-talking rule. Then the service would be led by the person picked for that week; the style depended on the particular person. Sometimes people developed a theme, possibly tied to the Torah portion of the week or to a holiday. They would bring readings and talk about these as a focus. Or they might choose psalms or prayers connected to that theme. And there was a great deal of music—Hasidic melodies, wordless tunes, or songs that were tied to the theme. You were supposed to give the person who ran the service feedback later. I think this worked as well as it did because some of the founding people were very good at this. There were experts on liturgy, like Zalman Schachter. In the first year, there were a lot of creative services. I was there once when, instead of reading the regular Torah portion, the person doing the service read a D. H. Lawrence poem. Some people brought in breathing exercises or meditation. Over time, though, the services became more traditional, in the sense of using the traditional prayer book and Hebrew. The point is, people were willing to grapple with the tradition, to deal with the tension between observing the traditional rituals and being creative and different. In the early years, if we wanted to do something that the tradition prohibited—

saying Kaddish for a non-Jew like John Lennon, for example—we just said, "Oh, yes, that feels all right, let's do it." Later, we wanted to know if there was something in the Jewish tradition that gave us grounds for doing something like that. If the tradition said no, we might *still* do it, but we would always take the tradition into account. For us, tradition had a voice but not a veto. *Halachah* had a voice, but no veto.

The *Catalog* happened when some of us were talking about how we actually couldn't remember how to build a *sukkah,** and we fantasized about a book that would tell people how to do things. Then Richard Siegal, who coauthored the *Catalog* with my wife and me, did a master's thesis at Brandeis University about what a Jewish *Whole Earth Catalog* would be like. So we said, "Let's do it, just for our small circle." We put notes in Jewish student newspapers. Someone knew Chaim Potok, who was at the Jewish Publication Society, and he was important in supporting us and seeing our vision. The first one came out in late 1973, and no one expected what happened. There was a little story in the *New York Times,* which helped sell out the first edition of 20,000. By 1982 over 250,000 of the first catalog were sold, and over 100,000 of the second one, which came in 1976. The third one came out in 1982. Obviously it was the right time. There was a search for something beyond what people have now. There was a desire for more meaning in life, a look back to religion, to tradition. And there had been the Six-Day War, the rise of Jewish pride, a feeling of comfort with being openly Jewish, the idea of ethnicity, black pride, and the search for roots. A significant thing is that now havurot exist in a lot of synagogues. Our ideas have spread.

During the sixties, when the havurot began their "experimental spirituality," the counterculture at large emphasized originality, new modes of ritual. Like contemporary aesthetics with its shock tactics, the ritual sensibility of the new religious innovations strove for powerful effects to avoid the danger of routine and conformity and to convey the immediacy of experience.

Thus the creation of new ceremonies was favored over repetition

*A hut of wood and branches built as part of the celebration of the holiday of Sukkot to symbolize the temporary dwellings of the Israelites in the desert following the Exodus from Egypt.

of traditional ceremonies. The usual answer to the question "Why do we do this ritual this way?" is "It has always been done this way." But proponents of creative spirituality found this response inadequate. Within Christianity, the spirit of sixties innovation reached heights that are difficult—and to some of those who were involved, embarrassing—to recall in these cooler times. There were, for example, enthusiastic young Catholics who strove to incorporate the entire range of secular culture into their religious services, as illustrated by the following account of a ritual happening at a Catholic college in 1968:

> About forty persons have gathered for mass on a Sunday afternoon in the dining room of a large house that serves as one of the dormitories for a Catholic college. Homemade posters and banners hang on the walls; the dining room table has been converted into an altar; the priest wears a sports shirt, and some of the nuns present wear bermuda shorts: the Epistle is a passage from the *New York Times* (Sunday edition, of course); the Gospel is taken from the writing of Daniel Berrigan, with bongo drums beating in the background; a Beatles song serves as an Introit, and a partially clad woman student, who is an accomplished jazz dancer, cavorts about at the Offertory. The homily is a collective effort; at its beginning, several marijuana cigarettes are lighted and passed around, and almost all of those present will offer a few thoughts before or after taking a hit.

A Protestant expression of the same spirit of inclusive experimental spirituality, sixties-style, was described by Harvey Cox of the Harvard Divinity School, author of *The Secular City*, a best-selling theological manifesto calling for the incorporation of secular modernity into religion. "The symbolic treasures of the full sweep of human history are available to us, everything from the oldest cave drawing to the newest image of Utopian hope," Cox wrote. Putting his ideas into practice, Cox organized an "experimental liturgy" for Easter at a Boston discotheque. As a basis for the ceremony, Cox made an unusual choice: "We wanted to surround the colorful Byzantine Mass with participatory liturgical dance . . . with light-and-music collages, with physical encounter movements—and also somehow to bring those powerful Old Christian symbols of New Life and shared bread more directly into the service of human liberation."

Nearly two thousand people participated, painting peace signs, crosses, fishes, and assorted graffiti on each other's bodies. They drew scenes of war and death and taped these to the walls. Free-wheeling liturgical dancers dressed in black-and-white leotards enticed people into "sacred gesture and ritual motion." Cox observed: "People who had never danced in their lives stretched out arms and flexed legs and torsos. The lithe solemnity of the movements made me think we should get rid of pews forever. . . . In one group, a teen began humming 'Jesus Loves Me' and soon her whole arm-and-leg-enmeshed group began to hum with her." There were choruses from Bach's *Saint Matthew Passion,* a gospel reading, and Handel's "Hallelujah Chorus." After more jumping, hugging, and moaning, communion was celebrated by a Roman Catholic priest, an Episcopal priest, two ministers of the United Church of Christ, and Cox, an ordained Baptist minister. Then the Hindu mantra "OM" was chanted and people fed each other the communion elements. Finally, the ceremony ended as the participants gathered outside the building to greet the dawn, chanting to the accompaniment of the Beatles singing "Here Comes the Sun."

Havurah-style innovation, deplored by Jewish conservatives as the "greening of Judaism," seems quite restrained when compared to this Christian exuberance. Substituting a D. H. Lawrence reading for the Torah portion of the service is relatively stodgy. It is notable, however, that even among those who were leaders in the search for originality, innovation, and "play" in ritual and ceremony, there has been a retreat to a more traditional stance. Harvey Cox, for example, published a work in the mid-eighties much more sympathetic to traditional religious thought and ritual, and more in keeping with the post-sixties zeitgeist, which found that the old rituals worked better in creating the desired mood and tone. Michael Strassfeld noted this trend among the veterans of havurot as well. The "innovation" that seemed to be most satisfying in the long run has been the deliberate and self-conscious choosing of traditional liturgy and religious forms. Ceremonial "traditionality" seems most effective in creating a sense of the spiritual, possibly because, as with the new Orthodox, it satisfies the desire for authenticity.

The innovative spirit of the counterculture has not, however, been entirely superseded by a new appreciation of tradition. On the contrary, it has survived and gone far beyond the original havurah practices. Rabbi Zalman Schachter, the acknowledged inspiration of the liturgical creativity of the first Havurah and of the *Jewish Catalog* more than twenty years ago, is now the spiritual leader of a network of "New Age" Jewish groups. A scholar of Judaism, a rabbi, and a professor of religious studies at Temple University in Philadelphia, Schachter has often served as the Jewish representative at ecumenical New Age guru gatherings, appearing with Baba Ram Dass, the Tibetan lama Rimpoche, the poets and mystical searchers Allen Ginsberg and Robert Bly, and others. Schachter upholds an inclusive spiritual perspective, treating mystical Judaism as the Jewish version of a universal spiritual truth, which may be found as well in other spiritual traditions: Hinduism, Buddhism, Sufism, Gurdjieffism, and so on.

New Age Judaism melds the styles of "human potential" therapeutic psychology with an inclusive modernist interpretation of mysticaltexts and practices borrowed from a wide range of religious traditions. In a journalist's description of a Rosh Hashanah retreat held by B'nai Or, Schachter's group in Philadelphia, he is pictured as a "reincarnation of the Sufi saint Rumi." The article continues:

> As I get my first glimpse of him in the barn that serves as a synagogue, he sits cross-legged in a white flowing kaftan and white pants, a *girtel* around his waist and a white turban over his gray hair, with earlocks hanging down on either side of his vibrant robust face. His two-day Rosh Hashanah retreat has the emotional intensity of an encounter group marathon, and Schachter uses Gestalt techniques to shift figure and ground in our sense of what is real. But there are also moments of Eastern-style cross-legged mediation, a somber walk to the beat of a Zen drum down to a lake for Tashlikh, the casting out of sins, and even Jewish chanting and circle dancing around two men who do Sufi spinning.
>
> An equally wide range of non-Jewish spiritual influences is represented in the group around Schachter, though most are Jewish by birth. One man, a dentist in the orange shirt and trousers of a Swami, is on his way to Muktananda's ashram in India; a schoolteacher has done Transcendental Meditation; several people wear Hindu meditation beads; two men have come from a Gurdjieff community in West Virginia. Whatever their spiritual practices during most of the year, however, they come together as Jews for the High Holy Days, gathering around

Schachter because he is one of the few rabbis who is pleased to make use of so many varied energies and influences.

Out in Berkeley, California, a long-lasting and active group called the Aquarian Minyan traces its origins to the work of Schachter. It credits him with seeing the importance of making the Jewish mystical tradition available to people unaware that a rich thread of mystical thinking is part of traditional Judaic doctrine. The Minyan, inspired by Schachter, has developed "a style of celebration at once innovative and spontaneous, with emphasis on singing, movement, chanting, storytelling, and sharing." The structure of the Friday-evening service and its underlying intent remain, but the specific details are decided by the worshipers who are present on any given occasion. "We believe that each one of us can be a vehicle for the Light, and that each can be a holy teacher and a holy student to one another at different times," declares an early credo of the Aquarian Minyan.

The spirit of the Minyan is conveyed by a flyer describing a summer program in the lovely Mendocino countryside of Northern California. "THE JOYS OF JEWISHING! IT'S FUN TO BE JEWISH IN THE COUNTRY! Explore your Jewish roots—a vision of the new age." The flyer goes on to invite the reader to join the Minyan and its teachers for a variety of activities, "new vessels" for the old faith, including "Hasidic Music and Dance, Social Awareness, Nature Study, Torah—Then and Now, Sensory Awareness and Movement, Massage, Davening, and Meditation."

The members of the Minyan are aware that from traditional Judaic standpoints their activities are questionable, even objectionable. In an irate letter to the editor, a traditional Jew, offended by the content of the Minyan bulletin, especially by a cartoon of Santa Claus as a Jew in *tefillin* and by the frequent references to Buddhism, Sufism, and Christianity, chastized the Minyan for not recognizing the essential difference of Judaism: "Well, Chanukah, it happens, is the celebration of the separation of the Jews from forms of worship that dominated the culture of the time. The Hellenistic age was a vibrant, cultured one. It had much to recommend it. Many cultures and religions have much to recommend them, too. But history has shown that the Jews must differentiate, define, and remain true to their own ways of worship."

The reply from a Minyan leader underlined the idea of universal spiritual truth and the Minyan's commitment "to emphasize the things that these religions have in common, rather than dwelling only on the differences." He explained: " 'Aquarian' refers not to a short-lived cultural fad, but to the dawning of a New Age, a time of great harmony among all peoples, in which the perfection of the individual is seen as commensurate with the progress of the human family. To this end, we accept any person who has the intention of davvening with us as counting toward a minyan, and encourage contributions toward an ideal of service, worship and teaching from all interested participants."

In line with sixties countercultural ideals, the Aquarian Minyan makes a deliberate effort to combine social awareness and spiritual concerns. During a Minyan Yom Kippur ceremony, the traditional list of sins for which each Jew must ask forgiveness was expanded to include sins appropriate to contemporary life. "Forgive us," the group reads in unison:

> for the sins we have committed before you and before us by being so preoccupied with ourselves that we ignored the social world in which we live.
> And for the sins we have committed by being so directed towards the political and social world that we ignored our own spiritual development.
> And for the sins we have committed by participating in a racist society and not dedicating more energy to fighting it.
> And for the sins we have committed by not putting more energy into the struggle against proliferation of nuclear energy throughout the society.

During this portion of the service, after a time of directed meditation, congregants were also asked to name personal sins, in their own words. One woman spoke of not having worked hard enough for world peace. Another was sorry that she had not been really supportive to a friend suffering from a serious illness. And one man, in perhaps the ultimate expression of a sensibility particularly associated with California—though hardly with Judaism—regretted "not having allowed myself all the pleasures I could have."

The membership of the organized New Age Jewish groups remains very small, but Zalman Schachter sees a meaning beyond numbers. "We're like the antennae of a bug. We don't know where we're going, but the rest of Judaism is following. . . . Monotheism was a big step out of polytheism. But now, with our increased access to higher states of consciousness, we have to evolve to pantheism."

As a vision, this is dubious. Aside from mystical intuition, there is no evidence that normative mainstream Judaism is following— or even noticing—the New Age movement. But the principle of free incorporation of forms that the Havurah began, and that groups like the Aquarian Minyan have pushed to an extreme, remains very broadly accepted. In fact, in a characteristically modern move, one need not even be part of a group to apply it. Now it is considered the right of individuals to shape and reshape traditional forms in whatever way suits them in order to construct the spiritual, ritual experiences that they find personally meaningful. "Do-it-yourself" kits like *The Jewish Catalog* enable anyone to put together his or her own occasional ceremony and ritual. There need be no authority in the realm of the spirit and no group need support the choice of ritual and ceremony: a subjective sense of truth and authenticity is the only required guide to proper practice. This spirit is much more widespread than the organized groups themselves. But by the nature of the case, we can cite only anecdotal evidence of the myriad variations that are being enacted in Jewish homes around the country.

Linda Shulman* teaches art history at a college in Pennsylvania. Her specialty is medieval Christian art. Long active in radical feminist politics, she had not continued her parents' mainstream Jewishness and returned to Jewish practice only after her marriage and the birth of her son, Joshua, and her daughter, Beth. Linda Shulman belongs to no group; she is her own havurah and her own *Jewish Catalog*.

"My Rituals"

I think that creating new ceremonies is something people have to do, because the old ones aren't pertinent anymore. New rituals have always been created. I can take what I want from the Jewish tradition, and add new things. As I get older I hope I will understand more and more, but at my age I already think I have a

*Pseudonym.

certain amount of wisdom about things, and no one is going to tell me what to do about ritual. I don't think there is an authority, not in the synagogue. I don't belong to a synagogue. I don't have a need for it in my life.

I think there is something positive about the sacred, about mystery. My grandmother was very spiritual. Every act in her kitchen was ritualistic. She wouldn't let me salt the chicken for fear I would do something wrong. When I teach about religious rites in my art-history classes, I always think about everything she had to do, how much knowledge was necessary. I feel lucky that I had someone in my life who had a feeling for the sacred, a sacredness that was in the home, not in some outside place. And I want to re-create that in my home, for my children. Before my children were born, I didn't do anything. Now I do a lot. I know all the holidays and I do things at home. On Friday night I make a good dinner, challah, wine, we sing all the blessings, we have guests, Jewish and non-Jewish. On Hanukkah I tell the children about the meaning of light back in earliest times, with the meaning of the Maccabees imposed thousands of years later. I dramatize the darkness, how scary it was, how happy people are when they see that it isn't going to get darker and darker and darker, and how important it was to make sure that it happened every year.

I'm excited now thinking about Beth's bat mitzvah. I've tried to suggest to her that she can do whatever she wants. She can decide what kinds of songs she wants—I don't use the word "liturgy"—and what kinds of things she wants me to cook. We're going to have it in my aunt's house, and we're going to have all women reading the Torah and women doing the service. This is what she really wants. It is going to be the women's side, the spirit of my grandmothers. We're going to decide what kinds of clothes to make. Both my grandmothers were seamstresses, and that is a Neolithic craft. You know, women have always worked with cloth, and it hasn't survived to be part of the history of art. The beautiful things that people wore—all that was done by women. But it was perishable. We're going to make altar covers and challah covers. It has got to be a ceremony that Beth feels comfortable with. I don't care about the authority of a synagogue. This is for Beth, just as Joshua's bar mitzvah was for him.

About God I take an agnostic stance. The way God has been visualized in the various mythologies is nothing more than a projection of our imaginations. I can't encompass the origin of all things, life, death, first causes. But this doesn't interfere with how I do my rituals. They are all part of my culture; they give interest and beauty to my life.

The spirit of individual creativity can possess even someone brought up in a framework of strict traditionalism. Daniel Jacobs* was born in Los Angeles thirty-five years ago. His parents are Holocaust survivors, and his father is a prominent administrator of Jewish education. He has been involved full-time in Jewish activities since his student days, and he is active in efforts to bring about Jewish-Palestinian understanding and peace in Israel.

"My Prayers"

Our home had a pattern of classical traditional practice—no travel or writing or handling money on the Sabbath, observance of all the holidays. My father prayed every morning. When I went to college, I wore a yarmulka all the time. I ate kosher, and I prayed every morning. I don't think my father really paid attention to what he was doing when he prayed every day, and I would have become just like him if I hadn't studied religion—I have a B.A. in the history of religion—and gotten into Buddhism, Hinduism, and other spiritual things for a while. After that I couldn't keep on just doing the prayers over and over again without paying attention. There are two concepts in Jewish prayer: *kevah,* the discipline, doing it over and over, and *kavanah,* the intention. I couldn't do it only with *kevah,* and I had no *kavanah.* I wanted to have a spiritual discipline in my life, but I had to change the way I was praying in order to continue praying. So now, sometimes, I put on a record and listen. There are a couple of songs I've been able to pray to: a song called "Long Promised Road," by the Beach Boys, and some James Taylor songs. Recently I've also liked to think about some good aspect of life in praying, so I listen to the old John Lennon song that he sings to his son, and I think about the relationship of a father and a child. I don't use the songs for background music; I give my attention to them and to what they are leading me to think about. I wear my *tefillin.* Sometimes I dance around, with my

*Pseudonym.

headphones on so I won't disturb the people next door or my roommates. I also sometimes do this praying to Dvořák, to a bluegrass version of one of the *Slavonic Dances.* I listen and either conduct or dance around. I mean, I really jump all over the place.

The woman thing has hit me hard. I've davened a lot less, recently. I just can't accept it. Sometimes I change the gender of God. The other day, I started to pray, and didn't have the motivation, so I wrote this letter to the prayer book. I think I wanted to focus my feeling on relationships between men and women. First I listened to an old Donovan song called "I Like You." Then I wrote this letter: "There is nothing in this prayer book to express my direct connection to another human being— my love for a woman, my sadness at our separation; my love for a man, my need for companionship. . . . God up there, come down here for a song and a tear."

I don't belong to a synagogue. I usually pray here on Friday nights. When I have guests over, we do the blessings around the table, and sing the songs. I've never been a big synagogue-goer; I have trouble with the melodies—every week the same melodies that were written hundreds of years ago—and there is never much creativity in the service. I'd rather sit at home and pray to different melodies to myself and add things and be creative.

The creative spirit of revival has not been without harsh critics within Jewish life. Take the response to *The Jewish Catalog,* a graphic expression of the revival spirit. Rather than welcoming the enormous sales of the *Catalog* as a sign that radical reform of Judaism into a contemporary idiom can appeal to people who otherwise would remain alienated from the Jewish community and Judaism, *Commentary* magazine, the most prominent Jewish intellectual journal, disliked the *Jewish Catalog* intensely. For the author of *Commentary*'s attack on *The Jewish Catalog*—Professor Marshall Sklare of Brandeis University, a prominent sociologist of American Jewry—the spirit of creative Judaism exemplified by the *Catalog* and by the havurot did not signify resurgence; rather it represented an unacceptable incorporation of a particularly obnoxious set of modern, secular, liberal values into Judaism. In his review, Sklare deplored the *Catalog*'s emphasis on the aesthet- ic dimension and its slighting of the ethical demands of Judaic doctrine. He argued that Judaism has a strong and coherent tradition and a clear set of theological doctrines and ritual practices, expounded and justified in classic texts, and that any reform that ignores these must be untrue to traditional Judaism, its ethos and values. Not surprisingly, this newest wave of reform, which draws from the most radical cultural trends of contemporary secular life and then claims that such borrowings are either consonant with or even inherent in Jewish tradition, is particularly galling to conservative defenders of the faith.

The conservative critique is rather like a sledgehammer trying to pulverize a sponge. The arguments are learned and well-founded, but they have practically no effect because they have no serious intellectual opposition. Neither the elite nor the masses who have become more involved in Jewish assertion through the creative style of the revival can adequately refute arguments about the untraditional tone and content of much of the Jewishness re-created by Jewish countercultural groups or by the unknown numbers of individuals who are "doing their own Jewish thing" informally, at home alone or with friends.

But what of it? The people involved are clearly committed to modern values, often of the most liberal and radical sort. They are humanists, which is why they feel little need to look to traditional values. The young Jews attracted to Jewish activity in this new style already have firm ethical and social values and outlooks; they do not need ancient Jewish texts and rabbinical interpretations to tell them what are the proper moral positions on civil rights or civil liberties or ecology or marriage and divorce or sexuality or sexual preference or anything else. They might want to affirm that the values they hold are truly Jewish, at least in spirit; and they might like to see those values reflected in some Jewish song or story or legend. They respect the idea of the "Jewish tradition," but as a reservoir of rituals, images, symbols, ceremonies and customs, holidays and festivals, not as divinely given law or as the authoritative determinant of cultural and ethical positions. Jewish traditions and ceremonies can be used in many ways. Aesthetically, they are lovely and moving rites of passage. Anthropologically, they give a sense of roots, the power of tradition, the connection to a community. Politically, they offer a historic Jewish heritage of social justice and sympathy for the oppressed. Therapeutically, the self-esteem they inspire can combat the self-hatred caused by anti-Semitism. And, of course, Judaism can also serve religious purposes, for those who still want that.

But the revival perspective does not acknowledge any authority that can determine which use of Jewish ritual is legitimate. In the history of religion, we can find numerous instances where disputes over the minute specifics of practice and ritual resulted in murderous struggle. But in the modernist perspective, it is the entire category of ritual that is valued, more than any specific content of the category. What is wanted is a "ritual experience," and it is characteristic of our eclectic times that one can have such experiences with a wide range of rituals, even those from cultures and religions far removed from one's own.

The angry and learned arguments of Sklare and others miss the point when they complain that much of what is incorporated into revivalist Judaism does not square with what the Jewish tradition and Jewish religion really are. The response to such arguments would be, typically: there are parts of Judaism that need to be changed because they are not relevant to us, or because they express outdated, inappropriate, or wrong values (though values perhaps explicable by the situations in which Jews lived back then). The high-minded accusation by conservatives that this way of treating religion and religious ritual is conceptually incoherent also misses its target. Since creative revivalists hold firmly to the basic modernist belief in the right of the individual to choose his or her own forms, their answer to the critic who says, "But this is not *real* Judaism," is, "Well, it's not what *you* mean by Judaism," or, with somewhat more sophistication, "Maybe that's what Judaism meant in the past, but much has changed, and Judaism should too."

The reason for bothering to create new forms is that the connection to heritage, to tradition, to the sense of a people and a history is perceived to be psychologically and spiritually rewarding. The incorporation of the new can cause some tension, especially for those who are knowledgeable about historic Judaism, but given enough latitude of interpretation—and that latitude is claimed without hesitation by the revival—it is always possible to achieve the happy inclusion.

There is no doubt that the creative energy of the new spirituality has had an effect on organized Judaism. Earlier we noted the proliferation of havurah-style groups within mainstream Reform and Conservative synagogues (though many of these, of course, do not reproduce the spirit of the original fellowship). A look at active Hillel groups on campuses around the country and at many of the synagogues that have been able to attract young, well-educated American Jews shows a similar openness to innovation. A recent advertisement for the Passover Seder sponsored by the thriving San Francisco Jewish Community Center, for instance, features the catchwords "innovative," "creative," and "participatory."

But can such creative modernizing stem or perhaps even reverse the drift away from Jewish involvement? Hopeful Jewish sociologists emphasize that the number of young Jewish-Americans expressing a desire to continue some active form of Jewish participation is larger than would have been predicted when the revivalists began their activities in the sixties, and that the new spirituality can help inspire a renewal of commitment to the Jewish community. They point out that traditional Judaism would never have drawn the hundreds of thousands of *Jewish Catalog* buyers who are delighted to have a little Jewish tradition and ceremony in their lives now and then. They point out that creative spirituality makes it possible for people to participate who might otherwise have completely forsaken religious Jewishness. But even these stalwarts admit that the number of those whose commitment has gone beyond occasional ceremonial observance remains small.

Creativity is problematic as a basis for establishing stable institutions and providing continuity over generations. The requirement that rituals and ceremonies "work" in a subjective sense can be difficult to fulfill (and even harder to pass on), with standards varying from individual to individual, and from time to time for the same individual. A religious commitment based on individual creativity and choice is inherently fragile, since it implies that if something does not work, then it can and should be dropped; and this modernist perspective, which validates the tendency toward privatization and individual combinations of bits and pieces, cannot but undermine the creation of enduring communal bonds.

7

The Jewish Radical

In 1980, a group calling itself the Committee for a New Jewish Agenda held a founding convention for a national organization of left-liberal Jews, which came to be known as New Jewish Agenda. According to Agenda's statement of purpose, "Authentic Jewish life demands serious and consistent attention to *Tikkun Olam* [the repairing of human society and the world]." In more mundane political terms, this meant a commitment to left-liberal political and cultural perspectives. Expressing the same spirit, in 1986 a journal called *Tikkun* began publication in California. It achieved wide visibility and a distribution of 40,000 copies within a year. An account of the journal's progress in New York *Newsday* noted, "To many of *Tikkun*'s readers and writers, the magazine represents nothing less than a resurgence of liberal Jewish opinion at a time when the era of Ronald Reagan and his once unchallenged popularity is drawing to a close." According to Michael Lerner, the editor of *Tikkun*, the historical relation of American Jews to "liberal and progressive" ideals had been blurred by McCarthyism, the cold war, and reaction to the radical movements of the 1960s. Like New Jewish Agenda, the journal called for a renewal of a Jewishness that placed liberal and radical political conceptions at its center, a set of values that assimilation and prosperity seemed to have obscured in the recent evolution of the American Jewish community.

The notion that connection to liberal and leftist perspectives is either a "new" Jewish agenda or one in need of resurgence is historically ironic. The prominence of Jewish participation on the

Left has been a commonplace observation in the study of European and American radical movements over the past century. Most recently, during the radical sixties, there was a disproportionately high representation of Jewish youth in the civil-rights movement and the New Left. It was widely noted that two of the three civil-rights workers who were murdered at the beginning of the Mississippi "Freedom Summer" of 1964 were Jewish; and the predominance of young Jews in the original membership of Students for a Democratic Society (SDS) is extensively documented. Arthur Liebman, in his study of Jewish connections with the Left, noted that "in the early to mid-1960s, during which time membership in SDS rose from 250 to more than 30,000, the percentage of Jews within it was considerable, ranging from 30 to 50 percent." At the 1966 SDS convention, 46 percent of the delegates who identified themselves as having a particular religious background were Jewish; this figure certainly underestimates the number of Jews, since specifying "none" for religious membership was considered to be more frequent for Jews than others. Liebman also notes that social scientists looking at the New Left broadly gave estimates that "students of Jewish background constituted anywhere from 50 to 70 percent of the New Left."

It was not uncommon for Jewish activists to locate the imperative they felt about commitment to radical social change in their vision of Jewishness and the Jewish historical experience. The identification of a radical ideal with Jewish tradition seemed so obvious a notion that no argument was needed. Mickey Flacks is a health worker in Santa Barbara, California. She and her husband, sociologist Richard Flacks, were founding members of SDS. In recent years while maintaining her involvement in progressive politics, she has become active in the local Jewish community.

"In Our Genes"

I was a "red-diaper baby" of the Yiddish variety, a subset of all red-diaper babies, even in New York. My parents were immigrants who came to this country in their young adulthood. They were Yiddish-speaking all their lives. They worked in the garment trades. My father came from Poland with a union card. Both my parents were deeply involved in Communist Party efforts in the union movement.

My father was from an Orthodox traditional home but had been a freethinker, even in Poland. My mother was born in Odessa in 1905. She was born in a basement, because that is where my grandmother went to take shelter when the battleship *Potemkin* was shelling the city in July 1905; so she was really born right in the middle of it. She was also from a traditional Orthodox home, but it was already beginning to break down. My mother came here in 1922, after the Revolution and the Civil War, to bring over my grandmother and a younger brother. My mother planned to go back on the next boat; she had no desire to come here. When they came, they found that not only was my grandfather living behind a laundry, which they knew, but he also seemed to be living with a laundress, which they hadn't known. So my mother had to stay to maintain the family—herself, her mother, and the younger brother.

My parents met and did *not* marry—because they believed that their union did not require the sanction of either church or state—and in 1925 they began to "cohabit." That was the date that we later celebrated in 1950 as their twenty-fifth anniversary.

I was born in 1940, and grew up in the northeast Bronx, near, but not in, "the Coops," the cooperative housing project built by the Communist Party in 1926. The Coops were mixed, with a large percentage of Jews. There were some blacks; it was probably one of the few integrated housing projects in the whole country then. The Coops were a focal point for a lot of the secular Jewish activities. Our Yiddish school was located in the basement. The basement was designed by the architect for political and communal activity; so to say we met in a basement isn't what it sounds like. There were classrooms and auditoriums and all kinds of stuff in the basement.

Yiddish classes started when I was about seven: four afternoons, an hour a day, and Friday the hour was reserved for singing. And on Sunday morning, we had drama, led by people who had been in the Artef—the Yiddish Workers' Theater—which was quite popular in the thirties. It was very big on performance, which was a way of continuing to relate to the parents. The children performed for the parents, the parents came to concerts and evenings of all sorts and saw firsthand that the children were maintaining the language and the culture. They could see it in the performances, and that remained important all the way through. The curriculum in elementary school was Yiddish grammar (we learned to read and write Yiddish just as you would any language), Jewish history, and the Bible (a secular interpretation, of course). In the high-school years, we had literature classes, where we read the classics: Mendele, Peretz, Sholom Aleichem, and the American proletarian Yiddish poets.

At school and also at home there was constant opposition to nationalism, Zionism, chauvinism of all kinds. Jews were not a "chosen people." They were a people like any other, and like all others they had their own history, tradition, language, and culture that we, because we were Jews, should know about. There was no specialness, except the way it snuck in was that Jews had a "mission." The fact that we were Jewish Communists was not accidental; somehow it all fit together. Being a Communist and being a Jew were part of the same ineffable thing. The connection wasn't something we thought about at the time, it was just a given. My own kids have the same feeling. My sons believed that there are Jews and there are Republicans; those are the two groups in the world. When they first encountered Jews they considered reactionary, they were shocked. They didn't quite know how to deal with it.

It was always a concern to us how to pass on our identity as Jews and as radicals to our children. When you live in a place like Santa Barbara, especially if you have kids, identity becomes a crucial issue. It never was for me earlier. In my childhood, the whole world was Jewish. In Santa Barbara, it's not. So I started a little secular Sunday school here. I began with a bar mitzvah class. When my elder son was ten or eleven, he had some friends who were the same age, whose parents were unhappy with the temple and were clearly not going to enroll their kids there because they didn't believe in it. The class met weekly to discuss Jewish things. And I taught it, trying to get the kids involved in their own biographies, roots, family histories, to give them a little flavor of Yiddish, music, some songs, the holidays. I was in it for my own kids, and to show others that it could be done. We did our son's bar mitzvah ourselves in the backyard. I invited the Jewish community, people who I wanted to show that they too could do it themselves, for their kids. The son of a friend of mine had a temple bar mitzvah, and I went to see what in the ritual I could rip off. And there was very little, actually, that interested me. The only thing I really liked was when the grandfather handed the Torah to the grandson. So we decided that we would hand not the Five Books of Moses, but five books, literally or figuratively, five works of culture that symbolized what our family was handing down to the next generation. We presented our elder son, Charles Wright Flacks (C. Wright Flacks, named for both C. Wright Mills and my father, Charles), a book by Sholom Aleichem in translation, a science encyclopedia from his paternal grandparents, a Benny Goodman record from his kid brother, because he played the clarinet, a plaque of the scissors my father used in his work—my mother presented this plaque essentially in the name of the international proletariat; it was quite a moving speech— and Dick and I gave him a manuscript written by Tom Hayden, actually his master's thesis, on C. Wright Mills. So this was our legacy to our son. And we had a party, which a bar mitzvah is. And our sons and their friends felt that this was a real bar mitzvah, just as much as anything that happens in a synagogue.

I know most Jews don't make the Jewish-radical connection as explicitly as we do, like in Chuck's bar mitzvah, but it's there anyway. I don't know where it comes from, quite frankly. Somehow it comes with mother's milk. Because the institutions that most American Jews grew up with are not the ones I grew up with; the suburban temple was no different than the Episcopalian church down the block. But somehow, there is something different. I remember in SDS keeping count of the number of Jews on the national council. And the day that the Jews were no longer the majority, I thought we had truly entered a new phase in American radicalism. Most of the other Jews in the group didn't come from my secular Yiddishist background; but the New Left clearly was founded and peopled by Jews—no question. Even now, the statistics still show that Jews are second only to blacks in their support for Democrats, and given their class situation, it is even more striking than blacks. There is something that works still, despite everything. For all I know, it may even be in the theology, in the democratic spirit of Jewish theology, that there is no intervener between a Jew and his God, that there is no church body, no priest class. All of those things may play a role in the Jewish consciousness in ways we don't understand. Maybe it's because, just as we carry Tay-Sachs disease, in our genes, we carry who we are and who we come from—unless it's destroyed by a Holocaust. It persists, it remains.

————

Mickey Flacks grew up in the immigrant Yiddish socialist milieu, which was adamantly anti-Zionist as well as antireligious. But, as she herself points out, such a background was in no way typical of most of the young Jews who were swept up in the political and cultural activism of the New Left from the late 1960s through the 1970s; nor does it explain the rise of a Jewish Left during this period. Rather, as African-American, Hispanic, and Asian-American radicals formed youth organizations that focused on the conditions peculiar to their own groups, small numbers of Jewish radicals also decided to form ethnically particular Jewish New Left collectives.

Reflecting the transformation of American Jewish life since the founding of Israel, the great majority of these groups were Zionist, in one form or another. The tradition of the Labor Zionist youth movements still flickered within the Jewish community, and it was the nationalist Jewish vision, matching the larger emphasis within the Left on "national-liberation" consciousness, that provided the ideological basis for the explicitly Jewish New Left groups. A network of radical Zionist groups emerged nationally, often on campuses with relatively large numbers of Jewish students and typically located in cities with significant Jewish communities. These groups maintained a dual radical commitment. As New Leftists, they were actively engaged in the political struggles of the day: demonstrating against the Vietnam War, marching for civil rights, urging radical university reform, supporting the general tone of cultural experimentation and liberation. Yet as socialist Zionists—inspired by the nationalist vision of a Jewish people in its own land, creating its own culture and history—they were committed to building their future in Israel. Accordingly, they were intensely involved with Israeli realities as well as with the immediate American political scene, and they wanted to see their New Left ideals manifested in their prospective homeland as well.

David Biale was born in 1949 in Los Angeles. He lives in Berkeley with his Israeli wife, Rachel, and their two small children. The author of a major study on the great German-Israeli scholar Gershom Sholem, he is a professor of Jewish history at the Graduate Theological Union.

"A Place on the Left"

My father had been active in Hashomer Hatzair, the far-left Zionist youth movement, when he was a young man in Poland. He came to Berkeley in 1928 to study agriculture so he could go to Palestine as a "pioneer," but he met and married my mother, who was born in Boston, the child of immigrants. They stayed here in California. My father was involved in a Labor Zionist intellectual circle in Los Angeles, formed to support the work of Hashomer Hatzair in Palestine. The group was Stalinist back then, like Hashomer, though they would sort of deny it now.

I was sent to a synagogue Sunday school, but this lasted only a very short time. I ended up having a bar mitzvah at home, after my father and I studied the Hebrew together. Since I had lived for a year in Israel when I was nine—my father was a biologist working for the UN then—I knew some Hebrew already. But I didn't really have much Jewish education. Most of my friends in high school were Jewish, and there was a sense of ethnic identity, but the Jewish thing was pretty unimportant. There was the sense that the smart kids in the school were the Jews and the Japanese-Americans, but that's about it.

The Six-Day War had an impact on me. That summer, I worked at a camp run by Young Judaea, the largest of the Zionist youth organizations, and this affected me a lot. There was obviously the heightened sense about Israel, and I had a strong feeling of connection. I began college at Harvard that fall, but I had a bad time there and transferred out to Berkeley, for personal and political reasons. I became very active Jewishly, and during the next year, 1969, I got involved in starting the Radical Jewish Union. The RJU people weren't spiritual, like the Havurah. Some had very good Jewish educations, but the flavor was political and Zionist. Actually, maybe 25 to 30 percent of that group ended up moving to Israel. We carved out a place on the Left for a radical Jewish ethnic identity. This was happening in other places too—Seattle, Boston, New York, Los Angeles. There was a network of these groups, journals being published and exchanged. There was the overlap with the Havurah in that there was the

Jewish cultural-religious context. We would meet for Shabbat, with a dinner—which was the main thing—and something of a service. But we were very much against the New Age stuff, like Zalman Schachter. There was definitely a nonflakey quality, and the people have remained that way to this day. Our Berkeley journal, the *Jewish Radical*, doesn't have any of that New Age spiritual stuff. I personally had been attracted to some of the spiritual concerns, and I even did some pretty traditional things, like Yom Kippur, with fasting and everything—but that was short-lived for me.

When I went back to Israel for half of 1973, I went to a desert kibbutz and I got involved in Siach, which was the fledging Israeli "New Left." I went to a demonstration in Tel Aviv that was broken up by Betar, the Likud youth group, and it was scarier than being at People's Park here in Berkeley, with those guys beating up on us. I went to a border kibbutz in the Jordan Valley because I wanted to see what the "war of attrition" was like. I read that this kibbutz was being shelled, and I thought, I need some excitement. And sure enough, the first night there, we were shelled, and I thought, I guess I don't need the excitement after all. But it did ground me politically. Even though we were being shelled by the PLO, it didn't move me to the right; it moved me more to the left. And on that kibbutz I met my wife.

During the next couple of years, I got married, did a doctorate in Jewish history at UCLA, and was very active in the RJU. During this time, we thought we would be going back to Israel. We were part of a group—a *garin*—that formed to go to Kibbutz Gezer, a young kibbutz with lots of Americans, mainly from Habonim, the mainstream Labor Zionist youth group. There are a lot of those Americans leaving the kibbutz and Israel now. We dropped out of the group after a couple of years, when it became clear we wanted to be in an academic world, but we continued to go through phases of wondering whether we should live in Israel. The question seems settled now.

I feel pretty alienated from the organized Jewish community, and I find it difficult to form ties to organized Jewish life. For nine years, I taught in Binghamton, New York, at the SUNY campus, and we had no connection at all to the Jewish community there. Berkeley has enough people with my perspective, so I can live comfortably as a Jew. The situation fits me politically and intellectually. I don't belong to a synagogue, and I never will. We light Shabbat candles and have some other rituals at home. We even bake challah—Rachel's challah recipe is in Mollie Katzen's *Moosewood Cookbook*. And we do holidays with our Jewish friends who want to celebrate, but aren't affiliated with synagogues.

My commitments, Jewish and political, are very personal. I think I understand how they grew out of my background. I feel that I have solved my identity questions, as a secular Jew. There is something about that Jewish-identity that drives me, and that motivates my professional and intellectual work. But I don't feel this is something my children need to do. If my kids decided that the Jewish-identity part wasn't actively important, that would be OK. I don't know really how I'd feel if it actually happened, and I would be disturbed if it came from bad personal relations with me; but if they just didn't have any real interest in it, I think that's all right. Most of the parents in the all-day Jewish school where one of our kids goes—it has all kinds of Jews and does Hebrew pretty well, and that matters to us—would say that they are sending them to the school so that they'll have a strong Jewish identity and won't assimilate and won't intermarry. In our family, we say that being Jewish is important, but so are other things. And the kids will have to make their own decisions and integrations, and some things will be dropped.

In the Radical Jewish Union, people had the sense of a connection between being Jewish and being radical. They felt an affinity with the radical Jewish movements that had grown up in the past. I remember that a lot of us had the same picture of Ber Borochov, a theoretician of Labor Zionism who had combined Zionism and Marxism, arguing that the Jews should go through their own class struggle and that Jewish workers should win their own revolution against Jewish capitalists. We identified with those earlier Jewish radicals, and we wrote about that turn-of-the-century radicalism in our journal. There was a real interest in Moses Hess, a colleague of Marx's who had the idea that Judaism was the original source of socialist visions. Our central concern was to establish the legitimacy of ethnic Jewish radical politics, just as other ethnic radicals were doing. But I think the Jewish student movement of that time was somewhat different in emphasis from New Jewish Agenda or *Tikkun*. Although all the different strands of ideas about Jews and radicalism were there, the idea that Jewishness was the *source* of one's radicalism was not really central. As I understood it, it was more a matter of compatibility than of essence.

I have two sisters. One is in Chabad, in London. She went into it here in Berkeley. She's been in it for ten years and is married, with three kids. My other sister is married to a Chicano construction worker, lives in the desert outside LA, and has no interest in either Jewish or leftist political things. Both their lives are rejections of what our home was like, whereas I'm basically replicating my father's position. We all gathered in Los Angeles last summer when my father was dying. There were these three Hasidic kids, and my Berkeley kids, and these two half-Chicano kids. It was crazy.

For New Left Jewish groups like the Radical Jewish Union, as well as for the Old Left milieu of Mickey Flacks's youth, the connection of Jewish identity and radical commitment was deeply felt and even articulated as doctrine. As one group, the Jewish Liberation Project, declared, "True commitment to the Jewish tradition necessitates participation in revolutionary struggles." Such absolute readings of Jewish tradition were not universally accepted even within the world of radical Jewish New Left groups; as David Biale recalls, there were radical Jewish activists who did not see the main source of their own political commitments in the Jewish tradition per se. But even for them, there was certainly the assumption of a historical and moral connection between Jewishness and radical commitment.

This sense that there is something deep in the tradition that makes liberalism, radicalism, and a commitment to social justice the birthright of Jews is only the latest version of a central conviction about the nature of Jewishness that, over the last hundred years, has been articulated so often and forcefully as to have achieved mythic status. What is mythic is not the connection of Jewishness with leftist and liberal movements, but the explanation of that connection by means of an essentially progressive Jewish identity. This explanation, which cites a passionate striving for a just society, often in opposition to the existing state, finds its sources in the words of the ancient Prophets, in the Talmudic prohibitions against the pursuit of power, fame, and wealth, and in the Torah value of charity, which is supposed to make Jews especially sensitive to the plight of the poor and unfortunate and especially responsive to proposals for social reform.

An early political creator of the myth was Moses Hess, a socialist philosopher, friend and coworker of Marx and Engels. In *Rome and Jerusalem*, published in 1862, Hess advanced the idea that the Jewish religion, with its denial of castes and classes, was the foundation of all egalitarianism and socialism. Judaism was the true source of the noblest social movements of modern times. This vision of the progressive essence of Judaism finds a later and more illustrious exponent in Albert Einstein, who himself looms large in contemporary Jewish mythmaking as part of that trinity of thinkers—Marx–Freud–Einstein—named with pride as representative of some particularly Jewish quality of mind and spirit. Einstein himself states part of the myth quite strikingly: "The bond which has united the Jews in the course of thousands of years, and unites them also today, is first of all, the democratic ideal of social justice, with the addition of mutual help and tolerance among all human beings." A variation on this is the "messianic people" image, the claim that the Jews are "chosen" to carry a message of the highest social ethics to the world at large.

Certainly, the facts require an explanation. The association of Jews and liberalism in recent American history has been so clear as to become a cliché. Jews of an older generation will remember their enthusiasm for Franklin D. Roosevelt. Jews not only overwhelmingly supported the Democratic Party, but were part of its left wing, in favor of civil rights, internationalism, fair employment practices, unions, Social Security, national health insurance, and other major welfare initiatives—all the most "socialistic" parts of the New Deal. In the 1956 presidential election, a Republican landslide with Eisenhower at the peak of his popularity, Jews voted much more Democratic than would be expected considering the relatively affluent social and economic status they had achieved as a group by then. Identifying with the underdog, Jews were Democrats as surely as they were Brooklyn Dodger fans. (Earl Shorris dedicates his book, *Jews Without Mercy*, —a passionate attack on the newly prominent Jewish neoconservatives whom he sees as betraying Jewish ethics—to the memory of his father, who "opposed Communism, Fascism, and the New York Yankees.")

In 1960, when the electorate chose the moderate liberal John Kennedy over Richard Nixon by a slender margin of 50.1 percent to 49.9 percent, the Jewish vote was 82 percent for Kennedy. Again, in 1964, over 90 percent of Jews voted for Lyndon Johnson; obviously, Barry Goldwater's Jewish ancestry did not win him much Jewish support. The Jewish vote for Hubert Humphrey in 1968, even with the antiwar sentiments that worked against him, remained very high, at 80 percent. George McGovern, in a Democratic debacle, got 66 percent of the Jewish vote and Jimmy Carter, in the close 1976 election, attracted 64 percent. Despite their growing wealth, high educational levels, and occupational achievements, Jews in the 1970s consistently took a more liberal line on controversial social issues—defense spending, welfare cutbacks, women's rights, school busing—than non-Jews. (These estimates have considerable margins of error, but the trend is clear.)

The association of Jews and radicalism is even more intense. Jews participated in the revolutionary movements of nineteenth-century Europe in numbers far out of proportion to their percentage in the population—a fact remarked upon by social observers, comrades, and anti-Semites. Many prominent figures in the ranks of socialist leadership were of Jewish origin: Karl Marx, Leon Trotsky, Ferdinand Lassalle, Eduard Bernstein, Rosa Luxemburg, Léon Blum—to choose some obvious examples. In the United States, the Jewish involvement in socialist culture on the Lower East Side of New York was far more widespread than that of other immigrant groups; Jews became a major and vital presence on the American Left from the early years of the movement. And, as noted earlier, the presence of Jews in the formation and growth of the New Left was obvious. The fact that only a small minority of Jewish New Leftists were like Mickey Flacks—the great majority were thoroughly unaffiliated Jewish-Americans who did not themselves evoke Judaic images or a Jewish background to explain their political and moral commitments, and who were hardly distinguishable in thought or style from the non-Jews with whom they marched and demonstrated—is not taken as a serious challenge to the myth, any more than is the fact that Marx himself had no Jewish upbringing and did not consider himself Jewish. If anything, this general fact seems to confirm some truth lying deep within the genes, or the collective unconscious—more profound than knowledge, more compelling than active choice, more transcendent than individual awareness. As Mark Mirsky, novelist and *Village Voice* writer on Jewish subjects, declared, "The appeal of

Communism to so many Jews is nothing but the reawakening of ancient Messianic dreams."

Despite the evocation of such ancient sources, if we look at premodern times we will find nothing like this modern image of the "Jewish spirit." In the past Judaism was synonymous with rabbinical Judaism, and deviations were not tolerated. Rabbinical Judaism was relentlessly Judeo-centered and communal; it did not purport to be a universal creed like Christianity or Islam. The Jews were God's "chosen people." Their holiness, of a different and higher nature than that of other peoples, lay in strict observance of Jewish religious law. To them had been given the Torah, which contained the sole revelation of God's truths, but conveying these truths to others was not part of their mission. On the contrary, a complex body of ritual practice and belief severely restricted friendly intercourse with non-Jews. Certainly, there was no aspiration to bring social justice to the rest of the world. Of course, the Jewish situation was almost always that of a despised and persecuted minority, hardly conducive to missionary or exemplary conduct. Still, it is worth noting that nothing in Jewish history during the premodern period parallels such outbursts of revolutionary, "messianic," political-religious fervor as the visionary calls for a world of universal equality and justice by the radical Protestant sects in England during the seventeenth century.

During the Enlightenment, when Jewish emancipation first became an issue in European politics, there was no preexisting image of any Jewish ethical genius. On the contrary, Enlightenment thinkers offer a harshly negative image of Jewish life, which they characterize as steeped in ignorance, benighted, and fanatic. To rationalist critics, the Jewish religion was a mass of medieval superstition and legalistic ritual, as deserving of the contempt of modern, enlightened minds as the medieval Christianity that the Enlightenment wished to destroy. And when *they* read the Old Testament, they found that it contained not only the high-minded declarations of a few prophets, but also, and more vividly, the chronicle of many cold-blooded atrocities visited by the Israelites on their neighbors and the inhabitants of the lands their God had given them, atrocities apparently approved by this God, including the deliberate slaughter of women, children, and captured prisoners.

Enlightenment liberals, Jews as well as non-Jews, felt the need for an apologetic analysis of the Jewish condition. They had no notion of a special Jewish dedication to social justice, nor did they cite such qualities, which would have appeared as a strong argument for emancipation. The apologists noted instead that the degraded condition of many Jewish communities, the concentration of Jewish activity in unsavory areas like money-lending, and the insularity of Jewish doctrine were all unfortunate products of the unjust Christian oppression of Jews. The hope was that when Jews were accepted as equal citizens and given rights and freedoms, these unpleasant "characteristics" would disappear.

In point of fact, the "true Jewish tradition" that liberal and radical Jews invoke goes back only about 150 years. The myth of the progressive Jew emerged in the late nineteenth century as part of the process of Jewish assimilation into modern European society. Within Jewish religious life, the Reform movement in the nineteenth century, faced with the dilemma of making Jewish religion and doctrine acceptable to modern Jews and nonoffensive to a surrounding gentile community that was hesitatingly offering emancipation, reinterpreted the particularity of the Jews; it no longer implied indifference to or withdrawal from the broader community, but rather a divine "mission" of universal significance. In this way, the "chosen people" idea could be purged of its disturbing connotations, and transformed into a duty carried on by Jews for the sake of others, a service to the world. Savants everywhere in the nineteenth century uttered vaporous language about national essences and racial spirits; modernizing Jews responded by ascribing "ethical genius" to their racial spirit.

But the offer of individual assimilation did not apply to Jews in Eastern Europe. Although many young Jews in Poland, Russia, and Austria-Hungary were rejecting Orthodox religion, the quick reversal of the liberalizing policies that had emerged during the earlier decades of the nineteenth century and the systematic application of anti-Semitism by the imperial governments meant that neither secularization nor internal reform could hold out any serious hope of equality, citizenship, or integration into the larger society. Significantly, it was in Eastern Europe that the phenomenon crucial to modern Jewish mythological thinking first developed: the mass attraction of Jews to socialist movements that were often outspokenly secular, even antireligious. Young Jews appeared in large numbers and rose to leadership in a whole range of radical organizations, from the Social Revolutionaries to the

Bolsheviks; masses of Jewish workers also belonged to their own socialist organizations, like the Bund, in prerevolutionary Russia and Poland. Many immigrant Jews brought this spirit with them to the movements, parties, associations, and unions they joined or formed in the United States.

One approach to explaining these distinctive cultural-political facts echoes the "transmuted spirit" notions of nineteenth-century Reform Judaism. Just as Edmund Wilson saw Marx as a "secular rabbi" thundering out in political terms the "traditional" messianic vision that inspired the Hebrew prophets, so other commentators, usually Jewish, assumed that some radical spirit in the Jewish tradition itself was the source of the appeal of radicalism to the Jews. But no such radical spirit existed at the time that socialism and the Jews first met in Russia. Neither the intelligentsia nor the people were moved by an affinity between Jewish tradition and socialist aims. Quite the reverse. Prominent Jewish revolutionaries were conspicuously what Marxist historian Isaac Deutscher, himself of Polish Orthodox background, termed "non-Jewish Jews," that is, Jews who had to go beyond the narrow, archaic, and constricting life of traditional Jewry in order to proclaim a message of universal emancipation.

Significantly, the early Jewish radicals came mostly from the semi-assimilated Jewish bourgeoisie created by late-nineteenth-century urbanization, and not from the shtetl, still deeply immersed as it was in traditional Jewish culture. They were exposed to the new currents of European thought in high schools and universities, not in the Talmudic yeshivas. They drew their socialist inspiration not from the Bible, but from the same contemporary sources as their non-Jewish Russian comrades. The vision of equality and justice basic to socialism attracted many deracinated Jewish intellectuals, who, no longer participating in the traditional life of the Jewish community, had found no entry into the larger society beyond it. They believed that the only resolution of this problematic situation lay in the creation of a secular, universalist nation in which such categories as "Christian" and "Jew" would lose significance—hardly a traditional Jewish aim.

The early Jewish socialists, far from having any presumptions about the revolutionary inclination of the Jewish masses, deplored the absence of just this spirit among the artisans and small traders who made up the bulk of the Jewish population. Just as Marx's essay "On the Jewish Question" shows that he did not accept any notion of Judaism as inherently inclined to support the Left, so the Jewish radicals regarded Jews as too materialistic, too ignorant, or too steeped in tradition to be likely candidates for conversion to socialism. One Jewish student radical of the 1870s expressed the feelings of his generation: "I am myself a Jew, but I have seen few Jewish workers. Russian Jews are interested only in petty earnings and they are ready to sell everything including their honor. It is not worth wasting effort on them."

When the idea of socialist proselytizing among the Jewish folk was first proposed in the 1870s, it was greeted with indifference and even hostility. The basic commitment of the Bund—formed in 1897 by a variety of labor and socialist groups dedicated to organizing the Jewish masses—represented a new direction, in large part based on the failure of Jewish radicals to reach the non-Jewish populace. The creation of "Jewish socialism" came in response to the problems posed to socialist revolutionaries by rising national consciousness. Since the fusion of all peoples into some universalist democratic culture was not a practical vision for the foreseeable future, organizing for socialism often came to mean working within national-ethnic communities. The Jewish revolutionaries who turned to the Jewish community to create socialism made a decision that was mainly pragmatic.

And here is where the myth comes in. To awaken the Jewish masses to a new consciousness, to reinvigorate these backward people by giving them a sense of their special contribution to the progress of humanity, the early revolutionaries intertwined the vocabulary of religious aspiration with a socialist vision. They affirmed the value of the new Jewish proletariat with references to historical Jewish resistance, invoking the Maccabees' struggle against the Syrian oppressors, for example, and the Bar Kochba revolt against Rome. They spoke of the messianic age, which in this incarnation became the socialist millennium: a classless society governed by universal justice.

The founders of the various Jewish socialist organizations shared in the creation of the myth, however much they disagreed on other issues. The adamantly anti-Zionist organizers of the Bund and the early Palestine-bound pioneers of Labor Zionism all supported this revolutionary reading of Jewish history and doctrine. Moses Hess's *Rome and Jerusalem*, which attracted little interest when it appeared in 1862, became an influential and much-quoted exposition of collective Jewish memory and experience, useful for mobilizing support. Hess was praised as the discoverer of the socialist content of Judaism, and others quickly amplified his discoveries. They found tribal communism in the desert period of Jewish history, communalist ideals at the center of the Mosaic code, an inherent commitment to messianism with a social dimension in the Maccabees and the Essenes.

A look at the real situation that confronted modernizing, acculturating Jews, however, suggests that Jewish progressivism has little to do with the dramatic recognition or rediscovery of spiritual essences. Jews lived in conditions that made them sensitive to the progress of democracy and social justice. It is not surprising that Jews in Western Europe gravitated toward a universalist liberal ethic that granted equality to all citizens and relegated religion to the private sphere, where tolerance was to be the rule. The congruence of Jewish aspirations with the liberal ideals of individualism and merit defined by achievement rather than ascription was further reinforced by the association of racial anti-Semitic notions with political conservatism. In Eastern Europe, where such a liberal politics was not possible, there was an equally realistic assessment that only a radically new society such as that envisioned by the various socialist organizations could provide a decent future for the Jews. Poor traders and craftsmen trapped in an intensely anti-Semitic environment, the Jews— short of leaving Eastern Europe—had no hope of escaping their oppression unless there were a revolutionary overthrow of the czarist system.

Eastern Europe was the source of the great mass of Jewish immigrants to America, and a secular Jewish culture that incorporated leftist values flourished in the United States. Even if American conservative thought was not obviously associated with the kinds of feudal "organic nationalist" and anti-Semitic doctrines familiar from Europe, Jewish interests were still allied with liberalism and its vision of a society committed to the civil rights and civil liberties of individuals, to the principle of merit, to ignoring invidious distinctions based on race, religion, or national origin. The community that grew up in New York and other American urban centers carried on for a while the leftist culture of Eastern Europe. This influence was not universal in the Jewish community even during the heyday of the Lower East Side, but it was, as we have seen, very widespread. Even as the next generations rapidly became middle-class and Americanized, and militant radical organizations of all sorts dwindled in membership and moderated their ideological fervor and rhetoric, a distinctively left-liberal culture remained, whose influence touched many young Jews, even those who never consciously identified themselves as radical. Many Jewish homes were connected to some extent and at some time to the enduring though diminishing network of radical Jewish institutions: schools, camps, unions, political organizations, newspapers in English and Yiddish. In the larger sphere of the American Left, Jews nurtured in this subculture formed a high proportion, sometimes a majority. (It should be noted that since the leftist groups in question had often been reduced to mere hundreds of members by the late, post-McCarthyite fifties, the number of Jews needed to dominate was only a small proportion of the five million American Jews of the period.)

When the civil-rights movement and the New Left began, it was hardly surprising that the visions of equality and social justice found resonance in young Jews who had been affected by the leftist Jewish subculture: a summer in camp singing socialist songs, stories from admired grandparents, aunts, or uncles who had organized the garment workers and marched for Sacco and Vanzetti, or memories of cousins who had died fighting Fascism in Spain.

It is to this diffuse generational influence and the cultural experience of significant numbers of American Jews rather than to any spiritual essence or religious ethic that we should look to explain why even today American Jews are statistically more liberal on most issues than their demographic profile would suggest. The retreat from the historic left-liberal inclination is not nearly as headlong as one might guess from a look at *Commentary* magazine, for example. Nevertheless, political shifts have certainly undercut the plausibility of the myth of the progressive Jew. One can read about the troubles of black-Jewish alliances, about right-wing Jewish organizations, and about Jewish publications that enthusiastically supported first Ronald Reagan, and then George Bush. That 39 percent of the Jewish vote would go for Ronald Reagan in 1980, especially when the rhetoric of his campaign was shaped by New Right concerns, the Moral Majority, and the right wing of the corporate elite, was a startling and important event in American Jewish political history. Undoubtedly, the pro-Reagan vote was motivated in part by the perception of

Jimmy Carter's stand on Israel as "questionable." But although the last two Democratic campaigns have not been vulnerable to this suspicion, Bush still got about 30 percent of the Jewish vote, a figure triple that of the sixties. Moreover, Jewish students are registering Republican at twice the rate of Jewish adults, another indication of the continuing "normalizing" trend.

Historical circumstance, in large measure, had led a majority among American Jews to be receptive to the idea of a progressive Jewish inclination. However, the social and cultural conditions that lent plausibility to the idea have changed. The Jewish community has moved away from the political subculture and the social conditions that generated and sustained traditional Jewish commitments to the Left. The argument that the Left not only is the morally decent position but that it will, as well, serve the long-run interests of the Jews (since anti-Semitism is a right-wing phenomenon) has also been seriously compromised. The anti-Semitism that surfaced in the Communist bloc severely challenged the older, simpler hypothesis. And the difficult situation of Israel in the international arena, the anti-Zionism associated with both the Communist bloc and a large majority of Third World countries (which, while sympathetic to Arab anticolonialist nationalism, also claimed to be heir to historic leftist ideas) similarly complicated the easy identification of Jewish sympathy with leftist rhetoric. Just as socialist language became sullied by its use in support of bad causes, so leftist language in general became problematic for many Jews, even those who still thought of themselves as progressive.

As the historical circumstances that engendered and nurtured the myth continue to change, its tenuous connection to reality becomes more evident. The "traditional" progressive inclination of Jews does not need to go all the way back to the Prophets for its sources, and the present-day evocation of spiritual essences distracts attention from the more mundane causes of political attitudes. (To take an analogous example, though relatively more blacks than whites in this country are and have been deeply committed to a belief in racial equality, it would be misleading to look for an explanation for this fact in African tribal tales or in the version of Christianity that the slaves adopted in America.) No doubt there is much in Jewish religious writings that expresses serious ethical concerns, and there are sublime passages in the Prophets. But the claim that Judaism contains higher ethical standards than other world religions is without foundation. Within any complex historical religious tradition, there are texts that can be called on to support ideas of social justice, liberty, equality, and other universalist values that many of us hold today. But there are other kinds of texts and interpretations as well. Texts cannot by themselves tell us why some people become liberal or radical, and others conservative or apolitical. And there is no good logical basis for choosing—and, if necessary, tendentiously interpreting— some passages and ignoring others, while paying little attention to the actual lived history of past and present Jewish communities to see where and how this "spirit" makes itself known.

Thus, for example, this assertion of a progressive Jewish essence systematically ignores the apolitical conservatism that has characterized the history of Orthodox Jewry. In fact, the most rigorously religious Jews then, as now, did not respond to universalistic ideologies or take an active interest in the injustices suffered in the non-Jewish world. Orthodox Jews have not generally been involved in struggles for social justice, and they show none of the supposedly deep traditional inclination toward liberal or radical political positions. It would be strange to conclude that the most devout and pious Jews have throughout history been deaf to the "authentic" Jewish spirit.*

The current expression of self-conscious Jewish radicalism and unapologetic liberalism, as exemplified by, among others, New Jewish Agenda and *Tikkun,* evokes the old Jewish agenda, so to speak. A well-advertised and well-publicized *Tikkun* conference in New York in December 1988 drew almost two thousand attendees. Much of the program was devoted to sessions on abortion rights, postmodernism, a "progressive political agenda for the nineties," and so forth—intellectual, social, cultural, and political concerns that do not have particularly Jewish aspects but rather are the common property of the left-progressive world whose ideas and positions have almost no ethnic qualities. New Jewish Agenda continues to insist on the essential link between leftist politics and Jewish identity, but those who hold such views

---

*In November 1982, three Orthodox rabbis formed their own "rabbinical court" and "excommunicated" all members of New Jewish Agenda and the signers of a *New York Times* ad criticizing Israel for its invasion of Lebanon. One of the rabbis claimed the court was simply carrying out Jewish Law against the accused, who had "violated the Covenantal destiny of the Jewish people."

are no longer compelled or even inclined to find their home in an exclusively Jewish organization. (And those who do, like David Biale, emphasize that "being Jewish is important, but so are other things.") Only that decreasing proportion of Jews who want actively to be part of the Jewish community will look to such organizations as the appropriate way of expressing their political commitments.

There may be a certain pleasure in associating politically leftist and liberal views with one's own Jewish identity, but this kind of symbolic allegiance to roots or mythic enhancement of identity is consistent with life in post-assimilation society and will not typically generate community commitment. The beliefs that sustain most people's leftist perspectives are derived from the integrated American, even international, culture of the Left, not from the particular Jewish radical world of earlier generations. As a major focus for Jewish identity and community involvement, the image of the Jewish radical has dimmed and offers little promise for revival. Only a generation or two ago, radicalism could provide a powerful basis for Jewish organization, identification, and community allegiance. That historical moment has passed, and changing historical circumstances make the occurrence of anything similar extremely unlikely in the foreseeable future.

8

Liberations, Jewish Style

Two social and cultural movements of the sixties that grew amazingly fast, spreading throughout society and challenging traditional beliefs and attitudes in all parts of the culture, are feminism and gay liberation. Naturally, the Jewish community has felt the impact of these movements.

The Feminist Movement

The conflicts between feminism and traditional Judaism are profound and wide-ranging. Orthodox Judaism is patriarchal, clearly defining different roles for men and women. Only men can be rabbis, only men count toward a prayer group, men and women must be separated in the synagogue, and only men may participate in fundamental rituals like reading the Torah in the service. The bar mitzvah is for boys; no such ceremony exists for girls. (The egalitarian bat mitzvah and confirmation are creations of liberal Judaism and are still not recognized by traditional Jews.) In "domestic" Jewish law, male dominance is affirmed. The man has authority over the woman; a man may divorce his wife, but not vice versa. Girls are considered incapable of study, and are still not educated as boys are; women should be wives and mothers, in the home. Conservative and Reform Judaism have been more liberal about gender rules: women and men have always sat together in temple, and women have regularly served on administrative boards. But until recently, more diffuse assumptions of male superiority remained: the all-male rabbinate, the male prerogatives in ritual, male dominance of Jewish organizations, except for the ladies' auxiliary–type groups that have been so important in Jewish community life.

From the beginning, the Jewish feminist movement was committed to reshaping Judaism in all areas: theology, liturgy, legends and prayers, religious and organizational roles. Over the last two decades, the absorption of feminism into Judaism has taken many forms: women's prayer groups, women's Seders with rewritten Haggadahs, feminist liturgies for women's services, ceremonies to honor the birth of daughters designed to match the traditional circumcision honoring the birth of sons, political organizations of Jewish women, and scholarly conferences on the woman's role in Jewish life and doctrine.

The most visible and dramatic change has been the woman rabbi. For Reform Judaism the question of ordaining women rabbis was relatively simple. After all, since Reform is based on the right to change even the most fundamental ritual requirements of traditional Judaism, it was hardly likely that Reform "male chauvinists" could find any serious grounds for opposing the inclusion of still more cultural modernity in an up-to-date Judaism. The situation within Conservative Judaism was more complex and contested. An intense struggle carried on for several years preceded the final decision of the faculty of the Jewish Theological Seminary to ordain women rabbis. Conservative Judaism is committed to a significant amount of observance, in contrast to Reform's rejection of traditional ritual requirements. (This is an "elite" issue; as noted in the section on the synagogue, it is obvious that the level of ritual observance, say, of the laws of the Sabbath or of *kashrut,* is much lower than official Conservative doctrine requires.) The demands of feminism are an obvious break with fundamental parts of Judaic doctrine and practice, an important consideration for Conservative religious leaders— though not for the bulk of the Conservative lay membership. In any case, the conflict was resolved in favor of feminist demands. There are now Conservative women rabbis, and the number is growing.

The energetic spirit of Jewish feminism is captured nicely by the Women's Minyan, a group of undergraduates at Brown University: "According to Jewish tradition, God has both male and female attributes. Yet, in most prayer books, God is referred to in exclusively male terms, and all the people referred to in the liturgy are men. This distorted view of God influences the way men and women view themselves, their roles in Judaism, and even their relationships with God. As a result, women may participate in rituals, lead services, and even become rabbis, and yet still not view themselves as having been created in God's image." To help rectify this situation, the student group constructed a women's prayer book that emphasizes the feminine aspects of God. For example:

> The Lord does not rest and does not sleep.
> She wakes up the sleeping
> and arouses the stunned to repentance and to new life.
> She gives speech to the mute, and freedom to the enslaved.
> She soothes those in pain and cradles the abandoned.
> To you alone we give thanks.

The book is an affirmation of the choice to remain within the tradition. "Our metaphors and ideas," writes the Women's Minyan, "come out of a wrestling with the liturgy—trying to make it embrace our experience. . . . In the process, we have arrived at concepts and interpretations which we believe in, and through which we can pray."

The new liturgy assumes that women will be counted as part of a minyan. It assumes their full participation in the Torah service, their right to recite the Kaddish, the mourner's prayer, and to perform all other rituals from which traditional Judaism—and official Conservative Judaism—explicitly excludes women. The students want to mark their newly claimed egalitarian participation in Judaism by using their own words in the prayers and blessings they recite at their own women's services, where, "isolated from men in worship, we are learning what it means to pray in and be part of a congregation of women."

On a more secular level, Jewish feminism now has a lively periodical, *Lilith*, that chronicles and advocates its cause in the style of *Ms.* magazine. An extensive and vivid Jewish feminist literature has also appeared, including autobiographical accounts by the first rabbinical students, manifestos by activist Jewish women's groups exposing the sexist dimensions of Judaism and the Jewish community, Jewish-feminist novels, poetry, and drama. This literature expresses anger, pain, sad memories, accusations, but surrounding such emotions is an air of triumph, of struggles that have already led to great victories and will surely lead to more.

Common to all Jewish feminist activity, from the most moderate to the most militant, is the assumption that feminism is "good for the Jews," that denying feminist demands will drive away women who actually want to be active members of the Jewish community, thus depriving Judaism of energy and talent. Only a Judaism properly receptive to women's equality and the need to undo doctrinal and institutional sexism will be able to call on the commitment and loyalty of women—and of men—for whom gender equality is a fundamental demand. And if feminism does find a welcoming response in Judaism, there is the expectation that women will become a major force in revitalizing an ailing Jewish community. In his survey of Jewish life in America, *A Certain People,* Charles Silberman, not atypically, sees great transforming power in Jewish feminism: "In the long run the energy being released by the Jewish women's movement is likely to provide the most important source of religious renewal."

Leslie Feinstein* teaches in the English department of a university in Chicago. She is married to a theoretical physicist, and is the mother of two adolescent boys. She grew up in Cleveland, in a very ethnic and religious environment. Having left a Jewish community that she experienced as sexist, she is now, once again, an enthusiastic participant; feminism was the vehicle for her return.

"*I Wear a* Tallis *When I Chant*"

My father was the president of a modern Orthodox synagogue in Cleveland; he had become quite observant, and willy-nilly, everyone else in the home became observant. I was just a child then, and I went to the synagogue's religious school. I had a very religious phase, around age ten to fourteen; and then, as with the two centuries of Jews before me, enlightenment pulled me away from religious Judaism. Looking back, I think that underneath the

*Pseudonym.

religious rebellion was the sense of being a peripheral person, what it felt like to be a woman in a Jewish community, to be on the outskirts, negligible, one's intelligence not counting. I had spent time behind the *mechitzah* or in the women's balcony, with the women chatting and showing each other baby pictures while the service was going on downstairs. I thought that if you're going to be there, you should be serious about it.

The community seemed to be saying, Who needs you? So I stopped going to synagogue for ten or so years. But I didn't lose my sense of Jewishness. I had been to Israel the summer I finished high school—it was my graduation present. I had relatives on an old leftist kibbutz. Though I hadn't ever been in a Zionist youth group, I came back with the spirit—I was going to leave college and go to the Hebrew University and live in Israel.

I didn't do that, of course. I got married while I was in college, and went to graduate school in literature while my husband got his physics doctorate and started teaching. We had our kids and settled in Chicago, where we could both have teaching jobs. All this time, I didn't want to have anything to do with "synagogue Jews." Jewish organizations, I thought, were the pits. But I had my own way of expressing my Jewishness and keeping a sense of the Jewish year. It was through what meant a lot to me—books and reading and the life of the mind. So I had this whole reading program: for Pesach, I read history; for Rosh Hashanah and Yom Kippur, classical religious sources. For Hanukkah, I allowed myself literature. Since Hanukkah was a basically frivolous holiday anyway, I could indulge myself.

Once I had the children, I became less comfortable with this eccentric, isolated Judaism. My husband had no religious background, or inclination: he still says that music is really his religion, which is basically true, I think. But he has been supportive of my concern to find a Jewish community or some way for the kids to have a real Jewish education. I found I couldn't do it by myself, at home alone. Luckily, just during those years after the Six-Day War, things seemed to be happening. Right here, at the university, where Hillel used to be a small, out-of-it institution, there was a big revival. A havurah-style congregation, mainly faculty and spouses, had begun and grown tremendously. People wanted something Jewish for themselves and their children. They started a Jewish school that they could feel comfortable with, and a congregation that reflected their values, including equality of the sexes.

I've thrown myself into this group with real excitement, and I've watched it grow. We don't have a rabbi, though the rabbi at Hillel comes as a member. I've become the *gabbai* [prayer leader of the congregation], and it takes up a lot of my time. Having the community means there is much more depth, excitement, and emotional satisfaction. It has immensely deepened Jewishness for us and the kids.

Since our group is egalitarian, my feeling about the place of women is supported. I've learned to chant from Torah. I never knew this, but there is a kind of intimacy with the word that is necessary to chant from Torah. Learning how to do it, and the melodic system, has been an amazing experience. It's like entering into that mythic self, like what Thomas Mann talks about in the beginning of *Joseph and His Brothers.* I wear a *tallis* when I chant and lead the congregation. The big "debate" on ritual at the moment is whether I should cover my head to lead prayer, like the men.

I get plenty of support for pushing for women's equality. For example, after I'd been *gabbai* for a couple of years, I announced that it would be a rule of this congregation that, when you're called to give the Torah blessing, you don't say the traditional "I am such and such, the son or daughter of this father"—of course, we had women being called to the Torah from the beginning—but you say the son or daughter of both of your parents. You'd be surprised how many people did not know their mother's Hebrew name because they had never used it. The regulars got used to it, but people who didn't come all that often would give me the father's name, and then I'd say, "Your mother's name?" and they'd look nonplussed. And some would be embarrassed and have to give it in English. You see, I think religion is about linking to the past, and so tradition is important. One of the major issues of Conservative Judaism is to have continuities for the essentials, and changes where they are needed. Many Orthodox argue that the difference between men and women in traditional Judaism is of the essence. I don't see that, and when you actually observe feminism functioning in the real life of the religious community, you see that the community is so much more alive because of the full and equal participation of women.

Part of the appeal of being an active feminist within Judaism is that I can make a difference in a world that is my world in special ways. Out in the non-Jewish world, I'm also active in women's issues. But there is something special to me about being able to maintain the religion and the tradition and still advance feminist ideas. I was in a feminist discussion group where we read Mary Daly's books, which are for chucking traditional religion as unredeemably sexist and oppressive to women. I don't think that, and I don't want to throw out everything in traditional religion.

In this congregation, there is no real opposition to the changes. If I were in a more normal Jewish community, it might be quite different, though I know that Jewish feminists are active and powerful throughout the non-Orthodox Jewish world, and there are real stirrings even in Orthodoxy. Probably, I'd get into a lot of battles. I'd find a few like-minded people and start pushing for change. I wouldn't just leave like I did as a girl. I've come to feel so strongly the importance of community to carrying on Jewish life that I'd fight and fight.

It's funny—I'm now, with some real changes, quite similar to my parents in my Jewish commitment and involvement in the synagogue and the Jewish community. I guess it's a sign of real maturity that I can do what my parents would have wanted me to do, without that being my reason for doing it. Although I did write my mother about our starting to keep a kosher home, and when she wrote back, gushing with enthusiasm, I thought, I'm going to convert to Islam.

Accounts like Leslie Feinstein's radiate joyful rediscovery in a congregation in which Jewishness and feminism are "synergistic," so to speak. Though part of a progressive vanguard, Feinstein is quite aware that forces for change are gaining throughout the Jewish community. But the effects are uneven.

In the founding havurot of the revival, the principle of sexual equality in religious status and practice was firmly and unequivocally established over two decades ago. In mainstream Judaism, with the general principle of reform established for over a century, change, though difficult to accomplish, was, in a sense, bound to happen. Since the modern, well-educated, and self-reliant women involved in making feminist demands on Judaism would not accept any arguments about the biological, social, or cultural justifications for the subordination of women in other parts of their lives, they were hardly likely to accept traditional or theological justifications for their status within Judaism. As mainstream liberal society has moved toward affirming at least parts of the feminist agenda of equality, so has the Jewish mainstream. Traditional doctrines and practices that reflect the old patriarchal essence of Judaism have been dropped. The principle of sexual equality is not subject to modification; Jewish practices, rituals, and customs are.

But Orthodoxy is a different story. For the new Orthodox, there is both activity and tension. Since many of the young women have matured within a world in which feminism has become a significant force, and since many of these women are well-educated professionals accustomed to equal treatment in the secular areas of their lives, it is understandable that they would want to change the status quo in their religious lives as well. This has happened. At the Lincoln Square Synagogue, for instance, several women formed a prayer group that does not meet in the synagogue and is careful to avoid the prayers that, according to *halachah*, require a legitimate (that is, all-male) minyan. But the group was still disturbing enough to elicit stern disapproval from the stricter members, who saw a threat in even the mildest assertion of feminist dissatisfaction.

The usual perspective of feminist women who are also committed to Orthodoxy is that there is much to appreciate about the place of women in traditional Judaism—that it is not all hierarchy, injustice, discrimination, and exclusion—and that change will come about, but must be pursued in traditionally accepted ways in order to preserve Orthodoxy. Writer and educator Blu Greenberg, perhaps the best-known Orthodox feminist, praises feminist advances within Reform and Conservative Judaism, and offers the prediction that there will be ordained Orthodox women rabbis within her lifetime. (This prediction is made with the knowledge that almost all of the present Orthodox rabbinate would disagree violently with both her prediction and the spirit behind it.) In her view, women can be loyal to the doctrine and practice of traditional Judaism while affirming the powerful claims of modern feminism. Her revision of the revelation at Sinai poetically conveys the new place of women:

> I have to ask myself, are women forever bound to that image of standing at the periphery with the children? We can't rewrite history, but perhaps we can renew some of its images. I've

determined that next year, on *Shavuot*, as I stand for revelation, I'm going to re-image myself standing at Sinai in the center. Perhaps I'll be standing among the men; perhaps I'll be standing in part of a women's semi-circle adjacent to theirs; perhaps I'll even be standing in an inner circle of women with the men standing behind us, to be closer to the center of awe but also so that men can try on a new role for size.

This confident sense of a future harmony of feminism and traditional Judaism seems less attainable the farther one moves from the "liberal left" of the Orthodox world. In the relatively isolated world of the old modern Orthodoxy, thoughtful, inquiring young women are absorbing the spirit of feminism and finding themselves caught in a very painful and lonely dilemma, without the exuberant sense of an exciting time of reform and eventual victory.

Rachel Adler, the wife of an Orthodox rabbi, responded to *Lilith*'s symposium query "What choices and changes have you made to live life as a Jewish feminist?" with a poignant confession of unresolvable conflict:

The experience which made me a Jewish feminist was my grandmother's death. I loved her greatly and I wanted her to have a *kaddish*. Since she had no male relative, I asked if I might assume this responsibility. I was told that I could not say *kaddish* because I was a woman, but that for $350 I could hire a man to say *kaddish* for her. For a teenager that was an astronomical sum. I told the rabbi I could not possibly pay, but I pleaded that someone say the *kaddish* just out of compassion, because she had been so good a person. The rabbi refused.

That was my first lesson in Jewish feminism: where there is exclusive privilege, abuse of privilege is inevitable. . . . In the case of my grandmother's *kaddish*, I wondered why the prayer of someone who learned her whole morality from the deceased and helped nurse her through her last illness should be less pleasing to God than that of a man who had to be paid $350 for his services. I have never been able to submit myself to the idea that *halachah* alone is the determinant of justice and injustice, and that my own deepest intuitions of right and wrong (conscience, if you will) are to be disregarded.

All this makes a firm and consistent basis for Jewish feminism—or would if it were all that I believe. The problem is that I am not antinomian, nor am I intellectually dishonest enough to make a *halachah* in my own image. . . . My observance of *kashrut*, Shabbat, *mikvah* are indistinguishable from that of an Orthodox Jew but I go to a service where I can participate equally with other Jews, and I will not sit behind a *mechitzah*. . . . I disapprove of the whole structure of Jewish marriage and divorce law with its assumption that women must be acquired and discarded by men.

. . . Consequently, I am a woman without a community. I can no longer go to the Hassidic *shtieblach* I loved, but I could no more *davven* in a Conservative synagogue than I could in a mosque. (I don't mean that disparagingly; it's simply that such services are alien to me.) . . . I find myself in the same bind, dealing with my three-year-old son. I am frustrated to think I'll be sending him to an Orthodox day school where he can imbibe all the sexism I've fought against, yet I am haunted by the fear that I may be teaching him to be an irreligious Jew.

. . . I try to remind myself that my concern with Jewish feminism has given me more than a dichotomizing tension. Under its stimulus I have learned to respect other women, to learn from them and to share with them. Without it I would never have learned the synagogue skills nor had the synagogue experiences which have so greatly enriched me. . . . It's ironic. I was always so convinced that my faith was a product of my reason. Now I have no reasoned defense for my faith, no consistency in *halachah,* no trust in intuition. I hold to the *mitzvot* I do and hang on for dear life. Am I a dreadful example of what happens when a wholesome Orthodox lady espouses feminism? . . . Maybe I'm a warning that if you're a stubborn and less-than-learned Orthodox lady, becoming a feminist will teach you and enrich you, but it may also let you in for a lot of loss and pain.

The dilemma is inevitable. If an Orthodox woman asserts feminist notions, contradictions must arise despite the fact that the process of compartmentalizing and avoiding the confrontation of ideas has been central to modern Orthodoxy. Where feminism is concerned, the hope that concessions to modernity can be absorbed without affecting the integrity of Orthodox faith and practice proves vain. For women who want to participate in key rituals—being counted for a minyan, saying Kaddish, reading the Torah, or, in Blu Greenberg's vision, fulfilling the role of rabbi— the Law seems clear and absolute. And the restrictions are certainly not arbitrary or unconnected; rather, they reflect a broad conception of the nature and proper roles of men and women in all aspects of life, not just the religious one.

Apologists for Orthodoxy claim that its traditional concepts are truly respectful of women, honoring them for their destined roles as mothers and homemakers. They argue that the exclusion of women from important ritual and prayer obligations is due to their supreme responsibility for child care, which could be adversely affected by the demands of rigidly scheduled ritual requirements; what women do is *more* important than the religious duties of men, and that is why the Law's exclusion of women from religious activities like Torah-reading or participating in a minyan or saying the mourners' prayer for a dead parent in the synagogue is not invidious. Instead, it is really an affirmation of the true holiness of women's role in Judaism.

This far-fetched excuse—itself a response to feminism's demands rather than inherent in the original exclusion—will not placate women like Rachel Adler who remain within Orthodoxy while continuing to support feminist values. It will be difficult for such women to suppress their strong feelings and beliefs about sexual equality, especially when these ideas are reinforced by almost everything found in daily life outside the Orthodox world.

This does not mean that Orthodox women with feminist inclinations will simply leave Orthodoxy. As Susan Levy commented, in describing her attraction to Lubavitcher Hasidism (which is even harder on feminist ideas than modern Orthodoxy): "I was never offended by the treatment of women. Anyone I would bring to services would almost collapse. 'How could you sit behind the curtain?' I had read Simone de Beauvoir when I was fifteen. Feminist themes were always part of my consciousness. But I never felt threatened or inferior. Which isn't to say I approved. I guess I thought that you don't throw out the baby with the bathwater. I felt that one had to distinguish between the theology and the practice. When I came across something that seemed outrageously sexist, they were able to explain it away to my satisfaction. To me the sexism meant that the religion had gotten into the hands of lesser people than the ones who created it. I'm not against male-female distinctions, but I'm against hierarchical ones. It is my belief that those are not intrinsic to Judaism, that the elevation of the functions of men to being the prestigious ones was a reflection of the society and the times. I feel that it was a wonderful system that had been made impure by the members. In

Chabad, you can't take it seriously that it is male-dominated, because most of those men are such pathetic, wayward souls, running around like roosters, dancing and trying to look important. I didn't feel that this was a serious threat to my own sense of self."

A similar sentiment was expressed at a conference, "Women of Faith in the 1980s," where nearly a hundred women active in Jewish, Catholic, Protestant, and Islamic organizations gathered to discuss the struggle of religious feminists. Inge Lederer Gibel, a program specialist for the American Jewish Committee, articulated a theme common to all women who choose to practice their religion while fighting for equality: "In spite of the fact that Judaism, like its daughter, Christianity, and its sister, Islam, has not given women complete equality, I cannot reject my heritage and its greatest scholars and sages because most of them were male, human, and fallible."

The response of Orthodox leaders to feminist ideas is not encouraging for feminists. In *Tradition: A Journal of Orthodox Jewish Thought,* a rabbi (who edits a publication called the *Journal of Psychology and Judaism*) cites contemporary theories about the "superiority" of women to argue for the social desirability of maintaining traditional sex roles. For heavy-duty secular support, the rabbi calls on the doctrines of right-wing pop philosopher George Gilder, whose work attacking feminism for sundry evils, like the psychic emasculation of men, was originally published by *Commentary.* The message of this rabbi-psychologist is that secular "knowledge" echoes the wisdom of the traditional Jewish perspective. Jewish men should hold the fort, he advises: "From a *halachic,* psychological, and societal view, the Jewish answer may very well be: 'to feminism, no; to women in their full uniqueness and authenticity, absolutely yes.'"

It is not likely that a combination of George Gilder and Torah will prove an effective defense against feminist ideas. Judaism, including the modern Orthodox form, will change; this is clear. With the continuing attrition of commitment and involvement in Jewish community life, it will seem foolish to alienate able and committed women who want to affirm and strengthen ties to the Jewish community. In any case, those who want to be Jewish and feminist will just *do* it.

But however lively the process of feminist reform of Jewish religion will be for those actively involved, its motivating force originates in feminist consciousness, not in religious questionings rising out of Judaism and its worldview. In fact, for some, taking up active Jewish involvement can even seem a direct, logical consequence of feminist understanding. Thus, Betty Friedan, a founder of the women's movement, has come to sense "a mystical connection between feminism and Judaism." Judaism, she feels, gives spiritual support to a continuing quest for human liberation. She says: "Becoming proud of my identity as a woman, I learned to be proud of this other part of my identity, my Jewishness. That taste for authenticity that I got with defining myself as a woman gave me a taste for authenticity that brought me to Judaism."

There are other unaffiliated Jewish-American women who might find the feminist message of pride and affirmation the path to active engagement in Jewish community life, Torah-study groups, religious ritual innovation, and the like. But this is obviously a very special path, not likely to attract many to the cause of Jewish-community renewal. More typically, absorbing feminism into Judaism will be necessary just to hold what there is, to avoid alienating women who are at the very least favorably inclined toward community involvement, and are often quite deeply committed to participation in Jewish life.*

To keep these women in the community will require the firm establishment of that most inclusive feminist principle: equality, an end to discrimination and subordination. Though interest in specific cultural and religious revisions may vary from woman to woman, the concern with equality is shared by all. Given how relatively recent the movement is, the growth and success of organized and articulate Jewish feminism have indeed been impressive. But, as in other areas changed by feminism, the fact of equality does not tell much about the meaning of equality. Dismantling systems of inequality is a worthy goal in itself. That there should be fair participation of women in areas from which they have been traditionally excluded seems like a good thing. But

*For illustration, *Lilith,* in its early years (1976), did a survey of its readers. Almost all of the women had some form of Jewish education, 57 percent were members of Jewish organizations, 48 percent belonged to synagogues, and more than half had been to Israel. This is obviously an elite group of committed Jewish women, and, as the *Lilith* editors stated, "Our readership is clearly concerned about Jewish life and eager for changes to enable all of us to participate in it fully and equally."

how much will Judaism or the Jewish community be changed? There is little reason to expect much change in the religion, since the demands are not, in essence, religious. The problems of Jewish culture and community also stay as they are—though whatever trends have affected the men will now equally affect the women.

The process of bringing sexual equality to Judaism, as in other areas of life, requires some struggle, and the fight is invigorating. But—as one might ask about law schools or corporate boardrooms or city councils—once the fight is won and women are participating in equal ways and even in equal numbers, how different will the institutions be, and how much will have been done about the deep problems that are not a result of unfair gender discrimination? The answers do not seem very encouraging. For Judaism and the Jewish community, the conditions of Jewish life in America will be pretty much as they are now; once the "woman question" is answered in the affirmative, there will still be the "Jewish question."

Gay Liberation

Like the feminist movement, the movement for gay liberation has spread, deepened, and gained in visibility and acceptance since its beginning less than two decades ago. On issues of doctrine and ritual, the gay Jewish movement does not mount a significant challenge to Judaism. Gay activists, unlike feminists, make no demands for extensive revision of ritual, rewriting of theology, creation of legends, additions to the liturgy, changes in ideas about the roles of men and women in family life, and so on. The main issue is the fundamental demand of gay liberation: *acceptance* of homosexuality as a legitimate and respected personal choice.

There is, of course, the biblical prohibition against homosexuality, found in Leviticus: "Thou shalt not lie with mankind, as with womankind: it is abomination" (18:22) and "If a man also lie with mankind, as he lieth with a woman, both of them have committed an abomination: they shall surely be put to death; their blood shall be upon them" (20:13). But more important is the general homophobia that Judaism shares with other patriarchal religions. In 1974, the Ad Hoc Task Force on Homosexuality (a group of rabbis, sociologists, and psychiatrists connected with the Commission on Synagogue Relations of the Federation of Jewish Philanthropies of New York) wrote a report that reasserted the biblical prohibition and went on to repeat familiar attacks on homosexuality, rooting them in the Jewish tradition's strong condemnation of all forms of "unnatural" sexual practices. The Task Force report called on the Jewish community to hold fast to the traditional Jewish position, which is based, as they put it, on a "transcendental source, possessing objective validity." It also called for "uncompromising and all-out opposition to any legitimization of homosexuality" and declared the establishment of gay synagogues an act of "spiritual self-destruction." The years since those words were written have been the years of gay liberation. Mainstream Jewish community views have shifted along with those of the wider liberal culture. There are now approximately twenty gay synagogues, and the Union of American Hebrew Congregations (Reform), has accepted gay temples as legitimate members of their organization. Indeed, San Francisco's Congregation Sha'ar Zahav in 1987 received the Union's annual award for exemplary social-service programs.

Emphasis on the biblical source of the opposition to homosexuality has hardly proved a winning argument for most mainstream Jews. That prohibition need not have any more weight than the other biblical commandments that have been cheerfully ignored or reversed in modern Jewish life. Among the Orthodox, there remain troubling questions of doctrine and practice, although the new Orthodox have accepted so much of contemporary liberalism that homosexuality also receives a rather modernist treatment from them. Naomi Stein expresses a spirit of generosity more characteristic of a contemporary liberal than of someone committed to the belief that the condemnation of homosexuality in Leviticus is God's word. She notes in her interview that the atmosphere of her congregation is decidedly "open." As long as homosexual preference remains private, it is not an issue, Jewish law notwithstanding.

But for many gay people, it is not enough just to have their gayness generously ignored. This kind of generosity was certainly dominant among the diverse group of rabbis whose panel, "Homosexuality in the Jewish Community," was reported in the newsletter of the New York gay synagogue, Beth Simchat Torah.

The range of rabbis was from very liberal Reform to modern Orthodox. Most found no problem in calling a gay Jew to the Torah, if only, as some put it, out of compassion for someone less fortunate. The gay participant in the discussion related being told that the open involvement of a gay person in synagogue life would not be welcome, with the exception of financial contributions. But generally the rabbis urged grudging toleration. Another report in the newsletter described the participation of synagogue members in a panel discussion on "Jewish Gays" held at a suburban New Jersey community center. The gay correspondent noted that the rabbi chairing the panel "was uncomfortable with the good impression we were making." The rabbi went on to assert that he could not agree with the view that homosexuality was merely an alternative life-style; as he saw it, it was a form of neurosis, yet hardly more significant than the neuroses suffered by 80 percent of the population, and equally beyond free choice or control. So, like other neurotics, gays deserve sympathy, not segregation. Such patronizing kindness, certainly not unique to this rabbi, was, needless to say, not at all welcomed by the gay delegation.

Liberation movements typically insist on full respect from the outside society as a necessary condition for their self-acceptance and group pride. Gays want this important aspect of their identity openly acknowledged. And they are aware that official toleration covers deep and contradictory feelings, many hostile and disapproving, and that the preference of many liberals, even today, would be to ignore homosexuality as an irrelevant and private matter. In keeping with the strategy of cultural liberation, many gay Jews have avoided the problems posed by anxious liberal acceptance and have started their own synagogues, most of them in major urban centers with large gay populations, such as New York, Chicago, Los Angeles, Philadelphia, and San Francisco. But it is also possible to find gay Jews gathering in the "provinces," as described in this item from the New York gay congregation's monthly newsletter: "Fort Wayne—In September, gay and lesbian Jews from Dayton, Columbus and Indianapolis met in Fort Wayne for Shabbat services. They got together for Yom Kippur, joined by others from Anderson and Marion, Indiana. (Yes, Virginia, there are gay Jews living in rural Hoosierland.)"

Both the participants and their straight observers emphasize the enthusiastic spirit that infuses gay congregations. Since gayness is typically the only true common thread, these congregations comprise the whole range of Jewish denominations and so a kind of inclusive innovation of ritual and services is required. The broad mixture of people is one of the attractions, says Steve Ashkinazy, an active member of the New York congregation: "The membership—and this is one of the things I've always liked about the gay synagogue—has a real cross-section, from the very old to the very young. We have teenagers, and we have many retired people. We have over 1,100 dues-paying members. Over 1,600 came to Kol Nidre last Yom Kippur. In most synagogues, in order to have your kids in Hebrew school, to have your kids bar mitvahed, to get a seat for Yom Kippur, you have to be a member. Here, we don't have a Hebrew school, most people don't have kids, our High Holy Days services are open, no charge. What you get for your membership dues is the satisfaction of supporting the synagogue.

"There are all the different religious styles, also. One important spiritual leader during the early days was a Hasid. No one in his community knew he was gay, and he found it very easy to stay in the closet because the Hasidim are such a closed community. He is a wonderful and spiritual man. For many people at the gay synagogue, he was the leader, although not officially.

"The Friday-night services are not conducted by a rabbi. There is a religious committee, and in many ways that has been very good for the synagogue because the members come from so many traditions. We have Sephardic as well as Ashkenazic Jews, we have Ethiopian Jews, we have a number of black Jews. We have Reform, Conservative, Orthodox, and even secular Jews—quite a few of them. It has been necessary to construct and design our own liturgy, our own customs, gathered from various sources and backgrounds. A lot of our service is in Hebrew. We use some very traditional liturgy, very Orthodox. Some is in English. Some of the English we've retranslated to take the sexism out of it, degenderize it, because there are a lot of people there who are feminists—men and women. Often we dance, which comes from the Hasidic tradition. After the lighting of the candles and a few introductory Psalms to welcome the Shabbos we'll dance Hasidic dances."

Participation and spirit are at levels unheard of in the normal mainstream congregations. It would be hard to imagine a straight, suburban congregation where the members could write—and believe—descriptions like this one, about High Holy Day services several years ago at Congregation Beth Simchat Torah:

> Our services for the High Holy Days were conducted not by paid rabbis and *chazanim*, but by members of our community who contributed their efforts and services together. More persons participated in major roles . . . and more persons attended than ever. . . . To just state that the *davening* was superb and the decorum excellent is an understatement—we rose to new heights of spirituality and closeness—to God, to each other, and to ourselves. . . . We were truly an extended family of gay and lesbian Jews coming together to be part of the community of Israel. After pounds of gefilte fish, chopped liver, chicken, and even vegetarian egg rolls, we were still able to sing and dance with great joy at the celebration of our Torah and our synagogue.

The sense of camaraderie and family is powerful. The freedom to be totally open about being gay while expressing an equivalent commitment to Jewish expression obviously underlies the remarkable participation and commitment demonstrated in the gay congregations. There is a sense of fun too, based on feelings of relief and safety, to be sure, but also connected to the way traditionally stigmatized homosexuality can be played with in Jewish forms. San Francisco's Congregation Sha'ar Zahav has a monthly newsletter, the *Jewish Gaily Forward,* and in 1987 published a Jewish cookbook, *Out of Our Kitchen Closets.* At the New York congregation, the *Purimspiel* becomes a transvestite bacchanal. As the curtain rises, the master of ceremonies explains that *Purimspieler* in the past had been boys dressed as girls. And tonight again, in a "return" to tradition, "boys will dress as girls." Indeed the story of Haman, Mordechai, and Queen Esther is a marvel of campy cross-dressing. "Who saved the Jewish people?" asks the master of ceremonies, relishing the special applicability of the Purim story for this congregation. The answer: "None other than a *queen.*" In the Yiddish songs that fill out the program, much emphasis is put on the word *freilich* ("gay" or "joyful"), which occurs frequently and is greeted by the crowd with cheers and whistles. The synagogue also sponsors well-attended social events, like the Hot Dog Gay Dance (a disco serving kosher franks), community-affairs groups, trips to Israel, a Zionist circle, and so on—a variety of activities as extensive as, if somewhat different from, what the mainstream synagogue offers. Of course, these congregations have become very active in the struggle against AIDS. Since 1986, at Beth Simchat Torah a special version of the traditional *hevra bichur holim* [the synagogue group for helping the sick] has offered Jewish spiritual counseling to people with AIDS or ARC and has visited the sick in homes and hospitals.

The central importance of the gay aspect of the congregants' identities can be felt in the way Jewish material is shaped and presented. In the weekly commentary on the Torah portion, printed in the congregation newsletter, a synagogue member interprets the "deceptions" in the story of Jacob and Rebekkah "stealing" Esau's blessing as speaking directly to gay people. The commentator writes: "For almost all of us, we have spent a part of our lives either deceiving ourselves about our true identity, or deceiving others, or both. Is this deception part of God's plan or is it selfish? Many of us believe that it is necessary to protect our livelihoods and our lives. Others, who have totally shed this deception, have proclaimed a liberation of spirit that overcomes the mundane fears and troubles of 'coming out.' Who is to say whether the deceptions we practice as lesbians and gays are selfish deceptions or are like the blessed deceptions of Rebekkah?"

Gay activists who have become more involved in Jewish identity often connect their experience of gay oppression with the more widely accepted sense of historic Jewish oppression. One account of a Jewish "coming out" noted that the first gay-liberation movement began in Auschwitz, where thousands of gays were murdered by the Nazis because of their homosexuality, and that the modern gay-rights movement was started by Jews, with Jews conspicuous throughout the leadership of the movement. Just as Betty Friedan credited her feminist awakening for leading her to appreciate and acknowledge her ignored and possibly suppressed Jewish identity, so gay Jews have found that the sort of "internalized oppression" that characterized their pre-liberation sense of self had also kept them from truly encountering their Jewish selves. For them, the claim to be Jewish and proud has come to have a psychic meaning similar to the assertion of being gay and proud. A spokeman for gay Jews, active in Congregation Beth Simchat Torah, told us: "Before I came to Judaism, I'd been through almost ten years of gay liberation. I mean, if I've internalized anything, it is a sense of being proud of who I am. I doubt that I would have had the same experience or been able to come to a Jewish identity if it weren't for the gay movement. The gay movement taught me to be proud of who I am; it taught me that honesty was all-important."

Steve Ashkinazy is a revival success story. Now in his late thirties, he is the founder and director of Harvey Milk High School, a New York Board of Education program for teenagers who have suffered at their former schools because of their sexual orientation. A gay activist since the early 1970s, he has over the last decade become deeply engaged with questions of Jewish identity and Jewish life, and currently runs a support group for gay Orthodox married men.

"Gay and Jewish, and Proud of Both"

I've really been through quite a number of renaissances, although I don't consider myself a person who fluctuates. I don't feel as if I've wavered. I just feel as if I've grown very steadily, never leaving anything behind, but taking the whole kit and caboodle with me. For years, I worked in theater, as a set and costume designer. I was very successful and very happy doing it. I started a number of cabaret-restaurants that used my theater experience. And then came the gay movement. I was kind of dragged down to the gay "fire house," the Gay Activist Alliance headquarters, and "politicized." So then I started splitting my time between work in the theater and in the restaurant business and political activity, gay stuff, some of it very militant. I even went back to school and got a social-work degree. I'm proud that I applied to schools openly as a gay person who wanted to work within the gay community. I was the first person in the country to be accepted into a social-work graduate school as a self-acknowledged gay applicant.

One of the things I did was to go around to all sorts of gay organizations and environments to have a sense of the different possibilities that were available to a gay person, so I could offer some suggestions to the people I was counseling about where they might fit in. I went to political groups, social groups, theater and singing groups, even gay churches. But I always found excuses to avoid going to the gay synagogue. For years, I was aware of its existence, and though I made time to get to every other gay

organization, I never managed to get to the gay synagogue. Why? I
don't know. I guess I thought Judaism was something I was
through with. Or maybe I couldn't deal with my own feelings
about being Jewish. I had put them safely away. And I had no idea
what strong, confused feelings I had.

I come from a very nice upper-middle-class family, assimilated
but Jewishly identified. Passover was very important to us. We
didn't observe it strictly, though we always had two Seders a year.
We also went to shul on Yom Kippur, and my brothers and I were
all bar mitzvahed. But I never heard of Shabbos until I went to
Hebrew school at age ten. And when I look back at some of the
historical events that happened even during my lifetime, it amazes
me how many of them I never heard discussed at home—we never
discussed the Six-Day War or the Yom Kippur War in Israel, and
the Holocaust came up very rarely. Jewish was just something that
we were. It made us different, but otherwise it was no big deal.
After bar mitzvah, I stopped going to shul altogether. I went to
high school and Brooklyn College and became a great rationalist,
very scientific. I decided the whole world could be logically
thought out, everything was explainable, within our grasp. Organized religion was of no interest to me; it was the opiate of the
masses and all of that.

Anyway, one night, about fifteen years ago, I did go to the gay
synagogue. Alone. I don't know what prompted me to go that
night. Even just talking about it now, I get overcome with emotion.
I cry just thinking about it, just remembering what happened to
me when I walked into that place. Because I don't know what
happened exactly. I just know how I felt. It was a Friday-night
service, and the synagogue was very crowded. I went in and I was
amazed. I thought, Who the hell have I been kidding! I mean, I've
done everything else. I've become the social worker who takes
care of the movement, but there's this whole part of my life that
I've been neglecting: I'm Jewish! There were faces that I recognized from other parts of the movement, and that made me feel
good. I thought, Oh, normal people come here. I guess I was
expecting fanatics, or people who needed an opiate. Since I had
fought my own Jewish feelings, I expected other sensible people
to fight their Jewish feelings as well. But as I looked around and
saw people who I had been calling brother and sister, I felt it was
okay, it was okay for me to be Jewish. Before, wanting to be Jewish
had been identifying with the oppressor, with the patriarchal

Judeo-Christian code that the gay movement was breaking away from. But I experienced the synagogue as a place that I belonged in, even though all of it was strange to me—I didn't understand the prayers, I had no idea of how to pray, I didn't understand the procedures, I didn't even know when to sit or stand. Still, I felt it was a part of me, and I should be a part of it.

I came back the following week, and the one after that, and the one after that. I had had a religious experience. In the rest of my life, I had community, purpose, comfort. But this was . . . identity. It's hard to put it into words, but what happened certainly had to do with my spiritual awareness. And it wouldn't have happened to me in any other synagogue. My defenses would have been much stronger.

I started to go regularly. And after a year I'd been through all the holidays once. I felt at home there; it was a place I wanted to be. Friday night became the high point of my week. It was a community experience as well as a spiritual experience. I became part of the group that didn't leave the shul until it was time to lock up, at 11:30 or midnight. And then I'd get a group of people together and we'd go someplace, like a restaurant or somebody's home in the neighborhood. And just continue to schmooze, just to extend Shabbos as long as possible.

The next big turning point happened when I went to Israel to an international conference of gay and lesbian Jews. People came from all over the world—about two hundred people came from about eighteen different countries. I'd never been to Israel. Most of my life I'd had this very negative feeling. I would hear about people who had gone to Israel and had this marvelous experience and wanted to live there, and I'd say, "I guess they were a little cracked before they went." It's sort of the way I felt about religion: it could not happen to me. I'd heard of friends of the family, kids who'd gone there and ended up staying, living on a kibbutz, but never anyone I knew very well. My mother would say, "Did you know that Jean's son lives on a kibbutz now?" And I'd think, Boy, he must be a fanatic!

But the experience of going to Israel was . . . for the second time in my life, I had the rush, like when I went to the synagogue. It was a very spiritual feeling. It didn't happen when I got off the plane or at the very beginning. It was an accumulation of feelings. Maybe the first time I felt it was at a very unreligious place, at the Museum of the Diaspora, in Tel Aviv. A beautiful museum that really was designed to break down the resistance within people about their Jewish identity, to make one feel a part of the chain of Jewish history. That might have been the first time I experienced it. But then, after the conference, some thirty of us, gay men and women, went on a ten-day tour—a wonderful communal thing, which tours always are because you spend all your time together. And here we had a lot in common: we were gay and Jewish, and proud of both! By the time I left Israel, I had the sense that I might want to live there someday. I also had a tremendous awareness of how little I knew—about Jewish history, religion, philosophy.

I came back from Israel really determined to start my education. I decided to learn Hebrew, and took a course for over a year. I began to keep Shabbos. I started to light candles. Next was keeping kosher. Wearing a yarmulka was the last thing and the most difficult. There were constant questions—"What are you doing? What's happened to you?"—which I couldn't answer because I wasn't quite sure myself.

Fortunately most people knew I was getting involved in Judaism, but this yarmulka, this was a mark, this was something that they could see, and to some people, it was the final step. I had crossed the line, and they related to me differently because of it. They became more formal, more careful about what they said in front of me. Gay and straight people both. A lot of straight people thought I was a nut anyway because I was gay, and now I was observant too. What'll it be next? To a lot of gay people, the yarmulka meant I had joined the enemy! The enemy is the Judeo-Christian tradition, which is what's turned society against homosexuals.

I personally don't think there is anything about homosexuality that is antithetical to Judaism. But homosexuality in Western culture is such an anathema that people are willing to see it as anathema to *whatever* they believe in. Here it's "pinko-commie-fag." And in Communist countries, in Cuba and China and the Soviet Union, homosexuality is classified as a sign of bourgeois-capitalist decadence. And people are quick to see homosexuality as antithetical to Judaism. People have said to me: "How can you be gay and Jewish?" Shocked, horrified. They say, "It's antithetical to *everything* that Judaism stands for." And I look at them and I say "*Everything?* You have the nerve to say *everything?* You call yourself a good Jew, but you don't keep Shabbos, you don't wear a yarmulka. I do." It's not a question of a particular observance. The important thing is that one make a really concerted effort to dedicate one's life to observance, making the effort and being aware. I do that.

Being gay or straight does not separate Jews from the rest of the world. Laws of *kashrut* and Shabbos do. As for family, many gays—especially women—are raising children. I don't think that being gay is antithetical to family life. I might adopt children some day. Part of my role as a parent would be fulfilling the mitzvah of transferring the culture to another generation. At this point, if I were to live with someone, set up a household, it would have to be someone who was Jewish. In the past this had never entered into my relationships. But my concept of a home now is of a Jewish home. At the same time, people on the outside, friends, don't have to be Jewish. Another one of the mandates of the Jewish people is that we should be a light unto the nations, which I think we have been through history.

As for the *halachic* prohibition against homosexuality, I think there just couldn't be a law in Judaism that is impossible to follow. That is a very important guideline. It is impossible for me to not be what I am. Like every other gay person, there was a time when I tried to stop being gay. When I discovered the Torah and became religious, I tried again. But over the years, I've met many people who are more learned than I, more committed to Torah than I, and more deserving of miracles than I, and I've watched them make greater efforts to change their homosexuality than I ever could and still to no avail. As a therapist, working predominantly with gay people, I've seen, more times than I can say, people who have tried to stop being who they are, only to suffer really devastating consequences. Judaism is against celibacy, which was seen as a deviation. It could keep you from studying Torah because of impure thoughts, fantasies, whatever, if you weren't fulfilled sexually. And a gay person can't be fulfilled heterosexually. The old prohibitions were made in relation to temple prostitution, not with any conception of the honest, caring love between two individuals who are of the same sex. So even though the rabbis have interpreted the law in the way they have through the centuries, it can't really be the clear command of God.

Some people have a more simplistic approach to it. Some of it is even funny. I know one man who is very Orthodox, from a Hasidic background, very fundamentalist, very literal. And he has managed to absolve himself of the conflict by taking "Thou shalt not lie with man as with woman" literally. And so he has sex standing up. And it works for him, and that's fine. Then there are some resolutions that are more rational. I know people who are gay, and not at all bisexual, who say, "I don't lie with man as with woman because I don't lie with woman." That's how they read the passage. These things all seem kind of cute, but they're meaningful too. It's different for me, because I've taken the issue out of the realm of just what it means for me and how I can get around it. But I don't think that the feeling that the only way you can put it together is as some clever game is necessary or inherent in the situation. There are many mysteries in Judaism and I can accept that it's not possible or necessary to resolve them all. That the Torah prohibits homosexual acts and that God has created me gay are two incontrovertible facts to me. Not allowing this one conflict to throw me off the main track is the challenge of my life. Being a religious person, feeling that the world is perfect even when we don't understand it, I really feel that if I was created gay, then it's okay.

For Jewish lesbians, the situation is more complex than for the men since gender as well as sexual orientation is at issue. In *Lilith*, Batya Bauman describes how she came to accept her gayness, which then reaffirmed the centrality of her Jewish identity. Inspired by the gay-liberation movement, she went through the painful and difficult process of coming out at the age of forty-three. The new involvement in women's and gay activities became a central part of her concerns, along with her Jewish commitment. Initially active at the gay synagogue in New York, she, like some other Jewish lesbians, ultimately found the synagogue too male-oriented and came to feel the need for a separate Jewish lesbian group: "Some of us who know Hebrew speak with each other in that language and it helps us to feel our Jewish roots profoundly. . . . We are rejecting in the man-created myths that which diminishes us as equal participants in our heritage as Jews. In digging deep in the sources of these myths, we are finding that our ancestors, in order to firmly establish the patriarchy, rejected and suppressed much which came before them; following their precedent after some 2,000 years, we are reworking existing myths for our own edification as women." But her long-range vision is of an ecumenical Judaism hospitable to all the new movements: "We pin our hopes on the evolutionary nature of Judaism and feel it must evolve more rapidly than it has, to embrace a wider range of human experience. I believe that the various Jewish countercultures will save Judaism from its present slide into obsolescence."

Certainly these movements were instrumental in her own "renaissance": "The Zionist movement, the women's movement, and the gay-liberation movement have been the most important factors in affirming myself and my identity as a Jew, as a woman, and as a lesbian. Zionism brought me out as a Jew. The women's movement brought me out as a feminist. The gay-liberation movement brought me out as a lesbian. All are self-affirming. All are life-affirming. All have made the difference between the denial of who I am and the affirmation of who I am."

The feminist part of the lesbian claim on Judaism will undoubtedly continue to achieve rapid success within the mainstream of the Jewish community. The specifically gay demand from those who feel part of the Jewish community and entitled to maintain their involvement in that community is a general expectation that lesbian identity will be respected and valued. Complete success here will be difficult to achieve in the immediate future, all would agree, though it is also clear that more liberal attitudes, composed of some mixture of real moral progress and hypocrisy (the need for which is itself a sign of moral shift), are dominant within the mainstream.

But even though no one talks biblically about "stoning" these days, within traditional "Torah-true" Judaism the liberated view of sexual orientation is still not acceptable. There is sympathy, compassion, even toleration, in some quarters—but no acceptance of the basic demand of gay liberation. *Tradition*, the modern Orthodox journal, in the same issue that explained how Judaism must say no to feminism, had a piece by an Orthodox psychologist who reviews theories concerning homosexuality in order to clarify Judaic doctrine for Orthodox therapists. His position is that therapists may try to help homosexuals to change their sexual orientation, but that Judaism forbids accepting the existence of an inherently sinful condition. So, for example, an Orthodox therapist is forbidden to treat a homosexual who wishes to get rid of guilt feelings about homosexual relations. The author concludes: "Maintaining this *halakhic* view in professional circles and in public may come as an embarrassment to many. However, *halakhah*'s obligations to society and the individual are not relativistic and must be understood as reflecting a higher understanding of human nature."

This is not a position that has much force outside the Orthodox world. Although liberal Jews might be uncomfortable with a proud and open insistence on being gay and Jewish, the acceptance of gay Jews and their organizations within mainstream Judaism has been accomplished in principle and increasingly in practice. As with feminism, the energy behind the gay Jewish movement is invigorating. But, similarly, although the gay Jewish movement may affect changes in custom and even increase membership, the deeper questions troubling Jewish life remain.

Feminism, gay liberation, countercultural spirituality, radical politics—can these be the sources of a *Jewish* revival? Can an even broader inclusion of secular modernity into Judaism renew the Jewish community? For participants, the revival shows that being actively Jewish can be integrated with all valued movements of contemporary universalist culture. Thus, the revival is sometimes presented as a creative way to thwart the historical trends of attrition and disaffiliation. We see something different: not a successful resurgence of Judaism, but rather its transformation into just another option for modern individuals constructing their identities in a post-assimilation culture. The impetus that might lead someone to choose that option, at least for a time and in part, has more to do with the dilemmas of modernity than of Judaism: the questions and discontents, yearnings and confusions that characterize thoughtful and aware individuals, whatever their cultural, religious, ethnic, or social backgrounds and involvements. A self-conscious creation, the revival expresses a typically modern effort of will, inherently fragile. And how could it be anything else, really? Revival remains problematic and contradictory, expressive of the very forces of dissolution it hopes to stem.

Epilogue: Choice and Self-Creation

The capacity to live comfortably as a self freely constructed from different pieces that need not fit together neatly is a characteristic of contemporary consciousness. Different parts of the individual's values and aspirations lead in different directions, and some of them conflict sharply with the attitudes that contribute to the survival of particularist ethnic and religious groups. Repressing the temptations of individual freedom of choice for the sake of traditional group loyalty goes against the modern grain. As the authors of *The Homeless Mind: Modernization and Consciousness* aptly note, "Individual freedom, individual autonomy, and individual rights come to be taken for granted as moral imperatives of fundamental importance, and foremost among these individual rights is the right to plan and fashion one's life as freely as possible."

The Jewish revival shows how Judaism can be refashioned to become a reasonable choice even for Jews who are well integrated into the larger non-Jewish culture. But modern identity, the sense that choice is open and that authenticity depends on individual choice—this is not chosen, this is a given. Of course, the right to self-creation might be taken as a source of strength rather than fragility for Jewish commitment. After all, as Philip Roth wrote, in *Commentary*'s 1961 symposium on "Jewishness and the Younger Intellectuals":

> One cannot will oneself into a community today on the strength of the miseries and triumphs of a community that existed in Babylonia in the 7th century B.C.E. or in Madrid in 1492, or even in Warsaw in the spring of 1943; and the dying away of anti-Semitism in our own country, its gradual ineffectiveness as a threat to our economic and political rights, further disobliges us from identifying ourselves as Jews so as to present a proud and united front to the enemy. And that is a good thing, for it enables a man to choose to be a Jew, and not be turned into one, without his free accession, by a hostile society.

But the idea that choice creates value is itself a key modern value. From inside traditional Judaism, a Jew is a Jew essentially, and that is destiny; choice is not what counts. Nor is it obvious that the principle of choice, however valued, provides the most powerful basis for identity. On the contrary, when choice permeates all commitments, the conditions for the maintenance and continuity of a separate historical community of faith are inevitably undermined.

Both the appeal of a "Judaism by choice" and its ultimate fragility as a foundation for communal and cultural continuity emerge vividly in our last two interviews. Bernard Altman* is a particularly eloquent and self-conscious shaper of an individual Jewish identity. His own life is a complex illustration of the tensions and inconsistencies that accompany the modernist commitment to "fashion one's life as freely as possible." A philosophy professor at a large urban university in New England, Altman is a scholar of classical German philosophy. He is also a Judaic scholar and has been religiously active throughout his life. His denominational identity would be impossible to specify. A short, stocky, bearded man in his early fifties, he is married and the father of two grown sons.

*Pseudonym.

"Different Worlds"

Where I was raised, out in the country in Northern California, we were the only Jews for miles. My father was an engineer building the Shasta Dam. We had no real religious upbringing in our home. On Passover we'd invite the Jewish boys from the nearby military base—and do the Seder in English. But my grandparents lived in Petaluma, in a community where everyone spoke Yiddish, and it was there that I got the sense of a mysterious world that I knew I belonged to. When I was thirteen, we moved into the San Joaquin Valley, near Stockton, and I was prepared for bar mitzvah. We joined a Reform temple, but my bar mitzvah was actually in a little Orthodox Yiddish shul in Petaluma. Even at thirteen, I felt that there was something going on there that wasn't going on in the Reform temple. It seemed real; the other seemed bullshit. All that feeling vanished the next year, when I went to a summer camp for Reform youth. I had an adolescent conversion experience. I made up my mind at fourteen to be a Reform rabbi, and from then to the first year of college I was sure that was what I was going to do with my life.

When I got to Berkeley in the early sixties and was studying philosophy, I began to really find out what the Orthodox thing was about. There was a group of about four of us getting together then to learn about it. (Now, when I go back to Berkeley, it is astonishing. I see forty or fifty people coming to the Lubavitcher shul on a Saturday, and fifty or so coming to this other Orthodox shul, and forty or fifty coming to Hillel for services.) To support myself, I worked as the cantor of the Hillel congregation, and even conducted services on Friday night. I was always a bit of an actor, and I could pull it off. Then my wife and I decided to go to Israel. It was there I encountered this incredibly complex yeshiva culture that I hadn't known about. I fell in love with it. I started wearing a yarmulka and *tzitzis*, keeping kosher. The only reason I didn't walk into a yeshiva and go the whole way was that I was married. You see, what my wife liked in Israel was that you could really be Jewish *without* being religious. There was something else too. We had both thought we could go to Israel and get rid of our alienness, be with our own. But when I got to Israel, I discovered I was "Anglo-Saxon," as the Israelis call American Jews—an American. I identified as an American, with Americans. And at some point, I chose being a Jew in America, rather than an American in Israel. I found I was alienated from where I had gone so as not to be alienated. I decided to go back to Berkeley and become a scholar of Judaic studies.

I didn't become a Judaic scholar, finally. I became a philosopher. But I always wanted to live a religious life, a life of sanctification. This is an absolutely critical and central feature of my life. I want to have a life with a sanctification of the seasons, of sex, family, the stages of life. I want the whole thing, and the Jewish mode is the one that presents itself to me. But I've realized that I can't survive in the *frum* world—it doesn't have a large enough circle of interesting, intelligent, imaginative members. So I've become almost shamelessly exploitative of the religious world. I stand outside of it and dip into it; I taste from it what I want. I don't live a responsible life in the middle of it or work for change within it. When I lived in Los Angeles, I moved near the Lubavitcher center. I kept Shabbos there. But I was living completely outside the community. I just couldn't live the Orthodox life. For one thing—the first thing that comes to mind—I couldn't stand their attitude toward sexuality. I love buying into the heavy male bonding when I'm in it, but, really, I find the situation with regard to men and women unbearable. I think of myself as a committed feminist. I feel deeply upset by the kinds of bad faith involved in Orthodox attempts to cover up the antifemale stuff rooted deep in Judaism. If I stand up in front of a minyan, as a prayer leader, I have a lot of trouble praying those prayers that thank God—"sh'lo asani isha, sh'lo asani goy"—that He has not made me a woman, that He has not made me a gentile. I won't read those words. I won't say, "Thank God for not making me a woman."

When I live near where there is a daily minyan, I'll go and put on *tefillin* every morning. Up until ten years ago, I used to drive to one in town. But when I'm not near, I can't bring myself to do it. So it works only when I can walk into a context where I can play it out, where I can impersonate a religious Jew, when I can be the person I might have been. I'd always hoped that when the belief became strong enough, I could do it honestly, without irony. But this hasn't happened. There isn't a day that goes by that I don't think at some level that I should go out, buy the *tzitzis*, and just do it, be Orthodox. You know, I carry my *tefillin* with me whenever I travel—even though I haven't put them on for years—because at any moment, I might realize that that is what I am. Now *that* is an insanity! I know better than that. A person *decides*—and I won't. I became a vegetarian because I could not ultimately make the commitment to keeping kosher, but I couldn't bring myself to eat *treyf,* either.

I don't think I can sort out what is the religious part and what is the enormous desire to be rooted in some ethnic world. I've actually been learning Yiddish over the past several years. I've started reading things. I'm still not good at it, but I love it. I love the way my mouth feels when I speak it. I throw in Yiddish phrases all the time at the university. Nobody I know speaks it. I don't have anyone to talk to. But it feels like home when I start speaking Yiddish.

My children went to Hebrew day schools; they know Hebrew. But neither of them is going to be an observant Jew. They held on to it a while after they left home, and they dig it, sort of. Sometimes I have a pang of guilt that I haven't done better by them. But then I think, What does it mean to "do better"?— what, turn them into yeshiva boys? Are you crazy? I'm blessed that my two sons are super human beings. I couldn't ask for better people than they've turned out to be. They had a really good mother, and I fathered them well, and then there was luck.

It's true, they respond to my ambivalence. Like, my sixteen-year-old, who was living with me, had some friends over on Shabbos afternoon, and they were up in his room smoking dope, and I said, "You know you can't do that." And he knows it. He can smoke during the week in the house, and I know he smokes outside on Shabbos, but he isn't allowed to smoke in my house on Shabbos, and he knows he can't eat *treyf* in my house. Once my kids leave home, it's their life. I couldn't object if they have non-Jewish girlfriends. There is a multiplicity of ways in which human beings have culture, and religious lives, and this is the one I'm in. This is my people, and family, and history. If my children leave it and embark on another one, I'll want to know, "Are you sure this is right? Are you sure this is authentic for you?" But I wouldn't dream of saying, "How could you?" One of my brothers is in a Buddhist monastery in Burma. That appealed to me— enormously. And still does. But I'm working out my karma of having been born a Jew.

I live in a lot of different worlds. A certain kind of American literary world—I write a lot of poetry that has nothing Jewish in it; I'm influenced by Ammons, Creeley, William Carlos Williams. The academic world of philosophy—I teach Kant and Hegel, Wittgenstein and Heidegger. And there's music—I get together with musicians and play a lot of bluegrass, and Jimmy Rodgers. I play mandolin and autoharp. Don't forget, in California I grew up among Okies. I experience my life as complex pieces that I am constantly weaving into a single life. I feel uncomfortable when I can't bring it all together. I love to introduce my friends to one another and bring my worlds together. And that's how it is for all of us. I don't feel there are any more worlds for me than for other people in my situation. That's what it is to live in contemporary Western culture. And I love it. I love the way I live my life. I feel it is right for me.

The texture of modern identity is well described in *The Homeless Mind:*

> Modern identity is peculiarly open. While undoubtedly there are certain features of the individual that are more or less permanently stabilized at the conclusion of primary socialization, the modern individual is nevertheless peculiarly "unfinished" as he enters adult life. Not only does there seem to be a great objective capacity for transformations of identity in later life, but there is also a subjective awareness and even readiness for such transformations. The modern individual is not only peculiarly "conversion-prone"; he knows this and often glories in it. Biography is thus apprehended both as a migration through different social worlds and as the successive realization of a number of possible identities.

Altman is a delighted exemplar of biography as a "migration through different social worlds and as the successive realization of a number of possible identities." His commitment to Judaism and Jewish identity is certainly central, and his involvement in Jewish thought is extraordinary and intense. Yet modern values not derived from Jewish religion and thought permeate his being and crucially constrict the scope and power of his Jewish commitment. Nothing outside his own chosen values is allowed practical moral weight: not the actual tenets of Judaism as a religion, not the demand on every Jew to be ultimately loyal to the Jewish people. In mundane terms, he can find no moral or psychological force in the commandment to marry someone Jewish or to make Jewish commitment an unquestionable requirement for his children. The path of Buddhism, chosen authentically, is as valid for a Jew—his brother, in fact, or himself—as carrying on Judaism. The consequences of such modernist undermining of religious and ethnic bonds of conscience are evident to Altman, but such a realization does not impose personal responsibility. He muses: "Judaism isn't going to last forever. It's not like you have some obligation to the past to keep it going. You should do it because you want to do it. But you don't have some obligation to the ancestors to keep it going, to keep it alive. It should be kept alive only if it should be kept alive, if it is powerful for you."

The last voice in this book is the most unlikely. Carolyn Craven is literally a "Jew by choice," as converts are called. A well-known media figure in the San Francisco Bay area, she also worked nationally as White House correspondent for "All Things Considered," the National Public Radio news program. In her mid-forties, she is lively, talkative, energetic, intense, and forceful. A single mother, she has a teenage son. She received national attention in a variety of media, including "Good Morning, America," when she went on a speaking tour on the subject of rape, after she herself was raped. Recently, she has been a producer and reporter on the television program "South Africa Now."

"Jewish by Choice"

I grew up in a nice, stable, black, upper-middle-class home in Chicago. My mother taught physics in the public schools, my father was a lawyer and a judge. My parents were basically unreligious, but my twin sister and I were sent to Sunday school in an interracial Baptist church around the corner. Our social peers, the other members of the black aristocracy, went to St. Edmund's Episcopal Church. My sister and I converted to Episcopalianism when we were twelve so we could get confirmed there. It was all black, upper-middle-class. The church was very beautiful, and we went with great regularity. I loved the service, like a Catholic mass in English, with religious fervor, in the quiet, sophisticated way that Episcopalians can have. It was a big part of our lives.

But most of our family's close friends were Jewish, and we went to Seders every year, and to zillions of bar mitzvahs. I knew the *Sh'ma* [the "Hear, O Israel" prayer] as early as I knew the Lord's Prayer. A good number of these Jewish families were religious, some Reform, some Conservative, some were even Orthodox and kept kosher.

I got hung up on some things in Sunday school, like transubstantiation. I was willing to accept a lot, but *that* was real hard. And there was this thing about being good because of the hereafter, heaven and hell. I knew that to be a good person among our Jewish friends—many of them were very political—was an end in and of itself. And forgiveness—in the Episcopal church, there was group confession. Everyone confessed before taking communion. I had a real problem with that. It seemed to me that a lot of people were sinning all week and then saying the thing on Sunday. But I hung in there. I was even president of the church club.

By the time I went away to college at Goucher, I wasn't interested in religion anymore. I was involved in politics and civil rights, I worked in SNCC [the Student Nonviolent Coordinating Committee] and helped to start an SDS chapter. In 1965, I left Baltimore, moved to the West Coast, became a student at Berkeley, and worked as an SDS organizer. That's where I was when the Six-Day War broke out. It was incredible. In one day, the campus divided down the middle. But I didn't have any doubts in my mind. I remember shaking with rage at my leftist friends who were anti-Israel. I knew I was in an untenable position with the Left. I was a national officer of SDS at the time. I resigned my job and resigned from the organization. And I was very aware of black anti-Semitism. People were being taught an unbelievable amount of bullshit. I'd hear black people saying things like "Rockefeller is a Jew." It was so outrageous. Some of it was just cynical. And some came from real problems. There was so much Jewish ownership in black neighborhoods. There were some black people whose only contact with Jews was with landlords and storeowners.

I remember people talking about religion in the early seventies. My generation was having children, settling down. And the "movement" had fallen apart politically. Maybe this is over-simplistic, but I think politics served in the place of religion for some people. All of a sudden, some of my very good friends started seriously talking about being Jews again and what that meant. Now, I'm sure there were Christians who were doing the same thing, but I happened to be around people who were Jewish. And when I started to think about religion, it was Judaism I thought of. I probably wouldn't have participated in similar discussions among Christians. At that time I was pretty thoroughly turned off to Christianity. Also all those other weird religions. Every former junkie or speed freak I knew had discovered religion, so they meditated or stood on their heads or rang bells or went on retreats. I had been active in civil rights and antiwar stuff. I could pass on the "human potential" movement.

I was real conscious that a lot of those people, like Baba Ram Dass, were ex-Jews. I thought that was a real betrayal. I remember being very embarrassed to say that what I was really thinking was that I wanted to learn more because I wanted to convert. I must have known people who converted for reasons of marriage, but no straight conversions. Maybe Sammy Davis, Jr., but he wasn't a buddy. Then I got sick and was in the hospital for a few months. A close friend brought me the Hertz edition of the Torah. I couldn't sleep in the hospital, and I used to stay up late at night and wake up early, and I read Torah a lot. I was fascinated. I read the annotations and was maybe even more fascinated by these foot-notes. Then, later, I started reading Jewish writers. Now I think I've read everything I. B. Singer ever wrote. And I read a lot of Holocaust stuff, especially Elie Wiesel. Then I got *Everyman's Talmud,* and I became more and more fascinated. I loved the *pilpul,* that convoluted kind of argumentation that's in the Talmud. My favorite stories in the whole world are in the Talmud. I use them when I speak in public. I love them.

Later I was talking to a friend from San Francisco, and I told her that I'd been studying and considering converting, but I didn't know what to do. Even though many of my friends were getting involved in Jewish things, none of them belonged to synagogues. She suggested Marty Weiner, a rabbi at Shearith Israel, in San Francisco.

So I called and made an appointment. I don't know if I told him I was black. And it was an advantage that he didn't know me from television; I wasn't "Carolyn Craven of Channel Nine News" to him. When I told him I'd decided to convert, he tried to discourage me, with all the kindness in the world, hinting, I think, Why would you want to be part of another minority? He talked for a long time about how hard the conversion process was, and how Judaism wasn't a proselytizing religion. And he asked, "Why take on the burden of becoming a Jew?'' I explained that the burden for me now was *not* being a Jew. We agreed we would continue meeting, and I would take the conversion class.

The class was given by an older woman, over seventy, taught on a one-to-one basis in her kitchen, at night. It went on for three or four months. There were books to read and papers to write, and work sheets. I just loved it. I started going to Saturday services at Shearith Israel. They were wonderful. What I hadn't anticipated was that a large proportion of the congregation were fans who watched my news show every day, so I was in a place where everyone saw me as a TV celebrity. I became the darling of the over-sixty-five set. At the end of the class I went back to the rabbi to continue the conversations we had started about faith. We talked about the Talmudic quote that says that faith isn't a large requirement, that much more important is obeying the rules and regulations set forth in Torah and Talmud. That is a good Jew.

There is a lot of rationality in Judaism. Unlike Christianity. There is a real difference. What you find among a lot of born-again Christians is that a personal catastrophe led to their religion, and that's not true among new Jews. In Shearith Israel, I met a lot of people like me who had converted because they wanted to convert. There are lots of us; we're not a rare breed. What I find is that there is a much more rational thought process that leads you to it. The religion doesn't offer the kinds of solace and comfort in terms of forgiveness that Christianity does. It's truly profound. On Yom Kippur, the only prayers of forgiveness are for sins committed against God, not for sins against man. Among the obligations for the time between Rosh Hashanah and Yom Kippur is the obligation to clean up your act with your fellow man, and you've got to do that on your own.

So the day came, and we went into the little chapel, with my teacher, and I answered the questions "Yes," and then we said the *Sh'ma* together, and a blessing, and it was over. The rabbi said that according to Jewish law this was the last time that I would be referred to as a convert. But then he was really surprised. I told him this wasn't enough, that I wanted an Orthodox conversion. He finally arranged it, including the *mikvah.* The new assistant rabbi also wanted to come. It turned out that Marty Weiner had been to the *mikvah* only once, and the assistant rabbi never. The Orthodox rabbi was really nice, and very moved that the Reform rabbis wanted to come, so he said to Marty: "Such a day! I make you an Orthodox rabbi, and you make the ceremony," and he gave Marty the book. So we went in, and the ceremony itself was lovely; the blessings and the immersion are wonderful. We were all surprised at how touching the ceremony was. Then we went to the court, the *beth din*. There were two other women being converted for marriage purposes. Then we went to the chapel and the ceremony there was like the one I'd experienced already. The reason I had an Orthodox conversion was that I wanted to make it real, absolute, so there would be no questions asked anywhere in the world, not even in Israel. Halachically, they can't touch you.

So I was a Jew, and I am a Jew. I went to shul regularly. I became involved in the sisterhood at the temple. I had Shabbos dinners, with candle-lighting. And ever since the conversion, things have happened that have reaffirmed my decision. One of the more dramatic was what happened when I was raped. First of all, the rape occurred on Shabbos, over ten years ago now. My seven-year-old son Gabriel was home. That Friday, I cleaned house, and baked challah. My sister was over, and she stayed for dinner. And then my friend Kate knocked on the door—she had come to borrow something—and I asked her to stay for dinner too. I had made tons of food—typical Jewish mother. After I'd said the blessings over the candles and Gabriel made Kiddush, Kate—who is Jewish—told me that she had never in her life had a Shabbos dinner. And we sang a little bit, and it was lovely. It was three women who really liked each other, and we talked, and it was a really fabulous night. And when they left, and I'd cleaned up the kitchen, I was thinking about getting up and going to temple the next morning, and I remember dancing around the living room and thinking, This is what Shabbos is all about; it's about being with friends and being happy and loving. It was a special Shabbos. And then, in the middle of the night, the guy got in and raped me. During the rape—it went on for over three hours—the level of fear was so great because I knew there was no way I could protect Gabriel if I got killed or hurt, so the thing became to keep my sanity. I couldn't believe I could survive this level of fear. I thought I would just flip out, and I remember thinking of two things: First, that God would not let me die on Shabbos, not tonight, not after this Shabbos. And second, what I kept saying was the *Sh'ma*, out loud, until the guy made me stop. It was like a mantra, and I kept saying it over and over. And I just kept praying that God would let me come through this.

The next morning, after the police and my sister got there, one of the people I had my sister call was my rabbi, and he came immediately, and he offered so much strength and love and support that it was just wonderful. He is a wonderful, ministering rabbi. I was still hysterical. At one point, he said to me: "You might not understand this now, but sometimes terrible things happen, not as a test, but as a way of allowing you to do something important, and I just think that you are going to come out of this much stronger, and you will do something real important." And he was right. I think that all of the talking I did after it, and all of the hundreds of talks and television appearances, was in part because I got a lot of support from Marty Weiner—that I could do it, that it would be a valuable thing. I ended up speaking a lot about rape to Jewish organizations.

In the years since then, I've become less observant. But, as with every other Jew I know, becoming less observant in no way diminishes my feeling of Jewishness. I think of Jewish history as my history. The shtetl experience is my experience. Do I talk to my sister about this? Well, maybe other Jews aren't like this, but I don't really talk about this a lot with goyim. There is too much they don't understand. See, I have a four-thousand-year history that my sister doesn't share. We have separate histories now, we really do. I have this rich and wonderful four-thousand-year history.

For Carolyn Craven, Judaism is much more than a religious creed; it is a people, history, culture, and sense of community. As she sees it, by becoming Jewish through conversion, all this fabric of Jewishness, religious and secular, has become hers. Those born and raised Jewish may find it strange to think that by going through a religious ceremony and study course, a person could become Jewish in the ethnic, cultural, and historical senses. But Craven genuinely feels part of the Jewish community and part of the four-thousand-year chain of Jewish history. She feels like a typical Jewish mother, shares the shtetl experience, feels some distance from goyim (including her twin sister). In fact, she is now so Jewish that, like millions of other Jews, she can stop worrying so much about practice without necessarily feeling that her Jewishness is thereby compromised or diminished.

This is not to say that Carolyn Craven leaves the non-Jewish world behind. She is a very modern convert. It is the secular rationalism of Reform Judaism that appeals to her, along with the ethnic sense of a long historical tradition. The conversion fits nicely into the identity the convert already had, her way of life, political and social values, and network of friends. Being Jewish is now part of her identity; but just as for her friends who were born Jews, it is only *part* of her identity. She still maintains the complex, multi-group social, political, and professional life that she had before conversion, and the values she brought to the conversion continue unchanged afterward. She will pass on her Jewish identity to her son, but he will also know that it is his right to mold his own identity just as his mother so imaginatively exercised her right to self-creation. And should the search for meaning move her—or her son—toward other identities, the claim of authenticity is certain to outweigh that of earlier ties.

Carolyn Craven's path illustrates simultaneously the power and the lightness of choice. Hers is a wholly unforced commitment— in a moral sense, the strongest commitment possible, but at the same time, the most fragile, since choice undercuts all imperatives that originate outside the individual consciousness. Life commitments are open to choice, in principle; and the range of choice is theoretically as wide as the world culture, limited only by the imaginative reach and capacity for identification of the individual. Craven's Jewish choice might seem unlikely or even bizarre to some, but, we suggest, hardly more so than that of an assimilated Jewish-American who makes a commitment to Orthodox Judaism. Indeed, if we focus on the degree of change, we risk missing the more profound and constant element. In modern culture, where identity is open, affirmations of the given and traditional are as much dependent on choice as more dramatic creations of new identifications and commitments.

Such choices are necessarily light—not in the sense that they do not matter for the individual, or that they are easy, or tentative, or without deep emotional meaning. Rather, the lightness is objective. In the public realm, all private choices of identities are equal: respected, accepted, in fact, valued. And while any particular choice is open to revision, the principles of choice and authenticity are not—even if one decides to enter a pre-modern world of fundamentalist belief, which is also a choice.

The contemporary rhetoric of identity, of being or becoming "what one really is," tries to make choices seem like destiny. But whatever the consolations of this rhetoric, it masks the reality testified to over and over again by the voices recorded throughout this book: Jews in America today are a people not "chosen" but choosing. This is true for the least affiliated as well as the most observant. And it is at the heart of both individual experiences and the apparently contradictory patterns of revival and assimilation that they generate. Identity, formerly objective and imposed, has become constructed and chosen—Jewish identity, like all others. There can be no return from this disposition to choose. The future of American Jews will continue to be determined by the place that individualism, modernity, and choice afford to Judaism—not the other way around.

Notes

INTRODUCTION

PAGE

3

For the most recent extensive survey of intermarriage and observance, see the front-page account in the *New York Times*, 7 June 1991, describing a study done at the Graduate Center of the City University of New York and released by the Council of Jewish Federations.

For community demographics and structure, see Daniel J. Elazar, *Community and Polity: Organizational Dynamics of American Jewry* (Philadelphia: Jewish Publication Society, 1980).

"Internal erosion": Leonard Fein, *Where Are We? The Inner Life of America's Jews* (New York: Harper and Row, 1988), xxi.

"Spiritual Jewish genocide": Marc Stuart Miller, "Conference of Jewish Activists Provides New Leadership," *Ha-Or*, Queens College (New York) Jewish student newspaper, February 1981, 1.

"End of American Jewish History" is the headline in *The New York Review of Books*, 23 November 1989, for an essay by Rabbi Arthur Hertzberg, "What Future for American Jews?" In the book from which the essay is drawn, Hertzberg suggests that, without a spiritual revival, "American Jewish history will soon end" (388).

4 Charles Silberman, *A Certain People: American Jews and Their Lives Today* (New York: Summit Books, 1985), 25.

For a more academic sociological work also claiming to have found a powerful revival, see Calvin Goldscheider and Alan Zuckerman, *The Transformation of the Jews* (Chicago: University of Chicago Press, 1984). Professors at the Hebrew University and Brown University, respectively, they write:

> Jewish vitality in America is reflected not only in secular political indicators. Since the mid-1960s there has been an enormous growth in Jewish activities, and new forms of Jewish identity and new sources of Jewish cohesion have emerged. These have been particularly concentrated among teenagers, college students, and young adults. The impressive growth of Habad houses, Jewish consciousness among students, kosher facilities, Jewish studies, and Israel–Zionism–Soviet Jewry activities, among others, have been revolutionary forces in American Jewish life. (185)

It is noteworthy that these intensely quantitative social scientists seem quite satisfied using terms like "enormous," "impressive," and "revolutionary" without providing any defining criteria or even a discussion of how the application of such terms could be operationalized so that all objective observers could agree on the appropriateness of their application. But we do learn how the authors *feel* about the state of the Jewish community.

A well-argued and powerful statement of the antirevival case from within the Jewish world is Hillel Halkin's *Letters to an American Jewish Friend: A Zionist's Polemic* (Philadelphia: Jewish Publication Society, 1977).

Jewish revival has also been noted in France and Great Britain. See Dominique Schnapper, *Jewish Identities in France: An Analysis of Contemporary French Jewry* (Chicago: University of Chicago Press, 1983), and Howard Cooper and Paul Morrison, *A Sense of Belonging: Dilemmas of British Jewish Identities* (London: Weidenfeld and Nicolson, 1989).

For a cogent account of the "optimist-pessimist" debate among Jewish-community intellectuals, see "Introduction, 1989," in Nathan Glazer, *American Judaism*, 2d ed., rev. (Chicago: University of Chicago Press, 1989).

5   Dr. Alvin Schiff quoted in Ari Goldman, "Poll Shows Jews Both Assimilate and Keep Tradition," *New York Times*, 7 June 1991.

8   Fein, *Where Are We?*

THE UNAFFILIATED

PAGE

9   Israel Zangwill, *The Melting Pot: Drama in Four Acts* (1914; reprint, New York: Arno Press, 1975). (First produced 1908).

11   Jewish population summaries are published yearly in *The*

American Jewish Year Book, prepared by the American Jewish Committee (Philadelphia: Jewish Publication Society).

12–13   A detailed analysis of how to interpret population estimates in terms of degrees of participation in Jewish life is provided in Elazar, *Community and Polity,* 71–77.

For a good analysis of long-term trends, as well as data like the Denver intermarriage figure, see Chaim Waxman, "The Emancipation, the Englightenment, and the Demography of American Jewry," *Judaism,* Fall 1989.

For a recent summary of demographic studies on intermarriage and Jewish practice, see Jack Wertheimer, "Recent Trends in American Judaism," *American Jewish Year Book 1989,* 63–162. This study is the source of the most recent figures used in citations in this book.

On Jewish emancipation and the Enlightenment, see Jacob Katz, *Tradition and Crisis: Jewish Society at the End of the Middle Ages* (New York: Free Press, 1961), and *Out of the Ghetto: The Social Background of Jewish Emancipation* (Cambridge: Harvard University Press, 1973). For a study of the particularly relevant subject of German Jewry and the Enlightenment, see Michael A. Meyer, *The Origins of the Modern Jew: Jewish Identity and European Culture in Germany, 1749–1824* (Detroit: Wayne State University Press, 1971).

14   Michael Berenbaum, *After Tragedy and Triumph: Modern Jewish Thought and the American Experience* (New York: Cambridge University Press, 1990), 157.

Arthur Ruppin, *The Jews of Today* (London: Bell and Sons, 1913), 155 (emphasis in original).

Meir Kahane, *Never Again: A Program for Survival* (Los Angeles: Nash Publications, 1971), 8. See also Kahane, *Why Be Jewish? Intermarriage, Assimilation, and Alienation* (New York: Stein and Day, 1977).

15   For an estimate of Jewish "repudiators," see Elazar, *Community and Polity,* 74.

1: ASSIMILATION, THE AMERICAN WAY

PAGE

20   *Night and Fog* is the 1956 documentary film about Auschwitz made by French director Alain Resnais.

30   Paul Cowan, *An Orphan in History: Retrieving a Jewish Legacy* (New York: Doubleday, 1982), 5.

Anne Roiphe's essay on Christmas appeared in the *New York Times*, 21 December 1978.

31   Anne Roiphe, *Generation Without Memory: A Jewish Journey in Christian America* (New York: Linden Press/Simon and Schuster, 1981), 17–18.

32   Popular autobiographies and novels about the experience of assimilation during the early decades of the century abound. In *The Promised Land* (1912; reprint, Boston: Houghton Mifflin, 1969), Mary Antin tells the happy and unconflicted story of an immigrant Jewish girl becoming a full American. More typical dramas of conflict, betrayal, guilt—and sometimes the redemption of return—include Abraham Cahan, *The Rise of David Levinsky* (1917; reprint, New York: Harper Torchbooks, 1960); Sholem Asch, *East River* (New York: G. P. Putnam's Sons, 1946); and Ludwig Lewisohn, *The Island Within* (New York: Harper and Brothers, 1928). A best-seller of the 1950s that painted a bleak picture of a deracinated, assimilated Jew is Herman Wouk, *Marjorie Morningstar* (New York: Doubleday, 1955).

33   Valuable works on the immigrant experience and acculturation include: Oscar Handlin, *The Uprooted: The Epic Story of the Great Migrations That Made the American People* (Boston: Little, Brown, 1951), and John Higham, *Strangers in the Land: Patterns of American Nativism, 1866–1925* (New York: Atheneum, 1966). For a detailed historical account of the process of acculturation through the second and third generations, see Deborah Dash Moore, *At Home in America: Second-Generation New York Jews* (New York: Columbia University Press, 1981). For sample accounts of the Jewish "success story," see Judd Teller, *Strangers and Natives: The Evolution of the American Jew from 1921 to the Present* (New York: Delacorte Press, 1968); Stanley Feldstein, *The Land That I Show You: Three Centuries of Jewish Life in America* (New York: Anchor Press/ Doubleday, 1978); and James Yaffe, *The American Jews* (New York: Random House, 1968).

Milton Gordon, *Assimilation in American Life: The Role of Race, Religion, and National Origin* (New York: Oxford University Press, 1964), 114. Gordon's influential study of assimilation defined "structural assimilation" as the confining of primary contacts to other members of one's ethnic group. Contacts outside the group took place on "secondary levels"— at work and in public and civic arenas. According to Gordon, "To understand that acculturation without massive structural intermingling at primary group levels has been the dominant motif in the American experience of creating and developing a nation out of diverse peoples is to comprehend the most essential sociological fact of that experience" (114).

See Judith Kramer and Seymour Leventman, *Children of the Gilded Ghetto: Conflict Resolution of Three Generations of American Jews* (New Haven: Yale University Press, 1961). The authors write:

> This second-generation community, located in the better neighborhoods of the city, emulated the structure of the general community with a multitude of institutions parallel to those of the larger society. Yet it retained its fundamentally ethnic character. It was, in effect, a gilded ghetto . . . whose social life was carried on exclusively with Jews of appropriate status. The institutions were all middle-class, but the participants were all Jewish. The social distance between the minority community and the general community had yet to be bridged. As a result of both exclusion and exclusiveness, second-generation Jews were well insulated from any but impersonal economic relations with non-Jews. The gilded ghetto thus furnished the prerequisite of social segregation essential for conformity to its special values. (11)

Popular fictional accounts of Jewish acculturation include Meyer Levin, *The Old Bunch* (New York: Viking Press, 1937); Philip Roth, *Goodbye, Columbus, and Five Short Stories* (Boston: Houghton Mifflin, 1959) and *Portnoy's Complaint* (New York: Random House, 1969); and Mordechai Richler, *St. Urbain's Horseman* (New York: Knopf, 1971). For a critical account of the literature of American Jewish life, see Allen Guttman, *The Jewish Writer in America: Assimilation and the Crisis of Identity* (New York: Oxford University Press, 1971).

34   See Gordon, *Assimilation in American Life*, 224–32.

2: IN SEARCH OF THE SELF-HATING JEW

PAGE

45   Lewisohn, *The Island Within*, 141.

Theodor Lessing, *Der Jüdische Selbsthass* (Berlin, 1930). For an analysis of self-hatred from a literary perspective, see Sandor Gilman, *Jewish Self-Hatred: Anti-Semitism and the Hidden Language of the Jews* (Baltimore: Johns Hopkins University Press, 1985). Gilman assigns the origin of the term to Arnold Zweig, writing about Austrian Jews in 1927.

46   "There exists today hardly a more tragic fate . . ." quoted in Jacob Neusner, *Stranger at Home: "The Holocaust," Zionism, and American Judaism* (Chicago: University of Chicago Press, 1981), 54.

46–47   Ben Hecht, *A Jew in Love* (New York: Covici, Friede, 1931), 5.

47   Kurt Lewin, *Resolving Social Conflicts: Selected Papers in Group Dynamics, 1935–1946* (New York: Harper and Row, 1948), 194. See especially the essays "Self-Hatred Among Jews," "Psycho-Sociological Problems of a Minority Group," and "Raising a Jewish Child."

47–48   George Simpson and Milton Yinger, *Racial and Cultural Minorities: An Analysis of Prejudice and Discrimination* (New York: Harper and Row, 1972).

Judith Weinstein Klein, *Jewish Identity and Self-Esteem: Healing Wounds Through Ethnotherapy* (New York: Institute on Pluralism and Group Identity, American Jewish Committee, 1980), 6.

See Price Cobbs, "Ethnotherapy in Groups," in *New Perspectives on Encounter Groups* (San Francisco: Jossey-Bass, 1972).

48–49   Lewin, *Resolving Social Conflicts,* 181.

"Helping Jews to Like Themselves," *San Francisco Chronicle,* 13 April 1982.

52   *Donahue,* 29 April 1982.

58–59   Myron Kaufmann, *Remember Me to God* (New York: J. B. Lippincott, 1957).

60   Christopher Isherwood, *The Berlin Stories* (New York: James Laughlin, 1945).

3: ANTI-SEMITISM, THE ULTIMATE TIE

PAGE

62   For historical and sociological descriptions of American anti-Semitism, see John Higham, *Send These to Me: Jews and Other Immigrants in Urban America* (New York: Atheneum, 1975); Michael Dubkowski, *The Tarnished Dream: The Basis of American Anti-Semitism* (Westport, Conn.: Greenwood Press, 1979); Carey McWilliams, *A Mask for Privilege: Antisemitism in America* (Boston: Little Brown, 1948); Stephen Steinberg, *The Ethnic Myth: Race, Ethnicity, and Class in America* (New York: Atheneum, 1981); Leonard Dinerstein, *Uneasy At Home: Anti-Semitism and the American Jewish Experience* (New York: Columbia University Press, 1987); Charles Stember et al., *Jews in the Mind of America* (New York: Basic Books, 1966). For discussion of the survey data and analyses of data covering the past half-century, see Harold Quigley and Charles Glock, *Anti-Semitism in America* (New York: Free Press, 1979); Gertrude Selznick and Stephen Steinberg, *The Tenacity of Prejudice: Anti-Semitism in Contemporary America* (New York:

Harper and Row, 1969); and the study of anti-Semitism carried out by the firm of Yankelovitch, Skelly, and Wright, prepared for the American Jewish Committee, *Anti-Semitism in the United States*, 2 vols. (1981). For the first major social-science study of anti-Semitism, done in a psychoanalytic-Marxist framework during the late 1940s, see T. W. Adorno et al., *The Authoritarian Personality* (New York: Harper and Row, 1950).

63 For the ditty and background on the issues, see Steinberg, *The Ethnic Myth,* particularly the excellent essays on ethnicity and the meaning of "revival."

63–65 For data on anti-Semitic ads and Catholic college faculty, see John Higham, "American Anti-Semitism Historically Reconsidered," in Stember, *Jews in the Mind,* 246.

Madison Grant, *The Passing of the Great Race; or, The Racial Basis of European History* (New York: Charles Scribner's Sons, 1921); Lothrop Stoddard, *The Revolt Against Civilization: The Menace of the Underman* (New York: Charles Scribner's Sons, 1923).

65 For polls, poll data, and change over this period, see Quigley and Glock, *Anti-Semitism;* Stember, *Jews in the Mind;* and Selznick and Steinberg, *Tenacity.*

65–66 Yankelovich, Skelly, and Wright, *Anti-Semitism.*

67–68 William Helmreich, "How Jewish Students View the Holocaust," *Response: A Journal of Jewish Renewal,* Spring 1975, 84.

69 Stanley Aronowitz, quoted in Ellen Willis, "Radical Jews Caught in the Middle," *Village Voice,* 4–10 February 1981.

Ellen Willis, "Next Year in Jerusalem," *Rolling Stone,* 21 April 1977.

78 Lenny Bruce's elaboration of the Jewish-urban identification springs to mind:

> To me, if you live in New York or any other big city, you are Jewish. It doesn't matter even if you're Catholic; if you live in New York you're Jewish. If you live in Butte, Montana, you're going to be goyish even if you're Jewish. . . .
> Evaporated milk is goyish even if the Jews invented it. Chocolate is Jewish and fudge is goyish. Spam is goyish and rye bread is Jewish. . . . Gentiles love their children as much as Jews love theirs; they just don't wear their hearts on their sleeves. On the other hand, Jewish mothers don't hang gold stars in their windows. They're not proud of their boys going into the service. They're always worried about their being killed. . . . Celebrate is

a goyish word. Observe is a Jewish word. Mr. and Mrs. Walsh are celebrating Christmas with Major Thomas Moreland, USAF (Ret.), while Mr. and Mrs. Bromberg observed Hanukkah with Goldie and Arthur Schindler from Kiamesha, New York.

Lenny Bruce, "On Jewish and Goyish," in *How to Talk Dirty and Influence People* (Chicago: Playboy Press, 1965), 73.

80–81　For general background on German anti-Semitism and the Jewish situation, see Donald Niewyk, *The Jews of Weimar Germany* (Baton Rouge: Louisiana State University Press, 1980); Paul Massing, *Rehearsal for Destruction: A Study of Political Anti-Semitism in Imperial Germany* (1949; reprint, New York: H. Fertig, 1967); Stephen Poppel, *Zionism in Germany, 1897–1933: The Shaping of a Jewish Identity* (Philadelphia: Jewish Publication Society, 1977); P. G. J. Pulzer, *The Rise of Political Anti-Semitism in German and Austria* (New York: Wiley, 1964); Frederic Grunfeld, *Prophets Without Honour: A Background to Freud, Kafka, Einstein, and Their World* (New York: Holt, Rinehart, and Winston, 1979); Gershom Scholem, *From Berlin to Jerusalem: Memories of My Youth* (New York: Schocken Books, 1980); and Peter Gay, *Freud, Jews, and Other Germans: Masters and Victims in Modernist Culture* (New York: Oxford University Press, 1978).

81–82　Jakob Wassermann, *My Life as German and Jew* (New York: Coward-McCann, 1933), 212.

82　Kahane, *Why Be Jewish?* x.

83–84　Some Zionists want to draw an important "Jewish-survival" lesson from the fact that the small number of European Jews who had accepted the Zionist idea and emigrated to Palestine survived, while trusting assimilationists remained in their German "homeland" only to be slaughtered. The polemical force of this observation depends on ignoring salient historical facts. Only Rommel's defeat at El Alamein kept the Nazi armies from overrunning the Middle East and subjecting captured Zionist Jews to the same treatment given Jews in other occupied areas. Furthermore, assimilation-minded Jews who happened to have chosen the United States, Canada, Australia, Argentina, and so forth, not only survived, but had much less close a call than the lucky Zionist Jews in Palestine.

84　Quoted in Niewyk, *Jews of Weimar Germany*, 84.

85　Peggy Dennis, "Am I a Jew? A Radical's Search for an Answer," *Nation*, 12 July 1980.

THE COMMUNITY

PAGE

91   Feldstein, *The Land That I Show You*, 542.

94–95   For the structure of the American Jewish community and indicators of affiliation, see Elazar, *Community and Polity*, and Steven M. Cohen, *American Modernity and Jewish Identity* (New York: Methuen, 1983).

      For recent accounts of the American Jewish community written by sociologists and historians who are also actively committed members of that community, see A. J. Karp, *Haven and Hope: A History of the Jews in America* (New York: Schocken, 1985); H. Feingold, *Zion in America: The Jewish Experience from Colonial Times to the Present* (New York: Hippocrene Books, 1974); Calvin Goldscheider, *Jewish Continuity and Change: Emerging Patterns in America* (Bloomington: Indiana University Press, 1986); Fein, *Where Are We?*; Hertzberg, *Jews in America;* and Charles Liebman and Steven M. Cohen, *Two Worlds of Judaism: The Israeli and American Experiences* (New Haven: Yale University Press, 1990).

95–96   *American Jewish Year Book, 1980,* 43.

96   Goldscheider and Zuckerman, *Transformation,* 222.

97   Hertzberg, *Being Jewish,* 136, and *Jews in America,* 388.

      See Steven M. Cohen, *American Modernity and Jewish Identity* (New York: Routledge, Chapman, and Hall, 1983), for data compilation.

4: LIFE IN THE MAINSTREAM

PAGE

99–100   For data, see Wertheimer, "Recent Trends," *American Jewish Year Book, 1989,* 63–162.

100   For comparative religious data, see Alan Fisher, "The National Gallup Polls and American Jewish Demography," *American Jewish Year Book, 1983,* 115. Recent Gallup polls show the same trends.

      Will Herberg, *Protestant–Catholic–Jew: An Essay in American Religious Sociology* (New York: Doubleday, 1956).

101   Charles Liebman, *The Ambivalent American Jew: Politics, Religion, and Family in American Jewish Life* (Philadelphia: Jewish Publication Society, 1973), 78.

      The survey data on self-definition was published in *Present Tense: The Magazine of World Jewish Affairs,* Spring 1982. The report describes a study by two sociologists conducted for the University of Judaism in Los Angeles in 1979. The survey of

413 Jewish households revealed that less than a third of those interviewed were affiliated with a synagogue. The sociologists noted that a generation ago most Jews would have defined "Jewish" primarily in religious terms, while today the great majority described "Jewish" as "ethnic-cultural."

Stephan Thernstrom, "Introduction," *Harvard Encyclopedia of American Ethnic Groups* (Cambridge: Harvard University Press, 1980), ix.

102   For judicious and well-informed accounts of the "ethnic revival," see the skeptical analyses of Richard Coleman and Lee Rainwater, *Social Standing in America: New Dimensions of Class* (New York: Basic Books, 1978), and Herbert Gans, *Popular Culture and High Culture* (New York: Basic Books, 1978). For popular, enthusiastic, and, as time has shown, wildly exaggerated manifestos for "ethnic revival" and its depth and importance, see Michael Novak, *The Rise of the Unmeltable Ethnics: Politics and Culture in the Seventies* (New York: Macmillan, 1971), and Andrew Greeley, *Why Can't They Be Like Us? America's White Ethnic Groups* (New York: Dutton, 1971). The most recent summary of how wrong these predictions about the future of ethnic politics were can be found in Mary Waters, *Ethnic Options: Choosing Identities in America* (Berkeley and Los Angeles: University of California Press, 1991), a study that analyzes census data on ethnicity from the 1980 census, concentrating on white, Catholic, suburban ethnics.

Phrase originally from Peter Laslett, *The World We Have Lost* (New York: Charles Scribner's Sons, 1973).

See Elenore Lester, "Yiddish Comes Out of the Shtetl," *New York Times Magazine*, 2 December 1979. The author noted that Yiddish courses were being taught on more than forty campuses, whereas earlier they had hardly existed.

103–104   Accounts of the Yiddish immigrant world include Irving Howe, *World of Our Fathers* (New York: Harcourt Brace Jovanovich, 1976); Ronald Sanders, *The Downtown Jews: Portraits of the Immigrant Generation* (New York: Harper and Row, 1969); and Moses Rischin, *The Promised City: New York's Jews, 1870–1914* (Cambridge: Harvard University Press, 1962).

Howe, *World of Our Fathers*, 16.

On Peretz, see Howe, *World of Our Fathers*, and Maurice Samuel's excellent *Prince of the Ghetto* (New York: Knopf, 1948). For a detailed study of the ideology of Yiddishism and its formation, see Emanuel Goldsmith, *Architects of Yiddishism at the Beginning of the Twentieth Century: A Study in Jewish*

Cultural History (Rutherford, N.J.: Fairleigh Dickinson University Press, 1976).

General accounts of Jewish left-wing and labor movements in America are in Howe, *World of Our Fathers*, and Arthur Liebman, *Jews and the Left* (New York: John Wiley and Sons, 1979).

110   *JFC Bulletin* (published by the Jewish Federation Council of Los Angeles), 15 September 1978.

110–111   The *Jewish Exponent "Inside"* (published by the Philadelphia Federation of Jewish Charities), Winter 1980–81.

111   *New York Times*, 15 May 1978.

111–112   Max Dimont, *The Jews in America: The Roots, History, and Destiny of American Jews* (New York: Simon and Schuster, 1978), 261.

113   Daniel Fuchs, *Homage to Blenholt* (New York: Berkley Books, 1965), 43.

113–114   Denis Prager and Joseph Telushkin, *Why the Jews? The Reason for Anti-Semitism* (New York: Simon and Schuster, 1983). Also note their other proselytizing work, *Nine Questions People Ask About Judaism* (New York: Simon and Schuster, 1981). In the authors' words, the explanation for anti-Semitism is that "as a result of the Jews' commitment to Judaism, they have led higher-quality lives than their non-Jewish neighbors in almost every society in which they have lived. . . . The quality of life of the average Jew, no matter how poor, was higher than that of a comparable non-Jew in that society" (23). And lest one bring up the issue of subjectivity in judgment, the authors assure us that "the higher quality of Jewish life is objectively verifiable" (56).

117–118   Interview with Leon Wieseltier, Cambridge, Mass., 1981.

John Murray Cuddihy, *The Ordeal of Civility: Freud, Marx, Lévi-Strauss and the Jewish Struggle with Modernity* (New York: Basic Books, 1975). For a critical account of the book and its context, see Robert Alter, "Manners and the Jewish Intellectual," *Commentary*, August 1975.

An account of the difficulties that beset the world of *Yiddishkeit* even during its most vital period can be found in Ezra Mendelsohn, *The Jews of East Central Europe Between the World Wars* (Bloomington: Indiana University Press, 1983).

119   Emil Fackenheim, *The Jewish Return into History: Reflections in the Age of Auschwitz and a New Jerusalem* (New York: Schocken Books, 1978).

120 Interview with Arnold Eisen, Stanford, California, 1990.

120–121 See Coleman and Rainwater, *Social Standing*, and Waters, *Ethnic Options*, for summaries of ethnic survey data.
Liebman, *Ambivalent American Jew*, 90.

121 Shlomo Avineri, *The Making of Modern Zionism: The Intellectual Origins of the Jewish State* (New York: Basic Books, 1981), 221.
Liebman, *Ambivalent American Jew*, 143.

122 Useful studies of the history of Zionism and its outcome in the present state of Israel include Ben Halpern, *The Idea of a Jewish State* (Cambridge: Harvard University Press, 1978), and Bernard Avishai, *The Tragedy of Zionism: Revolution and Democracy in the Land of Israel* (New York: Farrar, Straus, and Giroux, 1985). For a critical scrutiny of Zionist doctrine and practice from a non-Zionist perspective, see Noam Chomsky, *The Fateful Triangle: The United States, Israel, and the Palestinians* (Boston: South End Press, 1983), especially the section "Israel and Palestine: Historical Backgrounds."

123 Howard Sachar, *The Course of Modern Jewish History* (New York: Dell, 1958), 541.

124 Elazar, *Community and Polity*, 85–86.
Neusner, *Stranger at Home*, 200.
For a challenging inquiry into the nature of American "Zionism" and its meaning for American Jewish life and character, see Ben Halpern, *The American Jew: A Zionist Analysis* (New York: Schocken Books, 1956). For a general analysis of Zionism by one of the leaders of contemporary American Zionism, see Arthur Hertzberg, *The Zionist Idea* (New York: Doubleday, 1959).

129 Ahad Ha'am, quoted in Halpern, *Idea of a Jewish State*, 73.

133 For the manifesto, see the booklet *Telem: Movement of Zionist Fulfillment* (Los Angeles: Telem, 1979), 5.

134 Liebman, *Ambivalent American Jew*, 90–91.

135–136 Glazer, *American Judaism*, 155, 170. Glazer gives figures on post–Six-Day War contributions.
On "conversions," see Elazar, *Community and Polity*, 75–76.

137 For a recent summary of research on the return rate, giving the approximately 50-percent level, see Chaim Waxman, *American Aliya: Portrait of an Innovative Migration Movement* (Detroit: Wayne State University Press, 1989).

For burial numbers, see the *New York Times*, 10 June 1987. See also "More Come to Be Buried Than to Live," *Moment*, 12 September 1987, 13.

Interview with Steven M. Cohen, New York, 1981.

138   Interview with Alan Mintz, New York, 1981.

139–140   Anne Roiphe, "Marriage," *Present Tense*, May–June 1989, 57, 56.

For a thoughtful piece on the connection between "Israelism" and increasing political conservatism within the American Jewish community, see Christopher Hitchens, "Israel and the American Left," *Nation*, 5 December 1981. For an ongoing discussion on the issues of leftist politics and Jewish concerns about Israel, see any issue of *Tikkun* magazine since 1987.

140–142   Glazer, *American Judaism*, 24–59 and *passim*, gives a clear account from a sociological viewpoint of the evolution of the synagogue and its ideologies within the American Jewish community.

142–143   The data are presented in Marshall Sklare and Joseph Greenblum, *Jewish Identity on the Suburban Frontier: A Study of Group Survival in the Open Society*, 2d ed. (Chicago: University of Chicago Press, 1979), 181.

143   See the account of the development of synagogue-centers and community centers in Moore, *At Home in America*, where the author notes that "especially in the suburbs, synagogues served as ethnic facilities, with religious services often taking a back seat to recreational and educational activities" (237).

143–144   Steve Zipperstein, "Preface" to "The Reawakening of Jewish Religious Life in America," *Present Tense*, Spring 1980, 23. The revival of religious Judaism was also noted in Silberman's book, where the role of women in transforming Judaism was specified as the most potent source of religious renewal.

Ari Goldman, "More and More Young Jews Are Picking Careers as Rabbis," *New York Times*, 24 May 1991.

Bellah quoted in Fran Schumer, "A Return to Religion," *New York Times Magazine*, 15 April 1984, 90.

149–151   The discussion of secularization is dauntingly extensive. Some recent studies that are valuable and provocative include Peter Berger, Brigitte Berger, and Hansfried Kellner, *The Homeless Mind: Modernization and Consciousness* (New York: Random House, 1973); Ernest Gellner, *Legitimation of Belief* (Cambridge: Cambridge University Press, 1974); Bryan Wilson, *Contemporary Transformations of Religion* (London: Oxford University Press, 1976); Alasdair MacIntyre, *Secularization and Moral Change,* Riddell Memorial Lectures (London: Oxford University Press, 1967); Daniel Bell, *The Cultural Contradictions of Capitalism* (New York: Basic Books, 1976); Clifford Geertz, *Islam Observed: Religious Development in Morocco and Indonesia* (New Haven: Yale University Press, 1968); and Michael Harrington, *The Politics at God's Funeral: The Spiritual Crisis of Western Civilization* (New York: Holt, Rinehart, and Winston, 1983).

151   "Consumer preference" as applicable to religion is presented in Peter Berger, *The Heretical Imperative: Contemporary Possibilities of Religious Affirmation* (New York: Harper and Row, 1982).

153   Bernard Reisman, *The Chavurah: A Contemporary Jewish Experience* (New York: Union of American Hebrew Congregations, 1977), 113.

In the preface to the 1980 paperback edition of *Community and Polity,* political scientist Daniel Elazar summed up his sense of the movement:

> By the mid-1970s a number of mainstream congregations were experimenting with havurot within their established institutional frameworks. Though some of these fellowships were no more than study groups by another name, a few congregations actually reorganized themselves into a collection of small groups seeking satisfying Jewish experiences. The havurah movement has not stopped the decline in synagogue membership nor has it halted the widespread state of crisis that the American synagogue is in. But the havurot have offered some hope of new directions. (331)

158–159   Dean Kelly, *Why Conservative Churches Are Growing: A Study in the Sociology of Religion* (New York: Harper and Row, 1972).

159   Elihu Bergman, "The American Jewish Population Erosion," *Midstream,* June 1977, 9–19. Although critics like Goldscheider and Zuckerman, in *The Transformation of the Jews,* dismiss such disaster scenarios as "demographic nonsense," the predictions continue to be cited, for rhetorical effect, to be sure. The predictive power of simple straight-line projections is, of course, severely limited when the phenomena are human, social, and complicated. Still, showing the dimensions of what

would happen if rates and trends continue can be a useful exercise.

5: THE RESILIENCE OF ORTHODOXY

PAGE

162–164　For historically informed sociological description of American Orthodoxy, see especially Liebman, *Ambivalent American Jew*, and "Orthodox Judaism Today," in Reuven P. Bulka, ed., *Dimensions of Orthodox Judaism* (New York: Ktav, 1983). The essays in Bulka's collection give the range of positions on important issues within the Orthodox world. See also the descriptive anthropological studies of Hasidim: Solomon Poll, *The Hasidic Community in Williamsburg: A Study in the Sociology of Religion* (New York: Schocken Books, 1969); Israel Rubin, *Satmar: Island in the City* (Chicago: Quadrangle Books, 1972); and the "participant-observer" work by sociologist Samuel Heilman, *Synagogue Life: A Study in Symbolic Interaction* (Chicago: University of Chicago Press, 1976). More recent academic studies on the current state of Orthodoxy include Samuel Heilman and Steven M. Cohen, *Cosmopolitans and Parochials: Modern Orthodox Jews in America* (Chicago: University of Chicago Press, 1989); Samuel Heilman, *The People of the Book: Drama, Fellowship, and Religion* (Chicago: University of Chicago Press, 1983); and Herbert Danziger, *Returning to Tradition* (New Haven: Yale University Press, 1989).

164　For data on generational affiliation, see Liebman, "Orthodox Judaism Today," in Bulka, *Dimensions,* 109.

　　Natalie Gittelson, "American Jews Rediscover Orthodoxy," *New York Times Magazine*, 30 September 1984, 41.

165　Lis Harris, "Holy Days," *The New Yorker*, 16, 23, 30 September 1985.

　　Pittsburgh, Spring 1981.

167　Rabbi Shlomo Riskin, "Where Modern Orthodoxy Is At—and Where It Is Going," in Bulka, *Dimensions,* 403.

168　Reuven P. Bulka, "Orthodoxy Today: An Overview of the Achievements and the Problems," in Bulka, *Dimensions,* 9.

168–169　*Young Israel Viewpoint,* October 1980.

　　"Temple Tracker" ad quoted in Martin Snapp's "East Bay Ear" column, *Oakland* (Calif.) *Tribune*, 15 May 1988.

　　Dinovitz quoted in the *Los Angeles Times*, 5 June 1981.

178   Liebman, "Orthodox Judaism Today," 116. Liebman has developed the concept of "compartmentalization" applied to modern Orthodox Jews in the essay quoted as well as in several other works. See especially "Religion and the Chaos of Modernity: The Case of Contemporary Judaism," in *Take Judaism, for Example*, ed. Jacob Neusner (Chicago: University of Chicago Press, 1983), 147–164.

           Samuel Heilman, "Inner and Outer Identities: Social Ambivalence Among Orthodox Jews," *Jewish Social Studies*, Summer 1977, 238.

179–180   Liebman, *Ambivalent American Jew*, 197.

           "Jonathan Chaim Segal: A Fable," *Jewish Life*, Fall 1982.

180   Irving Greenberg, "Jewish Values and the Changing American Ethic," in Bulka, *Dimensions*, 285. For an accessible account of the rightward trends within the Orthodox world, see Wertheimer, "Recent Trends," *American Jewish Year Book, 1989*, 108.

           "Mixed dancing . . .", quoted in Wertheimer, "Recent Trends," 120.

181   Editorial, *Jewish Life*, Fall 1982.

           Marc Angel, "Orthodoxy in Isolation," *Moment*, September 1980, 61.

183–184   "Chabad" is the Hebrew acronym for *chochmah, binah*, and *da'at* (wisdom, understanding, and knowledge), the three levels of mind, according to the founder of Lubavitcher Hasidism. An account of the rebbe and the group in historical context can be found in Israel Zinberg's monumental *History of Jewish Literature*, vol. 9, *Hassidism and Enlightenment, 1780–1820* (New York: Ktav, 1976). According to this account, "God," declares Shneur Zalman, "contracted His infinite light and clothed it in the form of the limited world out of love for His people Israel, to raise the world to God, to 'illuminate the darkness with divine light,' and to fill the world with God's glory, through the aid of 'three garments'—thought, speech, and act. Thought and speech are the study of the Torah, and act is the fulfillment of the six hundred and thirteen commandments of the Torah."

           For detailed personal reporting on the Lubavitcher movement and its background, see Lis Harris, *Holy Days: The World of a Hasidic Family* (New York: Summit Books, 1985), based on a *New Yorker* series.

           Los Angeles Times, 18 April 1982.

191–192   Editorial, Chabad newspaper, 1982.

200   For a good discussion of the fragility of fundamentalist conversions within secular culture, see Berger, *Heretical Imperative*. He writes: ". . . . individuals now must pick and choose. Having done so, it is very difficult to forget the fact. There remains the memory of the deliberate construction of a community of consent, and with this, a haunting sense of the constructedness of that which the community affirms. Inevitably, the affirmations will be fragile and this fragility will not be very far from consciousness" (27).

201   See Paul Cowan, "A Renaissance in Venice," *Jewish Living*, March–April 1980. Cowan considered the "new Orthodox" efflorescence part of a revival of religious Judaism taking place all over America. He explains the appeal of this very modern Orthodoxy: "Increasingly, Jews—like other Americans—are searching for cohesive communities that aren't cults, for places that have a clear set of values, a clear set of limits, and still allow for personal freedom" (58).

Kenneth Briggs, "Synagogue Acts to Help Jews Renew Their Faith," *New York Times*, 28 March 1981.

207   Quoted in Cathryn Jacobson, "The New Orthodox," *New York*, 17 November 1986, 52–60.

210   The editions of Jewish religious texts and prayers with commentaries by Joseph Hertz, chief rabbi of Great Britain in the 1940s and 1950s, have been widely read over the past several decades by English-speaking students of Judaism.

THE REVIVAL

PAGE

219   Mark Jay Mirsky, *My Search for the Messiah: Studies and Wanderings in Israel and America* (New York: Macmillan, 1977), 11.

221–222   Arthur Waskow, *These Holy Sparks: The Rebirth of the Jewish People* (San Francisco: Harper and Row, 1984), xii.

For self-descriptions of what the revival activists did and why, see issues of *Response: A Journal of Jewish Renewal* and the collections of essays edited and written by activists, for example James Sleeper and Alan Mintz, eds., *The New Jews* (New York: Vintage Books, 1971), and Jack Nusan Porter and Peter Dreier, eds., *Jewish Radicalism: A Selected Anthology* (New York: Grove Press, 1973). In *Response* (Summer 1974), the departing editor, William Novak, looking back, noted that the first issue of the magazine had

> coincided with what we believe to be the second postwar era in American Jewish life. The fateful summer of 1967 was only the beginning of something even larger than we knew at the time . . . a persistent search for sincerity and authenticity in Jewish life. What began as political unrest among younger Jews has become something far deeper, and undoubtedly more positive. It finds expression in various ways: in the new religious impulse, the rise of various Jewish counter-institutions, the impressive growth of Jewish studies on the campus and elsewhere, and a new literary and artistic expression. (3)

6: THE NEW SPIRITUALITY

PAGE

224   *Seven Days*, 27 December 1989, 22.

For a detailed ethnographic study of the *havurah* movement by a participant-observer, see Riv-Ellen Prell, *Prayer and Community: The Havurah in American Judaism* (Detroit: Wayne State University Press, 1989).

227   Charles Fracchia, *Second Spring: The Coming of Age of American Catholicism* (San Francisco: Harper and Row, 1980), 47.

227–228   See Harvey Cox, *The Feast of Fools: A Theological Essay on Festivity and Fantasy* (Cambridge: Harvard University Press, 1969). Cox's current perspective, more appreciative of the force of traditional religiosity, can be found in his *Religion in the Secular City: Toward a Post-Modern Theology* (New York: Simon and Schuster, 1986).

229–230   Carol Ascher, "The Return of Jewish Mysticism," *Present Tense*, Spring 1980, 37.

230–231   Aquarian Minyan citations from *Aquarian Minyan Bulletin*, Berkeley, May–June–July 1981.

231–232   Schachter quoted in Ascher, "Return of Jewish Mysticism," 40.

235–236   Marshall Sklare, "The Greening of Judaism," *Commentary*, December 1974, 51–57.

7: THE JEWISH RADICAL

PAGE

239   Michael Lerner quoted in David Firestone, "A New Voice on the Left," *New York Newsday*, 7 July 1987.

For a participant-observer report on the founding conference of New Jewish Agenda, see Ellen Willis, "Radical Jews Caught in the Middle."

240   New Left Jewish estimates in Arthur Liebman, *Jews and the Left*, 67.

244   See Porter and Dreier, *Radical Jews*.

248   Jewish Liberation Project quoted in Robert Alter, "Appropriating the Religious Tradition," *Commentary*, February 1971, 48.

249   For Moses Hess, see Isaiah Berlin, *The Life and Ideas of Moses Hess* (London: Jewish Historical Society of England, 1959).
       Albert Einstein, "Just What Is a Jew?" in Saul Goodman, ed., *The Faith of Secular Jews* (New York: Ktav, 1976), 113.
       Earl Shorris, *Jews Without Mercy: A Lament* (New York: Anchor Press/Doubleday, 1982).

249–250   For numbers, and analysis of Jewish political behavior during the 1960s and early 1970s, see Stephen Isaacs, *Jews and American Politics* (Garden City, N.Y.: Doubleday). Isaacs points out the uncertainty of the data, noting that two different polls of Jewish voting in the McGovern-Nixon election, when the Republicans pushed hard in New York on their strategy of attracting Jewish voters, gave quite different results: 61–39 for one and 70–29 for the other. For the 1976 and 1980 elections, see Austin Ranney, ed., *The American Elections of 1980* (Washington: American Enterprise Institute for Public Policy Research, 1981).

251   On "messianism," see Gershom Scholem, *The Messianic Idea in Judaism, and Other Essays on Jewish Spirituality* (New York: Schocken Books, 1971).

251–252   For general background on Enlightenment ideology and the Jews, see works noted above on modern Jewish history and anti-Semitism, as well as Arthur Hertzberg, *Jews and the French Enlightenment* (New York: Columbia University Press, 1968).

252–254   An impressively documented and well-argued study of Jews and modern left-wing politics in Eastern Europe is Jonathan Frankel's *Prophecy and Politics: Socialism, Nationalism, and the Russian Jews, 1862–1917* (London: Cambridge University Press, 1981).
       See Edmund Wilson, *To the Finland Station: A Study in the Writing and Acting of History* (Garden City, N.Y.: Doubleday, 1940). Also see Isaac Deutscher, *The Non-Jewish Jew*,

and Other Essays (Oxford: Oxford University Press, 1968).

See Frankel, *Prophecy and Politics,* for detailed account of the evolution of Jewish radicalism in Russia during this period.

For a detailed analysis of Marx's famous essay "On the Jewish Question," see Julius Carlebach, *Karl Marx and the Radical Critique of Judaism* (Boston: Routledge and Kegan Paul, 1978).

"I am myself a Jew . . ." quoted in Liebman, *Jews and the Left,* 67.

256   Election figures on the 1980 election showing 45 percent for Carter, 39 percent for Reagan, and 14 percent for Anderson in Austin Ranney, ed., *American Elections of 1980,* At the Polls Series (Durham, N.C.: Duke University Press, 1981).

257   The figure on young Jewish Republican registration was given by Rabbi Chaim Seidler-Feller, UCLA Hillel director, during a talk at the *Tikkun* conference in New York, December 1988. Another indicator of this shift can be found in the recent opinion poll conducted by the Graduate School of the City University of New York, described in the *New York Times,* 15 April 1991. The two groups with highest identification with the Democratic Party were Jews and Baptists, both at 43 percent. Jews still maintained the lowest Republican identification, 22 percent, compared to 27 percent for Baptists. These figures confirm that Jews as a group remain predominantly Democratic and liberal. According to William Keefe in *Parties, Politics, and Public Policy in America,* the level of Jewish identification as Democrats declined slightly from 1952 to 1984, from 52 percent to 48 percent, while identification as Republicans almost doubled during that period, from 13 percent to 22 percent (Washington: CQ Press, 1988), 267.

For a sense of how concerns about Israel distanced American Jews from the Democrats during the Carter-Reagan election, see Cynthia Ozick, "Carter and the Jews: An American Political Dilemma," *New Leader,* 30 June 1980.

8: LIBERATIONS, JEWISH STYLE

PAGE

260   For background on Jewish feminism, see the anthologies on the revival noted above. Also see Charlotte Baum, Paula Hyman, and Sonya Michel, *The Jewish Woman in America* (New York: Dial Press, 1976), Susannah Heschel, ed., *On Being a Jewish Feminist: A Reader* (New York: Schocken Books, 1983); Susan Weidman Schneider, *Jewish and Female: Choices and Changes in Our Lives Today* (New York: Simon and Schuster, 1984); Blu

Greenberg, *On Women and Judaism: A View from Tradition* (Philadelphia: Jewish Publication Society, 1981); and Letty Cottin Pogrebin, *Deborah, Golda, and Me: Being Female and Jewish in America* (New York: Crown, 1991). For a recent survey of how feminism has affected the Jewish community, including a useful bibliography on the movement, see Sylvia Barack Fishman, "The Impact of Feminism on American Jewish Life," *American Jewish Year Book, 1989,* 3–62.

262   Naomi Janowitz and Maggie Wenig, "Selections from a Prayerbook Where God's Image Is Female," *Lilith,* Fall–Winter 1977–78, 27–29.

263   Silberman, *A Certain People,* 262.

267–268   *The Jewish Newsletter of the Conference on Judaism in Rural New England,* 1985. For a detailed account of the prediction, see Blu Greenberg, "Will There Be Orthodox Women Rabbis?" *Judaism,* Winter 1984, 23–33.

268–269   Rachel Adler, "The Way We Are," *Lilith,* Winter 1976–77, 4–5.

271   Gibel quoted in Charlotte Evans, "Feminists Trying to Deal with Religion's Confines," *New York Times,* 11 November 1980.

Reuven P. Bulka, "Woman's Role: Some Ultimate Concerns," *Tradition,* Spring 1979, 40.

272   Betty Friedan quoted in Bettyann Kevles, "A Feminist in the Late '80s," *Los Angeles Times,* 17 April 1987.

273–274   Task Force report described in Barry Alan Mehler, "Gay Jews: One Man's Journey from Closet to Community," *Moment,* February–March 1977, 23.

274–279   Citations from *Gay Synagogue News,* Congregation Beth Simchat Torah, New York, November 1981–June 1982.

284–285   Batya Bauman, "The Way We Are," *Lilith,* Winter 1976–77, 9–10.

285–286   Moshe Halevi Spero, "Homosexuality: Clinical and Ethical Challenges," *Tradition,* Spring 1979, 69.

EPILOGUE: CHOICE AND SELF-CREATION

PAGE

287–288   Berger et al., *The Homeless Mind,* 77.

Philip Roth, "Jewishness and the Younger Intellectuals," *Commentary,* March 1961, 33.

The discussion of "modernity" and its consequences for questions of identity, community, human agency, cultural and moral relativism, and related concepts has been a prominent theme in philosophical discourse. See, for example, Alasdair MacIntyre, *After Virtue* (South Bend, Ind.: Notre Dame Univeristy Press, 1981); Bernard Williams, *Ethics and the Limits of Philosophy* (Cambridge: Harvard University Press, 1984); Robert Bellah et al., *Habits of the Heart* (Berkeley and Los Angeles: University of California Press, 1984); Charles Taylor, *Sources of the Self: The Making of the Modern Identity* (Cambridge: Harvard University Press, 1989); and Anthony Giddens, *Modernity and Self-Identity: Self and Society in the Late Modern Age* (Stanford, Calif.: Stanford University Press, 1991).

292　Berger et al., *The Homeless Mind*, 77.

Index